QUEEN VICTORIA'S MYSTERIOUS DAUGHTER

Also by Lucinda Hawksley

Essential Pre-Raphaelites

*Charles Dickens' Favourite Daughter: The Life, Loves and Art of Katey
Dickens Perugini*

Lizzie Siddal: The Tragedy of a Pre-Raphaelite Supermodel

50 British Artists You Should Know

Charles Dickens

*March, Women, March: Voices of the Women's Movement from the First
Feminist to Votes for Women*

QUEEN VICTORIA'S MYSTERIOUS DAUGHTER

A Biography of Princess Louise

LUCINDA HAWKSLEY

Thomas Dunne Books
St. Martin's Griffin
New York

For Merle and Mei, with love

THOMAS DUNNE BOOKS.
An imprint of St. Martin's Press.

QUEEN VICTORIA'S MYSTERIOUS DAUGHTER. Copyright © 2013 by Lucinda Hawksley. All rights reserved. Printed in the United States of America. For information, address St. Martin's Press, 175 Fifth Avenue, New York, N.Y. 10010.

www.thomasdunnebooks.com
www.stmartins.com

Extracts from Whistler's letters are reproduced by permission of the University of Glasgow Library, Special Collections. Extracts from Wilfred Scawen Blunt's diaries are reproduced by permission of the Syndics of the Fitzwilliam Museum.

The Library of Congress has cataloged the hardcover edition as follows:

Hawksley, Lucinda.
Queen Victoria's mysterious daughter : a biography of Princess Louise / Lucinda Hawksley. — First U.S. edition.
p. cm.
Originally published as: The mystery of Princess Louise. London : Chatto & Windus, 2013.
Includes bibliographical references and index.
ISBN 978-1-250-05932-1 (hardcover)
ISBN 978-1-4668-6390-3 (ebook)
1. Louise, Princess, Duchess of Argyll, 1848–1939. 2. Princesses—Great Britain— Biography. 3. Great Britain—History—Victoria, 1837–1901. I. Title.
DA559.L6H39 2015
941.081092—dc23
[B]

2015025030

ISBN 978-1-250-13036-5 (trade paperback)

Our books may be purchased in bulk for promotional, educational, or business use. Please contact your local bookseller or the Macmillan Corporate and Premium Sales Department at 1-800-221-7945, extension 5442, or by email at MacmillanSpecialMarkets@macmillan.com.

First published in Great Britain by Chatto & Windus, an imprint of Random House, a division of the Random House Group Limited

First St. Martin's Griffin Edition: August 2017

10 9 8 7 6 5 4

Contents

Illustrations

Second picture section

1: 'The Princess Louise Polka', W. Smallwood (© Library and Archives Canada).
2: Princess Louise Caroline Alberta, Duchess of Argyll, Giulio Rossi, 1869 (© National Portrait Gallery, London).
3: John George Edward Henry Douglas Sutherland Campbell, 9th Duke of Argyll, after W. & D. Downey, 1870 (© National Portrait Gallery, London).
4: The Blue Room at Rideau Hall, Ottawa, decorated by Princess Louise, 1880; Princess Louise in Canada (© William James Topley/ Library and Archives Canada/PA-013031).
5: Marquis of Lorne, 1879(© Notman & Sandham/Library and Archives Canada/C-052047); Princess Louise's statue of Queen Victoria in Montreal (image courtesy of the author).
6: Princess Louise with the Mayor of Hendon at the opening of Brent Modern School, in 1935 (© Mary Evans Picture Library/National Magazine Company).
7: Princess Louise inspecting troops, 1909 (© Argyll Museum).
8: Princess Louise Caroline Alberta, Duchess of Argyll, Philip de László, 1915 (© Christies Images).

Acknowledgements

Very special thanks go to Nick and Sara Locock, Vicky Trelinska and Marek Trelinski, Basil Collett, Philippa Duckworth and Michael Gledhill QC for their enthusiasm, advice and selfless sharing of their own time and information. This book could not have been written without them.

Many thanks to Carolyn and Roger Taylor for generous accommodation, advice, gorgeous food and great fun in Ottawa. For the Bermuda section, I am indebted to Lord Waddington (what a serendipitous meeting), John Adams and Andrew Trimingham.

This book could not have been published without the lovely people at Chatto: Juliet Brooke, Clara Farmer, Penny Hoare, and my agents Christopher Sinclair-Stevenson and Broo Doherty.

In addition, I would like to thank (in alphabetical order) for guidance, advice and help, John Aplin, Simon Butcher, Caroline Dakers, Henrietta Garnett, Jake Gorst and Tracey Rennie Gorst (for Corsi information), Henrietta Heald, Sarah James, Anne Jordan, Dominique Kenway, Joanna Marschner at HRP, Genevieve Muinzer at HRP, Laura Payne, Vanessa Remington at the Royal Collection, Jane Ridley, Nicholas Robinson at the Fitzwilliam Archives, Sue Snell, Vanessa Story and Hugo Vickers.

Many thanks to the RSL Jerwood Award committee for their grant which helped with the costs of researching this book. Grateful thanks also to the hardworking staff at the Alberta Government archives, the British Library, the British Newspaper Archives, the Canadian Archives, Ottawa, the Imperial War Museum archives, Liverpool Central Library, the London Library, the London Metropolitan archives, Malta Tourism Authority, the National Archives, Kew, National Art Library, National Gallery archives, National Library of Malta, National Portrait Gallery archives, Rideau Hall, Ottawa, Swan Hotel in Lavenham (John Morrell, Ingo Wiangke and Kate Bourdillon), Tate Britain, University of Glasgow/Whistler archives and The Women's Library.

Many thanks as well must go to all those authors before me who have written about Queen Victoria's family, including those who have been given access to the royal archives in the past and have published excerpts of letters and journals in their books and articles.

Introduction: How it all began

The name of Sir William Blake Richmond is little remembered today, but in the late nineteenth century he was connected to almost everyone in the fashionable art world. As a painter who numbered amongst his friends William Morris, Robert Louis Stevenson and William Holman Hunt, Richmond moved with ease in the varied worlds that made up London Society. One day, as he was busy painting in his studio, he was annoyed to be disturbed by a servant announcing an unexpected visitor. Richmond yelled angrily, 'Tell her to bugger off,' unaware his visitor was close enough to hear. 'Not till I've seen you' was the mild and amused response from Princess Louise.[1]

I first discovered Princess Louise when researching my biographies of the Pre-Raphaelite model Lizzie Siddal and the artist Kate Perugini. This mysterious princess kept appearing in unlikely circumstances: visiting Dante Rossetti when he was ill (and deemed 'mad'); remaining friends with the difficult James Abbott McNeill Whistler, despite his financial and social embarrassments; arriving to see John Everett Millais on his deathbed, or taking tea with Arthur Sullivan, who called her 'my Princess Louise' in a letter to his mother. I wondered who this art-loving, aesthetically minded princess was. The more vague appearances she made in my research notes, the more I wanted to find out about her. When I discovered she was not only a friend to artists, but a sculptor in an age when few women broke into such a masculine field, I determined to discover more about her life.

[1] Richmond's comment varies depending on the source. A more sanitised version claims he said 'Tell her to go to the devil.'

Princess Louise was born in 1848 and lived until 1939; her life encompassed almost a century of extraordinary – and often terrifying – achievements, conflicts and societal change. At the time of Louise's birth, British women and girls were, legally, the property of either their father or their husband. (Queen Victoria might have been the most powerful woman in the world – but she was fervently against the majority other women who fought to be given the most basic human rights.) By the time of Louise's death, British women had gained the vote and were striving to achieve a world in which men and women could truly be equal. Louise had played an important part in the educating of these powerful new women. She was, as the daughter of a monarch, famous and celebrated in her lifetime, but, like so many women of her era, she has been all but forgotten since.

When I started my research, I mentioned it to a couple of fellow authors – who advised me against it. Both of them had attempted to look into Princess Louise's life themselves. One warned me, 'you will come up against a brick wall at every turn'. That intrigued me. They were quite right, of course.

After discovering the bare bones of Louise's life and beginning to read existing books about her, I applied to the Royal Archives. Many months later I received a response telling me I was welcome to visit the archives and detailing what times they were open and what I would need to bring with me. It all seemed very positive, until I reached the bottom of the letter. Almost as an afterthought was the comment 'We regret that Princess Louise's files are closed.' I could visit the archive buildings, but would not be allowed to view the files I needed to see.

I tried her husband's family's collection in Inveraray, Scotland, where my several applications (phone and email) were kindly but firmly rebuffed. On my initial approach I discovered that their archives were in the process of being rehoused and it would be over a year before they could be accessed again. More than a year later, I was told they were still inaccessible; and the same some months afterwards. My last two enquiries simply went unanswered. When I visited Inveraray as a tourist, in the summer of 2012, I was told by a curator inside the castle that the archives had not been rehoused. The curator also mentioned that it was 'almost impossible' for researchers to get into the archives; even people working at the castle itself were denied access.

I discovered that it was not only information about Princess Louise that had been hidden away, but information about a vast number of people who had played a role in her life, including royal servants and her art tutors. A great many items about these people that one would expect to be in other collections have been absorbed into the Royal Collection. Archivists at the National Gallery, Royal Academy and the V&A, as well as overseas collections in Malta, Bermuda and Canada, were bemused to discover that primary sources I requested had been 'removed' to Windsor. Over the decades, there has been some very careful sanitising of Princess Louise's reputation and a whitewashing of her life, her achievements and her personality.

Initially, this book was intended to be a complete artistic biography, but as it became apparent that this was not possible, I began to realise that one of the most intriguing aspects had become the journey to try and find her. My working title became 'The Mystery of Princess Louise'. There were so many rumours – some seemingly outlandish – that initially I had dismissed many of them as mere gossip, but the extraordinary secrecy that surrounds her life, and the many obstacles placed in the way of researching her, made me wonder if they were true. I have not been able to substantiate, nor could I disprove, the rumours that have been passed on to me from various people's oral family history as well as tittle-tattle of the era, but perhaps there really is no smoke without fire. I have drawn my own conclusions and shall leave you to decide for yourselves.

For some of the original research, I am greatly indebted to Michael Gledhill QC. As a law student in the 1970s, he became intrigued by Princess Louise and began working on a biography. In order to research her life, he placed adverts in national and local newspapers and magazines. Because Princess Louise had lived until 1939, he received fascinating responses from people who had known her and, in some cases, worked for her. He very kindly allowed me to see the letters. I am also indebted to the Locock family, who have been extremely helpful and generous with their time as well as sharing with me their family memorabilia.

It is important for readers to be aware that although Queen Victoria wrote letters and diary entries almost every day, those that are now in the archives and available online are *not* her original work. The queen's journals and letters were heavily edited, following her death, by her youngest child, Princess Beatrice. The princess went through them and removed anything that she considered controversial, then copied out the journal entries and many of the letters and destroyed the originals. At times when the queen's journals record extremely unpleasant comments about her family, it is astonishing to realise that Beatrice considered these acceptable. It makes one wonder just how much more controversial must have been the passages that Beatrice removed.

Queen Victoria is often described as a mother to her people. British schoolchildren learn that she was a great monarch, stateswoman and Empress and we see all around the country a preponderance of statues and monuments to her. Most date from her golden and diamond jubilees, so were created at around the same time, in 1887 or 1897, and as such they give a slightly skewed version of history, making one imagine not only that she was adored by everyone but also that she was adored all through her reign. This was not the case. When she became queen, soon after her eighteenth birthday, the public welcomed and idealised the young Victoria. When Albert, her prince consort, died in 1861, the young queen, bereaved so suddenly, was pitied and prayed for by her loyal subjects. People empathised with her pain and, in an age of high premature mortality, they could identify with her predicament.

As the years started to pass, however, and the queen remained in her 'widow's weeds' and continued to shun public engagements, she began to be resented by her subjects. By the time Princess Louise reached adulthood, her mother no longer had the love and respect of many of the people she ruled. Yes, she had lost her spouse to an untimely death, but so had many of her subjects, and, after all, the queen had nine healthy children. Even Prince Leopold, against the haemophiliac odds, was thriving. Those who, under her reign, still lived in terrible deprivation had become accustomed to watching their friends and family, especially young children, die. What was perceived as the self-indulgent behaviour of the 'Widow of Windsor' began to be seen as an insult to those others who suffered every day.

The queen's constant refusal to re-engage with her subjects and her ignoring of responsibilities jarred with her family too. Princess Louise, whose adolescence was blighted by the death of her father and by her mother's lack of interest in her children, as well as her constant criticism, found herself taking on many of the monarch's roles. In addition, Louise, in common with her sisters, had no choice but to work as her mother's companion, despite a heartfelt longing to leave the royal home and live as a professional sculptor. Unfortunately for the queen, Louise was the least compliant of her daughters and as the princess grew into adulthood she became increasingly antagonistic to the maternal bullying that Queen Victoria had mastered so ably.

It became apparent that Princess Louise had an intriguing personality. She could be adorable, generous and charming, or she could be stingingly unkind. She went out of her way to help people she liked, but froze out those she did not. She found it hard to forgive mistakes and could be hypercritical – although the person she was often most harshly critical of was herself. Louise had a desperate need to be loved. When she loved, she was fiercely loyal and, like her mother, continued that love long after the object of it had died. Because she was often ignored or belittled by her mother and other family members this need to be noticed, and needed, became thoroughly ingrained in her. I became fascinated by how history has tried to tame and trivialise this astonishing woman; how often she has been dismissed with comments that she was 'unhinged' or 'paranoid': there has been a concerted effort to try and make people believe that nothing Princess Louise said or did could possibly have any credence. The opposite is true. Louise was a powerful voice for women of her generation. She was a princess who sought not to be 'royal', a Victorian woman who strove to break into a masculine world, and a fiery, intriguing, often confusing personality. She challenges many preconceptions that we, in the twenty-first century, have of women who lived under the long reign of Princess Louise's formidable and – it has to be admitted – often extremely unpleasant mother.

As my research gained momentum, I found that much of the mystery surrounding Princess Louise was still to be uncovered. Why has she been locked away in the archives? What was it about her that is deemed too scandalous, or dangerous, to be revealed? Why should the life of a woman born in the first half of the nineteenth century be considered unsafe to be explored in the twenty-first century?

Prologue: A celebrity comes to Liverpool

> To her views [Princess Louise] was wont to give very forceful
> expression. She was a most amusing raconteuse, an inveterate
> though never a malicious gossip, and her indiscretions of speech
> were delightful . . . Her friendship and constant concern for my
> future had . . . very important effects upon my life.
>
> Charles L. Warr, *The Glimmering Landscape*, 1960

In the mayoral offices of Liverpool in the autumn of 1878, excitement
and tension were palpable. Within the next few weeks, the city would
welcome one of the most popular celebrities in Britain and every
detail of her visit had to be timed to the minute. At the city's docks,
preparations were equally feverish. The employees of the Allan Line
and the captain of the SS *Sarmatian* were fully aware of the import
of their upcoming voyage. Liverpool was buzzing with the news that
Queen Victoria's daughter was to visit the city – and she was the
country's favourite of the queen's daughters, the one who had stood
in so many times for her mother at official functions, her smiling,
pretty face replacing the dour expression of the black-clad queen; she
was the spirited daughter who had declared herself thoroughly British
and refused to marry a foreigner, unlike her sisters. The
journalists of Liverpool could not find enough superlatives to herald
the arrival of the artist princess.

On 12 November 1878, the *Daily Post* explained to its readers everything that would happen during the princess's brief stay. Carriages
would be waiting at the station to take the royal party from the sleeper
train straight to their hotel. After giving the travellers time to compose
themselves, the mayor would greet them at Liverpool's imposing town

hall, where there would be 1,000 invited guests. According to the *Post*, 'It is expected that the gathering will be a very brilliant one, as the good taste of the ladies will probably induce them to avoid dark colours, and display as many bright ones as the season will admit.' The paper published a map of the route for its readers, so that they could line the streets and wave to the princess and her handsome husband, the Marquess of Lorne. For several days, frenzied telegrams had been flying back and forth between London and Liverpool, in which every infinitesimal change to the princess's schedule was noted and explained.

At half past eleven on the night of Wednesday 13 November 1878, Princess Louise boarded a train at one of London's most impressive new landmarks, St Pancras station. With its magnificent hotel, designed by the architect Sir George Gilbert Scott, the station had caused a stir when it opened, two years previously, because of a truly innovative, and rather scandalous, addition: its Ladies' and Gentlemen's Smoking Room. This was the very first room in Europe in which ladies were permitted to smoke in public. It was the kind of place in which the bohemian princess (herself a smoker) would have felt entirely at home.

On the special train that rattled its way from London to Liverpool, the princess and her husband were accompanied by two of Louise's brothers, to whom she was extremely close: Arthur and Leopold. Their two Royal Pullman carriages were filled with every modern convenience and lavishly decorated with flowers, inside and out. Perhaps to avoid the crush of cheering crowds, the party had elected to leave late at night. This was not simply a royal visit to another city; it was the start of a brave and nerve-racking new phase in the life of the princess and marquess. They were moving to Canada for several years, for the marquess to take on the role of Governor-General. It would be the first time that a member of the royal family had lived in Canada. Louise's diplomatic role would be every bit as important as her husband's.

In Liverpool, the railway station and its surrounding streets were on red alert for the arrival of the princess. Flags decorated the station and the papers later reported that 'Ranelagh Street was illuminated by electric light by an enterprising firm of shopkeepers.' In the middle of the night, the people of Liverpool had started to line the streets in the hope of glimpsing the princess. According to the *Liverpool*

Mercury, 'the usual monotony' of a weekday in Liverpool would be pleasantly disrupted by the arrival of the royal party; businesses would be closed between 6a.m. and noon so that workers could have the chance to see the princess and her entourage.

The staff of the Royal Adelphi hotel had no sleep that cold November night. As one excited journalist wrote:

> The front of the noble building is literally covered with flags of all sizes and nations. The facade is surmounted by a magnificent Royal Standard, which is supported on one side by a Union Jack and on the other by a St George's ensign; while immediately above the principal entrance, and underneath the Royal Standard, an immense American flag[2] is displayed . . . A handsome porch, covered with scarlet cloth, has been erected at the principal doorway in Lime Street. This is surmounted by a shield representing the Argyll arms [the family crest of the Marquess of Lorne].

The princess and her party would enter the hotel by walking up steps covered with a 'rich crimson cloth'. Inside were 'festoons of flowers and evergreens'. Louise's Aesthetic soul would have appreciated the Japanese banners which had been chosen to 'impart additional variety and gaiety'. The staircase had also been given a makeover, with the addition of 'a rich Brussels carpet'. A large crowd had gathered and journalists reported that the princess and her husband were given rousing cheers; although many also noted with amusement that the two sons of Queen Victoria seemed to pass almost unnoticed. The princess was the person the crowds wanted to see.

The hotel had been issued with strict instructions on the protocol, and a number of rooms on the first-floor landing were set aside for the princess and her entourage. When the special train arrived at Liverpool, the sun had not yet risen, but the hotel's electric lights imparted, as one journalist wrote, to 'the strange early morning scene a brilliancy which the Royal party must have found very magnificent and surprising'. All of these preparations were for a visit which would last approximately four hours.

---

[2] A Canadian flag might seem more fitting, but the newspapers report that it was American.

When the royal train arrived, at six o'clock in the morning, it was met by an official party of 'prominent local gentlemen' including the mayor and the Commander of the District, General Willis. The proud mayor had travelled to London some weeks earlier for a private audience with the Marquess of Lorne, at which he had ascertained precisely how one should address the princess and whether she would be amenable to meeting local people. The answer was that Princess Louise would be very happy to undertake public duties. The royal party began its procession through the town, cheered on by crowds. Liverpool was proud of its maritime history, and the fact that the princess was beginning her new life from their docks was a moment to be cherished. The local hotels, restaurants and shops were equally pleased, their profits swelled by the journalists and other visitors flocking to the city.

The *Daily Post* claimed that a million people lined the streets of Liverpool that morning, cheering for their princess, and 'the weather was fine; frosty but kindly, and lit up with cheering sunlight'. The crowds of people waved flags as the princess, the two princes and the marquess were borne through the streets in magnificent carriages. By the time the royal party was ready to leave the hotel, for their 10.15a.m. meeting with the mayor, the numbers had swelled to include visitors from outside the city. Observers estimated that around a million people lined the royal route, desperate for a glimpse of the woman whose wedding had been such a popular event throughout the nation and whose loyalty to her people was legendary.

At this date, Princess Louise was more popular in Britain than her distant, stubborn mother (who, still mourning the death of her husband seventeen years earlier, made very few public appearances). The day after the princess's visit, the *Liverpool Mercury* reported: 'No event within recent years has caused so much excitement in Liverpool . . . although occupying but a few hours, [it] was characterised by an enthusiasm which could hardly have been more general or more significant.'

CHAPTER I

Born in the year of revolution

> The poor Duchess of Gloster is again in one of her nervous
> states, and gave us a dreadful fright at [Princess Louise's]
> Christening by quite forgetting where she was, and coming and
> kneeling at my feet in the midst of the service. Imagine our
> horror!
>
> Queen Victoria's diary, 16 May 1848

By the time of her visit to Liverpool, Princess Louise was a determined
young woman with a keen political mind and a career that she had
fought to be allowed to have. She was renowned by the public for her
good looks, her unusual artistic dress sense and her sense of humour.
Most importantly, Louise was also known for her compassion and her
many 'good works'. The princess was a forceful personality, who could
make herself adored, when she wanted to (and who could snub people
royally if she did not like them). She was regularly described as 'capti-
vating', 'charming' and 'clever'. People felt able to approach her,
members of the public wrote letters to her, or begged for her help
with charitable or political causes. Fellow artists were comfortable
enough to invite her to informal studio parties and men happily flirted
with her, in a way they would not have dreamt of doing with any of
her regal sisters. Even people who were not keen on the idea of a
royal family found Louise acceptable. She spoke openly and controversially about subjects that other people shrank from and she was
not above criticising the monarch. On one memorable occasion, as
she undertook, yet again, one of the queen's duties, Louise remarked
loudly that her mother 'was not too unwell to open Parliament, simply
too unwilling'. To understand why Louise should criticise her mother

so openly, it is necessary to look both at Queen Victoria and at Princess Louise's childhood.

Despite the fact that she is one of the most famous monarchs of all time, Queen Victoria was not intended to become queen. It was almost an accident that this young princess, whose father had died before she could even recognise him, ever acceded to the throne. The first link in the chain that led Victoria to the monarchy was the death in 1817 of one of the country's most popular royals: the much-admired Princess Charlotte. She was Victoria's first cousin, and the only legitimate child of the Prince Regent (later King George IV). When the news of Charlotte's tragic death spread the country went into extended mourning. She had died giving birth to her first child, a son who was stillborn after a protracted and stressful labour. To compound the tragedy, soon after the deaths of the princess and baby prince, one of the royal doctors who had assisted with the birth, Dr Croft, committed suicide.

Instead of gaining a much-loved and happily married queen, the country was left with its continued succession of dissolute Hanoverian kings. Following the death of King George IV, the throne passed to his brother, who became King William IV. Most people were angrily aware of the new king's former relationship with the actress Mrs Jordan – and of their ten illegitimate children. Aware he might become king, William had hastily ended this 'illegal' relationship and married Princess Adelaide of Saxe-Meiningen, but her two children failed to survive infancy. The country began to despair of its royal family, and the idea of a republican revolution was beginning to take hold.

The young Princess Victoria, who was the next in line to the throne, was perceived as a welcome and refreshing change after the excesses and debauchery of the sons of George III (one of whom, the Duke of Kent, was Victoria's father[3]). Initially, Victoria, who had

---

[3] There are suggestions that the Duke of Kent was not Victoria's biological father because of the presence of haemophilia in the royal family, which apparently began with Queen Victoria, who passed it on to her children. It has led generations of historians and geneticists to claim that Victoria's real father must have been someone whose family was cursed with haemophilia. For this reason, there were rumours that her mother's close advisor, Sir John Conroy, could have been her father. Other medical experts, however, point out that the disease can be acquired through a mutated gene and that Victoria could have been legitimate and have become a carrier

lived her childhood and early adulthood so simply, stiflingly and in genteel impoverishment, was seen as almost a reincarnation of the lamented Princess Charlotte. When William IV became ill, people were deeply concerned that he might die before his young niece reached her eighteenth birthday, thus leaving the throne vulnerable. The ailing king managed to cling to life until Victoria was just eighteen. The accession of this teenaged girl to the role of monarch was believed to be the dawning of a new golden age, one often compared to the Elizabethan era.

Almost immediately after she was declared queen, Victoria became an icon of morality and 'goodness'. Poets and artists immortalised her on canvas and in print and the country rejoiced in their new monarch and the changes she seemed to promise. When she married Prince Albert of Saxe-Coburg and Gotha, her love-match wedding – to a husband she had chosen and proposed to – was the ideal of fairy tales. Yet although Albert tried vigorously to celebrate all things British, he was never quite forgiven by his wife's subjects for being a foreigner.

Princess Louise was the sixth child and the fourth daughter of Queen Victoria and Prince Albert – and her birth was both agonising and terrifying. The queen would regularly recall its horrors, and as a child the young princess was made to feel dreadfully guilty about how much her mother had suffered to bring her into the world. The new baby was born at 8a.m. on 18 March 1848 and given the names of Louise Caroline Alberta. Louise was the name of her father's mother as well as that of her mother's aunt. Caroline was after her father's recently deceased step-grandmother – to whom Albert had been devoted. Her third name was after her father himself. On 14 April, the queen wrote in her journal: 'We have decided that our little girl's sponsors should be, Albert's Gt Uncle, Duke Gustoes of Mecklenburg Schwerin[,] Augusta Strelitz and the Dss of Meiningen.'[4]

During the pregnancy, Prince Albert had grown deeply concerned about his increasingly stressed wife, at what was a difficult time, politically. Royal families throughout Europe were being deposed, while in Britain, the working classes were agitating for higher pay, better

---

in this way. Had she been illegitimate, Victoria would have had no legal right to the British throne.

[4] In this instance, 'sponsors' means 'godparents'.

working conditions and more legal rights. Following Princess Louise's birth, Prince Albert wrote a letter to his brother saying how relieved he was – despite the irritating fact of the baby being female: 'I have good news for you today. Victoria was safely delivered this morning and though it be a daughter, still my joy and gratitude are very great, as I was often full of misgivings because of the shocks which have crowded upon Victoria of late.'

The new princess – nicknamed 'la nouvelle' by her siblings – came into the world during a very turbulent time. The year 1848 would be remembered as one of revolution and rebellion. In Ireland, revolutionaries were calling for an end to British rule and chaos seemed to reign throughout Europe as revolutions bred one another. The royal family grew used to the sight of beleaguered foreign royals and aristocrats arriving in London. These refugees, often possessing only the clothes they were wearing, brought stories of dissension and violence. Even Buckingham Palace could not cope with the influx: the royal children's bedrooms had been taken over by desperate distant relations of the queen, and Victoria and Albert's children had to sleep in servants' bedrooms.

By the time of Louise's birth, the queen was heartily sick of pregnancy and childbearing. In addition, her devotion to Albert allowed little room for her to love her children as they should have been loved. Many years later, the queen would reveal these feelings in a letter to her eldest daughter. When Vicky had been married for just a few weeks, she wrote to her mother of her longing to be alone with her husband and how tiresome she found it always having to carry out official duties. Her mother's reply explains a great deal about Queen Victoria's attitude to her children: 'You said in your long letter that the happiest time for you – was when you were alone with Fritz; you will now understand why I often grudged you children being always there, when I longed to be alone with dearest Papa! Those are always my happiest moments!'

Victoria, the Princess Royal, was nearly eight years old when the new baby was born. Vicky had been a true honeymoon baby, born on 21 November 1840, nine and a half months after her parents' marriage. By the time of Louise's birth, Vicky was a practised older sister and was accepted as the 'brains' of the family. Despite this, Vicky, in common with her sisters, was often made to feel a disappointment to her mother. Aware of how painful her mother's censure could be, Vicky grew protective of her younger siblings.

When Vicky was less than a year old, the queen had given birth to a son and heir. The future Edward VII, known as 'Bertie' to his family, was born on 9 November 1841. Almost from birth he was a disappointment to his parents, and his mother took every opportunity of letting him know how displeased she was with him. Bertie would become very close to Princess Louise, as the two often-neglected children bonded over their shared unhappiness. They would remain close throughout their lives.

The third of Victoria and Albert's children was Princess Alice (born on 25 April 1843); she was a caring sister and dutiful daughter, who strove not to upset her mother and who, during Louise's adolescence, often grew frustrated by her younger sister's wilfulness. Alice's behaviour in childhood was not remarkable – as Vicky's was by intelligence and Louise's by artistic temperament – but she would grow up to become an indomitable woman, devoted to furthering gender equality and championing the need for more, and better trained, nurses. Alice was especially close to the always naughty Bertie, but in many ways she was her parents' model daughter (until she grew up and became far too independent for her mother's liking).

Prince Alfred was born on 6 August 1844 and known in the family as 'Affie.'[5] Victoria and Albert made it obvious that they thought it a pity Bertie should be the heir to the throne, instead of the more promising Alfred. By the age of 12 Affie already knew what he wanted from life – he was going to be a sailor. He went on to have a distinguished career in the navy.

Princess Helena, known as 'Lenchen', was born on 25 May 1846. Her birth caused the queen to suffer 'longer and more than the other times', according to Prince Albert, and it was feared the baby would not survive. Helena was a tomboy, said not to cry when her brothers teased her, but to give as good as she got – famously punching one of her brothers back instead of bursting into tears. Helena was considered by her parents the least 'pretty' of the daughters and she grew up knowing her mother felt it would not be easy to find her a

[5] His titles would be Duke of Edinburgh and 3rd Duke of Saxe-Coburg and Gotha (his father's home).

husband. Indeed, Helena spent much of her childhood feeling a failure because she was not pretty enough.

By the time of Louise's birth, Victoria had an understandable horror of the pain of childbirth. She had few maternal impulses and famously detested the messiness and inability of young babies. She found their spasmodic movements – which she called 'that terrible froglike action' – physically repulsive. Louise's birth was followed by those of two more sons, Arthur (born 1 May 1850) and Leopold (born 7 April 1853). Louise was always extremely close to her two younger brothers, who adored her. None of the other princesses compared, in Arthur and Leopold's opinion, to 'Loo', 'Loosy' or 'Looloo', as Louise was variously known.

Arthur was named after his godfather, the Duke of Wellington (whose birthday he shared).[6] Louise made one of her first 'public' appearances at Arthur's christening, dressed all in white, like her sisters, and distinguished in her mother's journal as being 'very pretty & not at all shy, – very smart with her white gloves & little white & silver shoes' (she was two years and three months old at the time). The young Arthur showed an early interest in the military: it was claimed that even as a tiny baby he reacted with excitement when he saw a uniform. He was destined for the army.

The birth of Leopold in 1853 was remarkable as the first time the queen was given chloroform to help alleviate the agonies. Chloroform was an experimental new wonder drug and the physician who administered it had been in terror for weeks beforehand in case anything should go wrong. The new baby was named after Queen Victoria's beloved uncle and advisor, King Leopold I of the Belgians. From birth, Prince Leopold was sickly. When he was five or six, he was diagnosed with haemophilia. Unable to join in the energetic games of his brothers, he was usually expected to stay with his sisters and keep safe. He also suffered from an illness that caused him to have fits, perhaps epilepsy, something that was little understood and seen as an embarrassment. Throughout many of Leopold's 'bleeding' illnesses, which left him weakened and miserable, Louise was his childhood nurse, learning ably how to take care of him. The queen and prince consort wanted their children to be practical and useful and all their daughters grew up to be practised nurses.

---

[6] Later he became Duke of Connaught and Strathearn.

As had been the case with Leopold's birth, the queen's last baby, Princess Beatrice – born on 14 April 1857 – was eased into the world under the anaesthetic effects of chloroform. During the preparations for the birth, the medical establishment was divided firmly into two sides: those who admired Dr John Snow as a medical pioneer performing exciting work and those who thought that he was playing with the health of the monarch for his own glory.[7] One writer in *The Lancet* declaimed angrily, 'In no case could it be justifiable to administer chloroform in perfectly ordinary labour.' Snow suffered from the professional jealousy of his peers. When Prince Leopold had been diagnosed with haemophilia in the late 1850s, many doctors were quick to claim that his illness must have been caused by the use of chloroform. There was even a powerful lobby of medical men who insisted that God intended women to suffer in childbirth, and to die if necessary, and that any medication which alleviated the necessary pain went against the teachings of the Bible.

The queen and Prince Albert ignored the detractors; to them chloroform was a miracle. Victoria claimed that she felt 'better and stronger' after Beatrice's birth than she had after any of the others. As a result, she felt immediately more kindly disposed towards this baby than she had to any of her older children. Prince Albert described Beatrice as 'an extremely attractive, pretty, intelligent child – indeed the most amusing baby we have had'. Princess Beatrice was born a month after Louise's ninth birthday and seems seldom to have been written about in childhood without use of the phrase 'golden curls'. She was constantly favoured from the moment of her birth. The queen was delighted with how pretty her new baby was. Some years later, when Vicky (by that time married with children) censured her mother for disliking children, Queen Victoria responded: 'You are wrong in thinking that I am not fond of children, I admire pretty ones immensely.'

'Poor Louise' (as her mother usually referred to her), Arthur and

---

[7] By the time of Prince Leopold's birth, Dr Snow was one of the most famous medical men in Britain. He was from a non-medical background – the son of a Yorkshire farmer – but through intelligence and research he changed history and the medical profession. In addition to being a pioneer of anaesthesia, he was the first person to identify the cause of cholera (a very common disease in Britain at the time), saving millions of lives.

Leopold were all deeply affected by the arrival of the new and adored baby. In *Darling Loosy*, royal biographer Elizabeth Longford noted that it was around the time of Beatrice's birth that Louise began suffering from 'night terrors', an ongoing affliction that became exacerbated in times of stress.

Although the queen could have had no idea that Albert's life would end so soon, she knew Beatrice would be her last child. She was getting older and the gap between her most recent pregnancies had been wider than those between her first few. With the arrival of Beatrice, Queen Victoria finally discovered her maternal side. She petted and spoilt her new daughter and Beatrice was the one she wrote about glowingly in letters as the brightest star in her home. None of these comments and sentiments were likely to endear Beatrice to her siblings. Her relationship with them would be troubled throughout her life: Arthur and Leopold resented her almost from birth, and Beatrice had a particularly complicated relationship with both Bertie and Louise. Despite being almost 16 at the time of Beatrice's birth, Bertie found his mother's spoiling of her youngest child unbearable. When he finally became king, in 1901, Bertie began taking back from his youngest sister almost everything Queen Victoria had bestowed on her. Even in his sixties, Bertie still burned with the resentment created by his mother during his adolescence. Prince Albert's comment is very revealing: perhaps the reason Beatrice was such an amusing and alert baby was because she received so much more stimulus and affection from her mother than any of the other royal babies.

Louise was now pushed even more firmly out of the limelight. No longer the youngest daughter, she was not the most intelligent and she was certainly not the best behaved. She was simply one of those 'difficult' middle children, an overlooked, often ignored little girl. As she grew up, Louise would strive to become unique.

In 1848, while the queen was recovering from the ordeal of Louise's birth, the government was anxious about the monarch's safety. This fear had nothing to do with the possibility of puerperal fever or infection (a common cause of maternal mortality); what the government was worrying about was the threat of revolution. In 1848, one of its chief concerns was Chartism (the name arose from the People's Charter they had drawn up which demanded social reform). As the queen had been preparing for her 'confinement' (to use Victorian terminology) with her sixth child, the Chartists had been preparing to march from the north of England to London.

This march was the culmination of many years of protest. Between 1839 and 1848 millions of working people in Britain had signed petitions to the government, organised by the Chartists. A large percentage of those who had signed the petition were women (an unusual circumstance at a time when women had no political voice). Since 1839, many of the movement's most prominent activists had been imprisoned for their beliefs and protests, and by 1848 Britain's working classes were desperate and angry. The Chartists decided to march to London and hand in yet another petition to Parliament. It was rumoured that 150,000 protestors were on their way to the capital city. The government ordered strategic buildings, including the Bank of England and the British Museum, to be guarded against possible marauders. Thousands of new police officers were recruited to guard the streets of the city.

In the same year, a very different type of revolution had also begun in London. It would be a bloodless revolution and at the time was relatively little remarked upon, but it was to change the world in which Princess Louise grew up and it would have an enormous impact on her life and her career. A few months after the birth of the new princess, seven young men banded together to form a secret society. They called themselves the Pre-Raphaelite Brotherhood (or PRB) and they aimed to change the face of British art from within and, in particular, to challenge the antiquated views of the Royal Academy. The Brotherhood was composed of seven young men: John Everett Millais, Dante Gabriel Rossetti, William Holman Hunt, Thomas Woolner, Frederic George Stephens, James Collinson and William Michael Rossetti. They believed artists should not be stifled by the kind of restrictions that their Royal Academy tutors imposed; instead they longed for the freedom to create their own, unique style of art. These idealists would prove remarkably influential. They would spawn a movement that continued for decades and changed not only fine art, but the worlds of fashion, architecture and design and, through their 'social conscience' paintings, society at large. At the time of Louise's birth few people would have heard of their names; by her twenty-first birthday, they were famous. As an adult, the princess would come to know these young men and their circle both socially and professionally and they would have a positive impact on her life. By the time Princess Louise started to make her own mark on the art world, most of the PRB were pillars of the artistic establishment.

To the government, the queen and all those with political power, any revolution, be it political or artistic, was a threat to the social order. Those who ran the country were of course perfectly happy with the status quo and agitation was considered dangerous, subversive and in need of suppression. Throughout her reign, the queen would express fury with anyone who tried to usher in changes. Yet despite the early opposition to both movements, the Chartists and the artists changed British society.

Eight days after Louise's birth, on 26 March 1848, the order was given that a specially written prayer be read aloud throughout Britain:

> Almighty and merciful God, by whose Providence the whole world is governed and preserved; we yield Thee hearty thanks that it hath pleased Thee to deliver Thy servant, our Sovereign Lady the Queen, from the perils of childbirth, and to make her a joyful mother. We humbly beseech Thee to keep her under Thy fatherly care and protection; and enable her in the hour of weakness to feel the support of Thy everlasting arm. Defend the infant Princess from all dangers which may happen to the body and from all evil which may assault and hurt the soul; and grant that as she grows in years she may grow in grace, and in every Christian virtue.

Just days after the reading of this prayer for the health and security of the princess, the royal family was advised – some say ordered – to leave London in fear of their lives. The military commander and former Prime Minister, the Duke of Wellington, was so nervous of the Chartists, whose numbers were growing exponentially, that he genuinely believed that if the monarch and her family stayed in Buckingham Palace they would be in danger of being murdered. Prince Albert was fully aware of how many people posed a threat to his wife and children: he was so scared someone would harm his children that he was reputed to keep the keys to the nursery wing on his person at all times. People who would, in the twenty-first century, be defined as 'stalkers' posed a very real danger. Threatening letters were often received and Queen Victoria would suffer several assassination attempts. Despite the very young age of the new princess, the royal family and their servants made rapid arrangements to leave the city.

On 8 April 1848, the family party and its entourage travelled through a sodden, grey London to Waterloo station. This proud edifice, usually teeming with the public, was eerily empty – except for a large consignment of special constables. Records suggest that several hundred constables were employed to guard the family. A royal train and boats took the party to one of Prince Albert's favourite places, Osborne House on the Isle of Wight, even though the house was not yet ready for habitation. Due to necessity, the family moved in while the builders were still trying to finish off their summer home.

Prince Albert had fallen in love with the Isle of Wight a few years previously. He was a great lover of Italy and believed the view from Osborne House was like that of the Bay of Naples. The original eighteenth-century house on the site was not to Victoria or Albert's liking, so Albert hired the famous builder-architect, Thomas Cubitt, to replace it with his dream villa. Cubitt was told to emulate the style of Italian Renaissance architects, to lay out the grounds like an Italian garden and to fill the gardens and the house with classical sculptures. In 1848, when the royal party arrived for sanctuary, the original house was still standing, albeit vastly changed, and the new house was growing up around it.

In future years as Albert's Italianate vision took shape, Osborne House would become one of the royal family's most praised homes. The queen often bemoaned in her journal the necessity of having to return to London when they were all so happy at Osborne. Thanks to Queen Victoria's love of the island, the Isle of Wight gained a new status as a fashionable place to visit. It attracted poets, writers, artists and photographers and was immortalised by many of the leading names of the day. Alfred, Lord Tennyson (the Poet Laureate) and photographer Julia Margaret Cameron were among those who purchased homes there. The poet Algernon Charles Swinburne, who was born on the island, made regular trips home from his house in London. Famous visitors included Charles Dickens, William Thackeray,

Edward Lear, Lewis Carroll, the artist G.F. Watts and the illustrator John Leech. Osborne House, which is owned today by English Heritage, remains one of the island's chief attractions. When the family arrived so precipitately in 1848, however, the Isle of Wight was still fairly inaccessible and, in early April, the climate was markedly different from that in Naples. It was an arduous journey to undertake with such a young baby.

The Chartists had departed and the family had returned to London by the middle of May, for Louise to be christened. In her journal of 13 May 1848, the queen commented on the christening:

Another intensely hot day . . . Mama most kindly sent the Baby a string of pearls, to which was attached a locket with her hair, similar to what she gave Lenchen . . . I wore a silver moiré dress with my wedding lace wreath of acacias, with diamonds. The 4 Children came down with us into the Drawingroom [sic], Bertie, in a light blue velvet jacket, embroidered with gold, Vicky & Alice in white English lace dresses and Affie in a white and silver blouse . . . After the 1st piece of music (Albert's last Hymn, composed as a Christmas one) the Ld Chamberlain left, to fetch the child who was brought in by Mrs Bray the nurse and Ly Lyttelton [the governess] in attendance. I offered up my fervent prayers, that God would bless & protect through life, our dear little child. She looked very pretty, – so white plump. She cried a little at first, but behaved very well when the Archbishop took her up in his arms & christened her . . . We went upstairs in procession, excepting Aunt Gloucester whom Aunt Cambridge took up another way, as she had been seized by giddiness and faintness . . . The Baby and Lenchen were brought into the Throne Room where we were all assembled.

Despite the many laudatory illustrations and written accounts of the beauty and unity of Victorian family life, and the way in which the royal family was held up as an ideal to the rest of the world, the reality of life within the monarch's home was very different from the fiction. Initially, her journals would show an appreciation of a new baby in the family, mostly because of its connection to Albert, but Queen Victoria's later journals and letters regularly reveal exasperation, at times fury, with her children. She would praise them, but more often than not even her praise was marred by a backhanded compliment or a criticism in the form of an aside. For most of the time the queen found her offspring tiring and irritating. When writing about Princess Louise, the queen's initial comments were about the 'baby' as being sweet or pretty, or she would note that 'poor Louise' was 'still not well', but always she wrote from a guarded point of view, as though she were a casual observer rather than the baby's mother. As was considered normal at the time, the parents rarely saw their new baby; Louise lived in the nursery where she was cared for by servants and specially appointed ladies-in-waiting. In her journal the queen noted that the new baby was brought down to see her two or three times a day (usually at mealtimes); she and her clothing would be admired and then she would be sent away again.

As Louise started to grow up and develop a personality, the queen's letters began to make frequent mention to her daughter being 'odd' or 'difficult'. The queen herself often pondered if Louise's wilful personality was a direct result of her being born in that difficult 1848, the year of revolution. On Louise's fifth birthday, her mother commented: 'How well I remember all that eventful time when she was born, which timed with hourly news of revolution & civil war &c.'

On meeting Louise for the first time, the royal governess, Lady Lyttelton (known in the nursery as 'Laddle'), was entranced. She described the new baby as 'Extremely fair with white satin hair, large long blue eyes and regular features: a most perfect form from head to foot.' One of the ladies-in-waiting of the Duchess of Kent (the mother of Queen Victoria) wrote of the 'delicious baby, Princess Louise, it is a delight and a beautiful creature'. Sadly the baby's mother seldom went into such raptures, although on Louise's first birthday, the queen noted in her journal: 'May God bless the dear little child, who is so fat, strong & well again. She was born in the most eventful times, & ought to be something peculiar in consequence.' Louise was dressed in pink for this milestone birthday and had a table full of toys to play with in the breakfast room. Her siblings were dressed up for the occasion too, the boys in new kilts, and the queen noted with satisfaction that she also had two new dresses for the day, one for the morning and one for the evening.

The family was back at Osborne House for the birthday, where Louise was taken out to 'plant a tree, not far from the house' in commemoration of her special day. She took her first steps (or at least the first her mother knew about) a couple of months later, on 6 May 1849, at Buckingham Palace. It is likely she had already started walking in the nursery, but that the attendants wisely did not tell their queen that she had missed the event. In November, the queen wrote, 'Little Louise gets very amusing & says such droll things. She is very tall for her age & broad & fat.' From a very young age, Louise was noted to have a love of dancing – when she was seven the queen noted that she and Albert were 'quite astonished' at Louise's aptitude on the dance floor.

In the first years of her life, Louise appears in her mother's journals almost as a plaything, a pretty doll-like creature to be dressed up. It is also notable how often the queen writes that Louise 'sobbed bitterly' when her parents prepared to go away and leave her behind. While Prince Albert was alive, the queen, who would later become renowned for her refusal to wear anything except 'widow's weeds', took a great interest in clothing and fashion: the new gowns she possessed, which she described in detail, the matching outfits her children were wearing, and in which new styles the little girls had had their hair arranged. The princesses seem to have spent much of their lives being dressed and undressed and kept looking perfect, unable to move for fear of disarranging their outfits before they were taken to see their parents. Queen Victoria notes in her journal on 21 February 1852 that 'Lenchen & Louise had their ears bored [pierced] today, – very successfully.' From the beginning of their lives, royal princesses had to be beautiful and admired and were expected to make good marriages. There was to be no exception.

In the earliest years of Louise's life, the queen comments on her daughter being amusing or clever – on her seventh birthday, Louise was described in her mother's journal as 'so clever in many ways, affect[ion]ate, & a very pretty child' – but it did not take long for the queen to become far less enchanted with her daughter. More usually, the queen would write comments about Louise being 'backward', 'difficult', 'awkward', 'naughty' or 'rebellious'. Almost as soon as Louise was considered old enough to spend more time with her parents, her presence and personality began to irk her mother. At those times the queen seemed to forget that Louise had ever amused her and wrote of her daughter as if her development had been retarded since birth.

The queen's 'hands' off' attitude was demonstrated in 1855, when Louise and Arthur became ill with what the doctors diagnosed as scarlatina (also known as scarlet fever). They were quarantined. Fearful of catching it herself, the queen refused to see them. On 2 August, she noted that Louise was out of quarantine: 'Louise came down for a moment to my room, but I did not touch her.' Although the popular myth is that all Victorian aristocratic children were ignored by their parents and brought up by nannies, this was not always true. Most mothers, at least, took an active and tender part in their children's welfare, even though the routine work was expected to be performed by servants. Victoria was not a representative parent of her era. The queen's indifferent and hurtful behaviour would plague Louise into adulthood, but it had the effect of ensuring that Louise herself became adored by the children who knew her as an adult – she strove never to make the same mistakes as her mother.

CHAPTER 2

A royal education

Luckily the habit of moulding children to the same pattern has gone out of fashion. It was deplorable. I know, because I suffered from it. Nowadays individuality and one's own capabilities are recognised.

Princess Louise in a newspaper interview, 1918

That Louise was always considered the beauty of the family was mentioned regularly in contemporary accounts. Despite the country's loyalty to their queen and the often repeated belief that she was the woman on whom girls should model themselves, neither Victoria nor most of her daughters would have been considered great beauties had their veins not run with royal blood. Despite the fact that Louise was a very intelligent and able adult, as a child her mother refused to acknowledge these qualities in her. She had the same attitude to her eldest son and heir, Bertie, who spent so much of his childhood and adolescence fearful of letting down his parents that he went to pieces, academically. It is likely that Bertie suffered from an undiagnosed educational problem: some experts suggest he was dyslexic, others that he had ADHD. Bertie suffered the dual torments of having an extremely intelligent older sister and constantly disapproving parents.

The queen's lack of kindness to her children did not go unnoticed; and several members of the royal household were uncomfortably aware of it. In her biography of Princess Louise, written in the 1980s, Jehanne Wake comments: 'From an early age Princess Louise had to accept frequent admonishments, punishments and whippings for misbehaviour. Whereas the Lady Superintendent naturally hesitated before beating the princesses, the Queen knew no such qualms.'

The queen was not an easy person to appease. Although their marriage was essentially very happy, there were times when the monarch and prince consort became so furious with one another that they communicated only by letter. In later years, the queen would do the same to her children; they always knew they were in trouble when a servant arrived with a note. The queen would even use the servants to pass angry notes to people she was sitting next to. Prince Albert was frustrated by the queen's lack of maternal instinct and attempted to make her more gentle towards the children. In a letter written when Louise was a small child, Albert wrote to his wife: 'It is indeed a pity that you find no consolation in the company of your children. The root of the trouble lies in the mistaken notion that the function of a mother is to be always correcting, scolding, ordering them about and organizing their activities. It is not possible to be on happy friendly terms with people you have just been scolding.'

Alice was derided as 'backward', Helena was regularly criticised for not being pretty – especially for her face being too long – and, before Vicky became a dutiful wife and mother, she was regularly accused of being 'difficult'. The worst of the queen's caustic tongue however was usually aimed at Bertie, the son and heir, who could do almost nothing right. Bertie grew up in fear of both his parents, especially the queen. To the people of Britain he was a king in waiting, but to his parents he was an irresponsible child whose character was weak and needed to be moulded. In a letter to Vicky, dated 6 May 1863, the queen writes bitchily about Bertie and his new wife, the Danish Princess Alexandra ('Alix'). Victoria, outwardly so friendly to her new daughter-in-law, wrote privately to Vicky that Bertie and Alix were sure to have 'unintellectual children', because they both had small heads. The excerpt from her letter (and this is what remains after Princess Beatrice's heavy editing) reads:

> Are you aware that Alix has the smallest head ever seen? I dread that – with his small empty brain – very much for future children. The doctor says that Alix's head goes in, in the most extraordinary way, just beyond the forehead: I wonder what phrenologists would say.

The queen enjoyed expounding her theories about other people's brains. She wrote to General Grey (Albert's and then Victoria's private

secretary) that her physician had told her Louise had a 'peculiar consti-
tution of [the] brain'. She did, however, praise her daughter's beauty
and artistic ability. General Grey and his daughter Sybil were close
friends with Princess Louise until the end of their lives. Louise was
devoted to them both.

Prince Albert was extremely interested in his children and in shaping
them to become well-rounded, useful members of society. His sons'
testimonies show he was a very stern father, who insisted on physical
punishment and could be cruel, but he seems to have treated his
daughters with more care and less physical correction. When she was
10 years old and Albert was away, Louise wrote him a heartfelt letter:
'My dear Papa, How long it seems that you are away, I long very much
to see you again.' On Louise's eleventh birthday, the queen wrote in
her journal that Albert took Louise out in the afternoon for her first
'ride out'; it was just the two of them, something that Louise had
'begged for' as a special birthday treat. On this birthday, the queen
prayed almost resignedly that her already difficult daughter 'may . . .
turn out all one could wish!'.

Albert's ideas on education and child-rearing were fascinatingly
modern and he and the queen harmoniously agreed that all their
children should be brought up to have essential life skills, as well as
an academic education. The prince wrote to his brother after Louise's
birth,

> The education of six different children, for they are none of them
> the least like the other in looks, mind or character, is a difficult task.
> They are a great deal with their parents and are very fond of them.
> I don't interfere in the details of their upbringing but only superin-
> tend the principles, which are difficult to uphold in the face of so
> many women, and I give the final judgement. From my verdict
> there is no appeal.

It was not only his children whom Albert had grand ideas about
educating. He was passionate about educating the people of Britain;
a cause Louise would continue many decades after her father's death.
While Louise would concern herself with ragged schools and the
educating of girls to the same standard as boys, what Albert was
involved with was the higher ranks of education. He wanted Britain

to be the ideal country in which to live and for other countries to recognise it as such. He believed that art was one of the most important aspects of a well-rounded education.

That Princess Louise was artistic was not surprising. Both her parents were talented artists and Louise grew up in a home in which art was valued and enjoyed. Her parents took their roles as artistic patrons (a vital part of the economy before the creation of the welfare state) very seriously. Many of their presents to one another were in the form of art, often commissioned for special occasions, such as birthdays or wedding anniversaries. Although they had their favourite artists, including Winterhalter and Landseer, both Victoria and Albert also had a shrewd collector's instinct and made original and interesting purchases from new artists and artisans.

When Louise was three or four years old, she had her very first art lesson. The royal art tutor, Edward Corbould, had trained at Henry Sass's academy and the Royal Academy and was well schooled in the traditions of British art.[8] He was a painter and sculptor who was hired after Prince Albert bought one of his biblical paintings. Corbould taught the royal children from 1852 until the mid-1860s. After he had left her employment, the queen continued to pay him an annual pension.[9]

Corbould praised and encouraged his young pupil, recognising that Louise's art was an area in which she could shine. Because Victoria and Albert were such good artists themselves, they saw nothing particularly special in their daughter's talent. Louise would have to work very hard to gain recognition or be considered exceptional. In later years, she did this by dressing artistically and becoming part of London's bohemian artistic elite; as a child, however, she could simply keep trying to be noticed, and often that was achieved by being 'naughty' or disruptive.

[8] Sass's school was considered the preparatory training for the Royal Academy. It had been established, across the road from the British Museum, in 1818.

[9] Corbould died in 1905, and in the months before his death Princess Louise was one of his most regular visitors, taking him tempting foods to encourage him to eat. Corbould then lived on Victoria Road in Kensington, an artistic area of London not far from Edward Burne-Jones's house and studio and on the same road as the artists Carlo and Kate Perugini (the younger daughter of Charles Dickens).

Albert was the ideal consort for Queen Victoria. He was an intelligent and questioning man, interested in the affairs of state and yet wise enough to take a step back, out of the limelight, when necessary. One of his enduring legacies was the Great Exhibition of 1851 and the projects that were financed by the money it raised. The grand plan was to allow all countries to display their works of industry and manufacturing – with Albert secure in the knowledge that Britain was at the forefront of both. Ironically, he was more passionate than Victoria about Britain. It is common to read in Queen Victoria's letters complaints about her children being 'too English' and not as 'Germanised' as she would have liked. This was partly because, after Albert's death, she longed to cling to anything that reminded her of him, but even before he died she had less enthusiasm for the country over which she ruled than her 'convert' of a husband.

People travelled from all over the globe to the Great Exhibition, arriving at Hyde Park in their thousands. It was estimated that, in addition to the overseas visitors, more than a quarter of the British population attended. There were tickets in a range of prices, with certain days being affordable for those who could not manage the normal entrance fee. A visitor who walked past every single stall, along every single aisle, would have walked for over ten miles. There were representatives from almost every country in the world: 15,000 exhibitors showed off over 100,000 innovations. There were sculptures from France, textiles from India, watches from Switzerland, gold from Chile, armour from Russia, tea from China and furs from Canada.

Visitors could marvel at the inventions of science and engineering, and debates grew up about which of the many thousands of new ideas would become popular – and which could end up putting people out of a job. Brilliant inventions were showcased, many of them from British manufacturers. There were carriages, a working lighthouse, umbrellas that turned into weapons, the latest techniques for producing artificial limbs, innovatively designed false teeth, the world's biggest diamond and a wondrously powerful microscope. Before the exhibition, the organisers had worried about the need for 'public conveniences' for this vast number of anticipated visitors. An innovative idea won the day: individual water closet cubicles were provided, which had the great benefit of being able to pay for themselves. For one penny a customer could pee in privacy.

When the author Charlotte Brontë visited the exhibition, she was overwhelmed, as most visitors were, and wrote: 'Its grandeur does not consist in one thing, but in the unique assemblage of all things. Whatever human industry has created you find there. It seems as if only magic could have gathered this mass of wealth from all the ends of the earth.' The queen described the opening ceremony as 'one of the greatest and most glorious days of our lives . . . a day that makes my heart swell with thankfulness'. She returned to the Great Exhibition regularly and the younger children, including three-year-old Louise, were taken to it on the morning of 17 May 1851. The exhibition was a burst of colours, artistic styles and gorgeous textiles. The exhibition space itself – with its unusual architecture, waving palm trees, fountains and sculptures – was equally entrancing. It was a liberating and exciting place for children whose life was so tightly controlled. The queen's journal entry for their visit mentions 'fine black lace from Barcelona . . . beautiful richly brocaded stuffs . . . fine silks, some beautiful marble, particularly some of a rose-coloured tint which is quite lovely . . . carpets & tapestry . . . The taste & execution are quite unequalled, & gave one a wish to buy all one saw!' The queen did not expect her children to be able to take it all in, and was greatly impressed with Affie who talked about the amazing things he had seen for hours afterwards.

Lord Ronald ('Ronnie') Gower, with whom Louise would become closely connected in later life, was six years old when the Great Exhibition took place and in his memoirs he wrote of the wonders it had held for such a young child: the 'splendour and height' of the Crystal Palace and how cleverly the building had been constructed around the old elm trees in Hyde Park, which many people had feared would be sacrificed. He described the Crystal Palace as 'enchanted . . . [with its] crystal fountains and marble statues . . . also the vast crowds of peoples of all countries and nationalities, so full of variety and character'. He remembered 'the Turkish Court, where . . . we were given dates to eat' and 'the German department, where our childish fancy was charmed by stuffed frogs and weasels in every attitude of civilised life'.

The Great Exhibition was a great success and improved the prince consort's popularity. Although the idea for the exhibition had not been his, he had been a pivotal member of the committee and the public appreciated not only his work on the exhibition, but his plans for what to do with the profits. The exhibition raised almost £190,000, which was used to purchase land in South Kensington (then outside central London). Today, the land that Prince Albert earmarked for his educational programme houses three of London's most important museums: the Natural History Museum, the Science Museum and the Victoria and Albert Museum.

Albert constantly devised plans for his own children's education and enjoyment. He was determined they would not grow up to be pampered royals, but would become useful members of society, capable of running their own households as well as the country. Albert understood that the role of monarchy was changing and that the modern royal would need to be very different from Victoria's Hanoverian ancestors. This belief was passed on to Princess Louise. She was always grateful to her father for having provided her with such a well-rounded, and intelligently thought out, education.

In 1854, the year in which Louise celebrated her sixth birthday, the royal children were presented with a wonderful gift: a Swiss Cottage, in the grounds of Osborne House. This exquisite royal playhouse is no mere 'Wendy house'; it is a two-storey cottage designed perfectly in proportion for children to feel at home in. Inside was a real working kitchen, where the girls were taught to cook and bake. There was also a dining room, where they could entertain their parents or attendants and sample the food they had prepared. The children were encouraged to learn about nature, to go out into the park that surrounded Osborne House and the cottage and to learn about the world around them. The Swiss Cottage has been preserved and visitors today can see the remains of the little natural history collection, containing items that the children carefully sought out in the grounds, labelled and preserved. There are also specimens of their art, needlework and the boys' carpentry.

Outside the cottage remain nine neat little gardens, each marked out and named; they were expected to be kept beautifully by their royal owners. The children had their own tools and wheelbarrows. In their mini allotment, each child had dominion, choosing what vegetables, fruit or flowers she or he would like to grow. When their labours proved successful, Prince Albert would 'buy' them for use in the Osborne House kitchens or to decorate the tables, just as if they had been sold at a market. Louise became notable for her bakery and cooking skills. The children retained fond memories of the Swiss Cottage all their lives; it was an educational project, but it was also a place of fun and happiness. Shortly after her marriage, Vicky wrote to her mother, 'I must confess that I cried bitterly last night at the thought of your going to dear Osborne, and without me. My pretty rooms that I loved so much, the dear view out of the windows – the darling Swiss cottage, my garden, the tree I planted the day we left . . .' As its name suggests, the cottage was built in the style of a traditional Swiss home. It had working fireplaces, a balcony to sit out on on sunny days, a sleeping space for the house-keeper and a working loo.

For the royal children, life was spent travelling between Buckingham Palace, Windsor Castle, Osborne House and, once their mother fell in love with Scotland, Balmoral. Louise was desperate to pursue her art regardless of how often the family moved around and, as a young woman, she was granted a studio of her own at Osborne House. She decorated it with copies of works by Old Masters. Today much of Osborne House does not look like a royal home; following the death of Queen Victoria, it was handed over to the nation and became a naval cadets' training college, then, during the First World War, a hospital. Princess Louise's former studio was one of the rooms in which wounded soldiers were nursed. I was surprised, when I was allowed to see the room, at how very different it was from what I expected – and from what I imagined a budding artist would have needed. At Osborne House, the young princes and princesses were segregated by gender. The boys' rooms were on the second floor and the girls' on the first floor. The royal children had rooms that looked out on to the sea, and their attendants' rooms faced away from the sea. I expected that Louise's studio would have been a light, airy room with big windows and a beautiful view. Instead it was a very small room on the first floor, with the sole light source being one small window. Even with modern electric light, the room felt dark and cramped. It seems an uninspiring room in which to imagine an artist working, but for Louise, having her own studio in which to paint and sculpt was a much-longed-for form of freedom.

While Louise was taking her first lessons in drawing, the world was preparing for the brutal art of war. Despite the seemingly cordial relationships being played out in Joseph Paxton's palace of glass, at the time of the Great Exhibition, tensions were running high in Europe. Britain, France, Russia and the Ottoman Empire had begun to compete for influence and trade in the Middle East. As Catholics, Protestants, Muslims and Orthodox Christians battled over religious sites in the Holy Land the tension increased exponentially, until the vast might of the Russian and Ottoman Empires reached crisis point. In 1853, Turkey declared war on Russia. The following year, France and Britain became Turkey's allies and the Crimean War had begun.

Princess Louise was only five when war broke out, but the conflict was something no royal child was unaware of. Having enjoyed a brief couple of years of acceptance, Prince Albert found that his heritage was causing trouble. Newspapers published articles claiming Albert was 'intriguing' on the side of Russia. The royal family, with its relations in so many different royal houses all over Europe, were constantly entreated and harassed by supporters of both sides. In February 1854, Queen Victoria wrote to her beloved uncle, King Leopold of Belgium, that she feared war was 'quite inevitable'. Within a couple of weeks, Louise and her siblings were standing with their parents on the balcony of Buckingham Palace watching a parade of soldiers shortly to depart for the Crimea. The royal children spent the next two years, alongside their lessons, knitting for the troops. They made scarves and socks, stockings and gloves – anything that might be of benefit to the troops living and dying in the cold and harsh surroundings of a Crimean winter.

The Crimean War changed the way people in Britain viewed foreign conflicts. Thanks to innovations in communications and transport, news reports were sent home with much greater rapidity than in the past. This was the beginning of true war correspondence. The most celebrated journalist of the time, William Howard Russell, sent eyewitness reports to London from the Crimea. Russell's stories from the front line transformed how people viewed the military, commanders and war in general. 'The commonest accessories of a hospital are wanting,' reported Russell from the Crimea: 'there is not the least attention paid to decency or cleanliness . . . For all I can observe, these men die without the least effort being made to save them . . . The sick appear to be tended by the sick, and the dying by the dying.' It was this new style of groundbreaking journalism that inspired Florence Nightingale and Mary Seacole.

Thanks to Russell's pioneering work, the British public was aware that war was not a glorious thing that happened in far-off lands, that bred heroes and could be forgotten about in everyday life. Through the medium of the newspapers, it was now known to be terrifying, cruel and often inglorious. Those with sons, lovers, brothers and husbands away fighting had to live with the knowledge of what really happened on the battlefields. Russell's report from Balaclava inspired one of the most iconic of Victorian poems, 'The Charge of the Light Brigade', by Alfred, Lord Tennyson. Russell's report included the words:

> They swept proudly past, glittering in the morning sun in all the pride and splendour of war. We could scarcely believe the evidence of our senses! Surely that handful of men were not going to charge an army in position? Alas, it was but too true – their desperate valour knew no bounds, and far indeed was it removed from its so-called better part – discretion.

It was not only literature that took up the cause of the soldier fallen in the Crimea, artists were also inspired. Suddenly galleries were full of scenes if not of the fighting, then of families devastated by the death or injury of loved ones. James Collinson, perhaps the least well known of the Pre-Raphaelite Brotherhood, exhibited the poignant *Home Again* in 1856.[10] On first glance, it appears to be a joyous reunion of a soldier returning to his family. The large family is depicted in a poor but cosy home lit by a glowing fire. There are young children, a work-worn wife and elderly parents – all of whom are supported by his salary. On closer inspection, it becomes apparent that the soldier is not leaning forward to embrace his wife – he is stumbling forward with his arms outstretched trying to find her. The war has left him blind. Victorian viewers would have understood that he would be pensioned off at a fraction of the salary he earned when able-bodied. Now, instead of being the breadwinner, the soldier will not only be unable to earn, but he will also need someone else, someone of useful

---

[10] This painting is owned by the Tate Britain.

working age, to help care for him. The family's future looks frighteningly bleak.

Many artists focused on the royal family and their visits to the
wounded. The queen, Albert and their children were frequently
depicted visiting hospitals and talking to returned soldiers. In 1856, a
popular painting showed the queen, the prince consort and their two
eldest sons visiting disabled soldiers at the Brompton Hospital in
Chatham, Kent, a visit which had taken place in March 1855. *Queen
Victoria's First Visit to her Wounded Soldiers* by Jerry Barrett depicts the
two young princes listening to the tales told by a disabled soldier. His
clothing is worn and his beard unkempt, but he commands the full
attention of the royal family by his bravery.[11]

Once the shock of going to war had subsided, Queen Victoria's
letters suggest that she found the war exhilarating. By the autumn of
1854, she thrilled with the idea of her handsome young troops fighting
bravely and expressed the wish that she could have been a man and
fought with them. She busied herself with plans for a creating a Crimea
medal and, when it became apparent many more troops were needed,
the queen offered the royal yacht as transport, estimating it could easily
house 1,000 soldiers. As the war continued, the royal family became
increasingly aware this was not a simple skirmish from which they
could soon retire in glory. The monarch also began to realise what it
would mean for the many wounded soldiers who would be unable to
work; she started asking what schemes could be put in place to enable
disabled servicemen to find jobs on their return home.

Royal family life continued, however, much as before. In 1855, the
family travelled to the Isle of Wight for a summer at Osborne House
and the Belgian royal family came to stay – although it was an unfortunate time to visit, as the nurseries had to be quarantined due to
scarlet fever. The first to succumb were Louise, Arthur and Leopold.
Soon afterwards, Prince Albert was writing that Alice had caught the
illness from Louise. While the four invalids were recuperating, Victoria,
Albert and their older children travelled to Paris. It was the year in
which the city was hosting its response to the Great Exhibition, the
Exposition Universelle, on the Champs-Elysées. Among the British
exhibits was the much-celebrated painting *Ophelia*, by an artist who

---

[11] This painting can be viewed in the National Portrait Gallery in London.

would become one of Queen Victoria's favourite painters, John Everett Millais. Along with Dante Gabriel Rossetti and William Holman Hunt, he was a founder member of the Pre-Raphaelite Brotherhood, the rebellious art movement that had been established in the year of Louise's birth. Millais came from a wealthy family, so he was in the enviable – and rare – position of being an artist who did not need to worry about money. Within a couple of decades, Millais would be a member of Princess Louise's circle of friends.

In early September the reunited family journeyed to Scotland, and their new home, Balmoral. The queen recorded in her journal that as they entered the hallway 'an old shoe was thrown after us . . . for good luck'. The queen adored Balmoral, but many of her children were less enthusiastic. As adults, both Vicky and Alice would live overseas and the idea of Balmoral became to them a kind of talisman with which they could hold on to the past; both had rose-tinted memories of their Scottish home. For the younger royal children still living with their mother, the castle held fewer charms. Louise and Leopold particularly grew to dislike Balmoral as cold and unfriendly and for the bad memories they gained there – especially, after Prince Albert's death, of its association with the queen's adored Highland ghillie, John Brown (a bullying man who might have been loved by the monarch but who was despised by her children). As Louise grew into her teens and then adulthood, the family visits to the Highlands began to feel more like incarceration than relaxation and she longed for visitors to alleviate the boredom. During her early childhood years, however, the children were still captivated by their mother's enthusiasm for the Scottish Highlands. The family was at Balmoral in 1856 when they heard the news of an allied victory: the fall of Sebastopol. Albert led a party of revellers to the top of a nearby hill where they lit an enormous bonfire as a beacon of good news to all the villages around.

For the princesses, as for many girls and women of the age, one of the most exciting figures to emerge from the Crimean War was a young woman known as 'The Lady with the Lamp'. Florence Nightingale had become a legendary figure for Louise and her sisters. Queen Victoria was immensely impressed with the work carried out by the nursing pioneer and sent her a brooch and an invitation to visit the royal family on her return to Britain. At the end of September,

Florence Nightingale arrived at Balmoral. Lady Augusta Bruce (later Lady Augusta Stanley), one of the queen's mother's ladies-in-waiting,[12] wrote on 23 September 1856:

> Last night we did not return from Balmoral till 7.30 as there was a neighbour Ball to inaugurate the new Ballroom . . . The room lovely and the little Princesses exquisite. By the way, the most important addition was Miss Nightingale! . . . [who] spent a long time with the Queen on Sunday. – She is much less altered than expected – her beautiful countenance looks to me more beautiful than ever. – Her hair is short and she wears a little plain morning cap – her black gown high, open in front. The Queen and children delighted with her . . . She is so modest and retiring and fearful of notice . . . It is most touching to look on that slight delicate frame and think what it has been enabled to go through.

The queen noted in her journal on 4 October 1856: 'Had some long conversation with excellent Miss Nightingale, whose affection for my poor good soldiers is most touching, & whose philanthropy & truly Christ-like spirit of <u>true</u> charity are beautiful.'

For Louise, this meeting was thrilling. Throughout her life, she was intrigued by women who broke the rules. Florence Nightingale had been born into a wealthy family and was expected to follow the established journey of a well-born, middle-class Victorian woman. She had been born in Italy on her parents' extended honeymoon (and was named after the city of her birth) but grew up in rural England, where she felt stifled by the smallness of her world. One of her earliest battles was in persuading her parents to let her learn mathematics, a subject considered too masculine for a girl. It was a hard-fought battle, but she won. She would continue to fight for the right to make her own choices about life, often at the expense of family happiness. At a young age Florence had experienced what she described as a calling from God; her vocation was nursing. Her family was appalled, but eventually Florence achieved her dream. She not only learnt the craft of nursing but went on to fight for the right of other women to do

[12] Lady Augusta Bruce was the sister of Bertie's governor, Robert Bruce.

the same and she changed the profession dramatically, making it regulated, respectable and far more efficient.

When she met Nightingale, a woman of forceful personality and charisma, Louise was in awe of her. This was a woman who, before she found fame, had been shunned by many of her own social class for her 'unnatural' desire to work in such a lowly and unsavoury job, yet by the end of the Crimean War Florence Nightingale was universally hailed as a heroine. It had taken courage, stamina and determination. The opportunity to meet this legendary woman made a very deep impression. Princess Louise would always identify with, and want to associate with, women who did unusual or brave things. As she grew older, she made an effort to meet those whom society had shunned or who challenged the status quo, such as the novelist George Eliot (Mary Ann Evans), and the campaigners Harriet Martineau and Josephine Butler. She wanted to become one of those celebrated and controversial women herself.

CHAPTER 3

In the shadow of her siblings

Louise is very naughty and backward, though improved and very pretty, and affectionate.

Queen Victoria, letter to Vicky, 1858

The Crimean War ended in February 1856, shortly before Louise's eighth birthday (for which occasion a Mr Tanner brought his performing dogs to the Orangerie at Windsor Castle). Within a few weeks, the royal family had a secret reason to celebrate. Vicky had become engaged. Her fiancé was the Crown Prince of Prussia, Frederick, known as Fritz. Vicky was not yet sixteen so her mother requested that the news be kept secret for as long as possible and the couple wait a couple of years before marrying. By the middle of 1856, the secret was more generally known amongst friends and relations, yet Princess Louise and six-year-old Prince Arthur were kept in ignorance. Queen Victoria had decided that, although Louise was eight years old, she would 'not understand', so she insisted that no one tell her. By the date of Vicky's engagement, Louise usually appears in her mother's journal coupled with Arthur, with whom, by dint of age, she was most closely linked. The queen's standard formula when she wrote about her two children was 'Louise and dear little Arthur' or 'Dear little Arthur came in with Louise'. By the end of 1856, the news was such public knowledge that the engaged couple were honoured with waxworks at Madame Tussaud's, yet Louise was still expected not to know.

In the summer of 1857, a few weeks after Beatrice's birth, Louise was given the opportunity to go abroad for the first time. She was part of the family party when the royal yacht arrived in Cherbourg, and then Alderney, in the Channel Islands. The yachting holiday was only part of the great excitement of the final months of the year. At last Louise had been told about her sister's engagement and she knew she would be a bridesmaid.

Vicky and Fritz's wedding took place at the Chapel Royal at St James's on Monday 25 February 1858. The queen's dress was so magnificent that many of the newspapers wrote more about the bride's mother than the bride; particular notice was taken of the fact that the queen wore the world's biggest known diamond, the Koh-i-noor. Alice, Helena and Louise wore dresses of pink satin and white lace, with headdresses of cornflowers and daisies. Vicky's brothers all wore Highland dress and Prince Albert was resplendent in military uniform. This was one of the most exciting events in Louise's life so far and it fired her romantic imagination. The wedding cake towered over all the royal family (none of whom were particularly tall) at 'between six and seven feet in height', decorated with pillars, statues in ornamental niches and festoons of jasmine flowers. The decorations included profile drawings of the bride and groom and the English and Prussian royal families' coats of arms. Each slice of cake was decorated with a medallion bearing an image of the bridal couple.

Following the excitement of the wedding, the younger children soon lost the company not only of their eldest sister, but also of their two eldest brothers. Alfred joined the navy in 1858 and Bertie was finally permitted to start living independently at White Lodge in Richmond Park (albeit under such close guard by servants who reported back to his parents on his every mood that it was a spurious brand of 'independence'). When Bertie moved away, his relationship with his mother improved, but her words in a letter to Vicky are still damning: 'His natural turn and taste is very trifling, and I think him a very dull companion. But he has been quite altered, for the last few months (in short since he lived at the White Lodge) as to manner, and he is no longer difficile à vivre. Handsome I cannot think him, with that painfully small and narrow head, those immense features and total want of chin.'

In the year that Bertie, Vicky and Affie left home, Louise celebrated her tenth birthday. Despite her parents' continued belief that Louise was mentally deficient, comments from others suggest that she was a very artistic, sensitive and intuitive child, who misbehaved because of boredom and unhappiness, not stupidity. Louise had to contend with her parents' favouring of Beatrice, just as Bertie had had to contend both with the brilliance of Vicky (who he had assumed, until enlightened by his tutor, would inherit his mother's throne) and with his parents' very obvious preference first for Alfred, and then for Arthur. In 1858, the queen wrote to her husband of Arthur, 'This Child is *dearer* than any of the others put together.' (Beatrice being considered still a baby, not a child, did not fall into the same category as the others.) In the same year, she sent Vicky a report of her younger siblings:

> . . . As for Leopold he still bruises as much as ever, but has (*unberufen*) not had accidents of late. He is tall, but holds himself worse than ever, and is a very common looking child, very plain in face, clever but an oddity – and not an engaging child though amusing. I hope the new governess will be able to make him more like other children . . . Arthur is a precious love. Really the best child I ever saw. Louise is very naughty and backward, though improved and very pretty, and affectionate.

Louise and Bertie would often feel themselves allies. Both lacked self-confidence and were, as a consequence, often overlooked in favour of their happier, more confident siblings. When the family performed in plays or acted tableaux, the young Louise and Bertie were often placed together, in the less demanding (and less interesting) roles. Yet as an adult, Louise's acting ability was remarked upon favourably (although her lack of interest in learning lines made her a less than ideal thespian). A comment from Lady Augusta Bruce, the queen's lady-in-waiting, sums up Louise's childhood. Lady Augusta noticed that Louise blossomed when people were kind to her and paid her attention, something that happened rarely. While the family were at Balmoral in September 1861, Lady Augusta noted, 'Dear P.L. is very darling at present. She is so happy to be made a little of.'

That throwaway comment is a sad indictment of a childhood and adolescence in which Louise was often made to feel as though she were the least special person in the family. An indication of this can be found in the Royal Collection. The queen was very proud of two gold and enamel bracelets composed of miniature portraits of her children. Each child was painted (usually by Winterhalter) as a toddler.

The resulting portrait was then turned into a tiny but perfect miniature and added to one of the bracelets. Although Louise was born in 1848 and her portrait was painted by Winterhalter in 1851, her image was not added to the first of her mother's bracelets, the one dedicated to the six oldest children, until a decade later: 24 May 1861. All the other children's portraits had been added in shortly after they had been painted, while they were still toddlers. I wrote to the Royal Collection to enquire why this had happened; I wondered if an earlier portrait had been lost or damaged and needed to be replaced. The response was that there are no records of Princess Louise's portrait having been added at any time before 1861 or of any earlier miniature having been painted. For some reason, the queen chose to wear images of every one of her children except Louise. At Christmas 1850, one of Prince Albert's presents to his wife had been a bracelet whose clasp was made up of a miniature of Louise, but by the time Louise had begun to develop into her own person, she was no longer perceived as being quite so dear to her mother as she had been at that early Christmas, aged two.

After Vicky left home and became a married woman, the queen began to treat her eldest child in a quite different manner. Not only did she write multiple letters telling Vicky how much she missed her, but she began to treat her as an adult, on an equal footing to herself, someone in whom she could confide her feelings about the rest of the family – feelings that often made Vicky very uncomfortable.

A few days after Vicky's wedding, the queen sent a letter exclaiming 'Everything recalls you to our mind, and in every room we shall have your picture!' Just as she would do following a death, the queen began to idealise Vicky and to make a virtue of missing her. She did censure her daughter still – many of her letters contain a scolding for something – but she was also overly clingy, wanting to continue to exert control. Having found motherhood tiresome in the extreme for most of Vicky's life, the queen was now greedy to know all that her absent daughter was doing, plaguing her with daily letters insisting that she needed to know everything: no detail was too minute or prosaic. It was an odd facet of Queen Victoria's character that she made her children's lives claustrophobic by her constant intrusions into every area of privacy, yet she found their company irksome when they were with her. When Queen Victoria's mother, the Duchess of Kent, died the queen was plunged into a depression. Her relationship with her mother had been as difficult and frustrating as the relationships she had with her own children. When a friend enquired of Albert how the queen was coping following her bereavement, he responded: 'In body she is well, though terribly nervous, and the children are a disturbance to her.'

The queen's attitude to her family was engendered by her own unhappy childhood. Her father had died when she was less than a year old, after which her mother kept Victoria claustrophobically close and controlled every aspect of her life. As an adult the queen would relate how she was allowed to do nothing on her own; she slept in the same bed as her mother every night until the day she was proclaimed queen. She was forbidden to walk up or down stairs without holding someone's hand, in case she fell and hurt herself. She had an older half-sister, Feodora, from her mother's first marriage, to whom she felt very close, but when Feodora married, Victoria was left even more alone, reliant entirely upon the company of her mother and of her governess, Baroness Lehzen (whom Victoria regarded as a second, kinder mother). Much of Victoria's parenting problems were bequeathed to her by her own mother, who wrote regularly in her diary how disappointing the young Princess Victoria's behaviour had been, who could be bullying and unkind, and who had tried to control every aspect of her daughter's life.

Although the Duchess of Kent appeared to have mellowed by the time she became a grandmother, the damage was done, and Queen Victoria had inherited her worst traits. When Queen Victoria's daughters travelled with their mother the queen's controlling instinct became even worse than normal; they were forced to spend all day with her. Even though the queen so often complained that as a child she had known no privacy, and had had no space to call her own, she jealously guarded her own children's free time and, even when they were married, expected them to be at her beck and call. As sovereign she was allowed not only to request their presence, but to command it. It was often noted that she seemed to derive pleasure in thwarting her children's plans, particularly by insisting they attend to her on occasions when she knew they had already accepted another engagement.

The queen harried Vicky constantly for letters and criticised her for not including enough details, such as what people were wearing and what conversations had taken place. She expected to know everything about her daughter's private life, such as when she was menstruating and if her periods remained regular; perhaps partly because the queen hoped her daughter would not get pregnant as early in marriage as she had done. The queen's dislike of babies was so well known as to be a joke to those who knew her. She famously commented: 'an ugly baby is a very nasty object – and the prettiest is frightful when undressed'. Her most tactless comment about babies, however, was in a letter she sent to Vicky on discovering her daughter was pregnant for the first time. Complying with royal etiquette, the news had been sent by Vicky's husband in a letter to Prince Albert. This is the queen's astonishing response: 'The horrid news contained in Fritz's letter to Papa upset us dreadfully. The more so as I feel certain almost it will all end in nothing.' She then goes on to complain how little affection any of her children show her.

Victoria's prediction of a miscarriage was not fulfilled and her first grandchild, Wilhelm, usually called 'William' by his aunts and uncles, was born on 27 January 1859.[13] For Vicky's siblings, especially the youngest ones still in the schoolroom, becoming an aunt or uncle made them feel important. Even at a very young age, Beatrice would try to get out of schoolwork by insisting she needed to write to her sister's children. Shortly after Wilhelm's birth, Louise protested to a member of the household who had addressed them as the 'royal children' that they were no longer mere royal children: 'we are uncles and aunts'.

[13] Wilhelm's birth was difficult and agonising. Queen Victoria related that the Prussian doctors had given up on Vicky and her baby. It was the Scottish doctor, whom the queen had insisted be present, who had the presence of mind to be able to save them both. As a consequence of the birth, Wilhelm's left arm was permanently paralysed (probably as the result of Erb-Duchenne palsy). This injury would cause many psychological problems for the future kaiser and directly affected relationships in the royal family.

CHAPTER 4

An Annus Horribilis

> Helena was deeply involved in domesticity, Beatrice was growing
> to be a thoughtful child . . . while Louise, according to the Queen,
> needed watching.

Nina Epton, *Victoria and her Daughters*, 1971

Throughout 1859 and 1860, Louise continued to study art and her interest in becoming a 'real' artist increased. On her tenth birthday, she had been greatly impressed by being taken to the studio of John Rogers Herbert to see him working on a large fresco about the life of Moses. Herbert told his royal visitors that his art had kept him going following the heartbreaking death of his son. He had felt like giving up, but art, he declared, had 'kept him alive'.

Beyond the oppressive family home, Louise was noted to be less shy than many of Queen Victoria's children (this family propensity was often commented on). This seems to have stemmed from Louise's natural curiosity about people and a desire to find out more about those who interested her (though, throughout her life, if she found herself bored or irritated, Louise would willingly pretend to be overcome by the fabled family 'shyness' and use it as an excuse to leave a room). In 1858 she had shocked her family, but delighted a visitor to Balmoral when she stepped forward spontaneously to shake his hand. She loved the opportunity to meet new people and any variety they could add to what was often a very dull day-to-day existence was warmly welcomed.

While life for the youngest children continued as before, Bertie set off for an extended journey through Europe, where he studied art in Italy and was even granted an audience with the Pope. As was customary for the royal family, he travelled incognito, using one of the many titles he had inherited to make him seem like a little-known baron. This did not necessarily mean he travelled in secrecy or expected not to be recognised – often being 'incognito' meant simply that the royal personage was not there in an official capacity. All the while his parents kept a close eye on his behaviour, through constant communication with the tutors sent to guard him. Bertie never seemed to know how to handle his parents. His letters lack any kind of understanding of European politics and as soon as he mentioned going to a ball or anything that might suggest he had been in the company of women, his parents flew into a panic. While Bertie remained a disappointment to his parents, there was great excitement when Alfred came home to visit from his naval ship; and admiration not only from the family but in the newspapers.

In 1860, Vicky became a mother again, giving birth to a daughter. She was still attempting to settle into Prussian court life, something she would never find easy; Queen Victoria grew frustrated with Vicky's constant longing for England. Meanwhile Prince Albert shared with the family his enthusiasm for his new artistic hobby: photography. He arranged for a darkroom to be installed in Windsor Castle and Louise and her siblings were thrilled to discover this new form of art.

As Louise grew towards adolescence, her mother found her increasingly irritating. The queen's journal on 18 March 1860 reports, 'Our dear Louise's birthday, her 12th! May God bless her! We went to the schoolroom to wish her joy', but this is the version copied out by Beatrice and may not tell the whole truth. A letter written by the queen to Vicky the day before tells quite a different story: 'poor Louise's birthday, she will be twelve and is in fact only 6!' When writing to Vicky about Louise's sixteenth birthday, the queen could not help but sound patronising: 'God bless the dear child – who is so affectionate and has so many difficulties to contend with. I hope and trust she will get over them all in time and still become a most useful member of the human family.' The myth of Louise having learning difficulties or a personality disorder was still being perpetuated by the queen, despite the fact that no one else seemed able to see it. In 1866, the year of Louise's eighteenth birthday, when she was suffering from whooping cough, her mother wrote her a very tender letter: 'I can't say how grieved I am not to be able to be more with you and to *hold* you, darling, when those nasty coughs come on, – but it is a *trial* I *can't.*' Yet in the same year she was complaining once more to Vicky about Louise, 'she is not discreet, and is very apt to take things always in a different light to me', and again: 'she is very indiscreet and, from that, making mischief very frequently'. The following year the queen found Louise '*so very difficile*' and the year after that she was censured as being 'so vy wayward & unreasonable'.

Bertie was proving equally problematic, and Alfred and Arthur were held up to Vicky as examples of everything their oldest brother was not. The monarch was quite happy to tell anyone who would listen that Bertie would be a terrible king and in April 1859 she confided to Vicky: 'Bertie continues such an anxiety, I tremble at the thought of only three years and a half being before us – when he will be of age and we can't hold him except by moral power! . . . His only safety – and the country's – is in his implicit reliance in every thing, on dearest Papa, that perfection of human beings!' The queen's own ability to rely on 'dearest Papa' was, however, about to come to an abrupt end – and as far as Queen Victoria was concerned it was all Bertie's fault.

The year 1861 was to prove the most unhappy in Queen Victoria's life. She had always had a difficult relationship with her mother, yet when the Duchess of Kent died, Victoria went into a prolonged depression. She felt her mother's death so keenly, it was, she said, as if every aspect of her childhood had come back to haunt her. The duchess died two days before Louise's thirteenth birthday. It was to be the first of many miserable birthdays. The queen wept copiously over the gifts her mother had already delivered for Louise and wrote in her journal about her agony over the loss of 'such a mother, so tender, so loving' – a marked difference from the way she had usually spoken about her. Now the queen set about creating the myth of a perfect relationship with her deceased parent. It was bewildering for the children, and Albert confided to his friends that he was worried about how solitary Victoria had become, seemingly impossible to comfort. She refused to see her children, wanting only her husband. Bertie was berated for almost every thought and action. The queen became furious when Bertie – a man who had been taught not to show his emotions – did not openly shed a tear at the funeral for his 74-year-old grandmother. Bertie was a persistent worry: he was too wayward, his parents felt, and needed to settle down and become respectable. Albert threw himself into the task of finding his eldest son a suitable wife – and a suitable queen – while Bertie threw himself wholeheartedly into the army and its accompanying social life.

While still sunk under the grief of her bereavement, the queen became aware that Albert was also suffering. He was not looking well and was obviously feeling even worse. They had spent several weeks in a orgy of reading through her mother's private correspondence and journals and, in compliance with the deceased duchess's request, burning them afterwards. Victoria had been so caught up in the task, in her own grief, and in her need for Albert to be her rock, that she had not noticed the early stages of his illness.

In November, the couple were devastated to hear rumours that had been circulating in society: Bertie had slept with the actress Nellie Clifden, an affair that would soon be reported with glee in the newspapers. Albert was horrified. Victoria wrote that she could never forget the look on Albert's face when he heard the news: 'Oh!! that face, that heavenly face of woe and sorrow which was so dreadful to witness.' Albert was the son of a lecherous father and an unhappy mother driven to infidelity, and the brother of a man who was as debauched as their father had been. When he discovered that Bertie had lost his virginity to an actress, he overreacted, scarred by his parents' sexual behaviour. The nightmare he had sought to avoid by creating his own 'perfect' family within the cloistered atmosphere of the royal household was about to break through. Heredity had made itself known in Bertie and all that Albert thought he had ever taught his sons had been ridiculed. Despite feeling unwell, he set off for Cambridge to confront his son and his wife's heir.

The prince consort enjoyed an active sex life with his wife, but had what almost amounted to a phobia about the idea of sex outside marriage. 'You <u>must</u> not,' he admonished his son, 'you <u>dare</u> not be lost; the consequences for this country & for the world at large would be too dreadful! There is no middle course possible . . . you must either belong to the good, or to the bad in this life.' Although Bertie's behaviour was nothing abnormal, Victoria and Albert acted as though he had been guilty of the most evil of transgressions. Victoria declared herself physically repulsed by the very thought of her polluted son and even a couple of years later, when Bertie was about to marry, she rebuked him again with the loss of his virginity, which she described as 'the white flower of a blameless life'. She and Albert believed both men and women should be virgins when they married – a desire for equality in sexual experience that was a world away from the usual double standard of Victorian sexual behaviour, in which men were expected to be 'worldly wise' and women 'pure'. Although the younger children were kept in ignorance of the facts, Louise and her siblings were aware that their parents were furious with their eldest brother.

When he returned from his visit to the now-contrite and scared Bertie, the prince consort was feeling desperately ill. This was exacerbated by the fact that he had insisted he and Bertie take a long walk so they could talk, ignoring the fact that it was a cold November day and pouring with rain. By the time he reached Windsor, via a very uncomfortable carriage journey, Albert was feverish and complaining of dreadful pains all over his body. He was physically and emotionally depressed and it was Victoria's turn to become her husband's comforter. Nothing the medical experts could tell the queen about the nature of her husband's illness could persuade her that it wasn't Bertie's behaviour that had caused his father's illness.

The first time the public became aware anything was wrong was when a party at Windsor Castle was cancelled because the prince consort was unwell. In reality, Albert had been suffering from agonising toothache for several months and had seemed generally in poor health. He had had gastric trouble for many years, a situation that had worsened following his return home to Prussia the previous summer, and he had also been racked with what were described as rheumatic-type pains. Nevertheless the newspapers made much of his visit to Cambridge as the catalyst for his illness.

By 7 December 1861 both royal doctors, Sir James Reid and Dr William Jenner, were in permanent attendance at Windsor Castle. By 11 December, the queen was cheered enough by what was believed to be Albert's good progress to write a letter describing his illness as an inconvenience to her. In the same letter, to her uncle and advisor, King Leopold of the Belgians, she claimed that when she had typhoid at the age of 16 she had been far more ill than Albert: 'I can report another good night, and no loss of strength . . . It is very sad and trying for me, but I am well, and I think really very courageous; for it is the first time that I ever witnessed anything of this kind though I suffered from the same at Ramsgate and was much worse. The trial in every way is so very trying, for I have lost my guide, my support, my all, for a time – as we can't ask or tell him anything.' In her grief, the queen forgot that her children were likely to be as worried as she was about their father. For Louise, the whispered conversations, muted mumblings of the doctors and all the paraphernalia of the sickroom were frightening because everything was being kept from her. She and her siblings had no idea of how ill their father was.

The queen's optimism that she had survived a more serious bout of typhoid and her hope that her husband would be well enough to advise her again was short-lived. Three days after the queen's letter to King Leopold, her husband was dead. Ironically, on the morning of the day he died, the prince seemed to be rallying and at 10.40 a.m. a bulletin stated: 'There is a slight change for the better in the Prince this morning.' By 4.30 p.m. an update announced he was 'in a most critical state' and later that night a bulletin declared: 'His Royal Highness the Prince Consort became rapidly weaker during the evening, and expired without suffering at ten minutes before eleven o'clock.' There has been speculation in recent decades as to whether the royal physicians' diagnosis of typhoid fever was correct, but that was what it was believed to be at the time.[14]

Bertie was still in Cambridge, and in disgrace, when his father was dying. He was sent for and reached Windsor at around three o'clock in the morning of his father's final day. Throughout that last, agonising day, the older children were gathered around their father and Queen Victoria wrote in her journal:

I bent over him and said to him 'Es ist Kleines Frauchen' [it's your 'little wife'] and he bowed his head; I asked him if he would give me 'ein Kuss' [a kiss] and he did so. He seemed half dozing, quite quiet . . . I left the room for a moment and sat down on the floor in utter despair. Attempts at consolation from others only made me worse . . . Alice told me to come in . . . and I took his dear left hand which was already cold, though the

[14] Modern diagnoses include Crohn's Disease and cancer. Although Crohn's Disease itself is not normally fatal it was little understood in the nineteenth century and complications arising from the disease could kill.

breathing was quite gentle and I knelt down by him . . . Alice was on the other side, Bertie and Lenchen . . . kneeling at the foot of the bed . . . Two or three long but perfectly gentle breaths were drawn, the hand clasping mine and . . . all, all was over.

The younger children, including Louise, were taken to see their father before being sent to bed. They took his hand and kissed him, but by that time Albert was unable to recognise any of them. Lady Augusta Stanley, who was at Windsor at the time of the prince consort's death, noted that 'Poor Princess Louise did not learn of the end until the morning. Poor lamb.' Matthew Dennison, in his biography of Princess Beatrice, quotes an account given by one of the servants, about how Queen Victoria reacted to the news that her husband had died: 'The Queen ran through the ante-room where I was waiting. She seemed wild. She went straight up to the nursery and took Baby Beatrice out of bed, but she did not wake her . . . Orders were given at once for the removal of the Court to Osborne.'

After taking Beatrice from her bed, the queen wrapped her youngest child in Albert's clothes. For a long time after her husband's death, the queen would sleep holding tightly to her favourite child, still swathed in her dead father's clothing. Princess Louise felt keenly the death of her father and her inability to comfort her mother. As a sensitive 13-year-old, she had no idea how she was expected to behave or how to deal with her grief and convinced herself that the wrong person had died, wishing she could have sacrificed herself to save her father. She sobbed to the ladies-in-waiting: 'Oh, why did not God take me? I am so stupid and useless.'

The funeral was held on 23 December. It was an age when women and girls were not expected to attend. The queen did not choose to make an exception to the rule; feeling she could not cope with seeing her beloved Albert consigned to the ground, she took her daughters to Osborne, leaving Bertie and Arthur as chief mourners. The queen's letters following the death of her husband reveal the depth of her grief. As she said to Vicky, her world had revolved around her husband. She asked her daughter how she could be expected to live without Albert, how she could go on without the man 'without whom I did nothing, not moved a finger, arranged not a print or photograph, didn't put on a gown or bonnet if he didn't approve it[. How] shall [I] be able to go on, to live, to move, to help myself in difficult moments?' She told her uncle Leopold, 'the world is gone for me!' and kept the room in which he died, the Blue Room, exactly as it was in his last moments. When Charles Dickens had written about Miss Havisham in *Great Expectations*,[15] who kept her clothing and home precisely as they had been when she discovered her fiancé had jilted her, he could have been writing about his monarch. For the rest of her life, Queen Victoria insisted that the Blue Room remain unchanged: even the glass from which Albert had drunk his last sip was left beside his bed. This was not, she insisted, morbid; the room was preserved as a 'living beautiful monument'. She also commissioned a bust of her deceased husband, which was placed in the room beside the bed in which he had died. Vicky came back to England as soon as she was able to and comforted her younger siblings. When she was about to return to Prussia in early April 1862, Louise wrote to Arthur, 'I am so unhappy she is going.' Louise also told her brother that the five sisters had been photographed together, but the end result was so unflattering that the photographer had been ordered to do it again.

As the country went into mourning for the prince consort, the theatres and other places of entertainment were closed as a mark of respect. The streets were full of people wearing funereal black. According to Benjamin Disraeli, 'This German Prince has governed England for 21 years with a wisdom and energy such as none of our kings has ever shown.' The British public could have had no idea how long this mourning would last. Following the death of her husband, the queen suffered continually from depression – a condition that was not understood in her lifetime. Had she not been the monarch, she could have been in very real danger of incarceration: in nineteenth-century Britain most people suffering from depression ended up in lunatic asylums.

The mourning into which Queen Victoria plunged her family and her household would blight Louise's life and make her adolescence even more difficult than it might otherwise have been. At times the queen would insist that one of her daughters (usually Beatrice) slept with her; then just as suddenly she would push her away, wanting no

[15] *Great Expectations* was published in instalments from 1860 to 1861.

one except Albert. The queen seemed incapable of understanding that her children had lost their father – and a father who had been the less emotionally complicated parent. Albert had certainly not been averse to punishing his children (as Bertie's often desperately sad stories of his childhood attest), but he had been more understanding, kindly and empathetic than Victoria. King George V, Bertie's eldest son, would famously recount that he expected his children to be as frightened of him as he had been of his father and as his father had been of his mother. There was no mention of Albert as a tyrannical parent in that reminiscence, only of Victoria. In her memoirs, Lady Augusta Stanley recalled overhearing a conversation between the young Queen Victoria and her mother, the Duchess of Kent, that upset her. When Leopold was six years old and had been naughty, the queen wanted to beat him and the duchess wanted her to excuse him on account of his being so young. Lady Augusta wrote in her journal:

> The Duchess excused poor Leo tonight – 'he was so young, his passions would go off as he was six.'
> 'Oh,' said his Mama 'I don't know what we should do then – whip him well?' The Duchess said how sad it made her to hear a child cry, 'it makes an impression'.
> 'Not when you have 8 Mama – that wears off. You could not go through that each time one of the 8 cried!!'

Where most parents would have found their children a solace in grief, for Victoria, in the early days of her widowhood, her children became more of a trial, as they had been following the death of her mother. Bereft of Albert, Beatrice, her 'baby', was usually the only one she wanted near her. As the queen wrote to Vicky shortly after Albert's death, Beatrice was the only 'bright spot in this dead home'. It was noted by the household that the queen began taking almost all her meals 'tête à tête' with Beatrice and that Beatrice was allowed to behave as she liked, being 'impertinent' to the servants and members of the household, while the other children were scolded constantly.

In addition to the loss of their father, the younger royal children were subjected to their mother's violent fury with their oldest brother. The queen wrote to Vicky that she could not look at Bertie 'without a shudder' and that she wanted the world to know 'the real truth' about him; she urged Vicky to tell people it was all Bertie's fault: that Bertie's reprehensible behaviour had killed his father. A few weeks after Albert's death, Bertie left England for the Middle East, a journey that had been organised by his father in an attempt to educate Bertie in world politics. Many of the queen's advisors suggested the trip should be postponed, but Victoria was adamant that her son should go and break the 'constant contact which is more than ever unbearable to me'. Nearly a year later, Bertie spent his twenty-first birthday away from his family. Louise missed him dreadfully and wrote him a birthday letter, to which he responded, 'I was very sorry to have been prevented from spending it with you . . . But as this year is one of mourning and sadness, it is perhaps better that I should have been away.'

Something that been long anticipated and prepared for by Prince Albert in the final months of his life was the wedding of Princess Alice to Prince Louis of Hesse, at which Louise was a funereal bridesmaid. (When the engagement had been announced to Alice's siblings, Louise discovered that Alice had already confided in Lenchen but not in her; she was hurt by the snub, but simply told her mother she had 'expected it'.) Much as she longed to, the queen was persuaded not to cancel the wedding because her husband would have wanted it to go ahead. From the time of Albert's death to the end of the queen's long life, almost every mention of the word 'wedding' seemed a personal assault. Her letters are full of comments about how much she hates weddings, how bad marriage is for women and how few marriages are likely to last. Many years later, when her physician, Dr James Reid, requested permission to marry, the queen was furious and although she was not able to forbid the marriage, she tried to prevent the couple from being able to live together after their marriage. The queen, who did not attend the wedding, was highly irritated that her family and friends were all so pleased; she complained that on the wedding day she would have no one left to bring her tea, as all her usual companions (and many of her servants) were going to the ceremony.

For Alice and Louis's wedding on 1 July 1862 the chapel was swathed in black and the queen and Prince Alfred cried openly throughout. Although Alice was permitted to wear her white wedding dress, which had taken many months and many seamstresses to create, she was expected to change it for mourning almost as soon as the ceremony was over. Alice understood not only her mother's unusual personality but also that her mother was extremely depressed and she tried very hard not to show her how happy she was. The queen described her second daughter's wedding as 'more like a funeral than a wedding' and confessed that when Alice told her how proud and happy she was to have married Louis it was as 'though a dagger is plunged in my bleeding, desolate heart'.

When Alice left England to live in Germany, Louise lost another of her allies. Alice was renowned for being the peacemaker of the family. She was sweet to her little sister and, although she was angered by Louise's jealousy of Beatrice, she was understanding and kind to her. Before Alice's marriage, she had been the queen's amanuensis, a job that involved long hours at her mother's beck and call, answering her sackfuls of correspondence and working tirelessly to understand all the aspects of politics and state events. When Alice left home, this job fell to Helena, something 'Lenchen' had been dreading. In 1863, Louise wrote an amusing letter to Vicky: 'Mama gave a council this morning and the Archbishop of York did homage, Lenchen was present, she said that Mama held his hands up whilst he was taking [the] oath and then afterwards he kissed the Bible. Lenchen said she felt such an inclination to laugh.'

Despite this levity, Louise was all too aware that when Helena married it would be her turn to take on the cloying and claustrophobic role. Even before Helena left the family home, Louise could not avoid carrying out her mother's whims. A letter survives, dated 9 July 1863, which was obviously dictated by her mother and must have caused Louise distress. It was, purportedly, from Louise to her brother Arthur:

> Dear Mama wishes me to tell you that she will write to you soon, and she hopes you are working very hard for your examination. She is very anxious that you should pass it well, for if you did not it would make her very unhappy, she fears you are rather lazy. Believe me ever dear Arthur your most loving sister.

CHAPTER 5

The first sculpture

The much-to-be-remembered day of my first entering upon
Maid-of-Honour duties . . . the 2 Princesses . . . both kissed me.
Prss. Louise is very pretty.

Diary of Lady Caroline Lyttelton, 10 September 1863

In the year of Alice's wedding, 1862, a Hungarian-Viennese sculptor
named Joseph Edgar Boehm arrived in London with his wife. He settled
in the city and made his debut at the Royal Academy in the same year,
with a terracotta Bust of a Gentleman. Although he and Louise had
not yet met, he would have a great impact on her future. Following
Alice's wedding, Louise threw herself into her study of art. Her fourteenth birthday had been a muted affair, and she was finding increasing
solace in her pursuit of artistic freedom. Her new art tutor was William
Leitch, a landscape artist from Scotland, renowned for his watercolours.
Leitch was the art tutor to all the royal family (although the queen
stopped her lessons after her husband's death and did not resume them
for some years). Leitch taught only painting and drawing, but Louise
was continuing to improve her technique in sculpture, an art form that
had intrigued her from a very young age, when she first saw the sculptress Mary Thornycroft at work on a commission for her parents.
Thornycroft was commissioned to make marble sculptures of the royal
babies' hands, feet and limbs; in 1848 the sculptor had taken a plaster
cast of the baby Princess Louise's left arm and hand while she slept,
from which she produced a beautiful marble sculpture. It is still in the
Royal Collection.

By the end of 1862, the newspapers were buzzing with the news
of another royal wedding. The heir to the throne had become engaged

to Princess Alexandra, the daughter of the soon-to-be Danish king. 'Alix' was a welcome addition to the royal house of mourning. The queen and her youngest children had been travelling in Albert's home country when Bertie sent news of his engagement, in a desperate attempt to please his mother. At last he seemed to have done something of which she, tentatively at first, approved – although Albert's brother Ernst was not happy about the match. He and Albert had argued by letter when Albert first said that he hoped to secure the Danish princess for his son. Denmark and Prussia were not on amicable political terms and Ernst felt snubbed that Bertie had not chosen a Prussian princess. While they were in Prussia, the queen noted in her journal with a remarkable calmness that Leopold, her haemophiliac son, had suffered an accident. The top entry in her journal for that day was that she had gone out with Lenchen and Louise to try and interest herself in sketching again. 'Poor Leopold,' she continued, 'has a sore mouth, having by accident stuck a pen into his palate, which has caused severe bleeding which could not be stopped, & he could hardly eat anything. – Had luncheon with the 5 daughters. Drove with Alice and good Miss Hildyard to the Inselberg.' Her lack of concern is a mark of how self-obsessed the depressed queen had become. If a situation wasn't purely about her, she could not summon up interest.

In autumn 1862, the queen met Alix for the first time, and liked her. Alix's diplomacy was made explicit in the fact that she dressed in black: already she understood how to handle her intended mother-in-law. Although the public liked to believe this was a true, romantic match, it was actually the result of many years of planning. Initially, Victoria had been loath to accept anyone from the Danish royal family, because of past history and recent Danish hostilities with her beloved Germany. Prince Alfred also tried to prevent the alliance with Denmark, which had caused an argument between him and Bertie. The match, however, was a good one – and it was very popular with the British public, who were fed up with the queen's partiality for Germany.[16]

---

[16] A few days after Bertie's wedding, when Vicky wrote to her mother about how homesick she was, her irritated mother responded '[your] unbounded love for every thing English I own I can't share . . . when you write to Bertie and Affie don't write with frantic adoration of the Navy and all English feelings – for our sole object is to smooth that down and to Germanise them!'

Louise was enchanted by her brother's beautiful and poised fiancée. It was noted by several observers, including Queen Victoria, how different Louise was when Alix was in the room: she did not cause trouble – she sat and talked and behaved herself. Alix treated Louise in a way that few people had bothered to do before. Instead of starting their acquaintance with the usual assumption Louise was stupid or disobedient or deliberately difficult, Alix simply talked to her kindly, as a future sister-in-law. The awkward teenager blossomed and their relationship was close from the start. Alix had arrived in a foreign country, where she had to speak either German or English, never her native Danish, and she knew her future mother-in-law was formidable. She also knew that the queen considered Alix's parents scandalous and many of her close relations too immoral to be invited to the wedding. When she encountered sisters-in-law longing to be friends, it made Alix's transition to England much easier than she had feared. Towards the end of her life, Louise would describe Alix and herself as the closest of sisters. In Alix's letters to Louise she uses such endearments as 'My beloved Louise', 'My own dearest Louise' and 'my little pet'. She was one of the few people to take Louise's side in family arguments, writing to her during one of Louise's depressingly long stays at Balmoral that she hoped Louise was not being 'teased too much'.

Despite liking Alix, the queen was unhappy about the prospect of yet another wedding. While her children anticipated the wedding with excitement, the queen was being reminded of how happy she had been and how depressed she was now. She recorded in her journal the 'trembling voice' with which she had read to a small group of assembled ministers the declaration of Bertie's marriage. 'The children were quite distressed at my pale face when I came down to luncheon,' she wrote on 1 November 1862. She grumbled incessantly about the wedding preparations and said Bertie was far too 'noisy' and held him responsible for her 'bad headaches'. On 8 November, with the first anniversary of Albert's death looming, she wrote sadly in her journal: 'My sorrow seems to increase day by day, & my terrible loneliness overwhelms me.'

Louise too was suffering, and began to be plagued with headaches – such agonising pains that she was unable to leave her room. These became a regular problem for Louise and one that would continue into old age. Her physical health was always affected by nervous stress and emotional depression. Whether these early headaches were caused by stress, by a change in teenage hormones or by some other physical problem is unknown; perhaps she suffered from migraines. Or they may have provided a good excuse: sometimes a day alone in her bedroom was infinitely preferable to a day spent with her mother.

The public was thrilled by the prospect of a royal wedding – especially because it was the first time that one of Queen Victoria's children would get married without having to leave the country afterwards. The future Princess of Wales had won over public opinion from the start. The Corporation of London was believed to have spent £10,000 on preparations for her visit and wedding gifts arrived from all over the world, many of which were later placed on public display. Lady Caroline Lyttelton (who would soon join the royal household) noted disparagingly in her diary on 27 April 1863, 'Still warmer. The lilacs are all out. We went to the Kensington Museum to see the Princess's wedding gifts, which were hardly worth the exertion. Most of the jewels have been taken away, and many things were in very bad taste.'

On 7 March 1863 the Danish royal family arrived in Gravesend on board the royal yacht. Alix was greeted by enthusiastic crowds of around 80,000. The *Illustrated London News* reported a 'bevy of pretty maids, who, ranged on either side of the pier, awaited, with dainty little baskets filled with spring flowers, the arrival of the Princess, to scatter these, Nature's jewels, at the feet of the Royal lady' and much was made of the way the 21-year-old prince 'ran' to his fiancée and kissed her. (In reality, the prince was running not because of passion but because he had arrived late.) In 1864, Henry Nelson O'Neil, a member of the Clique artistic group[17] exhibited *The Landing of HRH the Princess Alexandra at Gravesend, 7th March 1863*. It shows fashionably dressed young women scattering flower petals over the red carpet along which the Prince of Wales leads his intended wife. The painting's popularity, and the artist's use of bright colours, emphasised

---

[17] The Clique was founded in the 1830s by artists studying at the Royal Academy and included Richard Dadd (a brilliant artist fated to be confined to a prison asylum after brutally murdering his father), William Powell Frith, Augustus Egg, John Phillip, Alfred Elmore and Henry Nelson O'Neil. At their weekly meetings they would discuss and study art, all drawing the same subject or object then critiquing one another's work.

how much this wedding meant to a public weary of the extended royal mourning.

From Gravesend, the royal party travelled to London, where thousands of people turned out in the drizzle and cold of an early March day. Lord Ronald Gower wrote:

. . . probably, since the day in Paris when Marie Antoinette[18] was acclaimed by the French populace in the gardens of the Tuileries, no princess ever had so enthusiastic a reception, or so quickly won the hearts of thousands by the mere charm of her presence. St James's-street was already densely thronged by nine o'clock in the morning, all about Pall Mall was bright with red cloth, banners and bunting, and garlanded with flowers. All the shops were transformed into places with benches and seats, which were filled by eleven o'clock . . . At two in the afternoon this part of London was hardly passable, and it was not easy to force one's way . . . past four, a carriage appeared coming from out St James's Street – first one, then a second and a third; but it was hardly possible to believe that these shabby, poorly-appointed vehicles formed the van of the royal procession for which all London had made holiday . . . These turned out to be the Westminster Corporation . . . they were certainly not ornamental . . . But now trot by a handful of Life Guards escorting an open carriage and four . . . and within, the Princess Alexandra, with her affianced husband . . . The Princess's lovely face has won all hearts.

The future Princess of Wales even proved herself a heroine. When a police horse became entangled in one of the carriage wheels, it panicked, unseating its rider. Alix managed to free the horse's hoof and calm the terrified animal. The respected journalist William Howard Russell, reporting on the day, was moved to hyperbole, writing, 'No generation of the British-born race had ever witnessed or ever taken part in such rejoicing.' After their successful procession through London, the party went by train to Slough, where they were greeted by Bertie's brothers and brothers-in-law and local dignitaries.

[18] It may seem strange that Lord Gower should make an allusion to the executed Marie-Antoinette, but he was working on a biography of the French queen.

Alix was welcomed into a waiting room 'specially prepared for her with great taste by the Great Western Railway Company, and adorned with the choicest flowers from Turner's Royal Nursery'. Six royal carriages and an escort of Life Guards was waiting and they began their procession to Windsor, cheered by enthusiastic crowds, including a party of fifty orphans from the British Orphan Asylum. The children had embroidered a banner for the princess – with words of welcome in Danish. The roads of Windsor and Eton were festooned with flowers, lanterns and banners, and houses and gardens that lined the royal route were lavishly decorated. Eton College spent a reported £400 on a triumphal arch decorated with 'medallions of the Prince and Princess of Wales'. The *Morning Post* commented that when the procession of carriages arrived at the castle, 'the Queen herself appeared at the window, and manifested the greatest interest on their arrival'. Inside, Louise and her sisters waited eagerly.

For everyone except Queen Victoria, the wedding day was glorious. The queen at least had the satisfaction of knowing that all was being done according to her plan – 'scandalous' relations of Alix, no matter how close the relationship, had not been invited. At the queen's insistence, the wedding took place in Windsor, not St James's Palace (the first time a Prince of Wales had been married at Windsor since the fourteenth century). Denmark had been offered no political benefits from the match (meaning the queen did not have to deal with Prussian anger) and even the Archbishop of Canterbury had been cowed: when the intended date of the wedding was announced, the archbishop had pointed out that it was during Lent, when weddings were not performed. The queen overruled him and the date was set.

On Tuesday 10 March, from the early morning onwards, London's Paddington station was thronged with immaculately dressed men and women waiting to board the special trains to Windsor. For Louise, it was a magical day that did much to dispel the gloom of the previous months. This marriage represented not only the arrival of a new and friendly sister-in-law, but also the much-craved opportunity not to wear black. The queen's insistence on her entire household continuing to wear mourning was lifted, albeit temporarily, for Bertie's wedding. Louise and her sisters were finally given the opportunity to dress in pretty, celebratory clothes. Their bridesmaid dresses were brilliant white, trimmed with pale purple, and Louise was allowed to wear her pearls, a necklace bequeathed by the grandmother after whom she was named, Louise of Coburg. At the end of the day, the happy couple were photographed with a mournful Queen Victoria and a bust of Prince Albert. The queen noted that Louise was the only one of her daughters not to cry and saw this as a sign of Louise's sullen, difficult personality – but there was no reason for Louise to cry. Her brother was happy, finally he had a wife to take care of him, and she adored Alix. For her, the wedding was a very happy occasion.

The month after Bertie and Alix's wedding, Louise became an aunt again when Alice gave birth to a daughter, Princess Victoria of Hesse. She was born at Windsor and the young princesses rushed to visit their niece. It was a year in which the royal family could begin to be happy, yet the queen wrote to Vicky that Beatrice was 'the only thing I feel that keeps me alive'. A few weeks after Bertie's wedding, the queen was in Coburg, visiting Albert's birthplace. In a letter to Louise, she wrote 'it is *all* the same – lonely and pleasureless – and *dreadful* without my own darling Angel! *Nothing* interests or attracts me *any more*.' In 1863 Lady Sarah Lyttelton, one of the queen's former ladies of the bedchamber, was invited to visit for the first time since Albert's death. She recalled that when she saw Helena and Louise, both dressed in the pale grey of mourning, she was struck by the fact that their 'poor plain faces' were almost the same colour as their dresses. The girls looked absolutely miserable and yet the queen seemed oblivious to their unhappiness. She talked to Lady Lyttelton about her own misery and all the physical ailments she claimed to be suffering from, which Lady Lyttelton felt was 'quite a delusion, poor thing'.

The effect that Queen Victoria's depression had on all her children is seldom mentioned or explored, yet it was profound and had long-term consequences for all of them. In 1867, when Victoria was disconcerted to realise her feelings of grief were beginning to subside, she wrote to Vicky about the years following Albert's death in which she 'longed' to die every day and every night. She noted in her journal her envy of a husband she had heard of, who had died a few weeks after the death of his wife. Even before their father's death, the queen's children had been nervous of offending her; now they lived in constant fear of displeasing her, terrified of saying the wrong thing or making their mother cry.

Louise at least had an occupation that could, temporarily, take her mind away from her mother's frightening behaviour. During the summer of 1863, Louise was at Osborne without her mother, as the queen was travelling overseas. It was a creative time, when the aspiring artist was able to spend more time than normal in her cramped little studio. Louise was interested in many forms of artistic expression and, for Bertie's twenty-second birthday, she made him a carpet, which she had woven herself. Her interest in sculpture had not dimmed as her parents had assumed it would and she took every opportunity to watch sculptors at work. Queen Victoria was not pleased that her daughter wanted to follow a pursuit she considered unfeminine, but as it became apparent that sculpting was where Louise's talent lay, she relented. In the mid-1860s, Susan Durant became Louise's first sculpting tutor. When she became ill, one of the queen's favourite artists, Mary Thornycroft, was engaged in her place. In addition to being a great sculptor herself, Mary Thornycroft (née Francis) was the daughter, the wife and the mother of successful sculptors. She had been trained by her father, John Francis, and had exhibited for the first time at the Royal Academy at the age of 24, with Bust of a Gentleman. Most of her later works would be modelled on children, such as those she made of the royal babies. She had made her debut in the royal household in 1843 after her father had shown the queen and prince consort examples of her work; it was then that she started to receive her first royal commissions. In 1840, at what was then considered the very late age of twenty-nine, Mary had married the sculptor Thomas Thornycroft. Her husband recognised the importance of her work and, for many years, put his career on hold in order to work as Mary's assistant.[19] Thanks to the patronage of the royal couple, Mary had been chosen to exhibit at the Great Exhibition of 1851 and at the International Exhibition of 1862. In her work and

---

[19] Mary and Thomas Thornycroft had seven children. Their daughter Alyce and their son William Hamo Thornycroft both became professional sculptors, with William being one of the most important members of the 'New Sculpture' movement of the late nineteenth century. Another of their daughters, Theresa, was a talented painter (and the mother of the poet Siegfried Sassoon).

in the way in which she lived her life, Mary Thornycroft was an inspirational role model for the young Princess Louise.

Mary helped Louise learn all aspects of sculpting, showing her how to sketch out designs on the block of marble – something Louise often felt nervous about doing – and giving her the confidence to make the first chip. Throughout her career, Louise often required help from her tutors and friends. Her work shows that she was a very talented sculptress, but she frequently lost interest in her creations before they were finalised; what she seems to have enjoyed was the early, physical work, the thrill of creating, not the technical 'finishing off'. Many critics unkindly claimed that none of her work was ever truly Louise's own, that everything was finished by her tutors, which was not the case. Even early in Louise's artistic career, Henry Ponsonby, not always Louise's greatest fan, wrote to his wife that he was very impressed with the princess's drawings and that he knew no one else had given her any 'help' with them.[20] At the end of 1863, Alix wrote warmly to her sister-in-law, 'The little statuette is really admirably modelled, and I strongly advise you to continue taking lessons with Mrs Thornycroft as you certainly have great talent in modelling, and may perhaps become some day an eminent sculptress.' She was particularly impressed when the sixteen-year-old Louise presented her with a sculpture of Princess Beatrice as a birthday present (noting in her journal: 'Louise's bust of Baby is charming and so like').

In 1863, in addition to enjoying the friendship of her new sister-in-law, Louise was cheered by a new face in the royal household. Lady Caroline Lyttelton had just been appointed maid of honour to the queen and she was only seven years older than Louise. Lady Caroline's grandmother, Lady Sarah Lyttelton, had been the royal governess for the first two years of Louise's life. Sadly for Louise, Lady Caroline was destined to spend just six months with the family, as she became engaged to Lord Frederick Cavendish (a son of the Duke of Devonshire). During her few months at court, Caroline and Louise became friendly – Caroline records in an unhappy entry in her diary that Louise was punished by her mother for taking Caroline riding

[20] Henry Ponsonby served in the royal household for most of Louise's life. He was Prince Albert's equerry from 1856 until the prince's death; extra equerry to the queen after her husband's death, and, from 1870, the queen's private secretary.

without having requested permission from the queen. Louise was a very confident and competent horsewoman and loved the freedom of riding. During one of their rides, she asked Caroline about her life before she came to court. Caroline and another member of the household (Miss Bowater) talked with glee about the fun of country house parties, whereupon Louise said wistfully, 'Ah, that is one thing we are deprived of.' Caroline was quite relieved to leave her life at court and admitted in her journal that she considered Louise's life 'rather monotonous'.

It was largely because of this monotony that Louise's adolescence was so troubled. When the queen was absent, she ordered her staff to inform her about all aspects of her children's behaviour, so the royal children grew up aware that they were being spied upon, knowing that Victoria was their servants' and friends' queen, and required from them absolute fidelity. Louise was excitable and enthusiastic: she would be praised for this often in adulthood but in adolescence it was seen as a serious defect – as a sign of mental illness. If the queen considered Louise too similar to Bertie it would explain why she believed her daughter needed constant correction and punishment. Louise was trapped in an atmosphere she found stultifying and depressing. She was fiercely loyal to those who showed even the slightest interest in her and this led to another of the queen's punishments. It was discovered that Helena and Louise had been reading novels, something of which the queen disapproved, but which they had been permitted to do by the French governess, Madame Hocédé, or 'Lina'. When she was questioned, Louise, fearful of getting Lina into trouble, claimed she had found the novel by chance. Lina was dismissed and Louise was punished both for reading a novel and for telling a lie – even though it was told to protect someone else. The queen insisted that Lina and the novels had caused Louise to become 'deceitful' and to have 'disobeyed orders'. She wrote to Vicky that Lina had done Louise 'a terrible deal of harm'.

Just as she had done with Bertie, the queen attempted to ensure that all members of her household understood the 'truth' about Louise's personality, telling them what they should think about the princess before they could judge for themselves. When Lady Caroline arrived in Windsor, her initial impression of Louise was that she was 'very pretty' and eager to be friendly. Yet Caroline was immediately informed by another maid of honour, the Hon. Horatia Stopford, to be on her guard: 'H.R.H. seems to be rather naughty, with a mischievous will of her own.' Despite Horatia's reservations, Louise, as a child starved of friends, had grown very fond of her. The following day, Caroline recorded that 'Prss. Louise sent for Horatia, and cried and sobbed at the thought of losing her on Monday, after their long bit at Osborne together.' Louise was desperate for close friends she could confide in. Her mother was equally insistent that Louise should have merely companions, not friends or confidantes; the queen's constant need to warn people how 'difficult' Louise was was an attempt to ensure they would keep their distance. This controlling tactic stemmed from the queen's jealousy when any of her children showed a desire to spend time with, or confide in, anyone except their mother.

Queen Victoria's attempt to prevent Louise from forming close friendships failed with one companion (who had been hand-picked by the queen herself). Sybil Grey, the daughter of General Grey,[21] formed a strong bond of friendship with the lonely princess. Sybil was Louise's secret ally against her mother and the two girls had confidential chats about the problems in the royal family. At the end of 1863, the Danish king died and Alix's father was crowned King Christian IX. Unfortunately his right to rule over the duchies of Schleswig and Holstein was immediately challenged by the King of Prussia (Vicky's father-in-law). Because of Louise's love for Alix, and Sybil's love for Louise, the two girls became fervent supporters of Denmark in the ensuing battle – although Louise had to keep this under wraps at home, as the queen made her partiality for the Prussian cause well known. This caused a great upset in the family. Alix was devastated by her mother-in-law's behaviour. Sybil's diaries contain girlish confidences from Louise, such as which of her siblings had fallen in love and with whom. The two girls had tea together as often as they could, and when they were apart they sent each other notes and letters. As they grew older

---

[21] General Grey had been equerry-in-waiting to the queen when as she attained the throne. When she married Prince Albert, Grey became his private secretary. After Albert's death, he became private secretary to the queen, until his own sudden death in 1870. He was replaced by Henry Ponsonby, who remained private secretary until 1895.

and Sybil was allowed greater freedom than the princess, they were saddened by how much time they had to spend apart. While Sybil was free to attend coming-out parties and balls, Louise was often forbidden to do so, so she lived vicariously through Sybil's descriptions.

Within a few weeks of joining the royal household, Lady Caroline had made up her own mind about Louise. 'She has an exceedingly pretty manner . . . compounded of dignity and kindliness,' she wrote in January 1864 and, as so many other people would observe, the princess made dull evenings fun, full of 'laughing and talking gaily'. This aspect of Louise's personality incensed her mother, who was determined that life without Albert should not be fun, or frivolous. Even Henry Ponsonby, who was very loyal to his monarch, began to realise that what he had been told by the queen about her daughter was not necessarily the truth. His son, Arthur, in a book about his father based on Henry's letters and journals, wrote that Louise 'found no more favour with her mother than any of the others and her rather Bohemian habits were watched and disapproved of. On her making some suggestion with regard to the heating of the new room at Osborne the Queen wrote: "Yes. But she must not interfere too much. She is not practical." . . . . [Henry] Ponsonby . . . repeatedly refers to the liveliness of Princess Louise's conversation at the Queen's dinner [parties] and the relief this gave to the too frequent dullness amounting sometimes to gloom.'

Louise spent much of her early adult life trying desperately to alleviate boredom, not only for herself and her siblings, but also for the household staff and invited guests, acutely and embarrassingly aware of how dull her mother's hospitality could be. The composer Sir Charles Hallé remembered visiting Osborne in the late 1860s, where the royal children still living at home were fulsome in their desire to talk to him, to play duets with him and to listen to him perform. The composer, despite understanding the great honour of this welcome, was nonetheless bored and frustrated by the atmosphere at Osborne and the lack of amusements. He wrote to his family: 'When shall I get away from here? That is the rub. The Queen speaks, and Princess Helena speaks, as if I were going to stay here for ever.'

The astute Lady Caroline was worried about Princess Louise; and in general she found all the queen's children neglected and unhappy.

By the time Caroline arrived at Windsor, Leopold had been diagnosed with haemophilia for some years, yet at times the queen strangely insisted on not giving him special treatment. On a day in which the royal party had endured a miserably cold carriage ride, Caroline wrote, 'Poor little Prince Leopold was full of talk and cheerfulness, but his small thin face grew pinched with cold; and I wished I cd take him into my arms and cover him warmly up.' Knowing the severity of her brother's illness, Louise talked to the medical attendants and made sure she knew as much as possible about his condition. The queen, who never seemed to feel the cold and had developed a passion for all things Scottish, was adamant her sons should wear kilts, even when they were not at Balmoral. In November 1863, while Arthur was being trained for the army, Louise wrote to tell him that 'poor Leopold has had the rheumatism in his leg, and it was very much swollen yesterday . . . he must be carried up and down stairs, the doctor says it comes from wearing the kilt in such cold weather, but Mama does not think so, poor little boy he says it hurts him very much'.

The siblings became united in their dislike of Balmoral and its associations, as later letters attest. Leopold wrote to his friend Walter Stirling of 'that detestable Scotland' and in a letter Prince Arthur told Louise, 'You must summon your courage and energy now for the amusements of your approaching Highland life . . . for if it is wet (a thing which occasionally happens in Scotland) it will be rather a bore.' A few weeks later, as he was about to join the family, he wrote again: 'The time when I am going to Balmoral is now fast approaching, but I do not know that I thoroughly appreciate the pleasure, for as you well know one is under a good many restrictions at home. There are also constant squalls and squabbles which give rise to a great feeling of bad feeling and jealousy . . . The only reason why I do not dislike the idea of going to Balmoral is that we two shall be able to see a little more of each other and that I shall be able to keep your company on long expeditions.' When Louise was overseas, Leopold wrote to her: 'The day after tomorrow we go to that *most* VILE and *most* ABOMINABLE of places Balmoral.'

In addition to her worries about Leopold, Lady Caroline was concerned about Helena who, since the departure of Alice, had become her mother's lackey. On 7 May 1864 Caroline wrote, 'I am much distressed about poor Prss. Helena who is cruelly overworked, the

Queen having no notion how her mind and body are strained, and indeed having no one to take her place.' Louise was equally concerned, knowing that Helena would be married as soon as a suitable match could be made; Louise would then be the one 'cruelly overworked' and have no time for art.

At the start of 1864, the royal family was waiting for a exciting event. Bertie and Alix were expecting a baby. It was due in the spring, so when Alix went into labour at the beginning of January, the worst was feared. She was only seven months pregnant and it is testimony to the skill of the royal physicians that a baby born so prematurely in the mid nineteenth century survived. The queen, in her letters to Vicky, blamed the baby's prematurity on Bertie's late nights and dissolute lifestyle and on Alix for trying to keep up with him. Even more shocking, to the queen, was the news that Alix's labour had begun shortly after she returned home from sitting in a sledge beside the lake at Virginia Water watching a game of ice hockey. The queen considered such an activity unacceptable for a pregnant princess.

The tiny baby, who weighed less than four pounds, was named Albert Victor (both of which names Lady Caroline derided in her journal as being far too 'foreign'), though he would become known as 'Prince Eddy'.[22] The circumstances of his premature birth had reached the newspapers and comedians, learning of the ice hockey game, quickly dubbed him not 'Prince Albert Victor' but 'Prince All-but-on-the-ice'. Like his father, Prince Eddy would suffer from poor academic skills and during his childhood his grandmother bemoaned that yet another heir was not living up to her expectations. She attempted to take charge of Eddy's education and the young prince experienced similar bullying to that which his father had suffered.

A few weeks after the birth of Prince Eddy, Louise celebrated her sixteenth birthday, which meant it was just one year until she expected to 'come out'. The following twelve months should have been spent organising her wardrobe, completing her education and preparing events to herald her arrival into adulthood and society. When she

---

[22] Bertie's son and heir was fated to die prematurely at the age of 28. In the 1960s rumours emerged that he had been Jack the Ripper – despite evidence proving that he was actually in Scotland when at least two of the murders were carried out. The rumours persist.

talked of her party for the following year, however, Queen Victoria announced that Louise would not have a coming-out ball. Despite the fact that Albert would have been dead for over three years by the time of Louise's seventeenth birthday, the queen made it clear that she thought her daughter selfish, forgetting she was in mourning for her father, and that she should not be thinking about parties. The ballroom at Buckingham Palace had been closed since Albert's death and the queen had no intention of opening it up for her wayward daughter to make an exhibition of herself in. Eventually she agreed that Louise could have a formal religious confirmation (for which she wore a white dress decorated with swansdown) after which she would be considered 'out' and therefore able to attend formal parties and balls held by other people. Her confirmation was intended to be at the end of 1864, but ill health intervened.

In the autumn of 1864, while staying at Balmoral, Louise became suddenly ill. She was treated by Dr Edward Sieveking who diagnosed 'meningitic complications' or tubercular meningitis, an illness frequently fatal, even today. In more recent years, this diagnosis has been challenged,[23] but whatever Louise was suffering from, it was a violent illness and one that left her considerably weakened. In October 1864, the queen was moved to write in her journal, 'Quite worried about poor Louise, who looks so ill.' The princess's headaches were so blinding that she needed to be kept in a darkened room as the light hurt her eyes. She was kept in bed and nursed carefully for over two months. Despite her daughter's illness, however, the queen insisted the household travel to Windsor. The train journey was agonising for Louise, who was too ill to make the full journey. She was carried off the train in Carlisle to sleep in a proper bed and continue to Windsor at a later date. It was not until December that Louise was able to move her head without pain and Sybil Grey wrote in her diary that even the sound of a rustling silk skirt was agony for the princess. For the rest of her life, Louise would suffer with intermittent health problems, often incapacitated by attacks of neuralgia; many of these were attributed to her severe illness at the age of sixteen.

By March 1865, a couple of days after her seventeenth birthday

[23] In his book *Royal Maladies*, Dr Alan R. Rushton argues that if Louise had developed tubercular meningitis she would not have survived, nor would her recovery have progressed as it did.

– which was marked in her mother's journal by the words: 'She is so handsome & talented, & has so much taste' – Louise had been confirmed and was considered 'out'. She was well enough to attend a ball at Marlborough House for Bertie and Alix's wedding anniversary, together with Helena. It was, as Louise wrote to Prince Arthur, her very 'first ball'. Alix was pregnant again, and would give birth to her second son, George, in mid-June. (Victoria described her grandson – who was to become King George V – as 'very small and not very pretty'.) That Alix hosted a ball while so heavily pregnant is interesting, as women were expected to hide away when their bump became visible. As fashionable women were increasingly reluctant to do so, however, a whole new industry had been spawned, which included corsets for pregnant women made to fit over the bump and then be tightly laced to create as small a waist as possible, despite the baby. Maternity corsets were terrifying-looking contraptions composed of buckles, straps and boning. For women whose pregnancy was advanced, an 'abdomen belt' could also be worn, under the corset.

Many medical specialists published articles on the danger of maternity corsets and abdomen belts – pointing out how often they resulted in miscarriage – but as long as society's rules dictated that pregnancy should not be discussed, or acknowledged in public, women had no choice but to try and conceal it, or to remain at home, hidden away. Fashion also allowed women to hide any aspects of their body that they chose to conceal by the judicious use of frills, pleats, padding and decorations, such as silk flowers, all designed to deceive the eye. Wearing a spectacularly low-cut dress was an intentional way of reducing the likelihood of anyone, in particular men, looking below a woman's bustline. The use of such artifice in combination with maternity corsets enabled many women to conceal a pregnancy entirely; it was often possible for an unmarried woman to hide an unwanted telltale bump.

When Louise was deemed well enough after her illness, she was taken abroad to convalesce. A family party travelled to Prince Albert's home town of Coburg, where Louise met many of her Prussian relations and stayed at Albert's beloved home, Rosenau. Louise wrote to Arthur about the journey, which she found exhausting and on occasion terrifying: 'I forgot to say that when we landed at Antwerp it was quite dark, and there was nothing but lanterns everywhere, and there was such a crowd of people, some men held torches: as we were getting into the carriage, a man put his head in, blew a quantity of smoke from his cigar in my face, and screamed 'God bless Victoria.' I think he was rather mad, he screamed the same thing out several times already when we were walking up the pier.' In Prussia she enjoyed herself. It was a family party, as Louise's siblings were in attendance for the occasion of unveiling a bust to Prince Albert. Before Arthur arrived, Louise wrote to him, happy to report that Leopold was 'much better' and chivvying him to hurry up and join them so they could enjoy 'some nice walks and drives together and rides'. Vicky loved the opportunity to see all her siblings and was longing for at least one of her sisters to move closer to her. She hoped Louise would marry a Prussian and, over the next few years, would suggest several suitable men, but Louise refused to show interest in them. Later she declared Prussian men were boorish and boring, and that they smelt bad.

Louise's brothers had a much better idea of the type of men Louise preferred. She confided in them in a way she did not with her sisters. In 1865, Louise had written to Arthur from the royal yacht saying, 'I have had nothing to do this morning so I have been drawing the sailors'; in 1867 Arthur sent her in a letter a sketch of a handsome Highland soldier, writing, 'I thought it would please you.' In the same year, he added a teasing postscript to another letter to her: 'I saw Capt. Rideout yesterday and he told me about all the fun you had on board the yacht together.'

Although she was unsuccessful in match-making Louise, Vicky did suggest a suitable match for Helena: she introduced her to Prince Christian of Schleswig-Holstein, a distant relative of the queen and fifteen years Helena's senior. (In appearance he seemed much older than that.) The queen had despaired of trying to find a husband for Helena: 'Poor dear Lenchen,' she wrote, 'though most useful and active and clever and amiable, does not improve in looks and has great difficulties with her figure and her want of calm, quiet, graceful manners. Nature certainly divides her gifts strangely.' In comparison, Louise was held up as a paragon: 'so handsome (she is so very much admired) . . . so graceful and her manners so perfect in society, so quiet and lady-like, and then she has such great taste for art'. What her mother lamented was that Louise's perfect behaviour in public was not exhibited at home. Vicky was thrilled with her successful match-making, but Bertie and Alix felt betrayed – Prince Christian's family had recently been at war with Denmark. The situation within the royal circle was miserably tense, and Louise was torn between her quarrelling eldest brother and sister.

In 1866, the year of Helena's wedding, Louise was heading inexorably towards the drudgery of becoming her mother's constant companion. At that year's Marlborough House Ball, Helena was noticed to be glowing with happiness; quite what Louise's feelings were that night were not revealed. After Helena and Christian's wedding, Louise wrote to Louisa Bowater, one of her few confidential friends, that she was 'low and sad' and spent much of her time alone in her bedroom crying. Her brothers, in particular, felt sorry for their usually vivacious sister, who was so seldom allowed to express her true personality and barely ever to attend balls or parties. Before Helena's marriage, the two sisters had stayed at home together, but now Helena was free to attend parties and events with her husband. Louise was feeling isolated and depressed.

Although the queen was very strict that her daughters remain in mourning, she allowed her sons a much wider rein; they could take part in the London season and were allowed to travel. The princes would try to compensate for Louise's lonely existence by sending long letters about people they had met, countries they had visited and events they had attended. These letters kept her tantalisingly close to the world she longed to enter. When Arthur was in Italy, Louise wrote longingly: 'I envy you having been to Naples, such a beautiful place, I should give anything to see it. We have had such dreadful cold weather here . . . it must be charming weather with you,' and 'You will get my letter when you are at Venice. Oh! what a lovely place to see, I will ask you to tell me a great deal about it, I have always longed so to see it.'

It seems, however, that Louise may have had a secret to help stave off the loneliness. For a few months of 1866, Prince Leopold had a new tutor or 'governor'. His name was Walter Stirling and for many years there has been speculation about just how important Stirling was to his charge's older sister, and why he was so suddenly dismissed.

CHAPTER 6

What really happened with Walter Stirling?

> I cannot say how I miss you, I always expect to see you come
> in the morning as you always did, and as I was carried down to
> breakfast Louise and I missed you looking over the banister at
> the top of the staircase at us.
>
> Letter to Walter Stirling from Prince Leopold, 1866

For the public, 1866 was notable as the year in which Queen Victoria
finally attended the opening of Parliament, for the first time since her
husband's death.[24] For Louise, the year began with the knowledge that
she was, once again, in trouble with her mother. Louise had been
thinking independently and making 'shocking' decisions. The princess
always liked to think carefully about what presents she should give to
the servants so, at Christmas 1865, at the age of seventeen, she
presented all the male servants with pipes or cigar cases, knowing
they had a fondness for smoking. Unfortunately smoking was a taboo
subject, as Prince Albert had abhorred it. Louise's choice of gifts, and
that she had bought them without consulting her mother, infuriated
the queen. It also shocked several of the household staff – a princess
was not expected to encourage such a vice. Bertie wrote his sister a
letter of support, telling her: 'I am very glad that your Xmas went
off well – tho <u>very</u> lively it cannot have been – I wish that you could

---

[24] The mourning was not over, however, and the family were made to honour not
only the anniversary of Albert's death every December, but the anniversary of the
queen's mother's death in March.

once spend it with us – how nice that would be and what fun we would have. I think you did quite right to buy pipes and cigar cases for the servants, although Sir Thomas[25] was very much shocked.'

The year 1866 was also notable for Louise as the year in which she completed her first unaided sculpture, a bust of family friend Lady Jane Churchill. She had been the queen's lady of the bedchamber since Louise was six years old and became a close friend of the young princess, a friendship that endured until Jane's death in 1900. The two women were often seen together and were even described on occasion as belonging to that curious elite known as 'professional beauties' (an odd description that encompassed everyone from actresses to bohemian princesses). Many songs and poems were written by admirers of the women who hoped to gain a patron. One such poem described Jane as a woman 'whose sweet tones make her the St Cecilia of the day' and coupled Jane and Louise together, including the lines '. . . warmly beautiful like the sun at noon, glowed with love's flames our dear Princess Louise'. Louise's sculpture of her friend was a significant artistic achievement and Mary Thornycroft determined to persuade the queen that Louise should receive more formal training. She also began to introduce Louise to other artists and, that spring, Helena and Louise visited the studios of the sculptors Baron Marochetti and William Theed.

In May, the princess's artistic desires were put on hold because, once again, Louise was ill, this time with whooping cough. She was visited regularly by Leopold, who understood how miserable it was to be an invalid. Leopold had also developed whooping cough, but luckily only mildly. Louise was exhausted and grateful for her brother's visits. At this time of his life, Leopold was unusually happy. The reason for this was the appointment of a sympathetic young army officer as his new 'governor', or tutor. Louise also warmed to her brother's handsome new tutor. On 25 March 1866, the queen had recorded in her journal that she had met Lieutenant Walter George Stirling of the Horse Artillery and declared herself 'much pleased' with him. Stirling and Prince Leopold became good friends as soon as Stirling took up his position, and Louise, who had just celebrated her eighteenth birthday, spent a great deal of time with them.

The queen's journal notes several instances of family outings,

[25] Sir Thomas Biddulph, Keeper of the Privy Purse.

parties and dinners at which Stirling was present, and there is no sign of disquiet in her jottings. To all observers, Stirling seemed to have become an important part of the royal household and the young prince blossomed under his care. So it came as a shock to many when the handsome young lieutenant was dismissed from his post in July 1866, just four months after being appointed. The queen's journal mentions him several times between March and May – then, in the journal that survives following Beatrice's heavy editing, his name appears no more until 4 August 1866. The queen wrote baldly: 'Breakfast in the Lower Alcove, after which took leave of Mr Stirling & gave him a silver inkstand & a bust of Leopold.' Later she took Louise and Leopold out for a 'nice drive', with no mention of what must have been their tears and fury about their mother's decision.

In the 1970s, the official explanation given for Stirling's dismissal by the Libraries at Windsor Castle was that 'After Stirling's appointment in early 1866 the doctors attending the Prince advised the Queen that he really needed to be in the care of a Governor who was more used to dealing with persons of delicate health, and the Queen felt she had made a mistake in appointing an army man to this post. Stirling therefore relinquished the appointment and returned to the Artillery.' Leopold was heartbroken, and the impetuous dismissal of Stirling, before another tutor had yet been found, is one of the mysteries that make researching Princess Louise so fascinating. The 1970s explanation is vigorously belied by the fact that for several weeks after Stirling's dismissal Leopold was not cared for by someone more aware of his 'delicate health'; he was at the mercy of the brutal Archie Brown, the bullying brother of John Brown, who regularly pinched and beat the prince and not only made his everyday life unbearable but seriously endangered the sickly boy's health. The reason for Stirling's dismissal was a mystery, and the 1970s letter just adds fuel to the fire of speculation that it was to do with a scandalous secret.

When researching Louise's life, the second half of the 1860s presents a great deal of intrigue. There is one particular rumour that persists and I had hoped to find the answer to it in the Royal Archives. Louise's files being closed made this rumour assume more importance. The decision to hide away her files indicates very strongly that there is something in them that the archivists, even in the twenty-first century, feel the need to conceal. Since the late 1860s rumours have persisted that Princess Louise gave birth to an illegitimate child. The father, it is claimed, was her brother's tutor. There are two names that come up in connection with Louise and the purported illegitimate son. One is Walter Stirling and the other is his replacement, the Reverend Robinson Duckworth (a friend of the author Lewis Carroll and the inspiration for the Duck in *Alice in Wonderland*). In 1960, one of Duckworth's nephews wrote down the oral history passed on in his family:

> Princess Louise always had great affection for this uncle . . . and wished to marry him. In those days such an idea was not to be thought of . . . [she] gave him a Bible with touching inscriptions also a peculiar signet ring (it contained a lock of her hair) which Uncle R wore. Also another ring containing 4 stones Ruby and Diamond for Robinson Duckworth & 2 Lapis Lazuli for Leopold and Louise. Inside an inscription: Forget us not Le. Lo. '67.

Elizabeth Longford also claims in her book, *Darling Loosy*, that Duckworth was Louise's 'first love'; Jehanne Wake writes that Louise developed a 'schoolgirl crush' on Duckworth and that he was 'her first girlhood love'.

Although Louise grew extremely fond of Duckworth, it seems unlikely that they became lovers. Duckworth too would be dismissed as Leopold's tutor, but not until 1870, after he had been in the post for three years. In addition, Duckworth was not sent away from the royal household, as Stirling had been. Once Duckworth was replaced as Leopold's tutor, he remained in the household as one of the queen's chaplains. The ring that Louise designed for him was made to commemorate the date on which he had arrived with them. It seems to have been a token of friendship rather than one proclaiming sexual love.

Duckworth's family revealed that, towards the end of his life, he was deeply saddened by the rumours that had emerged claiming he had slept with the young princess. In 1955, Captain Arthur Duckworth, nephew of the Reverend Duckworth, wrote to the Royal Archives to enquire whether there was any truth in the rumours that still dogged his uncle's memory. The royal archivist, Owen Morshead, wrote in response that there was no suggestion at all of a romance between Duckworth and Princess Louise. In his letter, dated 24 October 1955, he commented, 'After her [Princess Louise's] death I spent a fortnight in her residence, emptying the drawers and tin boxes, and reading every letter. I found nothing (and expected to find nothing) pointing to such an incident.' His letter also gives a fascinating glimpse into the way in which Princess Louise's life was to be carefully documented and then hidden away within the archives. Duckworth was the person who turned around Leopold's misery after the terrible months under the control of Archie Brown, and Louise loved him for that. As he was a close friend and confidant of both Leopold and Louise, it is possible she discussed with him her affair with Stirling. Duckworth was a gentle, kindly man who made it his mission to help the sickly Prince Leopold lead as interesting and fulfilling a life as possible; and under the command of the Rev. Duckworth, Louise was once more allowed to spend time with her brother. In 1973, Arthur Duckworth contacted the author Nina Epton, writing if there were any truth to the family rumour. He wrote, 'Leopold was devoted to his tutor and so, I believe, were all the royal family, and particularly Princess Louise, whom I have been told wished to marry him.' Nina Epton, whose book was about Queen Victoria and all her daughters, responded with a telling letter that reveals even she was kept in the dark by the Royal Archives about Victoria's mysterious fourth daughter. Her letter includes the words, 'I was so very short on material about Louise. I had hoped to be able to consult the Windsor Castle archives . . . Anyway I am sure there must be information which is still kept private, unless it was destroyed by the arch-inquisitor Princess Beatrice. This is most likely.'

It is possible that the rumours voiced for many years within the Duckworth family that Louise had wanted to marry the reverend had their basis in fact. It is also possible that the princess did consider marrying her friend, perhaps naively believing that to do so might enable her to adopt her illegitimate baby and raise him as their son. This would account for the persistent rumours within the family.

Despite all attempts to erase him from royal history, the most likely candidate for Louise's lover was Walter Stirling, welcomed into the family and dismissed just four months later. That Jehanne Wake makes no mention of him in her book – the manuscript of which was checked by the Royal Archives – is telling. When the Rev. Duckworth was hired to replace Stirling, the queen's one reservation was that she wished Duckworth had not been so handsome; it seems she had come to the conclusion that good looks were a dangerous asset in a royal tutor.

Following his dismissal, Stirling was sent back to the Royal Horse Artillery and was later posted overseas. Interestingly, the reason Elizabeth Longford gives in her book for Stirling's dismissal is different from the official explanation from the Windsor Castle Libraries. Longford, who was allowed access to Princess Louise's files under supervision, states that Stirling was dismissed because he had a 'quarrel' with Archie Brown. In the 1970s, Michael Gledhill wrote to Elizabeth Longford to ask if she could help him at all with his research into Princess Louise. In her kind response the author pondered, 'I felt that when Princess Beatrice transcribed her mother's diary she must have cut out almost as much about Princess Louise as she did about John Brown!'

It is documented that Stirling and Archie Brown did not get on well, but that was not particularly surprising. Archie's surly manner endeared him to few members of the royal household, so it seems unlikely that Stirling would have been singled out for dismissal. Stirling was also known to have quarrelled with Leopold's Scottish valet, Robertson, who was friends with and as much of a bully as Archie Brown and was equally unpleasant to the delicate Leopold. In an attempt to explain why she had dismissed Leopold's tutor, the queen claimed that Stirling did not understand the Highland temperament – forgetting that Stirling himself was Scottish.

The truth was that Stirling was defending Leopold, who found Archie Brown and Robertson frightening; the young prince described them in a letter to Stirling as 'the dreadful Scotch servants'. Archie seems to have been particularly cruel. A few years later, Leopold wrote a heartfelt letter to his friend Major Collins: 'that <u>devil</u> Archie, he does nothing, but jeer at, & be impertinent to me every day, & in the night he won't do anything for me though I order it, not even give me my chamberpot . . . the <u>infernal blackguard.</u> I could tear him limb from limb I loathe him so.' It is astonishing that the queen was so in thrall to John Brown that she allowed his brother to behave in an abusive and deliberately cruel manner to her sickly and vulnerable son, a child who was regularly unable to walk due to problems associated with haemophilia, and who needed to be able to rely on the kindness and understanding of his servants.

The story of Louise's life in the second half of the 1860s has been carefully sanitised and edited. Although the princess wrote constant letters – even at an early age she complained to Prince Arthur about the large number of people she had to write to every day – Elizabeth Longford does not seem to have been granted permission to reproduce many, and those published in her book *Darling Loosy* appear to have been very carefully hand-picked by archivists. Longford offers little explanation of who Stirling was. She does write about the rumour of Louise having an illegitimate baby, but she does so carefully, and only in relation to the Reverend Duckworth. After dismissing the rumours that Duckworth and Louise had an affair she comments 'there is no record of this . . . in the Royal Archives'. She does not mention whether the archives contain any reference to Stirling and Louise having an affair (although it seems unlikely that any such references would have survived Princess Beatrice).

In Longford's book, a joint letter is printed from Louise and Leopold to Walter Stirling, just after his dismissal, in which they talk about how he has been 'got out' of the household 'in an unpleasant way'. Louise and Leopold wrote alternate lines of the letter, so that Stirling should know it was truly from both of them and that they felt exactly the same way about the injustice of his dismissal:

> Today is Monday, Affie's birthday . . . breakfast was laid in the council room . . . Bertie for a *wonder* appeared at 9.30am, but Alix could not be up so soon, her usual time for breakfast being about 11am . . . We wondered what the new extra groom in waiting at the R.H.A. [Royal Horse Artillery] would be doing today; not having organs to grind or dogs to whip or cats to run after or pushing painters to sky daddle, *we* thought our best employment would be to write a joint comic epistle to our well beloved W.G.!!! a very kind friend of ours, in Scotch political troubles, but (thank God) is out of it now though got out of it in an unpleasant way.

After Stirling was dismissed the queen wrote to Major Elphinstone (who had been governor to both Arthur and Leopold and was instrumental in appointing Stirling) of her reasons for sending him away. As was usual, she wrote about herself in the third person: 'she does *not* think that Mr Stirling was *suited* for that post . . . the Queen must likewise own – that there is *that* in Mr S's manner – wh (& she felt it, tho she did not admit it – from the <u>very</u> 1st) wh wld make it <u>very</u> difficult for <u>her</u> to get on with him'. Elphinstone and another of the queen's advisors, Sir John Cowell, were saddened by the decision, knowing Stirling was good at his job and how attached Leopold was to him; they also felt it was deeply unfair to Stirling. Both men suggested Stirling be given the job of training Prince Arthur for the army, but, even though he would have been ideal for the role, the queen refused. It was apparent that she wanted Stirling out of the royal household immediately and was not prepared to explain her reasons to anyone outside the immediate family. There must have been a very pressing reason to dismiss Leopold's tutor before another suitable candidate had been found. Everyone in the household was gossiping and wondering about what this could be.

Leopold was heartbroken by the decision and became sullen with his mother. The queen was shocked by the force of her frail son's rage; she wrote in a sad letter to a friend, Lady Biddulph, that Leopold was being 'quite dreadful to me'. Leopold defiantly wore on his finger a gold ring Stirling had given him as a parting gift; this angered the queen, but Leopold refused to take it off. The queen took her revenge by refusing to allow Leopold and Louise to spend time together. Leopold wrote an agonised letter to Stirling, declaring 'I am no more allowed to stop with Louise as I used to do.' When the family were taken to Cliveden for a holiday, Louise 'broke down' as she wrote to her friend Louisa Bowater about her misery at the situation, 'a great grief to us both'.

If Louise did have a baby with Walter Stirling, the child must have been born towards the end of 1866 or the start of 1867. Louise was very fit and fairly tall; she was slimmer than her sisters, although not slender by today's standards, as photographs attest. If she had gained weight during this year, it would have seemed unremarkable, as Victoria and all her other daughters had a tendency to rotundity; Louise was in her teens, so any weight gain could easily have been assumed to be 'puppy fat'. Women used a great many fashion artifices to disguise pregnancies well into their seventh or eighth month, as Alix had done. It is interesting to see how many mentions there are in 1866 and 1867 of Louise's dresses as very highly decorated, with references to ribbons and bows and pleats. Unless Louise suddenly changed her fashion sense, and then changed it back again, these extra accessories could well have been disguising a pregnancy. As noted earlier, maternity corsets squeezed the foetus into such a small amount of space that a woman was still able to achieve a slender waist many months into a pregnancy. The voluminous Victorian skirts, often heavily decorated with swathes of material sweeping round to the bustle, went a long way to disguising pregnancy and, as the more advanced stage would have been in the winter, Louise could have worn numerous shawls and wraps – not to mention a large hand-warming muff, another common means of concealing pregnancy. Throughout the autumn and early winter of 1866, the queen and family spent a great deal of time in Balmoral, with their most trusted members of the household and very few visitors. Louise was often described as being in poor health, allegedly with recurrences of her crippling headaches.

There are many stories of Victorian women, in the servant class, who continued working right up until the moment they went into labour, and of their employers as having no idea that a pregnancy was being concealed. Many women succeeded in hiding all signs of pregnancy and childbirth, and if the baby survived they would continue to work without their employers finding out, leaving their child with family members. Women were moved to such measures by the harshness of society towards a woman who had a baby outside marriage – yet the same society did nothing to punish the fathers, even if the baby was the result of rape. If a working woman was discovered to be pregnant she would almost inevitably be dismissed without references or pay.

In 1864, the body of a stillborn baby was discovered in a field in St Ninian's in Renfrewshire. Its mother was a young servant, who had managed to conceal her pregnancy from both her family and her employers. Two years later, a servant named Helen Sutherland was found guilty of concealing her pregnancy and murdering her baby in an attempt to keep her job. The court was told no one had any knowledge the girl was pregnant and that she had given birth 'unaided'. In 1878, a servant named Margaret Brown, living in Aberdeen, was sentenced to nine months in prison. Although she had gone through a full-term pregnancy her employers had not noticed she was pregnant, and her condition was discovered only after she had given birth; the baby had died and her secret was uncovered when its body was found in a shallow grave. Margaret Brown was arrested for murder, but that was not proved and the baby was deemed to have died at birth. The crime for which she was sent to prison was 'concealment of pregnancy'. This was a recognised criminal offence and such cases regularly appeared in the papers. If a servant, wearing far more simple clothing than a princess, was able to use her clothing to conceal her condition, then Princess Louise, renowned for her unique fashion sense, who was able to sew and who had access to the best and most discreet dressmakers in the country, could certainly have done so.

It has often been claimed that Louise could not possibly have been pregnant at this time as she was recorded as having danced at a servants' ball, and the queen's Scottish diaries show that Louise was often encouraged to ride. Pregnancy would have been no barrier to dancing and at a Scottish ball Louise's dress would have been covered by a plaid shawl. If the queen had been hoping her daughter would miscarry, then energetic exercise would have been encouraged. One also has to remember that women of that era rode side-saddle, which would have been little more dangerous for a pregnant woman than being constantly jolted in a carriage, an everyday occurrence for the princesses.

It is notable that Princess Louise made few public appearances for several months at the end of 1866 and on those she did she met people who would be extremely unlikely to suspect that an unmarried princess could possibly be having a baby – as on her visit to the boys' parish school in Balmoral in October 1866 – or they were public appearances at which Louise was seen sitting inside a carriage, not getting out or walking around. In November 1866, Louise was with her mother when they visited the site for the Albert Memorial in London, but they simply drove up to the site to view it – and to give the public a brief glimpse of their queen. A couple of weeks later, Louise accompanied her mother to Windsor station, but when the queen disembarked from the carriage and took the train to Wolverhampton, for some reason she did not choose to take her daughter with her. While Victoria began her journey to knight the Mayor of Wolverhampton and unveil the town's statue of Prince Albert (sculpted by Thomas Thornycroft), Louise remained in the carriage, and as soon as her mother had departed, was returned swiftly to the confines of Windsor Castle.

Another interesting circumstance is that the queen noted in her diary for autumn 1866 that Louise did not require servants to help her dress, which seems extraordinary considering how impossible fashionable Victorian clothes were to get into and out of without help. The queen wrote that Louise was 'very handy and can do almost everything for herself'. In a household full of servants and ladies-in-waiting there was no shortage of people to help the princess dress. Louise spent the last couple of months of that year either walking or driving in a carriage with Leopold and the Reverend

Duckworth, or attending church – and although the latter sounds as though it was a public event, the royals had their own private entrance and sat in an enclosed area away from prying eyes. The pregnancy would almost certainly not have gone to full term if Louise had been wearing an abdomen belt and maternity corset. If that were the case, it is likely that she would have given birth to a premature baby (as Alix did) and would not have needed to hide the advanced stages of pregnancy for very long.

In December 1866, Leopold wrote a heart-rending letter to Louise: 'Loosey, I don't know what would happen to me if you ever went away, all would be over for me then.' Why was he so nervous? Until now, the queen had insisted that Louise stay with her, as companion, until Beatrice was old enough to take her place. What had made Leopold so scared that he was going to lose his sister? There were certainly no suggestions of marriage for Louise at this time.

By February 1867, Louise was very much in the public eye again. On 5 February, she attended the opening of Parliament wearing a dress of white satin. The day was not a success for the queen, who was shocked to hear booing from republicans and parliamentary reformists in the crowds. The following month, Louise was present to receive guests at her mother's first court of the season, and the newspapers described her outfit: 'a train of rich white silk, trimmed with tulle and white ribbons, and a petticoat of white tulle with white ribbons. Head-dress, feathers and veil; ornaments, diamonds and pearls, with the Victoria and Albert Order and the Order of St Isabel.' In a marked contrast to the previous few months, Louise attended the theatre and concerts, she went riding regularly and made a number of visits to Bertie and Alix, who were expecting another baby.

Bertie and Alix's first daughter was born on 20 February 1867 and named Louise Victoria Alexandra Dagmar. The queen was absolutely furious that the baby's first name was not Victoria and told all who would listen that it was yet another example of the fact that Bertie and Alix had no idea how things were 'done'. It was a minor victory for Bertie, but he braved the queen's wrath in order to name his daughter after her maternal, not paternal, grandmother. Yet although the baby was ostensibly named after Alix's mother, it delighted Princess Louise to know that she had a niece who shared her name and Bertie wrote to tell her she was the baby's namesake. Perhaps Bertie and

Alix did so not only to please the Danish queen, but also because they knew that Bertie's sister had been unable to keep her own baby. Giving her a niece named after her may have been intended to alleviate such a painful situation. Princess Louise would become very close to Princess Louise of Wales and, in years to come, the two women often attended social engagements together and could be found sketching or chatting at family gatherings.

Life for the new family was not idyllic. Alix's health was poor and she and Bertie were on increasingly bad terms. Alix was painfully and embarrassingly aware of her husband's infidelities and she was finding herself frustratingly disabled, often having to resort to a wheelchair. At around the time she gave birth to baby Louise, Alix succumbed to what was diagnosed as rheumatic fever. For ever afterwards she would be incapacitated, never regaining her former fitness. She had never enjoyed robust health and, following an operation on her neck as a child, was uncomfortable about the scar it had left. She would wear high necklines or chokers of pearls to hide the scar; both of which became extremely fashionable. (Alix was such a fashion icon that, once she began to walk with a stick, the sales of walking sticks soared and society women began to affect a limp, to emulate the Princess of Wales. It became known as 'the Alexandra limp'.) In the spring, shortly after the birth of Princess Louise of Wales, Bertie went away to Paris. He wanted Louise to stay with Alix and help with the baby – and to give her a respite from their mother – but the queen refused. Bertie wrote: 'I cannot tell you how sorry I am that you were not allowed to come and stay here with Alix while I am at Paris, but I was afraid that there would be difficulties in the way ... Both Alix and I are very anxious that you should be Godmother to our little girl, especially as she is to bear your name.' The queen did not want to let her daughter out of her sight.

The queen's major concern about the dismissal of Walter Stirling was that he would be indiscreet. The reason she gave to Elphinstone was that she feared Stirling would tell people of his grievance with the Highland servants and create damaging gossip about the way the queen ordered her household. Was she concerned that he might tell people about John Brown's position in the household? Or was there a far more serious need to rely on his discretion? The queen confided to Lady Biddulph, 'I dread his indiscretion & thought to wound.' To Elphinstone the queen sent a cautionary letter reminding him he had assured her of Stirling's discretion, with the undertone being that Elphinstone had better ensure Stirling's silence. Even within the royal household, however, the situation was being whispered about. When the queen's cousin visited from Belgium, two years later, he heard gossip about a man named Stirling. Whether he realised just how contentious he was being or not, the Count of Flanders made the mistake of asking the queen at dinner – surrounded by many other guests – what had happened with Stirling. The queen is recorded to have blushed.

Despite the queen's very obvious animosity towards Stirling, after he was dismissed, he continued to receive a salary from the royal purse.[26] Although he had worked with Prince Leopold for just a few months, he was given the official title of Royal Groom and continued to receive a generous annuity for many years to come. In return, the queen was rewarded with his silence.

---

[26] In 1875, Walter Stirling married Lady Clifden, a cousin of the Marquess of Lorne (Princess Louise's husband).

CHAPTER 7

The Locock family secret

The highest church court in the land is to decide whether a body can be exhumed from an overgrown Kent churchyard vault as part of a campaign to prove that it is the illegitimate grandson of Queen Victoria.

Ruth Gledhill in *The Times*, 22 March 2004

It was while looking into the rumours concerning Princess Louise's illegitimate baby that I came into contact with the Locock family. I read newspaper accounts of two court cases, in which a man named Nicholas Locock had attempted to gain permission for a MDNA (Mitachondria DNA) test to prove he was descended from Princess Louise. After twice going through the high courts, the Locock family's plea was refused.

The story of the Locock family and Princess Louise begins at the end of 1867, when a baby boy was adopted by the son of Queen Victoria's *accoucher* (in today's language he would be called a gynaecologist). The *accoucher*, Sir Charles Locock, had five sons; the one who adopted the baby was Frederick Locock. In the spring of 1867 Frederick moved into an apartment near St James's Palace. Nick Locock believes it may have been a 'grace and favour' apartment. Two months later, the family suffered a bereavement, when Sir Charles's wife, Amelia, died, yet in August 1867, just six weeks after the death of his mother, Frederick married his fiancée Mary Blackshaw. They married in a register office, not a church, in unseemly haste after such a bereavement (the mourning period for the death of a parent was expected to be one year). Four months later, the couple adopted their son; he would be their only child. The baby, who was named Henry Frederick

Leicester Locock, appears to have had no birth certificate – none has ever been found. The names of his biological parents are not included on any document (or, at least no documents that are in the public domain). In late December, Charles Locock wrote a letter to a friend in which he remarked that, unusually, he would not be able to have any of his sons with him for the end of the year and that he planned on taking a long holiday overseas. The letter suggests that he was shielding a secret and that he was unhappy about it.

Royal sources have been quick to refute the suggestion that Princess Louise was Henry Locock's mother, because she could not have given birth on the date written in the Locock family's Birthday Book, 30 December 1867. It seems likely that this was the date of the adoption rather than the baby's birth. At the end of December 1867, Queen Victoria's legal advisors were summoned to visit her. The newspapers reported that at this time 150 Scots Fusiliers were guarding the royal family, allegedly against the threat of Fenian attack. The Locock family believe that baby Henry was born at the end of 1866, or perhaps very early in 1867. It is probable that he was looked after by servants, with 'access to his mother'. Henry Locock would later tell his own children that he was Princess Louise's son and that his biological mother had 'access' to him in his boyhood years. Despite a seemingly happy marriage, Mary and Frederick had no other children; Mary's health was poor and perhaps she already knew she would have trouble conceiving. The couple made no secret of the fact that the baby was not their biological child and Frederick wrote in several legal documents about his 'adopted son'.

Mary and Frederick adopted their son at the end of December 1867. On 20 1867 the *Isle of Wight Observer* noted that Lady Stirling (the mother of Walter Stirling) had arrived on the island. She had come to stay eith Sir Charles Locock. July On 1 December 1867 Alix sent a sympathetic letter to Louise from Sandringham, in which she wrote: 'My poor little pet I am afraid you have not been enjoying yourself so very well lately.' If, as Henry would later attest, he remained with his mother Princess Louise at the start of his life, Alix's letter would have been sent as Louise was preparing to give him up. A year later, Alix would write to her again, worrying that Louise had been looking 'quite worn and sad' when they had seen each other. At Christmas in 1869, approaching the second anniversary of Henry Locock's adoption,

Alix wrote another supportive and suggestive letter to her sister-in-law: 'I hope my poor pet has not been worried and bothered lately about that tiresome old affair of yours! and that your sisters have given you a little rest now.'

Henry Locock's grandson, Nick Locock, was a six-year-old boy by the date of King George V's jubilee celebrations. Princess Louise was regularly in the news at this time, partly because she was a loved relation of the new king, but also because she was still so newsworthy, thanks to her great age and the story of her life as an artist. Nick recalls his father telling him during the coronation that they were descended from Princess Louise. The family's history, as it was told to Nick, was that his grandfather was the princess's son and that, although the baby had then been adopted by the Locock family, he had been given 'access' to Princess Louise all through his childhood. Nick's grandfather, Henry (who was always known in the Locock family by his middle name of Leicester), had died when his own children were still young, but Nick's father recalled his stories of childhood parties with all the royal children. One story that always made his children laugh was Henry's reminiscence of playing croquet on the lawn at Osborne House, when one of his royal cousins cheated. This infuriated the little boy so much that he hit his cousin with a croquet mallet: the cheater in question was the future Kaiser Wilhelm.

As he was growing up, Nick discovered that he was not the only Locock child to have been told what he describes as the 'family legend'. 'Subsequently,' he told me when we met, 'I realised that not only my brother and sister, but each of my eleven cousins had been told the same story by their parents. It was apparent that [Henry] had told each of his six children before his death in 1907, that his mother was Princess Louise.' Henry died young and was survived by his adopted father; Frederick did not deny Henry's claims that his adopted son's biological mother was Princess Louise.

The Locock family have in their possession a number of artefacts from the royal family. One of these is a bronze sculpture of a baby given to Dr Locock by the queen which may well have been created by Princess Louise. A photograph of Henry Locock as a baby has always been kept in a special frame hand-decorated with a border of flowers, in a style that looks very similar to Princess Louise's. The Locock family were keen to fight the court case, but not for material gain; as Nick explained, an illegitimate baby of the time would not have been entitled to any money, land or titles. What they wanted was to clear up a generations-old mystery and to be given, as Nick Locock said, 'the truth'.

Sir Charles Locock had been in attendance at the birth of all of Queen Victoria's children. He was one of her most trusted advisors and had proved over the years that he was fully capable of keeping secrets. He would have been the most natural person for the queen to turn to if her daughter became pregnant. As a senior member of the royal household, his presence with the family would have caused no comment, especially as Leopold's health was so often a cause for concern. If Sir Charles had delivered Princess Louise's baby, absolute discretion would have been assured. Following the death of his wife in July 1867, Sir Charles Locock retired, but he remained one of the queen's closest confidants. He owned a house near Osborne House and was a regular visitor when the family was in residence on the island.

It was in July 1866 (when she would have been pregnant with Henry, if my hypothesis is correct), that Louise wrote the letter to Louisa Bowater in which she confessed to being 'low and sad'. The letter went on: '[I] sit in my room and cry. I cannot write and tell you why, there are so many things ought not to be as they are . . . I am expected to agree with them and yet I cannot when I know a thing to be wrong.' In December she wrote to her friend again, 'I am often sad, but I never let others see that I am.'

In the autumn of 1867, Prince Arthur wrote a letter to his sister. He had been in trouble for mentioning a taboo subject and he now wrote to explain: 'As to the great secret, I did not know that I could not mention it to you, of course I would not speak of it to anybody else.' In his privately published book *Royal Mistresses and Bastards, Fact and Fiction 1714–1936* Anthony Camp dismisses the idea that Louise had a baby by suggesting that the queen's 'great secret' was that she was planning a trip to Switzerland. As Louise was the queen's personal secretary at the time and was travelling to Switzerland with her mother, she would certainly have known about the travel plans. A holiday could not have merited the words written by Prince Arthur, nor the secretive tone of his letter.

When Frederick Locock adopted his son at the end of 1867, he began to receive a mysterious large allowance. When Henry Locock died suddenly and unexpectedly in 1907, his personal estate was only

£800. Six months after Henry's death a deed was passed to his widow from the Public Trustee making over stocks to the value of £59,893. In 1911, when Henry's adoptive father Frederick, died his estate was in excess of £100,000. This money did not come from Sir Charles's estate nor did Frederick have an income that would have allowed such a generous settlement. It seems that someone with a pertinent reason for doing so was in a position to ensure that the children of the baby adopted by the son of the queen's *accoucher* would be provided for financially. When Dr Locock died there was a codicil in his will which changed Fred's allowance to a much smaller amount than that which went to his brother, to take into account the grace-and-favour apartment that Fred had been provided with alongside the large income he had been receiving. The codicil was drawn up by Arnold White, who happened to be Queen Victoria's personal solicitor. It was he who had the responsibility of drawing up all the Queen's daughters' marriage settlements. Arnold White would almost certainly have been the person the queen would trust to make the arrangements for the adoption of an illegitimate grandchild.

When Nick Locock began his court cases, what he was hoping for was to obtain a sample of his grandfather's MDNA. A few years previously, MDNA tests had been carried out on nine skeletons found in a shallow grave in Russia. The Russian authorities had, tentatively, suggested that these were the bodies of the murdered Tsar and his family, but there was no conclusive evidence. It was suggested that if a blood relative would supply a sample of MDNA, the identification could be carried out. The ill-fated Tsarina of Russia was Alexandra, one of Princess Alice's children and a granddaughter of Queen Victoria. The Tsarina was also the great-grandmother of Prince Philip, the husband of Queen Elizabeth II. Prince Philip agreed to supply a sample of his MDNA and as the scientific tests proved that he was blood-related to some of the skeletons, they were declared to be those of the Tsarina and her children.

The Tsarina was Princess Louise's niece and, therefore, if the Locock family legend is to be believed, she was also first cousin to the baby adopted by Frederick and Mary Locock. Nick Locock hoped to prove where his family came from. They had always known that they were not blood-related to the rest of the Locock family; now he wanted to find out the truth about his ancestry. Retrieving a sample of MDNA from his grandfather's grave would not have demanded disturbing the earth – Nick's grandfather's coffin is entombed within the family mausoleum at a church in Kent. As Nick told me, he himself will be buried there one day. Gathering the MDNA evidence would require unlocking the mausoleum, drilling a small hole in the coffin and removing a fragment of bone. No other graves would have to be disturbed.

The Locock family's case was fought in the British courts twice in the early years of the twenty-first century. The legal team won on almost every count, but lost their case on the point of 'The sanctity of Christian burial'. As Nick commented to me with a wry smile a few years after losing the court case, 'I wouldn't mind so much if the very same church hadn't recently moved about two hundred bodies to make way for a coffee shop in the crypt!'

When I contacted the church in question and asked them about the café, it was explained to me that the crypt, or 'undercroft', had repeatedly flooded and the bodies had had to be removed in order for essential maintenance work to be carried out. The bodies were then reburied in consecrated ground. The Locock family was told that the specific purpose of the building work was to build an under-croft for the café, not for essential work. They were also told that the skeletal remains were sent to a research department at the University of Oxford. As Nick Locock commented, 'So much for the sanctity of Christian burial!' Nick was told that after their sojourn in Oxford the bodies were returned to the church. I was told that they were reburied in consecrated ground. I did ask why they had not been reburied in the crypt once the work had been completed, but no one was able to give me an answer.

CHAPTER 8

An art student at last

> I think of thee, my sister,
> In my sad and lonely hours;
> And the thought of thee comes o'er me
> Like the breath of morning flow'rs.

From Prince Leopold's poem to Louise
written for her twentieth birthday in 1868

The year in which Louise turned twenty was to be as dramatic for
the royal family as the year of her birth had been. The year began
with Prince Leopold becoming very ill; he recovered, but the family
and the British public for several days expected to hear the news of
his death. Haemophilia was so little understood, and the doctors so
nervous about it, that it seemed this 'severe attack' might be fatal.
Louise nursed him as much as her mother would permit. Louise wrote
of Leopold's illness to Lady Augusta Stanley, who commented, 'There
is something so natural and true in Pss Louise's letter – so the reverse
of the wordiness characteristic of most of this young generation.'
Lady Stanley mentions in the same letter that she had recently taken
the American poet Henry Wadsworth Longfellow to Windsor where
he had met Louise, Leopold and the queen.

By the spring, Leopold was fully recovered, but within a few weeks
the family was shocked to hear that Alfred had suffered a close brush
with death. As the very first member of the British royal family to visit
Australia, in March 1868, Alfred was at Clontarf, in Sydney, when he
was shot by a would-be assassin, an Irishman named Henry James
O'Farrell. The Fenian threat to the royal family had long been worrying
their guards and in the autumn it was claimed that the family had been

besieged in Balmoral while troops outside prepared for the attack they were sure was to come. No one, however, had expected the Fenian threat to get so close to the royal family in somewhere as far away as Australia. The main demand of the Fenian movement was simple – Irish independence from British rule. Following the Irish potato famine of the 1840s, in which over a million people are estimated to have starved to death, anger against British rule intensified. The Fenian movement gathered force in many Irish communities overseas, most forcefully in North America and Australia.

The naval prince had been attending a charity picnic, held to raise funds for the Sailors' Home at Port Jackson. It was a public event, so there was little to prevent O'Farrell from getting close to the prince, raising his gun and shooting him in the back. O'Farrell was immediately grabbed, whereupon he fired again, painfully shooting in the foot one of the men who had arrested him. Prince Alfred had a miraculous escape, as the bullet just missed his spine. *The Lancet* reported that it 'entered the back half an inch to the right of the spine, struck the ninth rib, followed round the course of the rib, and lodged five inches from the umbilicus . . . having thus traversed a distance of twelve inches and a quarter'. It was considered astonishing that the bullet had caused so little damage and missed all of his major organs.

O'Farrell was arrested and very quickly brought to trial; he attempted to plead insanity, but the plea was refused. A few weeks after the attack, he was hanged. The newspapers claimed that O'Farrell was just one member of a gang and a large reward was offered for information leading to the arrest of his fellow conspirators. The incident caused an upsurge of anger in Australia against the Irish and Catholics, and a political headache for the government. Initially, the queen was understandably horrified by the assassination attempt, but the story soon began to pall and she became irritated with how much attention her son was receiving. In July, she wrote to Vicky: 'I am not as proud of Affie as you might think, for he is so conceited himself and at the present moment receives ovations as if he had done something – instead of God's mercy having spared his life.' By August, in a quite uncharacteristic manner, she was praising Bertie for being so much better behaved than Affie; he was being so affectionate to her, his only offence being that he was 'imprudent'.

While Alfred was recovering from being shot by an Irishman, Bertie and Alix were preparing to visit Ireland, a trip which could, very easily, have been a disaster. The question of Irish Home Rule was being fiercely debated in both houses of Parliament and all over Britain and, as had been proved in Sydney, there was a very real threat from the Fenians. Interestingly, despite the queen's belief that her son and heir was a buffoon who would never be capable of running the country, his visit to Ireland was a great success. People turned out in droves to see the Prince and Princess of Wales (who was heavily pregnant with their daughter Victoria) and the atmosphere was friendly and welcoming.

In August, the queen, Louise, Leopold[27] and Beatrice travelled to Switzerland to escape a heatwave in Britain; it was a holiday on which the mother and daughter would spend time more easily together than before, attaining a closeness they were seldom able to enjoy at any other time. Occasionally they travelled without the others, just the queen, Louise and a couple of courtiers. The absence of Beatrice helped the harmony, but even when they were all together, the atmosphere was one of happiness. The queen seems, in her journal entries, to have reached a level of contentment unknown since Albert's death. At the start of their holiday, she recorded: 'breakfasted together, in a charming spot, in the shade, near the house & I sat and wrote in a little summer house . . . The air was very pleasant, though the sun scorching. – After luncheon sketching the heavenly view from my window . . . Drove with Louise, Baby & Janie E. [Jane, Marchioness of Ely, lady of the bedchamber] through Lucerne & along the Lake, a most beautiful drive. Took our tea with us.'

The party left Osborne on board the royal yacht *Victoria and Albert* and sailed to Cherbourg. There, Emperor Napoleon III provided them with a special train, on which they travelled to Paris. After calling on the Empress, they continued to Lucerne, incognito with the queen as the Countess of Kent and Louise calling herself 'Lady Louise Kent'. (This caused some consternation amongst the royal entourage, none of whom

---

[27] It is interesting to note that the Reverend Duckworth was amongst the party, in his capacity both as Leopold's tutor and as a minister who often held private church services for the family during the holiday. His inclusion makes it even less likely that he was the father of Louise's baby.

could use their real title if it made them grander than the 'Countess of Kent'.) Amongst their number was the court physician Sir William Jenner, paranoid about foreign sanitation and fearful of typhoid wherever they went, and the now-ubiquitous John Brown. None of the royal children liked John Brown, Bertie in particular despised the influence the ghillie had over their mother and the lack of respect he showed for the queen's children. The diplomat and diarist Wilfrid Scawen Blunt recorded in his journal,

> Brown was a rude, unmannerly fellow . . . but he had unbounded influence with the Queen whom he treated with little respect, presuming in every way on his position with her. It was the talk of all the household that he was 'The Queen's stallion' – He was a fine man physically, though coarsely made, and had fine eyes (like the late Prince Consort's it was said) and the Queen, who had been passionately in love with her husband . . . got it into her head that somehow the Prince's spirit had passed into Brown.

As Louise would remark, in reference to the queen's unexpected displeasure with another royal servant, Sir John Cowell, as soon as John Brown took a dislike to anyone their card was marked for ever more.

Those accompanying the queen and princess to Switzerland expected the usual stormy relationship between the two women, and were instead pleasantly surprised by how amicable the atmosphere was. Henry Ponsonby, the queen's private secretary, recorded delightedly an evening in which everyone, including the queen, had laughed uncontrollably. Louise, he said, was 'choking' with laughter and he had never seen the queen laugh so hard. Their improved relationship on this holiday was helped by the two women's artistic affinity and the splendid opportunities for drawing and painting. The queen had begun to feel an admiration for her daughter's work and knew that Albert would have been proud to have an artist for a daughter. Even in 1866, a year in which the queen spent most of her time being cross with her daughter, she had been moved to write, 'Your print after Winterhalter's picture is quite lovely!' For some months before their holiday, Louise had been working on a sculpture bust of her mother; it had changed the balance of their relationship, because the queen had to sit still and quietly while her daughter worked. Now, on their holiday, mother and daughter happily painted, sketched and drew their way all around Switzerland's most picturesque sights. The queen's journal makes several mentions of walking with Louise, and of driving out with Louise and a lady-in-waiting to picturesque spots, where they would take tea and sit sketching until forced to leave either by the weather or the sun going down. It was a pivotal time in their relationship and, perhaps, indicates that the queen understood the depression her daughter had experienced in the previous twelve months. On several occasions, she permitted Louise to go off by herself (accompanied by courtiers, of course). Queen Victoria seemed, finally, to be gaining an acceptance of her daughter's independent spirit.

Although the Swiss holiday seemed idyllic, the threat of danger was ever present. The *New York Times* reported with relish while the queen was in Lucerne, that a Fenian would-be assassin had forced his way into her apartments and attempted to kill her. The story was grossly exaggerated and eventually reports began to trickle through that it was not a Fenian – not even an Irishman – it was an Englishman who had no weapons nor any apparently malign intent: he simply wanted to see the queen. Whether the 'madman' had even made it – or attempted to make it – as far as her apartments is also in doubt, but the story was a huge drama in the newspapers.

When the two women returned to England it was with an acceptance that, although Louise would continue to help her mother, her art was important as well and she needed to share some of her duties with Princess Helena. When Helena had married both she and Christian had understood that permission for their marriage was only being granted with the proviso that they remain living in England. The queen had not been happy at having to rely on Louise as her amanuensis, despite admitting reluctantly that Louise was more intelligent than Helena. Whenever Louise was ill or indisposed, Helena was expected to step back into her old role. The queen usually preferred to work with Helena, as Louise was too ready to challenge her mother and often made the great mistake of offering advice. The queen did not want advice: she wanted Helena's compliant meekness, not a daughter with a mind of her own. That aside, she was adamant that she would not hire a paid secretary and allow Louise to live her own life. By the time Louise was twenty, however, the queen's journal shows that she was growing increasingly pleased with her daughter, not least because she had 'such an affectionate heart'.

Despite Helena's occasional presence, however, Louise still had very little time to herself. She had been promised she would have every afternoon free to work on her art and to exercise. Louise was a great lover of exercise, something that bemused the rest of her family; she walked, rode and, when they had been invented, rode a bicycle as often as she could. Bicycling did not come naturally to her and her first efforts were said to be 'bad', but she persevered with lessons until she had mastered the art. (Louise loved speed and terrorised her milder sisters by driving a horse carriage as fast as she could make it go.) Those promised free afternoons were inevitably eaten into by work.

Louise was desperate to move out of her mother's home, to do as Bertie had done with White Lodge and have her own apartments. She wanted a proper studio, to go to art college and to become a full-time artist. In much of this she had the support of Mary Thornycroft, who had been trying to persuade the queen that Louise deserved more advanced artistic instruction. They were helped in this endeavour, unexpectedly, by the spectre of Prince Albert.

By 1868, Victoria had reached such a point of deification of her dead husband that she wrote to Vicky comparing Albert to Jesus Christ. She was, however, slowly starting to come back to life and was returning to the public duties neglected for so long. The newspapers had been printing angry articles about the queen's lack of interest in her people for years. Her advisors, well aware of the ever-present threat of revolution, told the queen that she needed to start earning her subjects' affection. That year she made several public appearances, including laying the foundation stone for the new St Thomas's Hospital in London. She also allowed Leopold to have a concert (albeit of 'sacred music') and a small celebratory dinner for his fifteenth birthday. Just a week later, Beatrice was allowed a dance for her eleventh birthday (which must have galled her older siblings, given the memory of all their uncelebrated birthdays, even important ones, since Albert's death). These changes were not enough to endear the queen to her subjects again, and in May

1868 there were calls for her to abdicate when she missed another very important parliamentary session.

The queen refused to listen to the newspapers. She was feeling proud of her latest achievement, a book entitled *Leaves from the Journal of Our Life in the Highlands*. She had had it privately printed for her family the year before (Bertie was derisive and scathing – although not to her face) and in 1868 she allowed it to be published commercially. The book was drawn from her diaries and contained her own illustrations. Some of her family may have scoffed, but it was an extraordinarily open thing for the queen to have published her own thoughts and drawings. Although the book grew out of Victoria's desire to praise the beloved home of her beloved John Brown, it turned out to be an important exercise in public relations. The elusive queen now seemed much more accessible to her people.

More important for Princess Louise was the fact that in 1868 her mother had mellowed enough to agree at last with Mary Thornycroft that Louise should be allowed to go to art school. The Thornycroft family had long had influence with the monarch and Victoria respected Mary because she remembered that Mary's father, John Francis, had helped Prince Albert learn to sculpt. Mary wanted her talented pupil to work with one of the most popular sculptors of the day, Joseph Edgar Boehm. It was under his tutelage that Louise would be attending the National Art Training School – and in doing so becoming the first British princess to attend a public school. The queen had been persuaded to give her approval because the National Art Training School had been one of Prince Albert's innovations, made possible with money raised by the Great Exhibition.

Although her mother had agreed to the training, the princess ended up missing a large number of her lessons because the queen would insist there was too much work to be done for her secretary to be allowed leave in order to go to class. As a result, Louise was constantly behind the other students and desperate to catch up; her classmates were astonished that a princess was made to work so hard: they had envisaged her as having an easy, privileged life. Louise loved the classes and the chance to study with fellow artists; she also relished the chance to make friends, real friends from the outside world. Her classmate

Henrietta Montalba,[28] and Henrietta's sister Clara (also a sculptor), would become important friends to the princess who strove so desperately for a non-royal life.

That Louise was entranced by Boehm is apparent from early in their relationship. He was a charismatic man, extremely talented and capable, and Louise longed to spend more time with him and to learn everything he could teach. She also had private lessons with Boehm, although she hated the fact that they were never allowed to be alone. Prince Arthur wrote a letter commiserating with Louise about the need for a chaperone in the studio, usually the German governess Fräulein Bauer.

For some time now the family and the outside world had been speculating about Princess Louise's future. Alix had hoped Louise would marry her older brother, the heir to the Danish throne, and the newspapers got hold of the rumour. For a few days in 1868, the story that Louise was engaged to a Danish prince spread around the country. The rumours were easily quashed, but speculation continued about who the queen's prettiest daughter was likely to marry. Louise found this stressful, as she confessed to Sybil Grey (who was now married and had become Sybil St Albans). Vicky wanted her to marry a Prussian, Alix wanted her to marry a Dane, and her mother wanted her to marry someone who was preferably German but who wouldn't require her to move overseas and would be content to live close to his mother-in-law.

Louise declared she disliked foreign men and would not marry a foreigner. Eventually, and somewhat surprisingly, the queen was won over and wrote to Bertie: 'I just wish to say that Louise is most decided in her wish to settle in her own country . . . and indeed I am equally of this opinion . . . and I have written to Vicky . . . that neither Louise or I would ever hear of the Prussian marriage, which must be considered at an end.' That the queen was willing to comply with Louise's demands lends weight to the suggestion that she was growing desperate for her difficult daughter to be married, and as quickly as

[28] In a letter dated 17 May 1875, the flirtatious Prince Arthur wrote to Louise about how much he had enjoyed meeting 'that Miss Montalbert (I don't know if that is the right way to spell it) . . . she is so clever and so pleasant in every way'. He asked Louise to take him to the art school one day, so that he could see her friend's work.

possible. Victoria's capitulation, however, led to a new problem: there was no one in the British Isles of a suitable rank to marry a princess. By this time, the queen was becoming more insistent that Louise find a husband and the clamour from all sides was very stressful for the princess. Still, Louise remained adamant she was not yet ready to marry. There may have been a very good reason for her stalling. It seems it was not the idea of a foreign man she was averse to, but the idea of having to leave England. It is possible that there was someone other than the members of her family whose company she was loath to part with.

CHAPTER 9

Falling in love with the Cult of Beauty

According to Mr. Boehm, we cannot be Greeks, for we have no mythology. Our art must be Christian and modern. 'It is vain to complain of the paucity of inspiring subjects in our age, of our ugly costume and the dearth of suitable figures for sculpture. You may regard objects and compose like Homer, but you may not inanely copy the antique. Do not return from Rome with some more bad nymphs, another Venus or another Cupid. Try to use the much-abused dress. Treat a coat-sleeve, a woman's gown, *con amore*, ennoble it by art, and it will be a pleasing object in the sight of those whose praise is worth having'.

W. Meynell, 'Our Living Artists – Joseph Edgar Boehm, A.R.A.', *Magazine of Art*, 1880

It is unsurprising to find that Princess Louise had a host of admirers. Not only was she the daughter of the queen, but she was elegant, pretty and charming. Louise could turn heads because of her looks, her unusual dress sense and her refusal to conform to conventionality, whether in her clothes or in the way in which she asked her maid to dress her hair. While her sisters wore the most 'safe' fashions and inherited family jewellery, Louise dressed in a style influenced by Pre-Raphaelitism – which meant less corseted, more loosely structured, flowing dresses, inspired by those in paintings by Pre-Raphaelite artists (which were, in turn, influenced by medieval fashion). By the late 1860s, Louise had started to ally herself to the artistic movement of Aestheticism. This was an exciting trend that had grown out of Pre-Raphaelitism and the Arts & Crafts Movement (founded by William Morris). By the 1870s Aestheticism was the most fashionable movement in London. Amongst its most famous exponents were Dante Rossetti, Oscar Wilde, James Abbott McNeill Whistler and Frederic, Lord Leighton. The movement, which became known as 'the Cult of Beauty', embraced not only painting and sculpture, but architecture, interior decoration and fashion. It brought to the forefront of public consciousness the art of China and Japan,[29] as well as that of bohemian France. The Aesthetic movement's famous motto was 'Art for Art's Sake' – their works did not need to be instructive or historic; they simply had to be beautiful and worth looking at. One of the most liberating aspects of the Aesthetic movement was its belief in 'rational dress', which meant not constricting the body with tight corsets, impeding crinolines and painful high-heeled shoes. Although Louise had to follow a very muted form of Aestheticism (her mother would never have allowed her to appear in public dressed in the style of the subjects who sat to G.F. Watts for his fashionable portraits), she became fascinated by the movement and particularly by its emphasis on beautiful objects, such as painted screens, fans and jewellery.

In the 1860s, when Louise, Helena and Beatrice were with their mother at Osborne, a local family was invited to visit the queen. They met all three of the princesses and were rather disappointed at first. Beatrice, who was still very young, struck them as slightly nervous and silent. Helena was pleasant but rather uninteresting, dressed in her dull mourning clothes. The visitors – especially the children – had expected something more glamorous from a princess. In their memory, it was Louise who stood out as 'delightful', 'gentle' and 'gracious'. She was 'tall and graceful . . . far the most perfect in beauty', and they agreed that, even if Louise hadn't been a princess, 'everyone would praise [her]'. They also noticed that she was wearing a beautiful large silver cross of an unusual beaten-metal design; she had made it herself.

Although Joseph Edgar Boehm's sculpture was not Aesthetic in style, he was closely linked with the movement, as he was friendly with so many of its key figures. In turn, he introduced Louise to many prominent artists of the time. Boehm's work had first been lauded,

---

[29] Until 1854, Japan had been closed off from the rest of the world for over 200 years, so when its ports were reopened and it began trading again, artists were enthralled by the artistic styles and treasures that began to appear.

in Britain, in the early 1860s and, in 1864, when he submitted to the
Royal Academy a bust of the popular novelist William Makepeace
Thackeray, he became instantly in demand. His work was refreshingly
modern and realistic: instead of the customary 'classical' style of
clothing of portrait busts, Boehm had depicted the author wearing
the fashion of the time. Boehm's exhibiting of the work in 1864 was
a timely decision, as Thackeray had died a few months previously.
The sculpture was an instant sensation, not least because it was
modelled in terracotta. Before moving to London in 1862, Boehm had
lived and worked in Paris, where terracotta sculpture was popular. He
enjoyed working with the medium and continued to do so in London;
it was a refreshing new way of looking at sculpture[30] and was one of
the techniques he would pass on to Princess Louise.

I was surprised to discover how difficult it was to investigate Boehm,
as an artist; remarkably little information is contained in the usual art
gallery archives. I made an appointment at the National Gallery in
London to look at the files concerning three of Louise's art tutors:
Edward Corbould, Mary Thornycroft and Joseph Edgar Boehm. The
day before my appointment, I received a phone call from a bemused
archivist. He had been attempting to find the relevant files before my
visit, but had discovered that everything, for all three artists, had 'been
appropriated by the Royal Archives'. His archives contained a single
letter written by Boehm – it was two lines long and the archivist read
it to me over the phone: it concerned the placement of one of Boehm's
statues during an exhibition. Yet again I had encountered problems in
trying to find the real Princess Louise; quite why the Royal Archives
felt the need to appropriate all information on Boehm from other
archives was intriguing.

It is not at all surprising that Joseph Edgar Boehm fell for his illustrious and very attractive pupil; and equally unsurprising that the
attraction was mutual. The couple was the object of a number of
rumours in the late nineteenth century. Rumours about their relationship gained momentum in the second half of the twentieth century
after the death of the Victorian writer and diplomat Wilfred Scawen
Blunt, who had lived a full and scandalous life, which he recorded in
great detail. On his death in 1922, his papers and diaries were

---

[30] Boehm also worked in other media, including plaster, bronze and marble.

bequeathed to the Fitzwilliam Museum in Cambridge, with the stipulation that they should be locked away for several decades. As soon as researchers were allowed to access Blunt's files (in the 1970s) a story about Princess Louise began to emerge. Blunt loved gossip and his diary is full of it. The source for several stories about Princess Louise came from a woman named Catherine Walters, better known at the time by her nickname of 'Skittles' (allegedly because her first job was in a bowling alley). She was born into a working-class family and became a high-ranking 'courtesan'. Amongst her lovers was Princess Louise's brother, Bertie, the future King Edward VII. Blunt was another of Skittles's lovers; she was the woman to whom he lost his virginity, and he remained a loyal friend to her, visiting her when she was elderly and very ill and writing down, at her request, all the stories she told him. When she related to Blunt the gossip about Louise, Skittles revealed that she had heard the stories from her friend Dr Laking, the royal physician, and from Bertie himself.

Skittles revealed that in 1869, when Boehm was working on a statue of John Brown for the queen,[31] he began to grow more 'intimate' with Princess Louise and that they eventually became lovers. Although when Louise had begun her private classes with Boehm, the queen had insisted she be chaperoned in the studio, by the time they were in Balmoral in 1869, sculptor and pupil were no longer chaperoned. Skittles believed that the first time Louise had met Boehm was at Balmoral, but in reality the couple were continuing a friendship and mutual attraction that had begun at the National Art Training School. Skittles related that during Boehm's three months at Balmoral, he and Louise 'became intimate, though not to the extent of actual love making'. This is not surprising; if Louise had recently given birth to a child she had been forced to give up, it would be natural for her not to want to risk getting pregnant again. Boehm was far more sexually experienced than Louise and moved in a world of courtesans and sexual freedom; when their relationship became fully sexual he would have been able to give her advice on avoiding pregnancy.

Skittles told Blunt that she had heard the following version of events

---

[31] This bust of John Brown is reportedly one of the items that King Edward VII ordered to be destroyed when he came to the throne. Elizabeth Longford claims he ordered it to be 'smashed up'.

from her friend Dr Laking, the royal physician. Laking told her that the queen and John Brown went into Boehm's Balmoral studio unexpectedly and found Louise and Boehm being 'intimate', whereupon a 'violent scene' ensued. Not only did the queen 'scold' her daughter, but John Brown was presumptuous enough to do so as well, causing Louise to react furiously. According to Laking, almost all the queen's children were convinced the queen and Brown were lovers and resented him deeply. When a servant saw fit to reprimand a princess, Louise decided the situation had gone much too far. As Blunt recorded in his diary: 'she told the Queen that she was not going to stand for [John Brown's] impertinence any longer and that either he or she would have to go away . . . whereupon the Queen too lost her temper and threatened to have her locked up'. In response, Louise threatened to cause a 'public scandal' about the queen's relationship with Brown. The row became so heated that a member of the household was dispatched to contact Bertie, who was then called upon to act as intermediary between his mother and sister.

A letter survives from Bertie to Louise. Written two years later, in 1871, it suggests that Louise had had yet another explosive row with John Brown while at Balmoral: 'I am so sorry to hear that that brute JB made himself disagreeable during your stay at B. I wish you would tell me what he did.' The popular belief about the queen's adored ghillie, ever since he was immortalised by the actor Billy Connolly in the film *Mrs Brown* (1997), is that he was a lovable rogue brave enough to stand up to an indomitable queen. In reality, his behaviour towards the queen's children, attested to by their letters and reminiscences, suggests he was a far more unpleasant character, who took pleasure in hurting the royal children both physically (when he was able to) and emotionally.

Despite the fraught circumstances of his stay in Balmoral in 1869, Queen Victoria took a great interest in Boehm. It seems likely that she had no choice. Louise was no longer as compliant as she had been during the Walter Stirling affair. She was older, wiser and had been hurt too much already to let another lover be forced out of her life. Her mother must have been aware that these were very different circumstances and that Boehm was not bound by the same loyalty to the royal family as a British army officer had been. The situation needed to be handled entirely differently. Boehm was accepted as a friend of the family; in 1881 the queen would name him her Sculptor in Ordinary (a similar honour to that of Poet Laureate). Louise's fury and the way she had stood up, not only to John Brown but also to her mother, worried the queen. She knew her daughter well enough to realise that she had reached the limit of her tolerance, so it seems she colluded in Louise and Boehm's relationship (just as it was suggested by Skittles that Louise had been forced to become privy to her mother's secret love life). Following the great row, Boehm continued to teach Princess Louise and, within artistic circles, their affair was talked about quite openly.

When Elizabeth Longford wrote *Darling Loosy*, she touched briefly on the rumours of the affair but rejected them, solely because Louise knew that Boehm was married. Longford refused to believe that either Louise or Boehm could have been what she described as 'the most extraordinarily insensitive hypocrites'. Longford, however, was looking at a nineteenth-century marriage from her twentieth-century viewpoint; her brief hypothesis does not take into account the unusual circumstances of Louise's birth: that even if Boehm had not been married, he could never have been considered as a husband for a princess, nor the fact that Victorian society insisted on hypocrisy in love affairs. Nor does her comment take into account the personalities of either Louise or Boehm. She admits that it was strange that the queen insisted, after they had initially been permitted to work alone together in the Balmoral studio, on Louise and Boehm again being chaperoned by Fräulein Bauer – for which she is unable to find an explanation.

Throughout this period of time, Louise turned down all proposed husbands and insisting she would only marry if she could find someone British and not move abroad. The queen eventually came around to the idea that her daughter might have to marry a 'commoner'; she began to consider the families of dukes and earls. In this she was encouraged by Bertie, who wrote to his mother, 'I must candidly confess that what I know of her character [Louise] would not be happy if she remained too long unmarried.' Bertie recognised in his sister the same sexual needs and appetite as he himself possessed – and perhaps he feared another unmarried pregnancy – yet despite his early approval of his mother's plans, he would soon try to prevent Louise's marriage.

CHAPTER 10

The people's princess

> The classes for drawing, painting, and modelling include architectural and other ornament flowers objects of still-life, &c., the figure from the antique and the life, and the study of anatomy as applicable to art. These courses of instruction are open to the public on the payment of fees; the classes for male and female students meeting separately.
>
> 'The National Art Training School' entry from *The Dictionary of Victorian London*, Charles Dickens Jnr, 1879

While her mother was searching through family trees, Louise was trying to establish her independence. She was beginning to make more friends and acquaintances outside her expected royal circle. She sought out, actively, the companionship of writers, musicians, thinkers and social reformers, as well as fellow artists. In March 1869, Louise was invited with her mother to a tea party at the Deanery of Westminster Abbey.[32] There they met the poet Robert Browning and the writer and historian Thomas Carlyle. The latter commented that the princess was 'decidedly a very pretty young lady, and clever too as I found out in talking to her'.

On the day of the tea party, Louise was looking forward to celebrating her twenty-first birthday. She intended to wear a beautiful brightly coloured outfit, as the queen had finally relaxed her rules on mourning for her husband (in 1869 she permitted her servants to stop wearing the black armbands they had been wearing since Albert's

---

[32] Lady Augusta Bruce was now Lady Augusta Stanley, the wife of Dean Stanley, who was the Dean of Westminster Abbey.

death in 1861). By the time Louise's birthday came around, however, on 18 March, the family had been plunged into mourning again, this time for their relation the Duke of Schleswig-Holstein.

The people of Britain had become used to the queen performing few public appearances and now actively looked forward to seeing the princes and princesses instead. Louise was always popular and after she visited the dockyards in Deptford, where she christened the HMS *Druid* (on 13 March), a laudatory article appeared in the *Illustrated London News*. The Prince and Princess of Wales and Princess Louise were rapidly becoming the royal family's most important PR tools. In the same month, the queen made a rare public appearance, when she visited the Albert Memorial in Kensington Gardens. A few weeks later, she and her family attended the opening of the new Royal Academy, which had recently moved from its home at Somerset House to Burlington House on Piccadilly (where it remains today). Louise was particularly nervous about this visit because a bust of her mother that she had sculpted was to be unveiled at the Academy.

During the official visit, she was thrilled to meet the President of the Royal Academy, Sir Francis Grant, and to talk both to him and to other artists about her work. Louise's position in the art world was certainly helped by her royal status, but she was also beginning to be taken seriously as an artist. She was working on a bust of her mother at the same time as Boehm was working on a full-length statue of the queen; his would shortly be unveiled at Windsor Castle to great acclaim. In 1868, Louise had been elated when the Royal Academy exhibited one of her pieces for the first time, a bust of Prince Arthur. In 1869, she exhibited the bust of her mother and in 1874 the Royal Academy accepted her bust of the recently deceased General Grey. She also produced *Queen Victoria* in 1876, a beautifully executed work in marble showing her mother as a stern but stoic queen (she donated this to the Royal Academy in 1877). The contours of the face and of the drapery that curls over the queen's left shoulder and ties beneath the bust (forming part of the pedestal) demonstrate just how talented Princess Louise was as a sculptor. Although she was often criticised for being slapdash in her approach and sometimes leaving Boehm to 'finish off' her work – usually because her royal duties never left her enough time to work the hours a professional sculptor could – her raw talent and the reason that Mary Thornycroft had recommended she be allowed to study at the National Art Training School is apparent. Louise captures the essence of the queen's personality in this bust. It is a fairly flattering depiction, compared to photographs of the time, but there is a realism to it, evinced in the slight double chin and the discreet but nevertheless present bulge of fat around the neckline. Louise has made the queen look better than she did in real life, but has not eliminated all her flaws. The expression on her face, especially the set of the lips, shows a woman of forceful personality.

In addition to her time in the studio and her long hours working with her mother, Louise was becoming increasingly interested in social reform and in deciding how she could use her position for good. She wanted to change the way that royalty viewed 'causes', to become properly involved, instead of simply viewing from the sidelines as her mother had always done. On 9 March 1861, when Louise was nearly thirteen, she and Alice had been taken to Wandsworth to visit the Female Military Orphan Asylum. The queen noted in her journal: 'delighted to find it all going on so well. It was a holiday & all the children looking so clean & happy & healthy, many pretty ones amongst them, were playing. The building is admirably arranged. We saw the fine Dining Hall, the nice tidy kitchen . . . the bakery &c – all attended to by the girls.' All the royal children were used to paying such visits, but they were always mere observers expected to say nothing unless directly addressed and to pass no comments nor add any ideas of their own. Visits such as these had engendered in Louise a desire to *do* something, to be constructive and useful. Now she was approaching the age of majority, Louise was determined to express her views.

The princess's friends General and Sybil Grey were closely related to a woman with whom Louise had become fascinated, the social reformer Josephine Butler (née Grey). The cause of women's emancipation was one that Vicky, tucked away in Prussia, had longed to be more active in and she encouraged her younger sister to take an interest in it; Vicky had already begun her own correspondence with Josephine Butler and suggested Louise do the same. At around the time of Louise's twenty-first birthday, Butler (encouraged by Vicky) contacted the princess and asked for her help. Louise asserted her independence by writing back and offering any assistance she could give: 'I do take great interest in the happiness and well-being of women and long to do everything that I can to promote all efforts in that direction . . . I feel pleasure in thinking you will let me know whenever any question arises in which my assistance and sympathy could be of any use to you.' Louise had started to realise that in spite of the many frustrations attached to her royal status, she could also turn it to her advantage. She *longed* to be useful. Understandably, Josephine was elated and she sent Louise a signed copy of her book, *Woman's Work and Woman's Culture*, as requested.

Josephine was the wife of an academic and church minister, George Butler, who was as passionate about his wife's causes as she was. Together they sought to fight injustice and to make people of their own social class aware of what was really happening in the world outside their comfortable homes. They campaigned for the abolition of slavery, they set up homes for 'friendless' women (sex workers, women who had lost their reputation and women who had become pregnant outside of marriage) – and even invited such usually shunned women into their own home, offering them a safe refuge and practical help to get their lives back on track. They fed the homeless and ill and worked tirelessly with prostitutes and single mothers. Much of their zeal was fed by the Butlers' own great sadness: the death of their six-year-old daughter in 1863, following a tragic accident (she died after falling down the stairs at their house).

At the time that Princess Louise contacted her, Josephine was involved in a cause that would bring her, her husband and their followers notoriety. In 1864, 1866 and 1869 Britain had passed three frighteningly misogynist laws: the Contagious Diseases Acts. In effect, these laws enabled the police to sexually assault any prostitute – or any woman they suspected of being a prostitute – in any of the towns named in the Acts. The Acts were concerned with protecting the sexual health of naval and military men (those of a lower rank were not allowed to marry while in service) and as such were enforced mainly in port and military towns. Women could be arrested and then forcibly examined for sexually transmitted diseases and if they were found to be contagious, they could be locked up. The examinations were supposed to be carried out by medical men, but many of the women detained complained that the police had carried out such 'inspections' themselves, forcing the women to strip and be 'examined'. Prostitution was one of the great social evils of Victorian England – seldom spoken of but always present. Prostitutes were seen as the greatest threat to family life; it was not only unmarried soldiers and sailors who were using their services – the number of wives infected with venereal diseases brought to the marital bed by their husbands was a serious medical issue. Refusing to accept that the problem actually originated with with the men who used the prostitutes, the Acts were worded in such language to imply that it was female prostitutes who threatened the fabric of English society – and not the men who paid them.

Louise must have realised how controversial her involvement in Josephine's work to repeal the Contagious Diseases Acts would be, but naïvely she hoped that, now aged 21, she would be allowed more autonomy in her decisions. It was a false hope. Despite her great admiration for Josephine Butler's work, she was forced by her mother to renege on her promise to help. Almost every member of her family, including the usually supportive Bertie, was outraged by Louise's decision to become involved with such a scandalous cause. She was eventually outwitted by the fact that Josephine's work was political: as a royal, she was not supposed to take sides.[33]

Unable to stand up against the full force of her family, Louise reluctantly returned Josephine's book. Unknown to her family, however, Louise continued to maintain her friendship with Josephine; as she always had to do with 'unsuitable' friends, she impressed upon Josephine the great importance that the queen should never find out.

Queen Victoria believed that she knew every aspect of her children's lives, but in reality she had turned most of her children into wily, practised liars, adept in the art of subterfuge. Marie Adeane, one of the queen's maids of honour in the 1880s, later described Louise as a consummate liar – unaware that it was a skill Louise and her siblings had been forced to adopt and one that became second nature. Josephine Butler and Louise also corresponded about the education of women and about the journal Josephine wanted to found, the *International Women's Review*. Louise responded with her concerns about the journal having the word 'Women' in the title, as she feared it would put men off buying it: 'I think all appearance of exclusiveness should be avoided

---

[33] Ironically, Queen Victoria meddled perpetually in politics, most obviously in her support for the Conservative leader Benjamin Disraeli, over his rival, Liberal leader, William Ewart Gladstone.

as it is after all only with the cooperation of the cleverest men that we can hope to succeed . . . I know the subject of women's rights, interests etc. has become so tedious to the eyes of so many, whose support it would be an advantage to gain.'

Louise had also gone to a great effort to contact, in secret, Elizabeth Garrett, who was determined to be Britain's first female doctor. She had heard that Elizabeth had attempted to attend medical students' classes while she was training as a nurse, but the male medical students protested about the presence of a female in their classes and she was banned. Undeterred, she sat the exam – and passed. The Society of Apothecaries immediately made moves to ensure women were banned from sitting the exam in future. By the time Louise met her, Elizabeth had decided she would go to France, where she would be able to qualify as a doctor. Louise contacted her and went to meet her – on the strict instructions that the queen should not find out. The visit was not a formal one in any sense: Louise simply turned up unexpectedly at the young medical student's house (and discovered her hanging wallpaper), and talked to her eagerly about her studies. Later Louise wrote to Josephine Butler about their meeting: 'it was a great pleasure to find her so enthusiastic in her work . . . she is one of those who can prove how much women can learn, if they put their whole heart, and soul, in what they are about'.

Louise had underestimated her mother's spy network – the visit was discovered and the queen was furious. She believed that women had no right to become doctors and was shocked that her daughter now appeared to be sanctioning such behaviour. People such as the progressive Garrett family and their talented and driven daughters were anathema to the queen, not least because they were strong supporters of one of her least favourite subjects: equal rights for men and women. In defiance of her mother, Louise kept in touch with the doctor, later sending Josephine Butler a note with the words 'I send you a letter from Miss Garrett on her successful examination at Paris.' After Elizabeth Garrett returned to London, she established the New Hospital for Women and campaigned, successfully, for women to be allowed to enter the medical profession.[34] She and Louise remained in contact.

[34] An Act of Parliament was passed in 1876.

Episodes such as these brought Louise to full awareness that she needed to escape her mother's house. Her pleas to be allowed to live in her own studio and work as a sculptor were never going to be recognised. The only way Louise would ever achieve any form of independence would be if she married – and if she chose someone less overbearing than Vicky's or Alice's husbands. Lady Ely summed up the problem that all Queen Victoria's children encountered: '[there are] struggles going on with Alice and Louise and others. The general tenor of which seems to be they want to do what they like not what the Q likes and want her to pay for doing what they like, while she is ready to pay if they will do what she likes.' It was stalemate. Just as her mother was doing, Louise began to look for acceptable suitors. Had Louise not been a princess, she would have had no shortage of offers. She possessed the type of looks that many Victorian men idealised: a trim but curvaceous figure, blue eyes and long, curling fair hair. The artist Edwin Landseer commented, 'If I were a young man, I should not rest until that lovely girl had promised to marry me.' Thomas Carlyle described her as 'decidedly a very pretty lady, and clever too'. Unfortunately for Louise, there were very few men who were eligible enough to be considered a suitable husband for a princess.

The fact that Louise would soon marry does nothing to quash the belief that she was having an affair with Boehm. Both she and Boehm knew she had no choice. Had the situation been reversed – had it been a single man in a relationship with a married woman – things would have been different; in Victorian England a single man was envied as a carefree bachelor; a single woman was an embarrassment. An unmarried *princess* was unimaginable – every member of the royal household had been keeping an eye on potential suitors almost since the moment of her birth. Louise *had* to marry – and it would be far better for both her and Boehm if she exerted some will over the decision. Just because Boehm was in no position to marry her did not mean he could not be her lover. They also recognised that, as a married woman no longer living under her mother's roof, Louise would have more freedom. She was already known to be Boehm's private pupil, so their meetings would arouse no comment from the papers or their families. This made conducting a relationship far easier than it would have been for most illicit couples of the time.

CHAPTER II

A controversial betrothal

The frivolity of the newspapers in speaking of France as if she were a child to be whipped or a blackguard to be flogged has been base. Does not this threatened siege of Paris rather recall the words of Christ weeping over Jerusalem? And must we not suppose Him, in human figure of speech, 'weeping' far more over that 'great city' Paris?

Florence Nightingale, September 1870

At the end of 1869, Alix safely gave birth to her third daughter, Princess Maud of Wales (who would grow up to marry King Haakon VII of Norway). This was not, however, the only piece of royal news that was being discussed. People in the know were gossiping about a visit paid to the queen by two of her subjects, the Duke and Duchess of Argyll.[35] The two families had been friendly for many years, but it was understood by members of the royal household that the duke and duchess were there to talk about the possibility of marrying their eldest son, the Marquess of Lorne (and future 9th Duke of Argyll; known in the Campbell family as 'Ian'), to Princess Louise. The royal family was immediately divided. When the engagement was finally announced (many months ahead at this stage) the papers would make a great deal of it being 'a love match', but, in reality, this was an engagement that was as carefully brokered as any business arrangement and one that was not decided on without a great deal of angst and argument. Amongst those members of the family who needed to be convinced that such an engagement was

[35] The Duke was the head of the Campbell clan.

a good idea was Louise herself and it would take some time, and a great deal of prevarication on the part of the bride, before the marriage could be announced.

Initially, Louise was intrigued by her mother's plan. Lorne was a very good-looking young man and he was different from and less formal than most of her suitors. These were attractive qualities to her, but soon she began deliberating, and this deliberation went on for the best part of a year. She confessed to her mother that she did not like him 'enough'. She did, however, form an attachment to the Duke of Argyll, Lorne's father, and she seems to have fallen in love with the very idea of the Argylls and their approach to family life, which was so different from her own experience. She had envied Sybil Grey, Caroline Lyttelton and Horatia Stopford for their uncomplicated and privileged family lives, and now she recognised that she was being given the chance to enter a similar family, where she could have the chance to be herself. Yet something still prevented her from saying yes.

Discussion of Louise's future was taking place at a time when tension was rife within the royal family. The year 1870 saw the start of the Franco-Prussian War – a conflict that split the royal family in two. Bertie and Alix – together with Alix's native Denmark and the majority of Britain – were fiercely loyal to France. Vicky's situation was appalling: married to the Crown Prince of Prussia, she was wife and mother to the next heirs to the throne, and as such was forced to be on the opposite side to the rest of her family. She did have an ally, however: Queen Victoria.

Although the queen had to pretend to be impartial, her pro-Prussian feelings were apparent to those who knew her – and to a large percentage of the sceptical newspaper-reading public. To Vicky, the queen wrote that she had to appear neutral, but 'My whole heart and fervent prayers are with beloved Germany! Say that to Fritz – but he must not say it again.' Bertie and Alix were aware of her allegiance and the situation within the family was quarrelsome and often explosive.

As the war escalated, however, even the queen, who had in the early months called the French position 'unjustifiable', began to realise what atrocities the Prussians were carrying out. From that time, her journal starts to reveal a sense of the queen's anger against Prussia.

The Emperor and Empress of France had always been kind and hospitable to Queen Victoria and she felt a responsibility towards them. She tried to reason with the Queen of Prussia, writing in August 1870, 'This frightful bloodshed is really too horrible in Europe in the 19th century.' When France was forced to surrender, the Empress and her son fled to England and the protection of Queen Victoria.

Louise, inspired by the example of Florence Nightingale, wanted to volunteer as a nurse during the war and go out to the battlefields to attend to the wounded, but she was thwarted by her royal status, again. For some time she had been deliberating over whether or not to marry Lorne or one of the other suitors her mother had suggested. Perhaps the queen's refusal to let her do anything useful during the war helped to tip the balance in favour of Louise agreeing to marriage.

In Britain, 1870 was to witness the beginning of a new era for women, with the passing of two vitally important new pieces of legislation. These were the first Married Women's Property Act and the Education Act. There was still a long way to go, but these two Acts of Parliament, concerned with women's rights and the rights of children, were some of the first significant steps towards equality. Louise was desperate to be a part of the new order – and as a married woman, rather than a spinster stay-at-home princess, she knew she would have more chance of achieving her goal.

Throughout 1870, Louise made a number of public appearances and the papers loved to comment on the clothes she wore and her artistic sense of style. She was the 'poster girl' for the royal family and as speculation mounted in the papers about her future, reports began to be leaked that Louise did not want to leave England, that she had refused to marry a foreigner, that she would only marry a 'Britisher'. The public loved her even more for this. The Prince and Princess of Wales were expected to attend a great number of social functions, but on the regular occasions when Alix was indisposed (her health was often poor as she was suffering from severe rheumatism and a hearing problem), Louise would attend official functions with Bertie. When the siblings appeared together for Bertie to open the new Thames Embankment in 1870, the crowds were ecstatic.

Thwarted in her intention to become a nurse, Louise threw her wartime energies into fund-raising and opening bazaars and fairs. She was also starting to gain confidence in her art, and when the New British Institution Gallery held its Winter Exhibition of 1870 – an exhibition of watercolours, with profits going to war relief work – Louise was one of the contributors. Interestingly, according to the National Art Library's archives, so was Vicky; it is strange to think that Vicky was sending her paintings to be exhibited in aid of war relief when her husband's family was responsible for the war itself.

Although Louise was now intending to become a wife, her mind was by no means made up as to who would be her husband. In March 1870, the Marquess of Lorne was told an engagement was not going to take place; Louise had changed her mind. As the queen wrote to Lord Granville on 13 March, 'while the Princess thinks Lord Lorne very clever and agreeable, she does <u>not</u> think she could have that feeling for him which would enable her to wish for any nearer acquaintance with a view to a further result. He is too young for her . . .'

The ending of her putative engagement to Lorne does not seem to have caused Louise much heartache. Soon afterwards, she was at a breakfast party hosted by the Gladstone family and Lady Lucy Cavendish noted in her diary, 'Sat by Princess Louise who looked very pretty and was charming and well-mannered as usual.' Rumours now suggested Lord Cowper as the princess's intended fiancé. At the start of October, however, all mention of Lord Cowper was at an end and the newspapers were about to get the story they'd been longing for. When the royal family was at Balmoral, Lorne arrived to stay. Within a few days of his arrival, the queen announced her daughter's engagement. The proposal had been carefully stage-managed by the monarch. Despite her later fiction that the marriage was a true love match and Louise would have no other husband than the future 9th Duke of Argyll, the ladies of the court recalled many years later that when Louise heard that Lorne had been invited to visit Balmoral she cried on and off for several days and, to those she trusted, confided that everything was 'so hard'.

On the day that Louise became engaged to be married, 3 October 1870, a small walking party set out with the promise of a good high tea at the end of their walk. The party included Lady Ely (a lady of the bedchamber and one of Queen Victoria's most trusted advisors),

Lord Hatherley (the Lord Chancellor), Princess Louise and the Marquess of Lorne. The queen, Princess Beatrice and other members of the party joined the walkers for tea – but they arrived, and left, by carriage. Louise and Lorne were both very fond of the outdoors, although he was less entranced by physical activity than Louise. When Louise thought of being outdoors, she thought of energetic walking or riding; Lorne was more content to be an observer. A year after their marriage, she would write to Lorne's mother, 'I make him walk as much as I can', but she admitted that she was seldom successful.

The princess was always happiest when she was physically active, the indolent lifestyle favoured by her mother and younger sister made her frustrated; she was also terrified of giving in to the Hanoverian tendency to corpulence. On the day of this particular excursion, the party ate scones and cakes and drank tea together while looking out over Dhu Loch, and then the queen and her party returned in their carriage, leaving the walkers to make their own way home. When Louise arrived back, she went dutifully to her mother to relate every minute detail of the proposal. The queen recorded in her journal the report Louise had given her: 'Lorne had spoken of his devotion to her and proposed to her and . . . she had accepted him, knowing that I would approve. Though I was not unprepared for this result, I felt painfully the thought of losing her. But I naturally gave my consent and could only pray that she might be happy.' The queen ordered a stone cairn to be erected in the grounds of Balmoral to mark the spot at which Lorne had proposed to Louise. The queen was grateful to Lady Ely for her help and tact and, as a memento of the occasion, presented her with a bracelet in a Celtic design, made of cabochon-cut local granites and silver; she also received a locket containing a photograph of Princess Louise.

On 4 October 1870 the queen received Lorne officially for the first time since his proposal and wrote in her journal, 'Saw Lorne for a few moments, who was much overcome, but spoke very nicely of his unworthiness, of his devotion to Louise, & of his anxiety to do all in his power to overcome difficulties & conciliate all.' He gained his future mother-in-law's approbation when he was taken to the family mausoleum for the first time, to pay his respects to the almost beatified Albert, and professed himself very much impressed with it. Like Alix, Lorne learnt very early on that ingratiating himself with the queen was the most important step towards harmonious royal family life. Despite her newly engaged status, Louise was notably not an excited bride-to-be. On 5 October, Henry Ponsonby made reference to Louise being 'moody' and 'absent-minded'. She was not as happy as her mother wanted the world to believe.

The queen ensured that her new son-in-law was aware of how things were expected to be right from the beginning – he might be marrying Louise, but it was Queen Victoria's happiness that Lorne was to consider above all else. She wrote to her future son-in-law, 'Mine is a nature which *requires* being loved, and I have lost almost all those who loved me most on earth' (an extraordinary statement for a woman with nine living children). She also noted with pleasure how worried Lorne's father, the Duke of Argyll, appeared to be when she met him shortly after the news of the engagement was made public. He dutifully expressed concern about how 'depressed' the queen must be at the thought of 'parting' from Louise upon her marriage.

The announcement of the engagement was popular with the public, but it caused an outcry in the royal family. The Prussian royals took it as a personal and political insult that Louise had chosen to marry someone British rather than a Prussian and Vicky was placed in a very difficult position. Bertie and Alix were equally angry, saying it was a disgrace that Louise was being allowed – and indeed encouraged – to marry a commoner, and the majority of their siblings seemed to feel the same way. The following month Bertie was at a house party at which Lorne's father, the 8th Duke of Argyll, was also a guest. Bertie snubbed him publicly, making his opposition to the wedding apparent. Meanwhile, Louise was feeling very sorry for herself. An accident had left her with a knee injury and for the next few weeks she would make a slow recovery; this was especially frustrating for someone so reliant on exercise to make her happy. When the family left Balmoral, she could not walk at all and had to be carried. She spent the next couple of months on crutches, which made the queen fret that Louise would never walk again, thereby making her 'unmarriageable'. (The injury would recur and plague Louise into old age, resulting in rheumatism in later years.)

One surprising thing about Louise's controversial betrothal was how much Queen Victoria supported it. While her other children were almost all displeased with their sister's decision, the queen was strongly in favour of the match, writing a long letter to Bertie to refute all his arguments – for example the difficulty of a princess marrying below her rank and that Lorne was known to be a Liberal and would therefore cause problems when the royal family was not supposed to be political. In her letter the monarch, mindful of the recent family heartaches during the Franco-Prussian War, commented:

> Times have much changed; great foreign alliances are looked on as causes of trouble and anxiety . . . You may not be aware, as I am, with what dislike the marriages of Princesses . . . with small German Princes ('German beggars' as they most insultingly were called) were looked on . . . As to position, I see _no_ difficulty whatsoever. Louise remains what she is, and her husband keeps his rank . . . only being treated in the family as a relation when we are together. It will strengthen the _hold_ of the Royal Family, besides infusing new and healthy blood into it, whereas all the Princes abroad are related to each other . . . I feel sure that new blood will strengthen the throne _morally_ as well as _physically._

The queen would later say with fond reminiscence how charmed she had been by the Marquess of Lorne when she had first encountered him as a pretty, belligerent toddler. Given the queen's usual feelings about small children, this seems unlikely, but Victoria began to tell the story – and soon the newspapers were using it to suggest that Louise and Lorne had been childhood sweethearts. The majority of royal family members might not have been happy about the engagement, but the British public – and the British press – were thrilled.

The queen must have had ulterior motives for 'marrying off' Louise as expediently as possible and to someone of a lower rank to whom the marriage would be an honour. Despite her fond reminiscences of the sweet little toddler, in reality when she met Lorne again as an adult her first impressions were nothing like as favourable. Most notably she complained that Lorne needed to wash more frequently. The queen did have her moments of indecision about the engagement, but whereas Bertie and Alix were vociferously against the match, the queen quite uncharacteristically supported it.

There is a more than mild suggestion that the queen knew there were very good reasons why Louise should marry as soon as possible – and to someone who would not be in position to 'pull rank'. This could have been because of Louise's love affair with Boehm, or because Louise had already borne an illegitimate child; most likely it was both. Although I was not granted access to the Campbell family archives, I have been told by a researcher who has seen these archives that they hold a letter from the queen to the 8th Duke of Argyll written before the wedding, in which it is stated that Princess Louise is 'barren'. How could the queen possibly have known that? Even if Louise's teenage illness had been tubercular meningitis, it was by no means a foregone conclusion that she was, as a result, infertile. Several other sources also mention this letter and some suggest a particularly unpleasant rumour. The rumour is that, when Sir Charles Locock helped to deliver Louise's illegitimate baby, the queen ordered the *accoucher* to ensure that Louise would be unable to bear any more children. This incredible rumour, however, is unlikely to be true, for several reasons. If the queen truly believed such an operation was possible, why did she continue to be so permanently laid low by her own hated pregnancies? The strongest refutation of such a suggestion, however, is that the Duke and Duchess of Argyll, as well as Lorne's siblings, made constant enquiries as to Louise's 'health' or 'condition'. Every time Louise was even mildly ill, the Campbells would solicitously enquire if she were, at last, pregnant. As Louise was destined not to have any more children, it is more likely that complications occurred during Henry's birth which made it impossible for her to have a successful pregnancy again, rather than that Charles Locock performed some mysterious procedure to make her 'barren'.

While the queen was in favour of Louise's wedding, why were Louise's siblings so opposed to the match? Vicky, one can understand – she was as conventional as her mother and felt that the marriage would reflect badly on herself and her family (plus, she had been desperate to have one of her sisters living close to her). Helena had a more personal reason to be against the match: she realised that if Louise married Lorne she would end up spending much of her time in Scotland. Having been forced to live very close to her mother, Helena was in real danger of having to resume her former role as unpaid secretary. At the very least, if Louise were married and she and Lorne were living in London, Louise and Helena would be equal again and it was likely they would end up sharing the role.

Why, however, was Bertie so adamantly against the match? Even when Louise had made up her mind and announced to her family that it was her desire to marry Lorne, Bertie remained angry. As unconventional as Louise, Bertie had always been her natural ally. One would have imagined that he would have backed her in her decision to marry and escape their mother's home. That Alix had wanted Louise to marry her brother, Prince Frederick of Denmark, was common knowledge, and she was disappointed when Louise said no, but that doesn't seem to have been the motive behind Bertie's firm opposition to the match. He gave as one of his reasons Lorne's Liberal politics, yet Bertie was usually happy about anything that would go against protocol. Could it have been that Bertie was more aware of Lorne's real personality than anyone else in the family?

Just as rumours persist about Louise, rumours about Lorne have been rife for well over a century. Marriage had not tempered Bertie and throughout his life he would continue to have affairs and to have friends who were equally scandalous. Bertie could tolerate most peccadilloes and indiscretions, yet for some reason was adamantly against Louise's engagement. Perhaps Bertie had already heard rumours about Lorne, rumours that made him want to prevent his beloved sister from marrying the future Duke of Argyll. Several historians have written that Lorne was involved in a sexual relationship with another pupil while at Eton, and, in less savoury rumours, that he was one of the 'favoured' boys of a paedophiliac master, William Johnson, who was dismissed very suddenly in 1872.[36] In the 1860s, Johnson composed a poem about two Eton boys and their love for each other. One of the boys in the poem was Lorne's close friend, Frederick Wood; the other, although not named, was believed to be Lorne, suggested in the poem by Johnson's reference to the Campbell family heraldic shield.[37] In adult life, Lorne numbered many of the well-known gay underworld amongst his closest friends.

[36] William Johnson later changed his name to William Cory and left the teaching profession.
[37] Although he was known as the Marquess of Lorne and would become the Duke of Argyll, his family were also part of the Campbell clan.

The researcher Michael Gledhill was sent a letter in 1977 from H.J. Cavendish Bentinck, who wrote:

My great aunt, who died ten years ago at an advanced age was a friend [of Princess Louise] . . . and the family still have several letters which we have always kept private . . . Firstly, to be frank, and you may already have found this out, there is the question of Lorne's proclivities, in the other direction, which needed the private 'handling' by Edward VII . . . Louise was a charming, gifted woman, but you will find a wall of silence regarding so much of the life and through no fault of hers.

Despite Bertie's concerns, the world at large was unaware of any problems between the engaged couple. While Prussia continued to destroy France, the newspapers had happily moved on to royal wedding fever. On 5 January 1871, the *Falkirk Herald* published a first-person article about the people's princess: 'I remember so well the day when I first saw Her Royal Highness the Princess Louise,' wrote the journalist.

'It was a day in the early spring, soft and brilliant . . . I had made a journey of some little trouble to go to the royal Isle of Wight, for the foundation stone was to be laid of a building belonging to an institution that was dear to me, and the Princess Louise was to lay the first stone . . . We waited some time for the sound of her horse's hoofs, for she had to traverse the whole breadth of the island on her errand of mercy. There was a throng of fair ladies present, but . . . there was no more sweet and intellectual face than that of the young Princess. Her duties were long and must have been fatiguing, but they were done gracefully and well.'

The writer also remembered standing with a young lady by his side, when Louise passed by; the princess 'gave us a gracious saluta-tion and a courteous glance of her candid eyes. It was but a trifle, yet one which we valued and treasured.'

Louise was determined to be taken seriously as an artist and continued her studies, despite the demands of her engagement. In the same year in which she would be married, she exhibited at the

Old Bond Street Gallery of the British Institution. It was an exhibition held on behalf of the 'destitute widows and orphans of Germans killed in the war'. Other artists and writers recorded the occasion of the royal wedding. The poet Robert Buchanan published a book entitled *The Land of Lorne* which he dedicated, with her permission, to Princess Louise.[38]

In the final months of 1870, the Franco-Prussian War had escalated, with terrifying rapidity, when the Prussians marched on Paris. After months of bloody fighting, the Prussians crowned their kaiser as Emperor of France and took control of the capital city. This became known as the Siege of Paris. Parisians suffered, became racked with diseases and starved in their thousands. Famous tales were told of the animals in the royal menagerie being slaughtered and eaten. Daring balloonists attempted to escape by air and specially trained pigeons were released, bearing desperate letters to the outside world, known as the 'pigeon post'. The Siege of Paris turned even those who had formerly supported Prussia into staunch sympathisers with the French. The people of Britain were incensed that their Princess Royal was married to the son of the warmongering Prussian Emperor. Queen Victoria wrote about her people's fury with Prussia to Vicky's mother-in-law. It is a diplomatically worded letter – ostensibly the queen appears to be offering Prussia her sympathy – but she is actually warning the Prussians how much they are now disliked overseas. The Franco-Prussian War, which ended formally in May 1871, had turned Princess Louise's wedding, and her choice of husband, into an act of patriotism.

[38] Later that year, Buchanan would publish a now-famous and scathing review of the poetry of Dante Gabriel Rossetti, entitled 'The Fleshly School of Poetry', in which he also criticised the works of Rossetti's friend Algernon Charles Swinburne. What Buchanan did not know would have made an even more sensational story – seven years after the death of his wife, the model Lizzie Siddal, Rossetti had retrieved the poems of which Buchanan so disapproved from her secretly exhumed coffin.

CHAPTER 12

'The most popular act of my reign'

Mr R.D. Blackmore, who died on Saturday last, had a hard struggle as a writer in the early days. His *Lorna Doone* . . . was rejected by no less than eighteen publishers. When Princess Louise . . . was married to the Marquis of Lorne, the public confused the names of Lorne and Lorna, to the benefit of the author, and the book began to sell at once.

The Era, 27 January 1900

In a letter to Vicky, Queen Victoria claimed that her announcement of Louise's marriage was 'the most popular act of my reign'. The newspapers concurred, with a journalist for the *Newcastle Guardian* writing that 'a feeling of satisfaction pervaded the country . . . that at last a stop was put to the practice of handing over our Princesses to petty German princelings'. The young princess's 'love match' to a minor Scottish peer became a vitally important exercise in public relations, not least because the queen's advisors were aware of the increasingly hostile feelings of a large sector of the British public towards the monarch. In Scotland, it was said that anyone with the surname Campbell or with any connection at all to the Clan Campbell was now allying themselves with the Argyll family and claiming kinship with the princess. The people of Balmoral sent Louise a necklace as a wedding gift, proud that she was marrying one of their country's sons. Her thank-you letter was reported in the newspapers:

I am deeply touched by your having so kindly thought of me on this occasion, and given me such a beautiful present. I thank you from my heart for it, and shall ever treasure it amongst my most valued gifts as coming from kind friends who will be associated in my thoughts with dear Balmoral, and who have known me from my childhood. Though I may no longer be so frequent amongst you as heretofore, I shall think of you often in my own new Highland home.

The royal wedding of 1871 was a bright spot in an extremely difficult year – although there were many republicans who were irate that the country was about to be subjected to yet another 'beggar' on the public purse. When the queen went to Parliament to ask not only for a marriage dowry for Louise but for an annuity for Prince Arthur, it was widely remarked upon that she only took any interest in the running of the country when she wanted money for her family. There was a great deal of opposition to both requests, and *The Spectator* published an irritable article in which it queried why people were against the princess's dowry:

> There is something very perplexing, and to us at least not a little irritating, in the sudden outbreak of popular feeling against the marriage of the Princess Louise, an outbreak so bitter that it may yet provoke a discreditable scene in the House of Commons . . . The subject is as embarrassing as the Permissive Bill, or the Contagious Diseases Act . . . What has the clever Princess done, or what is she about to do, that she should be treated with this exceeding discourtesy?

In constitutional terms, the wedding was not only controversial because it divided the royal family, it was the first marriage of a royal to a commoner since 1515. Louise might be marrying a marquess whose father was the 8th Duke of Argyll and whose mother was the daughter of the 2nd Duke of Sutherland, but her husband-to-be was still considered a commoner.

The Marquess of Lorne was a fascinating character whom many rumours surround, including that he had inherited a family gift of 'second sight'. Contemporary reports, in newspapers and letters, stressed that this was a romantic love match – and that was what the public wanted to hear. A popular cartoon in *Punch* at the time of their engagement showed the couple, with Lorne dressed in a kilt, looking at hordes of would-be suitors for the princess's hand. All the suitors wear Prussian or German army uniforms. The caption reads 'A (Real) German Defeat'. Engagement photographs appeared in newspapers and magazines and *The Graphic* commissioned portraits of the couple, which Louise and Lorne sat for, reproduced in a special 'wedding edition'. Wedding presents were sent from all over the empire, from lovingly crafted handmade items to jewel-encrusted regal gifts. The Mayor of Windsor was invited to hand over his gift in person: the people of Windsor gave the princess a diamond bracelet. The wedding preparations were not to be without political incident – Louise received a petition from 'the Ladies of Ireland' requesting her to intercede with the queen on their behalf to try and secure the release and pardon of Irish political prisoners.

The journalist Mrs Matthew Hall wrote gushingly about the intended marriage. This was to be a royal wedding to please the masses, and the message sent loud and clear to the nation was one that would not have looked out of place in a popular novel:

> Princess Louise, the fourth daughter of our gracious sovereign, whose name is at this time on the lip of every young lady in the United Kingdom, and who, being on the eve of her union with the object of her cherished attachment, engages the sympathy of all her sex . . . a perfect sympathy of taste in literature, music, and all the elegant accomplishments of refined life between the young couple, forms the basis of the ardent attachment which happily exists between them. So devoted, indeed, is the . . . Princess . . . that she has been known to declare should any unfavourable difficulty arise to prevent her union with the Marquis of Lorne, there was one thing she was determined upon: never to marry a foreign prince.

Mrs Matthew Hall's sentiment was rather different from that of Louise's sister-in-law. Alix wrote to her sister Minnie about the engaged couple two weeks before the wedding: 'She resents him like the devil, the poor man, I am sorry for both of them, and he is going to suffer for that!' However, Alix also wrote unpresciently of Lorne, 'He is in love with her *voilà tout.*' If Bertie was aware of Lorne's sexual preference for men, it was not something he had shared with his rather innocent and naïve wife. He had, however, managed to communicate his grave misgivings and Alix wrote with what she hoped was tact to her favourite sister-in-law: 'Let me now wish you all possible happiness for your future, and may you never have cause to regret the step you have taken! God grant that the husband you have chosen may prove worthy of you my dearest Louise in every respect!'

Three days before her wedding, Princess Louise celebrated her twenty-third birthday and awoke to a serenade by the band of the 2nd Life Guards. Bertie and Alix were conspicuously absent from her birthday dinner party that evening (although they arrived in time for the wedding). Louise and Lorne had already sat for their official wedding photographs and on the day before the wedding, excitement was generated by a local photographer who arrived to take pictures of the wedding cake. His photographs depict an enormous towering confection of white icing and sugar sculptures. Local newspapers were full of advertisements from businesses and warehouses announcing they would be closing early on the wedding day in honour of the royal couple.[39]

On the day before the wedding the crowds waiting outside Windsor Castle were thrilled to see, amongst the army of workmen and decorators, the queen, Princess Beatrice and Princess Louise walking across the castle quadrangle to check on the decoration of the chapel; they were attended by the Duchess of Roxburghe and guarded by the looming figure of John Brown. Crowds also gathered at Windsor's Great Western Railway station hoping to glimpse arriving royal guests, most notably the disgruntled Prince and Princess of Wales. The *Morning Post* made much of the fact that the bridegroom and his family passed unnoticed through the crowds into the queen's waiting horse-drawn carriages.

In the early hours of Tuesday 21 March 1871, many more people lined the streets of Windsor and Eton, to see the royal couple or their guests. The *Morning Post* reported 'windows commanding a good view of the procession are fetching fabulous prices. The enterprising occupier of a house at the bottom of the Castle Hill has let one window for seven guineas.' The marriage of Princess Louise and John George

---

[39] Another story that featured prominently in the papers in the run-up to the wedding concerned an earthquake that affected much of northern England and whose tremors were felt in the Channel Islands.

Edward Henry Douglas Sutherland Campbell took place at Windsor Castle's St George's Chapel. The chapel doors were opened at 11a.m. and the first guests soon started to arrive, with the ushers doing their best to ensure that everyone was seated according to rank and importance. The *Pall Mall Gazette* reported the progress of the wedding with bulletin-style accounts: 'By noon nearly all the seats were filled, and the scene was then excessively grand. Every gentleman was in full uniform, and most of them glittered with gold lace and stars and orders. There was great diversity in the dresses of the ladies, both in material and colour, from velvet to gauzy silk.'

At twenty past twelve, the music began and Helena and her husband Christian became the first members of the royal family to enter the chapel. The papers wrote avidly about the princesses' dresses: Helena wore cerise pink silk decorated with diamonds, Beatrice pink satin, and Alix was resplendent in dark blue velvet with an impressive train (the newspapers forbore to mention that Alix was heavily pregnant yet again and that her rheumatic knee was so unreliable that she fell painfully while getting out of the carriage on her way into the chapel). The Duke of Argyll's full Highland dress was remarked upon more often than his wife's white satin dress and diamond tiara. At half past twelve, Lorne and his party entered the chapel. There had been a great deal of public discussion beforehand about whether the groom would wear a kilt; he did not – he wore the uniform of the Argyllshire Regiment of which he was honorary Colonel. Princess Louise, in an elaborate but artistic dress of white silk and satin, was escorted up the aisle by her mother and Bertie. The *Illustrated London News* published a drawing of the wedding, in which Louise and Lorne are almost overshadowed by their bevy of bridesmaids (wearing dresses and veils similar to the bride's) who are in the centre of the picture holding up Louise's magnificent train. To the side, apparently keeping a critical eye on the eight bridesmaids, is a stern-faced Queen Victoria. Louise designed both her bridal veil and the vivid red bouquets of roses carried by the bridesmaids.

The wedding ceremony was performed by the Bishops of London and Winchester (with newspapermen waiting outside the gates in an attempt to hear the first eyewitness reports). Just before the entrance of the bride, a newly composed Wedding March, by Sir George Elvey, was played. Following the wedding ceremony, the queen invested her new son-in-law with the Order of the Thistle. The wedding breakfast was then served in the Oak Room at Windsor Castle. The wedding cake was reported to have taken three months to create, was five feet tall and 'decorated with figures representing the Fine Arts, Science, Agriculture, and Commerce'.[40] A special express train had been ordered for many of the guests to return to London from Windsor at 3.30p.m. The newly-weds left for Claremont House in Surrey, a beautiful Palladian mansion built in 1774 for Clive of India; its parkland had been landscaped by Sir John Vanbrugh, William Kent and Capability Brown. The house, once the home of the much-mourned Princess Charlotte, the ill-fated daughter of King George IV and Queen Caroline, had been a favourite place of the young Queen Victoria. Louise and Lorne left their remaining guests to enjoy what *The Graphic* described as 'a grand dinner party . . . at the Castle in the evening, after which there was a concert in St George's Hall'.

On their way to begin their honeymoon at Claremont House, the couple drove through Old Windsor, where the people had erected triumphal arches and Louise, now the Marchioness of Lorne, made a speech and was presented with a bouquet. Lord Ronnie Gower wrote in his diary for that day:

> A family party met at Cliveden the previous day, and on the marriage morning drove over to Windsor. Percy and I were the two 'supporters,' to use the expression of etiquette at these royal ceremonies. The day was brilliant . . . Lorne went through the ordeal with admirable self-possession. The bride very pale, but handsome. The whole scene was superb, full of pomp, music, pageantry and sunshine . . . At four the newly-wedded pair left the castle . . . under a shower of rice, satin shoes, and a new broom that John Brown, in Highland fashion, threw after their carriage as it left the quadrangle for the station.

Jane Ridley, Bertie's biographer, commented on how shocked Alix was by Louise's behaviour on the wedding day. Alix had expected her

---

[40] In 2009, a slice of Louise and Lorne's wedding cake went on sale at an auction in the UK. It was described as one inch thick and still in its original parchment wrapper. It was suggested that whoever bought it should not eat it.

sister-in-law to be demure and overcome with nerves and emotion, but instead Louise talked and laughed with her friends, often ignoring royal protocol.

All over the country, the queen's subjects held parties, lavish dinners, bonfires, balls and firework displays to celebrate the wedding of their princess. On the evening of the wedding day, 7,000 singers (one huge choir formed from many visiting choirs) performed on stage at the Crystal Palace in honour of the royal wedding, accompanied by the Crystal Palace Orchestra and an assembly of military bands. As with all royal weddings, the papers continued to print stories about the occasion long after the event. *The Graphic* published an illustrated guide to the presents, not only the lavish gifts given to the bride by her mother and by the Duke and Duchess of Argyll, but also a bracelet given to Louise by Lorne; it is a pretty and unusual design, which suggests he already understood her taste. The paper also showed the locket Louise gave to her bridesmaids (and which she had designed herself), a Celtic design bracelet given by the 'People of Mull' and the necklace and earrings 'given by the Upper Servants and Tenantry of Balmoral'. The princess even received a present from 'the Maidens of the United Kingdom of Great Britain and Ireland' (a casket and beautifully decorated bible).

For Louise, becoming a bride had made few discernible changes in her bid for freedom. Despite being married, the couple were still seldom alone. They were accompanied on their journey to Claremont House by upper servants and were greeted upon their arrival by two of Queen Victoria's 'spies', Colonel McNeill and Lady Jane Churchill; one very welcome member of the honeymoon party was Louise's pet dog, Frisky.[41] Two days into the honeymoon, the couple prepared for a visit from the queen, who claimed she could not cope without her beloved daughter and longed for them to return to Windsor and the bosom of the royal family. It was already time for Louise to resume official duties, such as receiving the Emperor Napoleon, recently arrived from beleaguered France.

---

[41] The National Portrait Gallery owns a carte-de-visite photograph of Princess Louise, taken by the fashionable photographers Hills & Saunders in the mid-1860s. Louise stands behind a chair, on which is a small terrier – the dog is standing contentedly on its hind legs while Louise holds its front paws. It seems likely this dog was Frisky.

At the end of March, just a few days after her wedding, Louise attended the opening of the Royal Albert Hall in South Kensington. Her fashionable white dress was the talk of the newspapers. In April, the couple set off for a proper honeymoon, taking the train to Dover and the boat to Ostend. Honeymooning in Europe was difficult with the war still raging and Louise knew it would be impossible to visit Vicky, but she had hoped to see Alice. The sisters met for the briefest of meetings in a railway station in Germany. Like many Victorian honeymoons, it was a strange journey. Louise was travelling with a man she barely knew and yet had pledged to spend her life with; it was an unsettling time, but also a time of great excitement. They travelled incognito as Lord and Lady Sundridge. The queen expected daily letters from her honeymooning daughter, but in this she was to be disappointed. The princess wrote regularly, but not every day: it was a small victory. Louise was determined to enjoy the independence of being a married woman.

In Italy, the Lornes indulged their shared love of art and Louise was able to visit the places she had written about so longingly in her letters to Arthur a few years earlier. The couple visited galleries and bought works of art for their marital home. In Florence, Louise made friends with the woman arranged by the queen to be her 'companion', Lady Paget, wife of the British Minister (who noted that she was always having to remind the princess that they ought to get back to their husbands – Louise's behaviour was not what she had expected from a honeymoon bride). At that date, Florence was home to a large population of British people; some went for the climate and their health, but many were there because it was so much more affordable to live in style in Italy. Louise and Lorne also visited Venice, a city that had inspired artists for centuries. Since John Ruskin had published *The Stones of Venice* in the 1850s, British artists and writers had been flocking to the city in even larger numbers than before. Whistler was amongst those who travelled regularly to Venice for inspiration. (In 1876 Louise would be amongst the elite few invited to see Whistler's Venetian-inspired works.)

Alice and Louise's brief meeting took place as the Lornes travelled back to London, and Alice was pleased to see how well her sister was looking. The knee injury was no longer troubling her and she had experienced her first, heady taste of freedom. The queen did not want her daughters to see each other, she was worried that Alice, who was known for her directness and medical knowledge, would talk to Louise about gynaecological matters. The queen wrote to Louise:

> I would rather you had _not_ met her _so_ soon [after the wedding], for I know her _curiosity_ and what is _worse_ and what I hardly like to say of my own daughter, – I know her _indelicacy_ and coarseness . . . Mary Teck, who _is_ very _nice_ in her feelings . . . told me _she never_ was _so shocked_ as she had been at the things Alice _said to her_!' A few weeks later, the queen cautioned Louise again with the unintentionally amusing postscript: '_Don't_ let Alice pump you. Be _very_ silent and cautious about your "interior".

The honeymoon journey seems to have been a success. There were many reasons why Louise and Lorne should have been compatible, not least because they shared the same Liberal politics. Lorne would become a Liberal MP and he and Louise shared an ideology: both wanted to improve the lot of Britain's poorest people and longed for educational and health reform. They were also strong supporters of women's suffrage – even at university, long before he met Louise, Lorne was renowned for his 'feminist' ideals, supporting women's education and parodying those who tried to keep female scholars out. It is likely, however, that they had too much in common. Two days before the wedding, Lorne had written to his beloved 'Aunt Dot'. He told her that he 'felt rather sad as I turn from independence to – we know what!' It is usually assumed that this meant sadness about being under the tyranny of his new mother-in-law. Perhaps he wanted to make a Victorian joke about the wonders of being a bachelor, but it also seems likely that it reflects his sadness about being married at all and the need to live a lie. This would tally with Lord Ronnie's comment in his diary that 'Lorne went through the ordeal with admirable self-possession.'

The rumours about Lorne's sexuality have persisted throughout the decades. Officially sanctioned books claim that Lorne was perceived as a 'ladies' man' by the local girls when he was growing up, and spurious claims were made that he had illegitimate children 'all over the Highlands', something that seems to have no basis in fact. In 1930 the diaries and letters of William Ewart Gladstone's daughter, Mary, were published and in them she revealed she had had a romance with Lorne before he married Louise. This is sometimes claimed as proof that Lorne was not gay, but a 'romance' to a woman of Mary's social status and era usually meant a flirtation and perhaps correspondence, not a sexual relationship. Within a short time of the 'romance', Mary's diaries reveal she was uneasy about spending time alone with Lorne and felt 'relieved' when they were with other people.

The inability to access the Argyll family's archive means I have been unable to clarify anything about Lorne's sexual behaviour before marriage (if there is anything left in the archive to reveal itself). A researcher attempting to write about Louise and Lorne in the 1970s told me that he was physically escorted out of the Argyll family archives by the then Duke of Argyll, after the researcher asked quite innocently if the archivist thought there was any truth to the rumour of Princess Louise having had an illegitimate baby. He had not yet touched upon the rumours about Lorne's sexuality. He was not allowed back again.

CHAPTER 13

The battle for independence

Our evening here consists in the Queen coming in to the drawing room for ten minutes or so and then we sit about and talk . . . [Lord Lorne] in his kilt and his belt studded with boars' heads, the skiff of Lorne etc., and adorned with the thistle ribbon, talks to the strangers; the Duchess presides at the tea table and Lady Dufferin, Lady Churchill and a daughter. Louise gets a Presbyterian Minister on a sofa near her; another Minister sings songs. Campbell of Islay wanders about, joining in the song, or sipping his tea, and I sit with an enormous book of the Argyll letters since 1660 which Lorne lumps into my lap.

Henry Ponsonby, letter to his wife, from Inveraray,
25 September 1875

Louise worked tirelessly during her first year of marriage. In addition to being at the queen's beck and call, she had her own public duties to perform, as the public wanted to see the royal bride and her handsome husband (as all the newspapers then described him). The queen, who was in Scotland when Louise moved into her new home in London, wrote officiously to her daughter: 'Pray _don't rush_ about in London, as you always used to do! Visiting and going to exhibitions, shops and studios . . . Pray be prudent and reasonable. And don't ever go out (when Lorne is _not_ there) without _some_ lady _or other_'. Louise ignored her mother, and what seems to be a badly veiled hint about not seeing Boehm alone, and enjoyed herself in London. She and Lorne had already realised the necessity of spending a great deal of time apart – which offended the queen, who wrote an angry letter to Lorne about how much she and Albert had longed to spend all their time together and saying that Lorne should never be happy when Louise was with her mother and he was elsewhere.

As soon as possible, Louise and Lorne set off on their marriage tour, travelling around the country and visiting Ireland. Lord Ronnie recalled the day that Lorne brought his new wife 'home' to Scotland:

> I went to Inveraray to be present at the 'Home-coming' of Princess Louise. It rained all the time, as it always does at Inveraray, in torrents . . . The Princess seems already quite at home, and very cordial to all . . . Highland games go on all day long in spite of the deluge, and Highland jigs, flings, and dances are the order of the night.

There was great excitement all around Inveraray and Louise was fêted. Twin girls who were born on the day the princess came to Inveraray were christened Louise and Lorne.

Louise was welcomed warmly by the Campbells; her parents-in-law and Lorne's siblings had taken to her and were pleased she was happy to be 'one of them', rather than insisting on stiff formality. The Duchess of Argyll would later write that her son's wife was 'a pleasure in our lives'. The Duke of Argyll and Louise had liked each other since before Louise had agreed to marry his son, and at the start of her marriage Louise's relationship with her father-in-law was one of mutual affection and respect (this would change in years to come when she considered the duke had behaved unkindly). In preparation for the couple's honeymoon, the duke had bought Benmore Lodge on the Isle of Mull. It is a pretty and pleasant house surrounded by lush parkland. During the honeymoon, Louise (and possibly Lorne) painted murals on its walls. Later residents are divided in their opinion of the murals, which range from 'excellent' to 'dreadful'. One resident who lived in Benmore Lodge for many years in the mid twentieth century commented that there were 'two splendid murals on the walls of the sitting room, which are still there, as well as two hideous others not done by her, at least I am fairly certain they weren't'. I was lucky enough to visit the house, thanks to the generosity of the family who were renting it for the summer when I appeared unannounced and asked them about it. Having heard the paintings described as 'murals' I expected them to stretch the length of the walls, but they are small in size. They differ greatly in accomplishment; two of the murals I saw are very pretty and accomplished and seem to indicate the freedom Louise felt for perhaps the first time in her life. As a married woman, her time of independence was beginning. The others, I would agree, were almost certainly not painted by Louise.

The year, however, was to prove tragic. While Louise and Lorne were away, Alix gave birth to a son, who died. Once again the Princess of Wales had gone into labour prematurely and the new baby boy was even smaller than Prince Eddy had been. He was baptised almost immediately after his birth, with the names Alexander John Charles Albert (but was always referred to as Prince John). He lived for only one day, dying inauspiciously on Good Friday. Louise would later hear how her beloved Alix had remained cocooned in bed with her dead baby, crying in misery. She wished fervently that she could have been there to comfort her. Prince John was to be Alix's last baby. Despite the fact that she was just twenty-six years old, her multiple health problems meant that she was extremely frail and the doctors advised the future king that his wife must never suffer pregnancy again. A short time after Bertie and Alix's tragic bereavement, Louise heard the shocking news that her friend Sybil St Albans had died in childbirth. Sybil's husband was left a single father to three children, including the newborn baby. Sybil had been one of the few members of the royal household whom Louise had been able to trust with her secrets. She missed her friend dreadfully over the coming decades.

In order to honour Sybil, Louise began working on a memorial; the project allowed Louise a physical expression of her grief. She sculpted a portrait medallion of her friend, a style of art that had become increasingly popular, thanks to the work of Thomas Woolner (the only sculptor in the now-famous Pre-Raphaelite Brotherhood (PRB)). The Brotherhood had become highly influential in the British art world, even though it had disbanded after only five years. It had come to an end in 1853 when Woolner had set sail for Australia hoping to make his fortune in the gold rush – certain he would never do so as an artist. Although he did find a small amount of gold, his greatest achievement while overseas was perfecting his technique of producing portrait medallions – portable round portraits, sculpted in relief. These became very fashionable in Australian society, with many local luminaries and their families commissioning them. He set sail for England in July 1854, encouraged by his success in Australia. He went on to become Professor of Sculpture at the Royal Academy – and was memorable for delivering not a single lecture during his tenure. His most celebrated works included statues of John Stuart Mill, Prince Albert and Sir Stamford Raffles. The last of these was erected in Singapore (today the precious original is in a museum, but a replica can still be seen marking the spot where it is believed Raffles first landed in Singapore).

While Louise was working on her portrait medallion and grieving for her dead friend, she was worrying about her mother. Queen Victoria was very ill – but as the queen had 'cried wolf' so often, the newspapers refused to believe that she was genuinely unwell. Once again the monarch came in for of criticism for not carrying out her public duties. This time, however, the queen really was ill: for some time she had been suffering from blood poisoning, she was unable to walk and had to be pushed around in a wheelchair, usually by the long-suffering Beatrice. Louise and Beatrice became exhausted by their mother's capricious demands and Louise and Lorne longed to go overseas to escape the British winter; the queen refused to allow this and an irate exchange of letters between mother and daughter ensued, with Victoria pulling rank and forbidding Louise to leave the country. Louise was starting to realise that marriage was not going to afford her the independence she had craved. The queen's illness was debilitating, but she was recovered by the end of the year – just in time for another family health scare.

For months, Queen Victoria's family had been dreading the tenth anniversary of Albert's death. Now, as the date approached, they were horrified to hear that Bertie had been diagnosed with typhoid fever. The whole family waited in trepidation and Louise stayed with Alix as much as possible throughout Bertie's illness. The house at Sandringham, where the future king lay on what was feared to be his deathbed, was overcrowded. Louise and Beatrice had to sleep in the same bed and the queen cruelly refused to allow either Helena or Vicky to visit their ailing brother. Lorne was snubbed by being pointedly not invited into the family drama. As the dreaded fatal date of 14 December grew close, the queen became convinced that she was going to lose her eldest son on the same date she had lost her husband. She began to spend more time with her son, and, rather pathetically, Bertie repeatedly told his mother through his fever how 'kind' it was of her to visit him. It was a terrible few weeks, but by Christmas, the crisis was past and Bertie was starting to recover. The family spent their first Christmas at Windsor Castle since Albert had died there.

Bertie's illness had two fortunate outcomes. He and his mother grew closer and the country began to exhibit patriotic fervour for the queen and her family. Victoria had been surprised and touched by the number of supportive letters and telegrams that had poured in from all over the country during her son's illness. For the first time in many years, the queen had started to elicit the sympathy and understanding of her subjects. Another positive outcome was that Bertie and Alix, whose marriage had not been happy, grew closer. The Princess of Wales confided happily to Louise, 'We are never apart, and are now enjoying our <u>second</u> "Honey Moon".' Louise and Lorne were, however, not so happy. An intriguing letter survives from Leopold in which he writes to his sister: 'I am very sorry also about other matters, but I <u>sincerely trust</u> that what you say will not be the case, and that you are taking a gloomier view of affairs than necessary.' Although it is not known what the 'other matters' were, it seems likely that they were to do with her marriage.

In the new year, thanksgiving services were held for the recovery of the Prince of Wales from the illness that was believed to have killed his father. Ironically, almost immediately after receiving so much love and affection from her subjects, the queen was brought face to face with the more terrifying realities of her reign. While she was returning to Buckingham Palace from St Paul's Cathedral, having just attended a thanksgiving service for Bertie's life, a Fenian terrorist leapt on to the queen's open carriage. Arthur and Leopold were in the landau with their mother and all three were rendered powerless by the shock. The man, Arthur O'Connor, was carrying a pistol. His intention, however, was not to kill (the pistol was later discovered to have been broken and quite useless as anything except a threat). What O'Connor wanted was to force the queen, at gunpoint, to sign a document he had with him, a petition for the release of Fenian prisoners. The queen and princes' rescue was effected by the ubiquitous John Brown who tackled and disarmed the attacker. Arthur O'Connor was later sentenced to a year in prison and given twenty lashes.

The attack on the queen was not the only royal topic being discussed at this time. If Louise had thought that once she was married speculation about her private life would end, she was disappointed. Within weeks of the wedding there were already whisperings about the expected pregnancy and with every month that passed without an announcement, Louise was placed under more pressure. Throughout her marriage, Louise would take regular overseas trips to spas and destinations renowned for their healthy air.

Spa trips overseas would become a regular part of Louise's routine. She would take the majority of her overseas 'health' trips with a female friend, usually Lady Sophia MacNamara. As the years progressed and there were no signs of the princess producing an heir, these trips were assumed to be Louise's attempts to improve her fertility.

Querying why there was no sign of a royal baby became a hot topic in the newspapers almost as soon as Louise signed her name on her marriage certificate. It is a sign of how accessible the people of Britain felt Princess Louise to be that she began to receive intimate letters from complete strangers offering her advice. Later she would say that she had received hundreds of such letters, many containing very private details of how her correspondents had managed to overcome infertility and what sexual tricks they had used to help them conceive. In a world where women were defined by marriage and motherhood, being a childless princess was a difficult role. Regular rumours were broadcast that the princess was expecting a child, such as the confident report in the *Manchester Evening News*, from 'our London correspondent', on 30 August 1873: 'It is stated that the Princess Louise, Marchioness of Lorne, will shortly make an addition to the house of Argyll.' Both the royal family and the Argylls also put pressure on her. In a letter of 1874 Vicky wrote to her sister that Louise and Lorne's country house, Dornden, in Kent, wanted for nothing except 'a few little fair heads looking out of the windows above – perhaps I may see that glad sight some day please God'. Louise's one ally in her childless state was her mother, who could always see the benefits of not enduring pregnancy and childbirth. Writing to Louise after the tragic death of a friend's daughter and her baby in childbirth, the queen commented that perhaps Louise's mother-in-law might realise 'that it is <u>not always</u> such happiness to have such prospects'. She added rather cryptically in the same letter that 'Lorne I know will'. She also sent Louise regular letters about boring christenings, in which the mothers looked a fright and the babies even worse.

In February 1872, she and Lorne were in Menton, a health resort in the South of France: they had a sociable time, with Alice and her husband, and several of Lorne's relations. Louise had been unwell for some weeks; the pain in her knee was troubling her again and she had been plagued by a persistent cough. She told friends she was struggling to deal with the damp greyness of a British winter and longing for sunshine and bright blue skies. Her illness was physical, but exacerbated by a feeling of emotional depression. Louise was obsessive about her health: she became renowned for the well-equipped medicine case she carried around with her, packed with homeopathic and conventional remedies, which she was always quick to offer if anyone in her party was suffering. Unfortunately the Hôtel Bellevue did not meet the princess's requirements – she described it as horribly dirty and unhygienic. Louise was especially shocked by the fact that there were no bathtubs; she loved her long, cleansing baths. The party, in the words of Louise's letters to her mother, made 'the best of it' and her spirits were raised by the warm, 'beautiful' weather. Leaving the sanitary disappointments of Menton behind them, Louise and Lorne travelled to Paris where Louise thrilled in the vibrant atmosphere of a city so recently released from the grip of the terrifying siege and a bloody war. The artists of London and Paris were closely connected and many travelled regularly between the two cities to study and to sell their works. Many young artists had fled to England during the Franco-Prussian War;[42] when Louise and Lorne arrived in Paris, they had returned and the city was buzzing with energy.

At the start of her marriage, Louise was happy to enjoy the novelty of being able to live as she chose. She had started to become involved in education reform and helped with the launch of the Girls' Public

---

[42] Among the artists who lived in England during the war were Claude Monet, who would continue to be inspired by London for decades to come, Camille Pissarro, Alfred Sisley and Charles-François Daubigny.

Day School Company, a charity with which she would remain closely involved. Both Louise and Lorne were passionate about the need for girls and boys to receive a proper education. Until now, it had been very common for girls to leave school after a few rudimentary years. Louise was determined to change this. She became friendly with one of Lorne's relations, Madeleine Wyndham (née Campbell), and was particularly interested in a new artistic project for women with which Madeleine was involved: the School of Art Needlework in South Kensington (of which Princess Helena would be appointed first president). The school aimed both to revive what was seen as a failing art, and to train respectable women, who had fallen on hard times, so that they could find employment and support their families.

Both Madeleine and Louise were patrons of Whistler, whose unusual modern work they admired. Visiting art galleries and other artists' studios was becoming a regular part of Louise's life and she often wrote to Leopold telling him about the works she had seen and the ways in which these artists ordered their studios. In the 1880s, Madeleine Wyndham and her husband, Percy, became part of a bohemian set that Louise was delighted to be involved with: the Souls. This was a group of aristocratic, educated men and women who met to talk about the issues of the day – the only rule being that the conversation should be intelligent or witty. One of their most celebrated members was Arthur Balfour, whose brother was married to Lorne's sister, Frances. Another was the beautiful Violet Manners, Duchess of Rutland, with whom Louise would become close friends. They were all in thrall to the work of Edward Burne-Jones, who was rapidly becoming one of the most famous artists in the country. The Souls were concerned with the great questions of life and death – particularly death, as they had all been greatly affected by the deaths of two of their friends, May Lyttelton and Laura Lyttelton (née Tennant – the sister of Margot Asquith). The group received its name when their friend Lord Charles Beresford commented, 'You all sit and talk about each other's souls – I shall call you The Souls.'

The new Marchioness of Lorne sometimes found it difficult to keep up with her brilliant and wealthy friends. Despite being the daughter of the queen and being married to the son of a duke, Louise had a relatively small income, especially when compared to her siblings, who had married royalty. A large number of expenses *had* to be met. It would have been impossible for a woman in her position not to have had an expensive house and the requisite number of servants. After all the necessary expenses and salaries had been covered, she had little disposable income. Her siblings pitied Louise for having to economise over things they would never have thought about.

Louise and Lorne's first home was 1 Grosvenor Crescent, owned by their relative, the Duke of Westminster. It was from this elegant town house that Louise prepared for her first London Season as a married woman. Like the other royal children, Louise had been granted by Parliament a settlement of £30,000 when she married, but unlike her siblings she had no great financial resources available from her husband as the Duke of Argyll had an expensive estate to keep. Louise learnt to economise early, discussing with her family and in-laws the merits of wallpapering versus painting – the former being cheaper – and whether it was necessary to open up all the rooms of the house when it was only she and Lorne and their small staff living there. There are no records of how Louise chose to decorate this first home, although it is known that she decided to keep changes to a minimum, in the hope that this home was temporary. Louise was not fond of the overstuffed, cluttered look that typifies so much of Victorian interior decor. She appreciated beauty and space and she wanted, more than anything, to make her home one in which she, Lorne and their friends would feel comfortable. The newly-weds were agreed that they wanted bohemian comfort, not the stiff formality of the royal homes. Louise loved bright colours – she was tired of feeling oppressed by the gloominess of mourning. Her home would be a place where creative, artistic and fascinating people could meet and talk and feel inspired.

Lorne's family had been concerned that his wife would be full of 'royal' ways and would not be content to be the wife of a marquess, but they were pleasantly surprised. The Argyll family, and the local people in their part of Scotland, were impressed with the ways in which Louise adapted to fit in with their lives. They could not have known how much she had been looking forward to being able to live with such a difference from the royal household as the Argylls' way of life provided.

They were also impressed that Louise was able to cook, sew and genuinely run a household. If a servant did not know how to do something, or the food was substandard, Louise did not just tell them to improve, she could go into the servants' hall or kitchen and put it right herself. No one had expected a princess to dirty her hands and cook dinner for the family.

It was a mark of how quickly the people of Argyllshire took to the princess that, within a year of her wedding, the 91st Argyllshire Highlanders changed their name and became known as the Princess Louise's Argyllshire Highlanders. In contrast, when the queen went to stay with the Argylls at Inveraray Castle, she managed to offend everyone – despite Louise's attempts at diplomacy. Victoria did so by peremptorily treating the Argylls' home as though it was her own and the family as her servants.

Louise's in-laws may have taken her warmly into their family, but the cracks in her marriage were already apparent. Even at this early stage, the Marquess and Marchioness of Lorne spent very little time together. Henry Ponsonby commented that it was 'absurd' that Louise and Lorne barely ever ate dinner together.

It was always assumed that Louise and her husband would soon leave Grosvenor Crescent and move into royal quarters, and in 1873 this became possible. Following the death of the Dowager Duchess of Sussex, the queen granted her daughter and son-in-law the dowager Duchess's apartments in Kensington Palace.[43] Immediately, Louise set about making them habitable. It was a long, laborious job in which she enjoyed playing an active role. The National Archives contain the many detailed accounts of the plans for Louise and Lorne's new home – and of the large amount of bureaucracy that had to be overcome for every change. Very little care had been taken over the apartments for many years; in particular, Louise insisted they had to have proper bathrooms before she and Lorne could move in. In Kensington Palace, the drains were poor, partition walls had been erected on a whim and the lighting was archaic, but that was all part of the project's charm.

The original palace had been built in the reign of King William and

---

[43] The palace, then as now, was divided into multiple apartments, which were allotted to members of the royal family.

Queen Mary, when Kensington was a small village outside London blessed with 'healthy air', so vital for the severely asthmatic king. The palace had grown up on the site of a former grand home, Nottingham House, and over the centuries had been added to and extended, with King George I hiring the best architects and designers of his day and making it one of the most important buildings in London. Since his reign, however, the palace had enjoyed only the most necessary of structural work and modernisation and Louise and her architects had an enormous task to make it suitably comfortable.

Until she was given her own home, Louise had been forced to live with her mother's choice of decor – and as one of her mother's companions, Lady Knightley, noted in her letters, Queen Victoria's idea of style was not something many others wished to emulate. In 1896, the queen's friend and former attendant would record her impressions of the queen's lack of artistic style following a recent visit to Osborne House:

Made a long expedition to the Isle of Wight to see Osborne . . .
I was immensely struck with the Indian room which had been
built, at enormous cost, since I was there and is certainly beautiful in its elaborate simplicity. But for the rest of the house –
well I never did admire Her Majesty's taste and never shall.
There are of course a good many beautiful and interesting things
scattered through the house but mixed with the most appalling
rubbish.

Every year at Christmas, the difference between Queen Victoria's and Princess Louise's taste would be made vocally apparent and the royal servants remembered constant squabbling about how things should be decorated. At last, with her own apartments, Louise had the chance to give her artistic mind full rein. She commissioned the newly fashionable architect George Aitchison to remodel the interiors of their new home. Aitchison had become famous in the 1860s for his masterful design of the artist Frederic, Lord Leighton's home. The house (which is now a museum) was a short walk away from Kensington Palace, in the newly fashionable artists' enclave of Holland Park. Louise's new home was in the heart of Aesthetic London. In Kensington Palace, Louise's interior decoration has not survived, but it is still possible at

Leighton's former home to witness how one of the leading lights of the Aesthetic movement chose to decorate his home. On entering the hall at Leighton House one walks into a visual feast of colour – rich peacock blue tiles, a brilliant gilt-covered ceiling and, at the end of the hall, the vivid blues, greens, pinks and golds of Leighton's now-famous Arab Hall. Every aspect of Leighton House was considered from the Aesthetic point of view: even the door frames are beautifully carved.

For Kensington Palace, Louise and Aitchison settled upon: 'green woodwork and green and red walls in the ante-room; brown woodwork and dull pink walls in the small dining-room; green woodwork and gold walls in the drawing-room; red woodwork and gold walls in the large dining-room'. Louise also looked to contemporary furniture designers, including Richard Norman Shaw and Edward William Godwin (the former lover of the actress Ellen Terry and the father of Ellen's two children). He was the most innovative architect and designer of the Aesthetic movement, and Louise had been introduced to him by her sister-in-law, Janey Campbell. In 1877 Godwin produced an expensive catalogue of his furniture designs; he dedicated the catalogue to Princess Louise.

At Kensington Palace Louise built her first proper studio. It was built in the palace gardens, at a secluded distance from prying eyes, and designed by Edward Godwin, who consulted both Louise and Boehm while drawing up the plans. The original plans are now in the National Archives, drawn up by Godwin's hand. The studio was designed in red brick with a green slate roof. Godwin gave the following description of it to his students:

> I built a studio 17ft high and put over it a kind of Mansard roof, with windows looking onto the garden. It is about 25 ft square and has an ante-room attached for the Marquis of Lorne, a little hall and three entrances . . . All the light is reflected so as to reduce the horizontal ceiling as much as possible. This studio seems perfectly satisfactory to the Princess, to Mr. Boehm, the sculptor (for it is a sculptor's studio), and also to myself.[44]

---

[44] Sadly, Princess Louise's studio was dismantled after her death, when the palace and its gardens were being remodelled. Princess Louise's apartments and garden

The studio was built close to the old wall of the palace garden and its roof was fitted with an enormous north window – north light being a vital source of natural light for an artist, as it does not change throughout the day, no matter what position the sun is in.[45] Once her studio was completed, Louise had her own place in which she could work as she pleased on her sculpture and where she could meet Boehm without fear of gossip.

It was not only her introduction to the artistic elite that made Louise happy: she revelled in the chance to run her own home. In the early years of their marriage, the Lornes also had their country house, Dornden. Vicky, in a homesick moment writing to her sister from Prussia, recalled, 'You cannot think with _what_ pleasure I remember the lovely balmy sunny evening when I saw your sweet little country house in its nest of ivy, how picturesque, how inviting it seemed!' The queen was less impressed than Vicky, reports had reached the queen that local newspapers were commenting on the influx of people visiting the area, in the hope of seeing Louise, and she was concerned that her daughter would be unable to move around without being 'molested'. One of Louise and Lorne's frequent, and welcome, visitors to Dornden was Ronnie Gower.

Gower was actually Lorne's uncle, but as they had been born just two days apart they were more like brothers than uncle and nephew. Gower was a charming and amusing man, who won over Queen Victoria far more easily than most. The queen wrote in her diary, shortly after Louise's engagement, that Lord Ronald was 'very pleasing & amiable'. Gower noted Louise's strong attachment to her home (which Lorne nonetheless sold within a couple of years, despite Louise's pleas to him not to) and wrote,

> it is pleasant to see the busy German housewife strongly developed in her here; she bustles about all day, looking after and superintending all the domestic arrangements, carving at meals,

---

were being divided in two, and the studio was considered a hindrance to the division.

[45] A good example of a 'north light window' at an artist's studio almost contemporary to that of Princess Louise's can still be seen on the house once lived in by the artist Marcus Stone at 8 Melbury Road, a short walk from Kensington Palace.

and making herself generally useful. After dinner we stroll out in the grounds of the pretty little domain, and visit the stables and the kitchen-garden; and generally finish the evening by a game of billiards or pool, on a capital table, given them, when they were married, by the Prince of Wales.

Louise always loved the domestic duties she had been taught in childhood and amazed Lorne's sisters and nieces by teaching them basic household tasks, including how to sew on buttons.

There could also have been another reason why Louise so loved Dornden. Until recently, the house next door to Dornden had been owned by Sir Charles Locock and Frederick, Mary and Henry had been regular visitors. At the end of August 1874, Mary Locock died after a long illness; at the end of her life the family were staying at a hotel in Seveonaks, and she died there. Louise would have known that Henry Locock would be left motherless very soon. With the family staying close to Dornden, the princess could spend time with her son without anyone becoming suspicious. It would be quite acceptable for her to want to help take care of the grieving son of a family friend.

Louise's obvious contentment in her new life prompted the queen to exclaim that the only one of her daughters she could rely on was Beatrice, as 'no married daughter is of any use'. Louise did, however, continue with her public appearances and assisted her mother when needed. In 1873, she was present when the Shah of Persia and the Grand Vizier of the Ottoman Empire visited England. In his book about his mother, Lady Augusta Stanley, the Dean of Windsor commented: 'In June of 1873 the Shah of Persia came to England and although he later amused Aldershot by appearing on a horse with tail dyed pink, and . . . was said to have slaughtered a sheep as a sacrifice on the floor of his room at Buckingham Palace, his arrival was a splendid occasion.' The dean's mother's journal recorded a conversation she had had with the queen about his visit, 'Does your Majesty know one of the Shah's titles "Asylum of the Universe"!!' Louise was fascinated by the visiting dignitaries and their entourage. This was the era when the 'exotic' and 'oriental' were fashionable artistic subjects and Louise was enthralled by the different materials and styles of clothing that the Persian party wore. After they had left, she painted a portrait of the Shah from memory.

In Queen Victoria's family, dogs were considered as important as people and many were immortalised in portraits. *Princess Louise often travelled with her dogs and even took Frisky on her honeymoon.*

Even after Prince Albert's death, he remained a constant presence in the royal children's lives. This family photograph of Bertie and Alix's wedding day includes a sculpted portrait bust of the deceased prince consort.

Princess Louise and Prince Leopold were always the closest of allies – especially when it came to their shared dislike of Queen Victoria's most trusted servant, John Brown (pictured below with the queen and Princess Louise). It has long been rumoured that Brown was the queen's lover.

Princess Louise was an integral part of the London art scene.
Her closest friends included her tutor – and lover – Joseph
Edgar Boehm (above) and the flamboyant James Abbott
McNeill Whistler (self-portrait, below).

Windsor Castle by Whistler. Princess Louise was a great admirer of Whistler's work, but many of their contemporaries considered his art controversially avant garde.

Louise's statue of her mother at Kensington Palace gained critical acclaim.

This ring was a present to Duckworth from Louise and Leopold.

The Reverend Robinson Duckworth was Prince Leopold's trusted tutor, and he became one of Princess Louise's close friends.

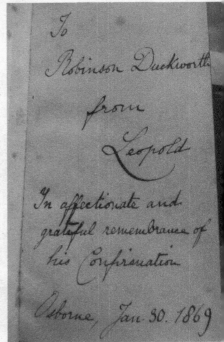

To
Robinson Duckworth
from
Leopold
In affectionate and grateful remembrance of his Confirmation

Osborne, Jan. 30. 1869

The inscription is from a bible given to Duckworth by Prince Leopold.

This sculpture of a baby may have been by Princess Louise; it was a present from the queen to Sir Charles Locock, whose son Frederick adopted the baby Henry Frederick Leicester Locock.

Henry photographed as a child, with a border possibly painted by Princess Louise, and in his army uniform.

Louise posed for the society photographer Alexander Bassano several times. This photograph dates from the early 1880s and emphasises the princess's role as a leader of fashion.

Later that year Louise travelled incognito, with her maid but without Lorne, to a party in a chalet in Switzerland. Henry Ponsonby wrote tellingly to his wife, 'I believe [Louise and Lorne] get on as well as possible' – but they got on much better when they were apart, free to pursue their own interests. The Swiss chalet was owned by Jacques Blumenthal, the pianist and composer, and his wife Léonie. The guests included Gertrude Jekyll, with whom Louise became good friends, and her brother Walter.[46] The guests at the Blumenthals' chalet were pleased to discover a princess without pretensions. As on her honeymoon, Louise travelled as Lady Sundridge, one of her favoured incognito names, and was nicknamed 'Hoheit' by her fellow guests. (Gertrude was nicknamed 'Stiegel'.) The group spent their days sketching, walking and enjoying the gardens, while in the evenings they played games, listened to music and sang to entertain one another. The Blumenthals had invited one of their artist friends to be the art 'tutor', the impressively named Hercules Brabazon Brabazon (a friend of John Singer Sargent and soon to become one of the New English Art Club). Writing to his sister about the party, Brabazon told her what a good artist Louise was and commented, 'we are all a most pleasant party'. In common with several of Louise's artistic friends, Brabazon was homosexual, something that was no secret to his friends.

Several of Lorne's friends were also known to be gay, including Ronnie Gower, who was said to have inspired Oscar Wilde's character Lord Henry Wotton in *The Picture of Dorian Gray* (1891). Lorne was an important part of Ronnie's circle of friends, which included the artist Frank Miles (who once shared a house with Oscar Wilde), Wilde himself, Frank Shackleton[47] and other members of the homosexual 'underworld'. It has been claimed – usually by historians who insist that Lorne was heterosexual – that neither Louise nor Lorne knew Ronnie was gay until much later in their friendship, and that they

[46] Walter Jekyll was a friend of Robert Louis Stevenson, who used his friend's surname in one of his most famous books, *The Strange Case of Dr Jekyll and Mr Hyde* (1886).

[47] The brother of the Arctic explorer Sir Ernest Shackleton. Frank was known to be gay, and believed to be a criminal involved in the theft of the Irish Crown Jewels in 1907. According to rumours, Louise's brother, by then King Edward VII, suppressed the investigation of the theft in order to protect Louise and Lorne, Shackleton and others of his friends from being implemented in the scandal.

were deeply shocked when they discovered it. This is an unconvincing assertion. Ronnie was a regular visitor to their home, they travelled overseas together, and Lorne and Ronnie had been holiday companions for years; Lorne also went on holiday with Ronnie and his lovers. Amongst his friends, Ronnie made no secret of his sexuality. That a couple firmly ensconced in the world of Aestheticism, the Souls and the artistic elite of London and Paris could possibly have been shocked by the realisation that someone they knew very well was gay, seems highly unlikely.

Although in the twenty-first century we look back with hindsight at how homophobic Victoria's Britain was, as the queen presided over laws to make life as unpleasant as possible for homosexual men (while refusing to believe that homosexual women existed), those people living at the time, in the artistic worlds of music, the theatre, literature and fine art, would have known that certain members of their circle were homosexual. It was expected not to be talked about to strangers, and behaviour was expected to be discreet, but no one in that circle would genuinely have been 'shocked' at the discovery that Lord Ronald Gower, a 'confirmed bachelor', was interested in men rather than women.

While Louise and Lorne were fitting into each other's lives – working out the best way to live as individuals, often separately, within their marriage – Louise's siblings were getting married, having children or, in the case of Beatrice, being thoroughly cosseted to the point of stiflement and not permitted even to think of marrying and leaving her mother. In 1874, Prince Alfred married Grand Duchess Marie of Russia, the daughter of the Tsar. Very few family members were able to attend the wedding, which took place in Russia, and Louise did not meet her new sister-in-law until the couple had been married for some weeks. The two women did not get on well. Marie did not endear herself to many people in the family by insisting that as the daughter of an imperial tsar she ranked higher than anyone else in the family. The queen, however, was won over by her new daughter-in-law and wrote, when the couple had left, that 'everyone' must like Marie but 'not one likes' Affie. As usual, she was the harshest critic of all when it came to her own children. The marriage was to prove miserably unhappy and Affie would sink into a world of alcoholism and depression.

Affie was getting married, Beatrice was to be confirmed and Helena, who had four children, was preparing for motherhood again, although she would be tragically thwarted twice, giving birth to a son who died after a few weeks, in 1876, and having a stillborn son in 1877. Meanwhile Bertie was getting into debt – and having his scandals gossiped about all over London (*The Times* published an article about his debt-ridden lifestyle). He was also made a Grand Master in the Freemasons. His mother was not amused by Bertie at this date, writing to Louise that he was 'not in a satisfactory state – so stout and puffy'.

Almost all the royal children seemed to be creating lives for them-selves, except for Beatrice – who was still young enough for her mother's possessive behaviour to be considered acceptable – and Leopold, who was hampered in his bid for independence by debilitating ill health. The extent of the pain Leopold's condition caused him was made explicit in letters to Louise. In 1870 he had written to her: 'I am mad with pain . . . I am in such agonies at this moment', and 'I go on as usual suffering frightfully, at this moment I am in agonies of pain; my knee gets worse daily and I get more desperate daily.' At times the pain was so bad that he would have to break off from writing; he told Louise that he was 'tortured' and worried that the constant pain would cause him to become insane. That Queen Victoria was horribly jealous of the closeness of Louise and Leopold, to the point of cruelty, was demonstrated in the winter of 1874–5.

As expected, Louise was spending Christmas of 1874 with Lorne's family, in Scotland. The queen and several of her children were at Windsor, when Leopold became extremely ill. He was desperate to see Louise and regularly called out for her. When she heard he was unwell, Louise was equally anxious to visit him – but she had to request permission from her mother, as queen, to leave Scotland and visit her brother. The queen refused to grant her permission, ordering her daughter to stay with her husband's family. The distraught princess was trapped in Scotland, a long journey away from her ailing brother, who she knew would be getting more ill from the stress of not seeing her. Major Robert Collins, Prince Leopold's tutor, recorded his disgust at Queen Victoria's callousness and lack of maternal feelings. He knew that Louise's presence was urgently needed and was incensed to witness the deliberate cruelty of his monarch, who seemed to take a malicious pleasure in being able to punish her son and daughter for the disobedience of loving each other more than they loved her. Major Collins even tried, bravely, to reason with the queen, but she was stubbornly resolute. He was a good friend to both the prince and princess, sending secret letters to Louise to keep her up to date with Leopold's condition.

Despite the queen's letters to Louise, insisting Leopold was in no danger, the household knew that the young prince might die at any time; as Major Collins wrote to Walter Stirling, Dr Jenner thought that Leopold was 'dangerously ill'. When Leopold lost a large amount of blood in a haemorrhage from his bowels, the doctors were convinced he was dying. The queen finally relented and allowed Louise to begin the time-consuming journey from Scotland. Beatrice wrote to tell her to come and she recorded Leopold's 'look of delight' on hearing that he would finally be able to see his favourite sister. It defies belief to think that a mother should take such an active part in ensuring the unhappiness of two of her children. Major Collins was convinced that Louise would arrive too late; he confessed in a letter to a friend that his feelings towards Queen Victoria had become 'a loathing dislike' which he concealed with great 'difficulty'.

Louise reached Windsor in time to see Leopold make a very slow and painful return to health. After Louise's arrival the queen remained domineering. Louise wanted to be useful in the sickroom by helping to nurse her brother, as she had done so many times before, but their mother refused. The queen also enforced a strict limit on how much time the siblings were allowed to spend together, permitting them around an hour of contact a day; however, when the queen was not present, the doctors allowed Louise to visit for as long as she liked. On those visits, she read Leopold his favourite books and they talked for hours. She wrote to her brother-in-law, Archie Campbell, 'I am a good deal with my poor brother . . . he takes interest in all that goes on.' The whole household noticed how much happier Leopold was when his sister was around, and how much his health improved under her care. The household was in collusion with the siblings, keeping their time together a secret from the queen. Major Collins noted, 'It was an immense pleasure to him to have his sister sitting with him.' As soon as Leopold was out of danger, the queen sent Louise back to her husband; as Collins wrote in a letter, 'Alas! She is gone again. The Queen was I think waxing jealous, at any rate she wouldn't let her tarry any longer.' A few months later, the queen sent Vicky a letter in which she warned her that she would discover as her children grew up that they would be a bitter disappointment to her.

In the summer of 1875, the queen would again attempt to exert her control over both Leopold and Louise, this time attempting to gain Louise as an ally in a bid to curb Leopold's attempts to gain independence. He was studying at Oxford and had, without telling his mother, gone to London for a few days to stay with Louise and Lorne. The queen was incensed that she had not been consulted and insisted that Leopold's health made it impossible for him to live an adult life free from his mother's strictures. Louise responded to this furious letter tactfully, but included the words: 'at his age he cannot unfortunately be told [what] to do, and not to do . . . Leo is old enough to use his own discretion.' In the letter, the queen had accused Lorne of being a bad influence on both Louise and Leopold because he subscribed to that 'unfortunate idea which all British young men, especially in these days, have of being independent of their parents and doing just what they like'. Louise defended her husband (and herself) hotly against such an accusation and told her mother that she had burned the letter as it was so upsetting (the letter survives only because the queen kept a copy of most of her correspondence).

It has often been claimed that Leopold's first love was Alice Liddell, Charles Lutwidge Dodgson's inspiration for his book *Alice in Wonderland*, whom he met in Oxford. Alice was the daughter of the Dean of Christ Church, Oxford, and Leopold had met her when he arrived in Oxford as an undergraduate in 1872 (when Alice Liddell was twenty). The two certainly became very good friends and in a few years' time Alice would name her first son Leopold, and ask the prince to be his godfather. Leopold attempted to assert his independence on a number of occasions while at Oxford. Each time, this infuriated the queen and she inevitably blamed Louise for being the bad influence on Leopold and encouraging him to defy her.

While Leopold was at Oxford, Bertie set off on a trip Leopold could only have dreamt about: a tour of India. (The queen complained throughout the trip how 'boring' Bertie's letters to her were.) On 15 October 1875 Louise recorded the circumstances of her brother's departure for her mother:

The last day the 11th was a most painful one for Bertie, and I know he was thankful when it was over. He was dreadfully overcome when he parted with the children; and he said goodbye to all his servants and Alix's people. They drove in an open carriage to the station, and there were crowds of people all along the streets, and in the station. Dear Alix kept up wonderfully, she was fighting with herself all the time. On her return from Calais she was looking calmer, and better than I could have expected, but she was very tired; she was looking forward to a quiet time with the children at Sandringham [this comment was perhaps written to stop the queen insisting her daughter-in-law and grandchildren stay with her in Bertie's absence]. I never thought dear Bertie would have felt it so deeply as he did leaving, it was dreadful to see him but at the same time it brought out all his warm kind nature, which was very touching to see.

In his absence, Bertie's siblings took on some of the duties the Prince of Wales would have been expected to undertake. Louise was a great success when she launched HMS *Inflexible* at Portsmouth docks on 28 April 1876. The *Inflexible* was clad in thick iron and carried bigger guns than any British warship before her. Shortly after launching this 'monster' of a ship, the princess had a lifeboat named after her at Campbeltown in Scotland. She was not there for its launch, but Lorne was; once again, they were apart. Usually Louise and Lorne spent several months of the year at Inveraray; this year was an exception. Neither wanted to go to Lorne's ancestral home, probably because they did not want to be forced to spend so much time together. Louise came up with an excuse that she knew her mother would agree with: 'I mentioned in one of my former letters that one of the elder girls was I think <u>unintentionally</u> rather rude to me.' This letter neatly let Louise out of a winter in Scotland, as far as her mother was concerned. Instead of going to Inveraray, Louise wanted to go to Dornden. As she explained to her mother, with more than a trace of irony about the queen's insistence on visiting Balmoral every year: 'I hope to be happy at Dornden. For two years we were 7 months in Scotland, life becomes monotonous if one does the same thing every year.'

After Bertie returned from India in May 1876, the Prime Minister,

Benjamin Disraeli, announced that the queen would also be known as Empress of India. Although the title was not made official until 1877, it was a controversial topic of discussion for a year beforehand. Louise wrote to her mother about the furore on 14 March 1876, attempting both to give advice and to soothe her mother's anger: 'There is a great deal of bother and talk about your title of Empress. The people will not understand it. They think you wish always to be called so in future, instead of Queen, it is too stupid; of course there is no title so fine as that of our British Queen: and calling us the Imperial Family instead of Royal gives a very <u>unEnglish</u> sound and which the people are so against but I always say that you never <u>thought</u> of such a thing.' Louise was far more in touch with the people than her mother.

CHAPTER 14

Politics and Aestheticism

You have been one of my <u>few true</u> friends that I have looked up
to all my life & from whom I have always had encouragement
& sympathy & from whom I have learnt much besides art tho
[*sic*] art was the foundation of all things. When I am married as
I have the great happiness of remaining in my beloved country
& amongst my friends & acquaintances I shall hope often to see
you & that our interest in each other[']s works will not diminish
but increase if possible.

Princess Louise to Edward Corbould, 25 October 1870

In the years since their wedding, Lorne had been pursuing his political
career, as a Liberal MP. It was a career he would eventually excel at
(though he would have to give it up when he inherited the dukedom
from his father and entered the House of Lords). Louise was proud
of her husband's egalitarian principles and shared most of his political
beliefs. While her mother firmly supported Disraeli, Louise's husband
joined Gladstone's party.

By the mid-1870s, Princess Louise was not only the daughter of the
queen or the wife of an MP, she was at the forefront of the Aesthetic
world and one of the most fashionable women in London. In 1877,
Arthur Sullivan (of Gilbert and Sullivan fame) wrote enthusiastically
to his mother about 'My Princess Louise' coming to his house the
next day and all the preparations he needed his mother to help him
make for Louise's visit. 'I had better do all I can to make her happy!
Bring a *lot of roses* – never mind what it costs – I don't get her every
day. I want nothing but roses about the rooms – masses of them, and
one in every single thing I have got. Hooray! Blow the expense.' Louise

embraced Aestheticism even more than she had the style of dressing in a Pre-Raphaelite-inspired manner. She met many of the top artists and craftspeople of the movement and was renowned on informal occasions for eschewing the conventional family jewels worn by her sisters in favour of modern jewellery designed by master artisans she had met through her artistic friends (including Carlo Giuliano and Robert Phillips).

As her husband immersed himself in party politics, Louise continued to work with numerous charities and to undertake 'good works', not simply opening new schools and hospitals but taking an active role in helping to fund-raise and set them up. At this time, Princess Helena was a vice-president of the children's hospital in Great Ormond Street, London and enlisted her sister's help with the hospital. In addition to raising funds and awareness, Helena and Louise sewed and knitted items of clothing for the children and encouraged their friends to do the same – many of the children arrived at the hospital dressed in what were little more than rags.

No longer cowed by her family, as she had been during the incident with Josephine Butler, Louise set about meeting the people she wanted to meet – regardless of whether society deemed them 'acceptable' or not. George Eliot (Mary Ann Evans) was considered a scandalous woman no 'respectable' lady of the time should have agreed to consort with, because Eliot had fallen in love with George Henry Lewes, a married man. Lewes's wife was already in a relationship with another man, so the situation was worked out amicably between the two couples; yet London was scandalised that Eliot and Lewes chose to live together 'in sin', and even more scandalised when it became apparent that they refused to be ashamed of it. Louise was a fan of George Eliot's work, so she asked a mutual friend, George Goschen, to invite the author to a party. Then, breaking all expected protocol, Louise introduced herself to the author instead of waiting for a formal presentation. The two women talked for a long time and Louise was obviously entranced by Eliot's intelligence and independent spirit. Her mother would have been incensed had she known.

Louise did follow her parents' example in becoming a patron of many of her favourite artists. That Louise was moving in circles which included Millais and his great friend and rival Frederic, Lord Leighton can be seen in a letter from Bertie at the start of her marriage. In

1872 he thanked her for sending him descriptions of her visits to the studios of Millais and Leighton. The princess supported Whistler through very public scandal and serious financial problems; she was one of the first people he invited to view his now-famous Peacock Room in 1876. She also remained friends with Dante Gabriel Rossetti, when he was already considered 'mad' by many of his former friends (he attempted suicide in 1872 and was known to take drugs). Rossetti was used to hearing unfounded rumours about his behaviour and most of the time he did nothing to correct them, partly because he could not be bothered to concern himself with them and partly because they added to his aura of artistic eccentricity. On one occasion, however, he went out of his way to extract an apology. An article had appeared in *The World* in which it was claimed that when Princess Louise had called on him, Rossetti had told his servant to tell her that he was not at home and nor was he at the command of royalty. Rossetti wrote to the paper and demanded that a correction be printed. He also sent a letter to *The Times* to set the record straight, in which he wrote: 'It is true enough that I do not run after great people on account of their mere social position, but I am, I hope, never rude to them; and the man who could rebuff the Princess Louise must be a curmudgeon indeed.'

In 1877, the Aesthetic world was thrilled by the opening of a new art gallery, one that would rival the stuffy formality of the Royal Academy. It was founded by Sir Coutts Lindsay and his wife Lady Blanche. Both were talented amateur artists; in addition, he had the business acumen and she had the money – Blanche was an heiress to the Rothschild fortune. The gallery was intended to look like a fashionable and wealthy home. As well as the works of art, there was a library and a billiard room in which visitors were invited to make themselves at home. The gallery was heralded as a much-needed saviour of modern artists. Oscar Wilde wrote an article in which he described the idea behind it:

The origin of this Gallery is as follows: About a year ago the idea occurred to Sir Coutts Lindsay of building a public gallery, in which, untrammelled by the difficulties or meannesses of 'Hanging Committees,' he could exhibit to the lovers of art the works of certain great living artists side by side: a gallery in which the student would not have to struggle through an endless monotony of mediocre works in order to reach what was worth looking at; one in which the people of England could have the opportunity of judging of the merits of at least one great master of painting, whose pictures had been kept from public exhibition by the jealousy and ignorance of rival artists.

Louise was amongst the stars of the artistic world who on 1 May 1877 attended the opening of the much-anticipated Grosvenor Gallery on fashionable Bond Street. It was a glamorous and avant-garde night at which the luminaries of the artistic and musical worlds were prominently in attendance. Most of the conventional newspapers and magazines wrote cool or scathing reviews of the inaugural exhibition, but for the artistic world the gallery was one of the most exciting things to have happened to London in years. Despite the hostile press, the gallery had its own pet writers: Oscar Wilde and Henry James both attended the opening (Wilde in a 'cello-shaped' coat made specially for the occasion) and wrote glowing reviews. The Grosvenor Gallery was intended to be a fashionable meeting place and, as such, it boasted of being the first commercial art gallery in London to have its own restaurant (or 'dining room', as it was called, to continue the theme of visiting a fashionable home).

Rapidly, the Grosvenor Gallery became *the* place to be seen. Because it was a joint effort of husband and wife, and because Blanche had as forceful a personality as her husband, the Grosvenor Gallery became renowned as one of the few exhibition spaces in London to which both male and female artists were encouraged to bring their works. Artists whose works could be seen on the walls included Louise Jopling, G.F. Watts, Marie Spartali-Stillman, Edward Burne-Jones, Evelyn De Morgan, Lawrence and Laura Alma-Tadema, and Louise's friends, Henrietta and Clara Montalba. One star in attendance was John Everett Millais, who had strongly encouraged the Lindsays to open the gallery in opposition to the Royal Academy. Both Louise and Boehm exhibited at the Grosvenor regularly and Louise became close friends with Sir Coutts and Lady Blanche Lindsay. This new and fashionable gallery proved an immediate success and was recognised at once as the spiritual home of the Aesthetic movement. The Lindsays knew they had made it when Gilbert and Sullivan parodied Aestheticism in their 1881 operetta *Patience*, in which a song includes the repeated line: 'Greenery-yallery, Grosvenor Gallery' ('greenery yallery' being the name the composers gave to the unique yellowish-green paint that the Lindsays had had made for the walls of the gallery).

It was also in 1877 that Louise presented the bust of her mother to the Grosvenor Gallery's rival, the Royal Academy – she was being careful not to identify herself with only one artistic movement. Shortly after the opening of the Grosvenor Gallery, Louise took Bertie to view Millais's latest exhibit, *Effie Deans*, which was on display at the King Street Gallery. Louise wanted to see the painting because it was by her friend and an artist she admired; Bertie because the model for the painting (based on the tragic heroine of Sir Walter Scott's novel *The Heart of Midlothian*) was Lillie Langtry. He wanted to meet the model: he did, and she became one of the most famous of his many lovers.

Louise was also making regular visits to Scotland. In the autumn of 1877, the entire Campbell household, including Louise, narrowly escaped being burned to death when a fire swept through Inveraray Castle. The fire was spotted in the early hours of the morning when one of the duke's tenants, a fisherman, woke up and suddenly had a desire to go out and check on his boats. He raised the alarm and, astonishingly, no one was killed. Every member of the household was alerted, and Lorne was hailed a hero when he returned into the burning castle without a thought for himself having heard that there were people still inside. Louise's great contribution was to take control of the fire-fighting and suggest they form a human chain to pass water buckets; later she attributed her suggestion to a story she remembered Prince Albert telling her in childhood. In letters afterwards, members of the Campbell family and household praised her for her quick thinking (she had a clear head, when most of them were still in shock) and it was said that her idea had saved a great many of the family's treasured possessions. Newspapers around the country reported that the duke owned a fire engine which was 'brought up with all speed, and, after the hose had been adjusted and led up to the roof, a stream of water was soon directed upon the building. A column of flame was now rising from the central tower the roof of which had fallen with a tremendous crash . . . By great exertions all the most valuable paintings, and most of the furniture, books, &c., were saved from the fire, though much spoiled by the water and debris.' Although the castle was devastated, it was not completely ruined, thanks to the fact that the walls were extremely thick and the staircases were made of stone.

Louise wrote to her mother about the fire:

All was perfectly quiet and peaceful till about 5 o'clock a.m. when I was woke by our big dog barking and making a great fuss. A few minutes after, Mrs Campbell of Isla's Scotch maid came to the door, and one of the men shouted 'the castle is on fire' – then Lorne woke, and jumped up and said we must be off that moment (not knowing whereabouts the fire was) – and so with only our dressing gowns, not even slippers, we went downstairs and found all the inner part of the Hall was illuminated, and large sparks falling as we went; when we passed through the big hall, where the billiard-table is, large bits of the flaming roof fell on the furniture and set it in a blaze; most of the roof fell in about three minutes after Lorne and I had passed. All the others passed outside . . . It was a bitter cold night; as the morning broke, we found all the hills white with snow . . . It was a curious sight to see us all huddled together, walking away from the burning house . . . Not a being knew (I mean those in the Castle) that it was on fire, till alarmed by some people outside. A fisherman was the first to see it . . . Had he been a quarter of an hour later we should none of us been able to get away.

Following the fire, the castle was completely rebuilt – but the castle today dates from much more recent times, as another devastating fire would decimate the building in the 1970s. Inveraray Castle remains the seat of the Dukes of Argyll, but it is now open to the public and remains proud of its association with Princess Louise. Amongst the items on display are an equestrian sculpture of the Black Prince by the princess, some of Louise's baby shoes (red ballet-style pumps), a presentation slice of Louise and Lorne's wedding cake (adorned not with the happy couple, as Vicky and Fritz's cake had been, but with a medallion of Queen Victoria) and the gorgeous clothes worn by Louise at the coronation of King Edward VII and Queen Alexandra in 1902. The dress shows how remarkably slim Louise was in late middle age; it is lavishly decorated in gold embroidery and gemstones, together with a velvet and ermine robe. The dress seems surprisingly sexy for such a solemn occasion.

After their return to London, Louise threw herself into her work, trying to finish items to be exhibited both at the Royal Academy Summer Exhibition and the Grosvenor Gallery, in the same year. Louise had become close friends with Blanche Lindsay. The two women would paint and sketch together and talk for hours and Blanche painted a portrait of the princess. Louise was welcomed into their circle, and also became friendly with Sir Coutts Lindsay's cousin, a fellow artist, Violet Lindsay (who would become the Duchess of Rutland and one of the Souls). Violet was renowned as a great beauty and Louise immortalised her looks in a small statue; it was reviewed by the *New York Times* in 1879 while it was being shown at the Grosvenor Gallery. It was described as 'one of the prettiest bits of sculpture [in] the exhibition'. The princess had seldom been happier, her life was full of things and people she loved and she was free to create great works of art. When Disraeli attended a dinner party at the Belgravia home of Percy and Madeleine Wyndham, Louise was one of the guests, as was Robert Browning. Disraeli, himself a well-received novelist, wrote afterwards that at the dinner no one talked about anything except 'pictures and art and Raffaelle'. For years Louise had longed to be a part of this world: now, finally, she had her wish. It helped that one of her sisters-in-law was the beautiful Aesthetic beauty Janey Campbell (née Callander), the wife of Lorne's younger brother Archie. The couple had been married since 1869, but marriage to the son of a duke did not prevent Janey from keeping up with her artistic friends and their circle and she was thrilled to be able to present the princess to so many of her friends.

Not everyone in the artistic elite, however, was pleased to welcome Louise. Many considered that she was accepted only because she was royal, and felt she had not done enough to 'prove' herself as an artist, despite her training. There were many who refused to believe that any of her work was her own, but there were also plenty of artists who recognised the princess's talent and treated her as a fellow artist; the latter consisted mainly of those who had worked alongside her and knew that she did not, as was rumoured, give every one of her projects to be finished by her tutor. Those who were not so close to her wanted to scorn a princess for daring to attempt to be bohemian. One who was scathing about Louise's work was William Rossetti, the only non-professional artist of the Pre-Raphaelite Brotherhood. He was the younger brother of Dante Rossetti, and lived his life in awe of his sibling and his talented friends. William longed to be an artist and described himself as one, but in reality he was the chronicler of the group, the man of letters who dabbled with painting but would never be an artist. By the late 1870s, he was filled with self-importance and jealously guarded his position as the ultimate authority on Pre-Raphaelitism in particular and art in general.

In 1878 William Rossetti reviewed an exhibition at the Grosvenor Gallery, at which Louise had exhibited *Geraint and Enid*; he wrote contemptuously that it attracted the 'most attention' of any of the sculptural exhibits, not because of its style but for being the work of a princess: 'There are seven horses close together here, and an eighth in the distance: of course, anything but an easy matter for even a skillful [sic] hand to manage. The movement is instantaneous, not however particularly vigorous; but the work of a lady and a princess is assessed from a point of view rather different from that which applies to a professional sculptor.' As a member of the royal family, Louise was prohibited from becoming a professional artist, but amongst her peers she was considered amateur only in name. She insisted on being paid for her work and on being taken seriously.

Louise exhibited paintings as well as sculpture at the Grosvenor Gallery, and was gratified, some years after William Rossetti's damning review, to read in the *Illustrated London News* the following description of her portrait of Colonel Charles Lindsay:[48] 'The work is far above that which one is accustomed to find amongst amateurs' (again, her royal status had refused her the privilege of being called a professional). A couple of years later, in 1882, the London correspondent for *The Argus* in Melbourne, Australia, wrote glowingly of Louise's portrait of her friend Clara Montalba: 'The "prentice-hand" is not seen here at all; the work is firm and assured, full of character, and the colouring is of a superior order.' (The same critic praised the work of Louise Jopling and Walter Crane, but was scathing about paintings exhibited by Lord Leighton, Lawrence Alma-Tadema and Edward Burne-Jones.) Despite an undercurrent of sniping from those artists and critics who

---

[48] An uncle of Sir Coutts Lindsay.

disliked a princess attempting to enter their sphere, Louise made strong and lasting friendships within the London art world. Everything was turning out as she had hoped, but, frustratingly, just as she was making her entrance into the 'real' world she had so longed to be a part of, her life was about to be turned upside down.

At the end of May 1878, Lorne's beloved mother, Elizabeth, died. The family was distraught. Lorne and his siblings had adored their mother and they would be horrified when their father, the duke, announced his second marriage less than a year after Elizabeth's death. Like several members of his family, Lorne had long believed that he had the gift of 'second sight' and, shortly after Elizabeth's funeral, he had a vision. He told Louise that he had been drifting in a boat on a quiet loch when he saw with perfect clarity Disraeli offering him a post overseas. Some months later, his psychic vision came true.[49] In the autumn of 1878, Lorne was invited to become the next Governor-General of Canada.

---

[49] Lorne's pyschic abilities were not always so finely honed. One Christmas, after reading a verse that came out of a cracker, he became obsessed with the morbid belief that he was going to die at the age of sixty. For years, he would tell everyone that he had a presentiment about his death. When he lived beyond his sixtieth birthday, he quickly changed his 'prediction' to the age of seventy.

CHAPTER 15

The first year in Canada

When [Princess Louise] returns to England, she will be able to boast herself above all her sisters. She will have seen more of the world than any of them. She has seen the Continent pretty well. She knows Canada better than most wives of Governors-General, for she is an artist and strays into its forests. She has also seen something already of the States, and she is now on her way to California where she will discover what a *canon* is, and learn something of the people who live in the wilds.

Portsmouth Evening News, 12 December 1882

Shortly after Lorne's appointment as Governor-General of Canada was announced, Lady Dufferin, whose husband was just coming to the end of his time as Governor-General, confided to Henry Ponsonby that she did not think Louise and Lorne's appointment was a good idea. As Ponsonby recorded, 'the real difficulty was, how Louise would treat people in Canada – if as royalty, there will be trouble, but if in the same way Lady Dufferin did, they will be flattered'. The newspapers had more faith in Louise than Ponsonby; as the *Montreal Gazette* declared: 'With a Princess as chief lady of the dominion, her Royal mother would be as fully represented as by a Prince, and by all accounts, Her Royal Highness is . . . just the one we should choose . . . Accomplished, intellectual, and amiable.'

Despite the fact that this was, at last, Louise's chance of the independence she had craved for so many years, she was nonetheless perturbed at the thought of going to Canada. This was not because she feared the people would not take to her, but because she was leaving all her friends, her family and Boehm to spend five years on the other side of the world with a husband she was not in love with. If she and Lorne had had a different kind of marriage, the prospect would have been less daunting. On 7 November 1878, Louise gave a farewell dinner party at Kensington Palace. The guests included a saddened Leopold, the Coutts Lindsays, and Benjamin Disraeli who noted that Lorne was 'rampant' with excitement but that Louise was 'in low spirits'. Lord Ronnie Gower also wrote in his diary that '[Louise is] very sorry to go and looks forward apparently with great dislike to her life there.'

Louise was leaving London at a time when the artistic world was in uproar and when Aestheticism was reaching its most exciting heights. Before she left, however, she helped her friend Whistler with a problem he was having. He had commissioned their mutual friend Edward Godwin to design his new home, the White House on Tite Street, but was having trouble with the Board of Works, which was reluctant to agree to such a modern style of building. In his correspondence, Whistler recorded: '[Princess Louise] greatly sympathized – and I made a grand stroke! I said that if her Royal Highness would only drive past and say how beautiful she thought the house that of course that would put an end to the whole trouble – She laughed saying that she didn't believe her influence was [as] strong as that! but afterwards said in a reflective way that "Lorne knows Sir James I think" . . .' Louise persuaded Lorne to speak to the head of the Board of Works and Whistler and Godwin were granted permission to carry on with the building works.

The day after Louise's farewell party, Whistler wrote a chatty but poignant letter to Louise which he sent with one of his paintings as a gift (a landscape which he took great pains to point out was without fog, unlike so many of his London scenes). Although purporting to be formal, it is a teasing, flirtatious letter, which demonstrates how at ease Whistler felt with her: 'Madam – I feel it incumbent upon myself, as your Painter – by devotion, if not by office – to right myself, if possible, in the eyes of my Royal Mistress.' The letter was written while Whistler was embroiled in a famous court case with John Ruskin, the art critic who had accused Whistler of 'flinging a pot of paint in the public's face'. The painting Ruskin so abhorred is now considered a masterpiece, *Nocturne in Black and Gold: The Falling Rocket* (1875). In 1877 it was exhibited at the Grosvenor Gallery, which was where Ruskin saw it. He then published his scathing letter, in which along with his damning description he called Whistler a 'coxcomb'. The artist was incensed and sued the critic. The court case divided artistic London. Both men were well known and had many friends and colleagues in common. Ruskin, who was beginning to suffer mental health problems, was decreed by his doctors unfit to appear in court and an unhappy Edward Burne-Jones was deputised to appear on his behalf. As Ruskin's legal team instructed him to say, Burne-Jones gave as his expert artistic opinion that the painting was a 'failure' in its effort to recreate night and he did not consider it worth the asking price of 200 guineas. When cross-examined, however, he was compelled to comment that 'Whistler had an almost unrivalled appreciation of atmosphere, and that his colour was beautiful, especially in moonlight scenes'[50] which seemed to give the lie to his earlier statement. Like many of his fellow artists, Burne-Jones had hated taking sides. William Rossetti was asked to appear for Ruskin and reportedly pleaded not to be made to do so, saying it was hard to take either side. His sentiment echoed that of many London-based artists.

In the letter to Princess Louise in which Whistler begged her not to believe Ruskin's defence team's arguments, he described himself as

one, who, if indifferent absolutely to the judgement of all others, has the ambition to be seriously considered by the Artist Princess whose high opinion he has made it his duty to acquire. It saddens him to think that she, who has been so often most gracious and indulgent in her protection, should at all accept the popular belief of meretricious and wilful eccentricity in the work of the painter she has been so kind to! May I venture to offer Your Royal Highness as a tribute of devotion and gratitude a favourite picture of my own – which has successfully resisted the danger of sale on more than one occasion – and which I send herewith? In it, I would timidly hint that, while I recognise nature's masterly use of fairy fog – 'when the evening mist clothes the riverside with poetry, as with a veil' – I still do love to look at her when she is beautiful without it.

[50] *The Times*, 27 November 1878

His efforts appear to have worked, as Whistler – or his defence team – leaked a story to the papers. In a section entitled 'London Gossip' local newspapers around the country published a sarcastic paragraph declaring that 'Princess Louise has turned Whistlerite, and is now an enthusiastic admirer of Nocturnes and Symphonies and "arrangements".'

While Louise was saddened at the prospect of leaving her life in London, Lorne was enthusiastic about Canada. He had longed to travel widely. As a young student at Cambridge, Lorne had grown bored with the stuffiness of academia, so had left university early and travelled to Jamaica, America and Canada with his close friend Arthur Strutt. His father had then paid for him to study for a year in Berlin, where he developed a superb social life but few academic skills (and where he had renewed his family acquaintance with Vicky and Fritz), before travelling on to Austria and Italy. He had also visited Canada on that trip, although his impressions then had not been favourable. This was about to change.

Louise's introduction to her new life was not auspicious: she had never been a good sailor and the November seas on the journey between Liverpool and Halifax were extremely rough. The *Sarmatian* was a luxurious ship fitted with every modern convenience. Journalists had been invited to view the ship and the *Liverpool Mercury* ran a long article about it, describing the ship as 'in every respect a most substantial specimen of marine architecture . . . The saloon . . . a gorgeous palatial apartment . . . [is] copiously lighted by a lantern cupola . . . This is augmented by an abundance of side lights . . . which, united with the gorgeous furnishing, produces an effect at once gratifying and dazzling. The ceiling is delicately panelled in French white, enriched with golden mouldings.' The bedding was the most remarkable feature of all. It was made of a special material (which the Allan Line was in the process of patenting). Rather disconcertingly the pillows – of a material 'with a greater floating power than cork [and] a softness almost equal to feathers' – could also be used as a floating life preserver, should the need arise. Despite the newspapers' fulsome reports, the princess was horribly seasick for a week.

Included in the party's entourage were Sir Richard Moreton (Lorne's Comptroller), his Greek wife Janie (acting as Louise's lady-in-waiting), and their eight-year-old daughter Evelyn. Janie's mothering style seemed to be similar to that of Queen Victoria: she was far more interested in her husband than her child. In her memoirs, published under her married name Viscountess Byng of Vimy, Evelyn recalled a funny but poignant story about how disappointed her mother was when she was born, as she had been longing to have a son she could call Rupert, and had been insistent that her child should be blond and beautiful like her husband. According to Evelyn, her mother never quite forgave her for inheriting her dark Greek hair and features. When Evelyn was three, her mother ordered the nanny to bleach her daughter's hair so she could finally have the blonde child she craved. Whenever anyone commented on Evelyn being pretty, her mother would say, in front of her child, what an ugly nose she had and that it ruined her face. As a result, Evelyn grew up, in her own words, 'fiercely resentful of my appearance'. As Evelyn recalled, 'I was reared in that same fear of my elders which had characterized [my mother's] own youth.' Louise empathised with the little girl and befriended her; she was always happy in the company of children, and the presence of Evelyn made those first months in Canada more bearable.

Several decades had passed, but her adoration of the princess remains palpable. The young Evelyn would lie in her cabin and listen to the groans of her seasick mother and governess; she could even hear the moaning of the princess in a cabin some way off. Louise was so ill that a 'special bed', which sounds from descriptions like a hammock, had to be suspended from the ceiling of her cabin. Evelyn remembered that a man fell, or threw himself, overboard on the journey and that, despite the crew's best efforts, he was never seen again. 'A short time later more hurrying and talking . . . A baby had been born! . . . I knew nothing of it then, since it was the era when the young were told that babies were found under gooseberry bushes, and there were no such things in mid-Atlantic.'

On Saturday 23 November 1878 the *Sarmatian* arrived at Halifax. The weather was so appalling that the ship was unable to make it into the harbour for several hours. Prince Alfred, the Duke of Edinburgh – already in Halifax, on his ship *The Black Prince* – became frustrated by how long it was taking his sister's ship to appear. The fog was thick, and telescopes were useless, so he ordered his ship to set sail and try to find the *Sarmatian*. He was unsuccessful.

Eventually, the captain of the *Sarmatian*, whose signals for a pilot to guide them to the shore had gone unanswered, took the brave decision to enter the harbour without a pilot. Some months later, a story emerged that Louise first set foot on Canadian soil incognito, that she borrowed her brother's launch and went in secret to Halifax so she could attend church, heavily veiled, to give thanks for surviving the horrendous crossing and to compose herself before her official arrival and the pomp and ceremony that would attend it. On the Monday, 25 November, the new Governor-General and the princess were officially welcomed to Canada, by Prime Minister John Macdonald. Louise wore a black dress and kept her face veiled throughout – the woman renowned for her beauty was not prepared, after so many days of seasickness, to show her face in public quite yet.

Lady Dufferin's concern that the people of Canada would not like Louise could not have been more wrong. From the moment she arrived, Canadians were thrilled to have a child of Queen Victoria living amongst them. Louise's relationship with Canada would become a love–hate relationship on both sides for a large part of Lorne's term of office, but she started and ended her years there with Canadian adoration.

From Halifax, Lorne, Louise and their entourage journeyed to Ottawa, the seat of the Governor-General, by the Inter-Colonial Railway.[51] They arrived at the beginning of December, but the rain was so heavy and the weather so cold that the planned welcoming ceremonies had to be postponed for twenty-four hours. It was not a propitious start for a princess who always felt happiest when the sun was shining. Added to this, she was soon to receive the very worrying news that her sister Alice and Alice's baby daughter, May, had contracted diphtheria. Alice died in Darmstadt on the anniversary of their father's death, 14 December 1878.[52] Alice's baby died too. Louise

[51] Although sections of the line had been opened some years earlier, the railway was not finished until 1876, two years before Louise and Lorne's arrival in Canada. The Inter-Colonial Railway spanned over 700 miles.

[52] According to Matthew Dennison, Princess Beatrice's biographer, Bertie began to think that Alice's widower, Prince Louis of Hesse, would be a good husband for Beatrice. As such he became a fervent supporter of the Deceased Wife's Sister's Marriage Act, currently going through Parliament and supported by, amongst others,

grieved for the loss of her gentle sister and niece thousands of miles away from the rest of her family. She and Lorne spent a subdued Christmas in Ottawa. The queen was moved to write in her journal on New Year's Day 1879, 'My poor dear Loosy far away in a distant land, in another quarter of the globe.' The deaths of Alice and her daughter would be followed just three months later by more tragic news from Germany: that of the death of Vicky's eleven-year-old son Waldemar, from a heart condition.

Despite her sadness Louise soon became 'a great favourite' with her husband's subjects, as the British Minister, Sir Edward Thornton, reported at the start of January 1879. Before her arrival, one of Lord Dufferin's staff, terribly nervous about how to deal with a princess, had issued orders on how to dress and behave, which angered the local people. Francis de Winton, who was acting as Lorne's private secretary, earned the couple a lot of very bad press when – without their knowledge – he took the peremptory decision to force several journalists off their train when the couple first arrived. When Louise heard about this and about the concerns people had about not possessing 'regal' enough clothes to wear to the official gatherings, she was angry, commenting that she wouldn't mind if they 'came in blanket coats!'.

Within days of her arrival, people had begun to realise that their fears were unfounded, and Louise was greeted even more warmly than she had anticipated. In January 1879, she held a party for the local children at their home, Rideau Hall in Ottawa (also known as Government House), and a few weeks later she proved to the Canadians that the queen's daughter was unaffected and practical. When an outbreak of scarlet fever hit several of the servants and household at Rideau Hall, the other servants refused to nurse the patients, for fear of getting ill themselves. Louise, who had survived scarlet fever as a child, immediately took charge and nursed her staff and household back to health.

Her culinary skills also surprised her guests. The lessons Louise had learnt in the Swiss Cottage at Osborne House had not been forgotten. One guest related to his family his astonishment at

---

the Pre-Raphaelite artist William Holman Hunt (who had been forced to marry his dead wife's sister in Italy as their marriage was considered illegal in England).

discovering the oyster pâté had been made by the princess. A long article appeared in an American magazine, telling the story of a dinner party in London at which Louise had happily shared her recipe and cooking tips. As *The Hour* (described as a New York City 'society journal') reported:

[Princess Louise] is a lady of much good taste, with a large fund of commonsense. The supervision of her household affairs is upon the model characteristic of all well-appointed English households. A gentleman who has a weakness for apricot tart dined with her a short time before she left England. To his delight, apricot tart was included in the *menu*, and he expressed his fondness for it. 'I am so glad you like it,' replied his hostess, 'because I made it myself. Let me give you the recipe,' and with genial interest she detailed its ingredients. 'Remember, when you get home, to tell Mrs J— that apricot tart should always have an upper crust'.

Louise became renowned for the ease with which she addressed people, chatting to everyone she met and shaking hands – people did not expect a royal to permit any physical contact – including with native Canadians and their wives. This was at a time when most local white settlers were both terrified of the native Canadians, and looked down upon them. In October 1879, the *Toronto Globe* reported 'an amusing incident which occurred at the reception held by the Princess Louise at Hamilton. Chief Waubuno, of the Six Nations Indians, and a brother red-man, both arrayed in Indian costume, mounted the dais and shook hands with the Princess, who, though somewhat startled by the sudden appearance of such warlike-looking individuals, evidently enjoyed the novelty, and cordially returned their well-meant greeting.' A similar incident had happened to Bertie, while travelling in North America, and he had received his native American visitors with the same aplomb and friendship.

The stories of Louise's 'common touch' continued to be talked about for decades after her time in Canada. A newspaper article of 1912 recalled how 'on one occasion, in a Canadian cottage, the daughter of Queen Victoria peeled potatoes, while sheltering from a storm'. Not everyone was pleased by this, however, as several members of

Ottawan society had been thrilled at the thought of how elevated society would become with a princess at its helm. Jehanne Wake reports in her book on Louise how cross one Ottawa luminary was when he discovered that despite having been invited to a viceregal party, he was expected to share the dance floor with his grocer. There were also grievances about the fact that Louise and Lorne spoke French fluently – in terms of diplomacy, this made the French-Canadians far more welcoming to the vice-regal couple than had been expected, but it made the non-French speakers complain of being 'left out' of conversations. The division between French-owned, French-speaking Canada and British-owned, English-speaking Canada was marked and politically difficult. Louise and Lorne made their best attempts to close the vast rift between the two.

If for Louise being in Canada meant being away from those she loved, it was also a welcome release from the stifling social conventions in Britain and her mother's court. For Lorne, it was the start of an exciting new era and one which he embraced wholeheartedly. In England, Lorne was constantly made to feel second best: he was the commoner son-in-law of the queen; at certain official functions he was not even permitted to sit at the same table as his wife. In Canada, however, he was the most important person in the land. His and Louise's roles had been switched, as she was now his subject and expected to behave as such. It was noted with wonder how easily Louise adjusted to being subservient to her husband. Marie von Bunsen, a German aristocrat and family friend of the Campbells, wrote in her memoirs:

> Government House was ugly, but comfortable and dignified; but the Court struck me as odd. All the honours were paid to him as the Sovereign's representative; the Princess Louise, the Queen's daughter and a Royal Highness, played second fiddle on every occasion. She took her seat and walked on his left, entered the room behind him, rose with all the rest of us when he came in and, like all the rest, remained standing until he was seated . . . [Lorne was] a fair, cheery man, not a personality, but keen, and with many interests; she, tall and slight, a handsome figure in black velvet with diamonds and emeralds in the evening. She was clever and had artistic tastes [and was] most likeable.

Marie von Bunsen was available and willing to spend time with Lorne, so Louise used the opportunity to cry off social engagements, such as the theatre, suggesting Marie went in her place. This had the effect of making Marie side with Lorne. She seemed to think that Louise was terribly cruel to Lorne and that this must have been because she was in love with someone else. It seems likely that Marie was flattered by the attention Lorne paid to her, and perhaps saw herself as Louise's rival in love. It was soon being whispered that Louise was not happy with her husband and that she was having an affair, using the numerous times she did not accompany Lorne to engagements to meet her lover. I discovered in the archives in Ottawa that many men had their names coupled with Louise in the gossip of the time – and in gossip printed several decades later, when people were still telling stories about the princess. The newspapers certainly elaborated over the years and the rumours grew in the telling. It is unlikely that she could possibly have had quite so many lovers in Canada as have been attributed to her – certainly not without the news getting back to England – but whoever she was or wasn't having an affair with, the problems in her marriage were apparent to most of their circle in Ottawa.

Louise and Lorne were keen to see Canada. One of their first sightseeing trips was undertaken with Edward Thornton and his wife; they visited Niagara Falls and the newspapers in America and Canada sent reporters in their droves. No one was fooled by the incognito of Lord and Lady Sundridge. An illustration of the viceregal couple (though neither is easy to recognise) walking across the 'ice bridge at Niagara Falls' appeared in a number of newspapers. Both the Lornes and the Thorntons grew weary of being constantly stalked by journalists and laughed out loud when one reporter fell over in the snow while trying to sneak up on them.

In February 1879, Louise was upset at missing her beloved brother Arthur's wedding to Princess Louise of Prussia ('Louischen'). Her future sister-in-law had written her a very sweet letter, just before Louise and Lorne left for Canada, commiserating with Louise's 'low spirits' and saying 'Arthur and I will miss you _terribly_ and it is so sad that his favourite sister should not be there for our marriage.' In an attempt to raise her spirits, Louise hosted her first proper party since Lorne had taken office. It was to be a 'uniquely Canadian' event – an ice-skating party. Louise had learnt to skate as a child, but she needed to brush up her skills. Instead of taking private lessons, she endeared herself to her household by learning alongside them – and hooting with laughter every time she fell over. She also oversaw the decorations for the party, ensuring the grounds were lit with flaming torches and oriental-style lanterns. As there was to be dancing on the ice, as well as in the ballroom, a band was hired to play alongside the ice rink. Well versed in the habits of Canadian winters, the band insisted that a large stove be provided and the musicians took regular breaks to thaw out their frozen musical instruments.

Rideau Hall was a forbidding property when Louise and Lorne arrived, and Louise took immediate action to make it less ugly and more habitable. The original stone house had been built as a private family home in the 1830s. In 1865, it was leased to the first Governor-General and was eventually bought by the government. By the time of Lorne's residency, the house had undergone a number of extensions and changes. Evelyn Moreton recalled its appearance in 1878: 'cramped inside, monstrous outside . . . the Tent-room and ball-room already flanked the front door, which was a squat affair – more like a stable entrance than a Governor-General's residence'. The 'tent-room', an innovation added during the tenancy of Lord Dufferin, was an indoor tennis court that could be, according to one contemporary report, 'converted in a few hours into a splendid supper-room'. Lord Frederic Hamilton, the brother-in-law of Lord Lansdowne who would become Governor-General after Lorne, recalled how the room could be transformed: 'a red and white tent is lowered bodily from the roof; a carpet is spread over the floor; great white-and-gold electric standards bearing the arms of the different Provinces are placed in position, and the thing is done'. Several other visitors to Rideau Hall also commented on a peculiarity that Hamilton noticed. 'The thing most surprising to strangers was that it was possible in winter-time to light the gas with one's finger. All that was necessary was to shuffle over the carpet in thin shoes, and then on touching any metal object, an electric spark half an inch long would crack out of your finger.'

When she wasn't carrying out official duties, Louise filled her days with walking, riding, shopping and art. Depressed by her new home's dark, dull interiors, she set about decorating Rideau Hall, painting pictures to hang on the walls and painting the walls themselves. As part of their entourage, Louise and Lorne had invited the artist Sydney Prior Hall to Canada; he was a talented portrait painter and book illustrator and Louise and he often painted and discussed decorating ideas together. (During their first Christmas in Canada, Louise asked Hall to sit to her so she could paint him.) Inspired by Japanese art and Aestheticism, she decorated her own boudoir in peacock blue, and painted sprays of apple blossom trailing over the doors. Other artist friends who visited Louise during her first months in Canada were Henrietta and Clara Montalba. The three friends worked happily together on paintings and sculptures of one another and on recreating scenes of Canadian life (Henrietta also sculpted a bust of Lorne dressed in Canadian furs).

Louise decided that the woods around Rideau Hall were too dense, obscuring the beautiful views around them when she went for walks. So she ordered what became known as the 'Princess Vista', a swathe cut through the woods so that a glimpse of the Ottawa River could be seen in the distance. Evelyn Moreton, who spent her weekdays having lessons with the de Winton children, recalled with great fondness her Sundays with Louise.

There were sedate Vice-Regal walks on Sunday afternoons during the winter, when in a solid phalanx, we sallied forth in sealskin coats, the women and children with their heads shrouded in white woollen mufflers called 'clouds' and worn over our caps, a blessing to one's ears, though we must have looked funny trudging along, headed by Lord Lorne, talking in his high-pitched, nasal voice, with Princess Louise, young and beautiful, by his side. It was she who nicknamed me 'Little Seal', because she said I was seal-coloured all over – eyes, hair, and coat. And I was full of importance as I trotted along with the grown-ups on those Sunday afternoons!

The grounds of the house were spectacular, with two skating rinks, which were also used for curling matches, and an aviary. Something that Louise found especially touching was that Lord Dufferin had left specific instructions that the artist's studio he had had built for his own works be preserved for the princess. He also left painting and sculpting equipment, knowing how much she would miss her own studio in the years she would be away from London.

Louise took every opportunity to be outside sketching. She commissioned a special 'sketching hut' to be made, a portable shed which could be moved around the grounds but which was warm enough for her to sit inside and shelter in on inclement days. It sounds as though it was similar to a bird hide, on wheels, although one wall was made entirely of glass to allow the princess and her companion to sketch even when the weather was bad. Her love of ingenious devices to enable her to paint on the move was well known, begun in childhood when her tutor Edward Corbould encouraged her to carry a sketchbook wherever she went. The artist Arthur Severn (whose wife, Joan, was Ruskin's cousin and housekeeper) created three of what were described by the artist Henry Stacy Marks as 'the tiniest paintboxes in existence'. In an interview with the journalist Harry How in 1891, Marks said that the three paintboxes were owned by him, by Arthur Severn and by Princess Louise. He described the box as: 'in the shape of a charm for a watch-chain but, on opening it, it is found to contain all the necessary colours in miniature for painting a picture'.

The princess also indulged one of her favourite new pastimes: fishing. In 1974, the owner of a junk stall in London's Camden Market sold 'a very tatty canvas bag containing a rather heavy greenheart salmon fishing rod'. The man who bought it was intrigued to discover that the butt was engraved with the words 'H.R.H. the Princess Louise, 18th March 1879' – it was a present for her thirty-first birthday, which she spent in Canada. It was obviously well used – in autumn 1879, a ship returning to Liverpool from Canada was entrusted with a consignment of 'nine fine salmon', caught by Princess Louise and sent as a gift to her mother, siblings and members of the royal household. The National Library and Archives in Ottawa contain a large number of Louise's sketches and drawings, many of which depict figures fishing, often from a canoe. In several of these the people fishing are identifiable as herself and her husband. Louise's one grievance while fishing was that mosquitoes and other insects plagued them as they fished; so she invented a 'mosquito helmet', an uncomfortable-looking contraption. One observer recalled seeing Louise smeared all over with a dark tar-like substance, said to be impenetrable to biting insects.

The newspapers in England had not forgotten their princess and waited eagerly for stories to appear in the Canadian press, so they could repeat them. In the spring of 1879, the *Manchester Evening News* reported that the princess

> may be seen in the dull grey mornings, of which we have had so many since her arrival, at as early an hour as 8.30, vigorously walking in the romantic neighbourhood of Rideau Hall. She comes to town nearly every day, not in a carriage, but in good stout English walking boots, in which she tramps through mud and slush with a bold firm step . . . A few days ago she was seen suddenly to stop before a small tinshop. She saw something in the window which attracted her attention, and after observing it for a moment, walked into the very humble place. Now, what do you suppose had struck her fancy? A small tin teapot. A little common thing, with a capacity of about one cup, and worth about 25 cents. She bought it, put it in her capacious pocket, and trudged on.

In May 1879, Louise and Lorne travelled to Quebec, visiting Montreal – where they opened the new gallery of the Arts Association – and Quebec City. In Quebec Louise was instantly popular because of her superb French (she learnt from babyhood to speak German, French and English equally fluently), and the couple decided to make their summer home the Citadel in Quebec City. A few weeks later, the Argyll family arrived to stay in Canada. They loved the countryside and decided that they should all go camping. The journalists, who noted their every move, were amazed that the queen's daughter was happy to 'rough it' in a tent.

Following their summer at the Citadel, to which Louise and Lorne returned once the Argyll family had left, the viceregal couple travelled by ship to Nova Scotia, visiting Prince Edward Island, and on to western Ontario. Lorne was determined that he should see as much of 'his' country as possible. He would become a respected Governor-General, but it must have been galling that, no matter how tirelessly he worked, the person his subjects really wanted to see was his wife. In a letter sent when Louise and Lorne had been in Canada for nearly ten months, Disraeli wrote that although Lorne was not as popular as Lord Dufferin had been, Louise was 'a great success . . . she is extremely gracious, speaks to everybody and is interested in everything and skates divinely'.

For some reason, Lorne was never quite as popular as he should have been, and it seems that this may have been because people in Canada (and America, when he visited), had their suspicions about his sexuality. While the women of Britain were writing letters to the princess suggesting how she might overcome her infertility, the women of North America may have been rather more aware of why the marriage was childless. In the 1980s, Sandra Gwyn, a Canadian academic, published *The Private Capital*, about the history of the Governors-General. In most books, when one reads about Lorne, the words 'allegedly' and 'perhaps' often appear in references to his sexuality. In Gwyn's book it was refreshing to discover that the chapter devoted to Lorne's time in Ottawa is simply entitled 'The Gay Governor-General'. Gwyn comments:

> Lorne was, almost certainly, a homosexual, and not always one who remained in the closet. As a schoolboy at Eton, as the British scholar Timothy D'Arch Smith has revealed . . . he had been involved with a relationship with another sprig of the aristocracy, Frederick Wood, the future Lord Halifax . . . In later years, Lorne was well-known as an habitué of certain illicit London clubs and to attend what were discreetly described as 'masculine parties'.

Louise was tired of living a charade with Lorne and was not looking forward to a second Canadian winter. She was homesick, she wanted to see her family, she wanted to see Boehm and her friends, and she wanted to be apart from her husband. Most of all, she couldn't bear the idea of the long months of ice and snow, in a home that was even harder to keep warm than Balmoral. On 18 October 1879, she boarded the *Sarmatian* in Halifax and travelled back to England. Lorne remained in Canada. The story given to the press was that Louise had been advised by her doctors to spend the winter in a less harsh climate, and that she would return to Canada and her husband as soon as her health permitted. She reached Liverpool on 30 October to a triumphant welcome, and took a special train to London. The newspapers made a great deal of the fact that the Duke of Argyll was not amongst those waiting to greet his daughter-in-law at the station; as there was no special reason why the duke should have been there, the newspapers can only have been using his absence as an oblique way of hinting at a rift between the princess and her husband.

Although she spent Christmas with her mother and siblings at Osborne House, Louise spent very little time on the Isle of Wight. She divided her months in England between London (where she was based at Buckingham Palace, her apartments in Kensington being unavailable) and Windsor. She and Prince Leopold took every opportunity to be together, attending parties and visiting galleries, and going to see an exhibition of work by William Morris, at Westminster Hospital. (Louise and Lorne were admirers of Morris's work and politics, often attending his famous lectures.) When Leopold was unable to accompany her, Lord Ronnie Gower became Louise's escort. Louise also carried out official duties, such as opening 'a new middle-class girls' school' in Blackheath. She attended parties at Whistler's studio and spent as much time as possible with Boehm and her friends. Boehm and Louise seem to have been realistic and pragmatic about their relationship: whenever they were in the same country they would spend time together; but both were aware of the importance of their own marriages, reputations and social position. In nineteenth-century Britain, for those with land, property, money or titles to think about, marriage was almost always a business proposition between families rather than a romantic love match (despite what the novelists of the time wanted their readers to believe).

Louise was able to comfort her mother and the deposed Empress of France who had suffered the tragic news, while Louise was away, of the death of the Empress's son, the Prince Imperial, who had been killed in the Zulu Wars.[53] Not only had the Empress lost her son, but it was widely believed that Princess Beatrice had hoped to marry the ill-fated prince. Beatrice's future was looking increasingly bland.

Following the death of the Prince Imperial, a new face had been seen at the royal court, a young man who had served with the prince and had been chosen to go to the palace and give the queen his report on the prince's death. His name was Arthur Bigge and he would later

---

[53] In 1880, the Royal Military Academy was presented with a bust of the Prince Imperial to be displayed alongside Louise's bust of Prince Arthur.

become an important member of the queen's household. He was a good-looking young man, to whom Louise was introduced by their mutual friend, Lady Sophia MacNamara (who was nicknamed 'Smack'). Some years later, Louise and Bigge's names would be linked in a scandal, but for the moment, he was simply a young man whom the queen liked the look of and had decided to help in his career.

Return to Canada was inevitable, and Lorne was there to greet Louise as the *Sarmatian* docked in Halifax on 3 February 1880. Louise was given a warm greeting by the waiting crowds. Once again they travelled by special train to Ottawa via Montreal, where the train was delayed for some time by heavy snowstorms. In the Canadian national archives is a painting on a piece of bark, which was presented to Louise on her return. I assume this is the item that was referred to in a newspaper article: 'We understand that the chief of the Aberacke tribe of Indians, situated at St. Francois-du-lac, county Herville, has lately presented to the Princess Louise, in the name of his tribe, an address congratulating her Royal Highness on her safe return to Canada. The composition is that of the chief himself, and embodies strong proofs of loyalty.'

Louise's return was not entirely without rancour, however, for in her absence rumours had started to circulate and gain momentum. It had been noticed by several observers that all was not as it should be in the Governor-General's marriage. Louise's flirtatious nature had been commented on and it was said that she had gone back to England to give birth to a baby that was not her husband's. Another story was that she hated Canada, and this story was one that rankled amongst the people who had made her so welcome. Yet another rumour, and one that would persist for years, was that she and Lady Macdonald, the wife of the Prime Minister, were embroiled in a bitchy feud. Whether there was any truth to this is difficult to fathom; according to the evidence available, the two women were on perfectly amicable terms and were both very upset by the rumours. One researcher in Canada suggested to me that papers 'proving' the feud might have been destroyed. There is, of course, the possibility that, like so many wives, Lady Macdonald disapproved of the effect Louise had on her husband – including the gossip that Louise had taken against Lord Macdonald after he got drunk at a party and had 'taken a liberty'. This was repeated in the 1912 memoirs of one of Macdonald's political opponents. The former finance minister, Sir Richard Cartwright, wrote gleefully that Princess Louise had 'very just cause' for taking offence against Lord Macdonald and that she had been 'obliged' to leave the room when he entered it. It seems Lorne and Lord Macdonald also had their political differences. Yet, when so much of the problem seemed to centre on Lord Macdonald, why is it that gossip perpetually saw the two women as the source of the problem? It seems there were problems between all four of the Macdonalds and the Lornes, but the newspapers, of course, found a feud between the wives far more noteworthy.

Within days of Louise's return, the discontent towards her that had been building in her absence had been replaced by shock and sympathy. On 14 February 1880, Louise and Lorne were travelling in a horse-drawn sleigh on the icy roads. Unfortunately, their driver was English, not Canadian, and not used to the driving conditions. As they approached a sharp corner, the driver lost control. One of the horses – which had been made to go much too fast to be able to slow down – took fright. The sleigh crashed, twisted and was dragged for several hundred metres along the road. Louise took most of the impact as her husband was flung out of his seat and on to her. Lorne was barely injured but unable to move because of the position of the sleigh; Louise thought she would suffocate as the weight of her husband's body pressed on to her chest and lungs. After smacking her head on the bar that held the sleigh roof in place, Louise was knocked unconscious. Lorne was terrified she had been killed. In a letter home, Lorne reported: '[Louise] has been much hurt, and it is a wonder that her skull was not fractured. The muscles of the neck, shoulder, and back are much strained and the lobe of one ear was cut in two. As we pounded along, I expected the sides of the carriage to give way every moment, when we should probably have been all killed.' For the rest of her life, Louise was assiduous at ensuring that her hair covered up her ears, as she had lost part of an ear (although rumours suggested her entire right ear had been ripped off).

A few days after the accident, Arthur Sullivan arrived to stay. He was on a tour of America and Canada with *The Pirates of Penzance* and had been greatly looking forward to spending time with 'his' princess. Although relieved she had survived such a terrifying accident, he was saddened that Louise was so ill, meaning he was able to see very little of her during his stay. Lorne had written a poem that he intended to become the new National Anthem of Canada; he had called it his 'Dominion Hymn' and asked Sullivan to compose the music. It was not his most popular work. A 'society journal' in New York reviewed the hymn – and Lorne – scathingly: 'He has written one or two things which are chiefly conspicuous for their mediocrity. His latest attempt in poetry is his "Canadian National Anthem," which Arthur Sullivan has set to music, and redeemed it from absolute failure. As a sample of poetic inspiration it is very moist.'

Initially, the unfortunate decision was made to play down the severity of the accident – even Queen Victoria was not told the truth about how badly her daughter was injured. This was deeply damaging to Louise's and Lorne's reputations: until the extent of her injuries was known, Canadians began to talk about Louise in much the same way that Britons had discussed their queen, accusing her of malingering and shirking her official responsibilities. When the nature of her injuries became common knowledge, Louise was once again adored by the public, who felt guilty, not least because politicians had been making unflattering or derogatory comments in Parliament. The MP who wrote, 'Except the cut in the lower part of the ear I think there was no injury done worth mentioning' must have been mortified when he realised how close to death Louise had come.

On 6 March 1880, Louise was able to leave her bed for the first time. Her first public appearance was on 11 April, when she and Lorne attended a church service. Although to outward appearances she was fully recovered by May, the sleigh accident would have repercussions for the rest of Louise's life: the headaches she had long been prey to became more frequent and more painful and she began to suffer from neuralgia and occasional deafness. All of these symptoms were exacerbated at times of stress.

Positive things were happening as well. Most notably, one of Louise and Lorne's plans was coming to fruition. The couple were keen to improve the artistic life of Canada, as Canadian artists currently had very few opportunities to forward their careers. Thanks to the viceregal couple, in the spring of 1880 the school that would become known as the Ottawa School of Art hired its first instructor. It was also in this year that they helped to found the first Canadian Academy of the

Arts.[54] Louise and Lorne also picked the works that would feature in its first exhibition; these items later formed the nucleus of the National Gallery of Canada collection. When the gallery was complete, Lorne was proud to declare it open. At the time of the first exhibition, Louise was too ill to leave her room, but as Lorne revealed in a letter she 'insisted that I should bring up to her room nearly every one of the pictures exhibited, in order that she might judge the position of Canadian art at the time'.

While Louise was recuperating, Prince Leopold was also recovering from an injury and was longing to see his sister. As soon as he could, he travelled to Canada on the *Sardinian*, arriving on 23 May. Louise was overjoyed to see him – although she and Lorne were nearly involved in another serious accident on the way to meet Leopold in Quebec. As their special train was travelling through Quebec it narrowly missed a collision with the Montreal–Ottawa Express. Louise was badly jolted and scared by the experience.

Once she had recovered, Leopold and Louise set off together, without Lorne. Just as Louise had once made such desperate bids for independence from her mother, now she was equally desperate to achieve independence from her husband. The visit of her favourite brother was the perfect excuse to escape.

Louise and Leopold went first to Toronto, from where they travelled to the Niagara Falls, then into America, visiting Chicago, Milwaukee and Detroit. They had planned to visit San Francisco, but that idea was dropped – in the Canadian archives there are a number of references to Fenian activities and threats to Princess Louise in Canada, which the Prime Minister took very seriously. It seems that San Francisco was considered too dangerous for the son and daughter of Queen Victoria. At the end of their travels, the siblings met up again with Lorne and his brother Archie in Quebec City, having stopped in Montreal on the way. They all went to the Citadel and then for a fishing trip on the Cascapedia River. Leopold hankered for an outdoor life, to do all the things that other men of his age were able to, but

---

[54] In his book *Painting in Canada*, J. Russell Harper discusses the squabbling that marred the founding of the Academy: 'The new academy was born in a "marvellous amount of bitterness and bad language; half the artists are ready just now to choke the other half with their paint brushes".'

although Louise was eager to let him realise this dream, the holiday nearly ended in disaster. While they were staying with a Mr and Mrs Stephen, at the couple's holiday cottage on the Matapedia River in Quebec, the haemophiliac prince fell and hurt his leg. His doctor insisted that he should return to England, not wanting the responsibility of caring for such a delicate member of the queen's family. Louise was determined to go with him: still feeling unwell, she was dreading another icy winter. Major Collins, who was travelling with Leopold, noted that she was 'unstrung and restless'.

Before she left, however, Louise carried out several official duties, with Leopold accompanying her on visits to hospitals. Shortly before she set sail, Louise laid the coping stone of the new 'Louise Embankment' in Quebec, at which Lorne made a speech. In it, he defended his wife's decision to leave Canada again so soon, explaining that she had been 'ordered' to return to Europe and urging the people of Canada to look on the princess's injuries in the same way as they would those of a soldier; he pointed out that she had been injured 'in the performance of a public duty'.

The newspapers reported that Leopold looked better than expected but that his accident had had 'a weakening effect upon him'. It was obvious that he needed to return to his doctors in London. The prince and princess set sail on 31 July 1880 on the steamer *Polynesian*. Louise had been in Canada for barely six months. She was, however, genuinely unwell, suffering from debilitating headaches and neuralgia, gastric troubles (probably caused by stress) and insomnia. The royal entourage on board the ship included two ladies-in-waiting and the ever present Colonel McNeill, who seems to have spent much of his time sailing back and forth between England and Canada: it was said by many in Canada that he was in love with Louise, and several gossips claimed they were having an affair. That seems a valid possibility. While Louise was separated from Boehm, she needed a lover. For a woman who had as strong a need for affection as Louise did, being trapped in a sexless marriage would have been unendurable. As Bertie's earlier comments to their mother about Louise needing to be married made explicit, he was aware that his sister had a similar sex-drive to his own. Bertie was rarely without a lover as well as a wife; the children of the unmaternal monarch may have been able to value themselves only when they were being valued and desired by others. As the wife of the Governor-General and daughter of the monarch, Louise would have been wise to choose someone from the royal household, whose discretion was assured. Colonel McNeill was just one of the many names suggested as Louise's lover in later newspaper articles. There was also gossip that she had a 'favourite guide' from the Micmac tribe. This tribe lived at the mouth of the Grand Cascapedia River, one of the princess's favoured fishing spots, which she and Lorne visited regularly. Local gossip claimed that her guide was also her model, that he posed naked for her and that they became lovers. According to journalist Alex Shoumatoff,[55] who writes about the region today, there is still a rumour that when Louise left Canada, she bought this alleged lover a ranch in Alberta.

When their ship arrived in Liverpool, on Monday 9 August, the yacht *Victoria and Albert* was waiting to transport the siblings to their mother on the Isle of Wight. A special train was also laid on, just in case 'the princess preferred to go by rail', as a tactful journalist noted – Princess Louise's tendency to seasickness was well known.

Bertie and Alix came to Osborne to see Leopold and Louise, after which Louise chose to cut short her reunion with her mother. On 12 August, she left the Isle of Wight, accompanied by Colonel McNeill, and headed to London, in preparation for a holiday 'for the benefit of her health'. She left for Cologne accompanied by Captain Collins and his daughter. She took the waters at Marienbad and convalesced at Salzburg. She also travelled to Darmstadt, to spend time with Alice's bereaved husband and children, as well as Alfred, Marie and their children, who were in Germany at the same time. By the end of August, the papers were predicting that Louise would set sail again in the late autumn – but it would be well over a year and a half before Louise would return to Canada and her husband. As she was on her way back to England from Germany, the press reported, 'There are

---

[55] Shoumatoff also notes, sadly, that Louise's love for the area was the cause of one of the greatest problems for the Micmac tribe in the future. She and Lorne built a 'fancy fishing camp' (known as Lorne Cottage) and as a result the salmon in that part of the river became the property of the Governor-General. This meant that, during all succeeding governor-generalships, the tribe was forbidden to fish there. 'Many departed for factory towns in New England,' wrote Shoumatoff in 2006. 'The bottom fell out of their culture, and they remain deeply demoralized and marginalized to this day. While I was there, the chief's teenage daughter killed herself.'

rather disquieting reports as to the health of the Princess Louise . . . in consequence of which her return to Canada is postponed to an indefinite period. The shock sustained on the occasion of an accident to the sleigh was much more severe than was realised at the time.'

CHAPTER 16

A marriage lived in different continents

What was the true nature of the relationship between Lorne and his wife, the Princess Louise? Was it because Louise detested Canada or because she detested Lorne that she spent so little time at his side here? . . . In hindsight, the years of the Lornes at Rideau are a conundrum. In terms of tangible results, few governor-generalcies have been more productive: . . . two landmark instruments of Canadian culture, the National Gallery and the Royal Society were established in the space of two years. Yet [never] has a governor-generalcy been marred by so much acrimony in public and nasty whispering in private.

Sandra Gwyn, *The Private Capital*, 1984

On 13 October, Louise sailed into Dover and took an immediate train to London. The very first visit she paid was to the studio of Joseph Edgar Boehm. After several days of seeing her friends, Louise spent a morning with Bertie and Alix, before boarding a train to Scotland. The Duke of Argyll had been suffering from gout and was unwell and grumpy, but for several days at Inveraray Louise played the dutiful daughter-in-law. At the time of her arrival, the Campbell family was in crisis: Lorne's younger brother, Colin, had fallen in love with a beautiful but middle-class woman named Gertrude Blood – he had become engaged to her within three days of their first meeting. His father was incensed. When Lorne heard the news, and that the wedding was inevitable, he too was angry, writing that Colin had no right to ally himself with 'a pennyless and groatless grenadier of a girl'. It seemed that the family thought it acceptable for the son of a duke to aspire to marry the daughter of a queen (and rely on her financial aid to save the family fortunes), but when the situation was reversed and the son of a duke married a woman lower down the social scale, the Campbells did not like it at all.

Soon after Louise's return to London, the newspapers were whispering that the queen was displeased with her daughter and that the two women had had an argument. To add fuel to the fire, instead of staying at Buckingham Palace, Louise chose to stay with Leopold at Claremont House. Then she spent the next few weeks with friends and carrying out the kind of official duties that had made her so popular in the past, visiting hospitals and planting trees, as well as attending her friends' exhibitions and concerts. A fulsome letter survives from Whistler (the date is unknown but it is likely to be from this time) on behalf of the Incorporated Society of British Artists. It was sent to Captain Arthur Collins (who was appointed Louise's equerry in April 1880) and invites the princess to tea:

> I do so want the most charming of Princesses to be gracious and kindly intentioned to this most respectable and hitherto dreary dank and most grown body of British artists whose wisdom was in their despair – when they called upon me to join them! I mean to bring upon them and into their very midst the unknown success and joy . . . and so have created a tabernacle of 'sharp bright gaiety' in Suffolk Street to which I venture to entreat the Princess to give her gentle countenance. Do my dear Collins say things nicely for me to H.R.H. She has been so good and indulgent that I really have not the hardihood to trouble her with a note to answer. Tell her that you know how dainty and pretty are our Sunday afternoons – and say that if she would only pass through the galleries next Sunday at about five o'clock or so and touch a cup of tea in the place our triumph would be complete!

Louise responded to say that she would attend – and received a gratified response containing the suggestion, 'I hope also that perhaps Mr Boehm may be able to come at about half past four.' Evidently the love affair between Louise and Boehm was no secret to Whistler as he sent Boehm's invitation not to the sculptor's own studio, but via princess Louise. Whistler also had confidence in Louise's work, writing to her a year after his request for her to visit Suffolk Street to remind her of her promise to send them one of her own works. He finished the letter in characteristic flowery style: 'I pray you bring to us the joy that inaugurated with your own work would attach itself to our Society and distinguish us among all others as the one whom Your Royal Highness has delighted to honor [*sic*].'

Wherever the princess went, the crowds flocked to see her. On 17 December 1880 the *Manchester Evening News* quoted an American magazine which bemoaned Canada's loss of the princess. Lorne on his own, they suggested, was not a resounding success: it was Louise who was making his reign memorable: 'The Marquis is neither popular nor unpopular. He may be termed rather of the goody type of young man. Neither his vices nor his virtues entitle him to any remarkable prominence. In fact his individuality is lost in the superior position and attainments of his wife.'

Louise settled back into life in England, but Canada had made her impatient with the conformity and stiffness of London regal life. Rumours began to circulate that Louise was kicking against the formality of her mother's court. For the first time in her life, Louise was living exactly as she had always wanted to do. She was an artist, working professionally, visiting whom she pleased and, although she had the status of a married woman and therefore the social freedom of that status, she did not have the encumbrance of a husband. For Louise, 1881 was the year in which she finally attained liberation. It was also the year in which Queen Victoria named Joseph Edgar Boehm Sculptor in Ordinary to the royal household. This honorary position, which effectively made Boehm the most important sculptor in Britain, gave the lovers greater freedom to spend time together. As an official member of the royal court, Boehm would be an even more acceptable presence in the princess's social life and court life than he had been as her tutor. (In the same year, Leopold was made Duke of Albany.)

In the spring, Louise left England again, travelling incognito to Italy. Despite the fact that her holiday had been intended to be a secret, her mother's government consistently sent word to each of her destinations warning that she would be arriving and requesting 'all the honours due to her rank'. She visited Rome, Venice and the popular tourist resort of Ventimiglia. While Louise was away, the Duke of Argyll paid a visit to Osborne House. It was assumed by journalists (many of whom wrote erroneously that she was present at Osborne) that Louise had returned to her family, so when it was discovered she was still in Italy, several newspapers hinted that she was deliberately snubbing her father-in-law and that the Lornes' marriage was in serious trouble. Immediately, the royal physicians issued a statement that Louise was in Italy for medical treatment and too unwell to make the long journey back to England.

It is likely that Louise *was* avoiding her father-in-law. The duke's children had been deeply hurt by his decision to marry again. His second wife was the widowed Amelia ('Mimi') Anson. Initially, Louise had attempted to play peacemaker, but the situation became so explosive that she had found herself caught in the middle and attacked by both sides. It is possible that she stayed in Italy to prevent herself becoming any more deeply involved in the Campbell family feud. On 19 March 1881 the *Gloucester Citizen* made a veiled dig at the fact that the princess was away from her husband for their wedding anniversary: 'Yesterday was the 33rd anniversary of the birth of Her Royal Highness Princess Louise . . . Her marriage with the Marquis of Lorne . . . was solemnised on March 21st 1871, and Monday next will accordingly be the 10th anniversary of their marriage. The Princess is now in Italy, where she is travelling as Lady Sundridge.'

Louise returned to England before the end of April, in time to take care of her mother who was in mourning for Benjamin Disraeli. She spent the summer months travelling around the country, staying with friends and keeping out of the public eye as much as possible. She was unwell, and unhappily preparing to see her husband for the first time in over a year. Lorne sailed back to England in November 1881. Louise, it was claimed, had intended to meet him in Liverpool, but when his ship was delayed, she went instead to Eaton Hall in Chester, as the guest of the Duke of Westminster. Lord Ronnie Gower was at Liverpool to meet Lorne and together they travelled to Eaton Hall. Both husband and wife must have been relieved that their reunion did not happen under the watchful eyes of the British press. At the end of November, they travelled to Windsor to see the queen; the monarch was depressed, as she recorded in her journal, because Leopold had announced his engagement (to Princess Helen of Waldeck-Pyrmont).

Lorne remained in Britain until early January 1882, but he was longing to get back to Canada, having grown extremely fond both of the country and his exalted life out there. When he sailed from Liverpool on 11 January Henry Ponsonby wrote to his wife that Lorne was 'apparently happy' without Louise. In Canada, the suspicions about his sexuality were gaining force, mainly because he seemed to be so much more content living as a 'bachelor' than he had been when his beautiful and vivacious wife was sharing his home. The archives in Ottawa have been carefully purged of any but the most vague references to the Lornes' extramarital love affairs in Canada, although time and again one reads that there was unspecified 'gossip' about these as well as about Lorne's sexuality. Apart from the general tantalising gossip, there is no record of a specific man (or men) whom he was linked with. There was talk of his relationship with his male servants (again unspecified). This is unsurprising, as if Lorne had been known to be what was termed a 'practising homosexual' he would have been punishable by law, and likely to get a harsh and severe sentence. The son of a duke, and especially the son-in-law of the queen, could never be allowed to have such a scandalous private life exposed. In his book, *Royal Rebels*, Robert Stamp asserts his belief that Lorne was known to be gay and that it stemmed back to his time at Eton and the culture of homosexuality that pervaded the British boarding school system.

Perhaps Lorne's unusual personal habits also worked against him in Canada. His family seem to have found his eccentricities charming and overlooked many traits that others would consider odd, such as the fact that he often refused to wash and that he regularly wore inappropriate attire. He might turn up for a formal dinner in old clothes or, conversely, dress in full military regalia for an informal occasion. Nina Epton recorded an interview with one of Lorne's nieces who said he was a 'little odd in his behaviour . . . [he might] appear at breakfast wearing the Order of the Garter'.

Charles Warr, who knew Louise and Lorne only in old age (when he was a young man), described the princess's husband as 'an affable and amusing man, simple and unaffected, immensely knowledgeable, who loved the company of his chosen friends . . . He was attracted to spiritualism and the investigations of psychic phenomena.' This description seemed sweetly eccentric when it was published in 1960, but in the mid-Victorian period, a man who spoke of his psychic visions and advocated spiritualism would have been considered distinctly strange.

In London, Louise slipped easily back into life as an independent woman, although the queen did all she could to prevent her daughter from living as she chose to, regularly requiring her assistance. On 2 March 1882, Louise took lunch with her mother at Buckingham Palace on what was to prove another dramatic day in the life of the longest-reigning monarch. After lunch, the queen travelled to Windsor, where yet another attempt was made on her life. The would-be regicide was Roderick Maclean, described in the papers as 'an unsuccessful poet'. He was alleged to have a personal grievance against the queen, having sent her his poetry and not received a satisfactory reply. Maclean aimed a pistol at the queen, but the shot went wide. At his trial he was found 'not guilty, but insane' (a verdict the queen was not happy with as she insisted he was guilty despite being insane); he spent the rest of his life in a prison asylum.

With Lorne back in Canada, Louise was thoroughly enjoying being in England. She attended the christening of yet another niece, visited Harrow School (in the company of the Gladstone family) and met the Crown Prince of Denmark on his official visit to Britain (the man to whom she had allegedly been engaged in 1868). She also inspected the preliminary excavations of the proposed Channel Tunnel; but more exciting than all of these duties was the chance to spend time with Boehm.

One of the reasons Louise had wanted to remain in Britain was to attend her favourite brother's wedding. Leopold married Princess Helen of Waldeck-Pyrmont at St George's Chapel in Windsor on 27 April;[56] Louise's presents included a Dutch landscape in oils and one of Lorne's paintings of Canada. After Leopold's wedding was over, Louise had run out of excuses to remain in England. She was preparing to return to her husband – and feeling nervously unsure what kind of reception the Canadians would give her. She sailed from Liverpool on 25 May, missing Oscar Wilde's visit to Canada. If Louise had been there it is likely she would have taken the opportunity to spend time with him, but for some reason Lorne snubbed the visiting writer.

Much has been made of the fact that Lorne spent the few days of Oscar Wilde's time in Ottawa being 'otherwise engaged'. Claims have been made that Lorne avoided Wilde because of the risk of being

[56] Just over a week after Leopold's wedding, the country was shocked by the news of the Phoenix Park murders in Ireland – one of the victims was a cousin of Lorne. The queen blamed Gladstone for the tragedy.

'outed' as homosexual. This cannot be true, however, as Wilde, although a flamboyant figure, was, in 1882, not yet known to be bisexual. He had, in fact, recently met the woman who would become his wife, the aptly named Constance (née Lloyd). Wilde had a history of falling painfully in love with women who rejected him, including Lillie Langtry (whose husband famously fell over Oscar Wilde, huddled in misery on their doorstep) and Florence Balcombe (who declined his proposals and married Bram Stoker, author of *Dracula*). Even though Wilde was not yet suspected of being a 'somdomite' (in the ill-spelt accusation that would later be hurled at him by the Marquess of Queensberry), at the time he visited Canada, some of his writing was already being claimed to be 'dangerous' to both men and women. In his travels around North America, Wilde confounded all his would-be critics. Those who had heard about his 'effete' reputation were stunned to encounter a man well over six feet tall with the physique of a soldier. He might dress like a dandy, but there was nothing about Wilde's physical features, except his flowing hair, that could mark him out as 'unmanly'.

Lorne cannot therefore have been avoiding Wilde in case he was 'tainted' by his reputation; as Wilde's biographers agree, he did not have his first sexual relationship with a man for a number of years after his visit to Canada.[57] He did already have a number of 'scandalous' friends – but so did Lorne. So why did Lorne refuse to meet Wilde, especially when it seems an invitation had already been issued? They had a number of mutual friends, thanks to Lord Ronnie Gower, and Wilde was under the impression that he had been invited to Rideau Hall. On 15 May 1882 Oscar Wilde wrote to his friend Norman Forbes-Robertson claiming, 'Tomorrow night I lecture Lorne on dadoes at Ottawa.' Yet the meeting did not take place. Was it because Wilde's writing was already considered 'dangerous'? Or because Lorne knew a number of Wilde's associates were also a part of Lord Ronnie's gay underworld? Or was Lorne frightened that Wilde, renowned for his acerbic wit, would pick up on a facet of Lorne's personality that he

[57] Wilde's first male lover was the poet Robert ('Robbie') Ross, who remained his loyal friend throughout all the miserable times Wilde was forced to endure. Ross later became his literary executor. Their relationship began in the late 1880s, following the birth of Wilde's two sons with Constance.

was anxious to keep hidden? Wilde was well known for parodying people in his writing.

Canadian academic Sandra Gwyn wrote that Lorne 'made a point' of not inviting Wilde to Rideau Hall and that he spent the two days of Wilde's time in Ottawa deliberately out of his office and playing golf. She believed the snub was deliberate: 'Not only was [Wilde] not invited to dine at Rideau Hall, the Governor General did not even bother to interrupt a round of golf to ask him to lunch. Nor did Lorne attend Wilde's public lecture at the Grand Opera House.'

Louise arrived back in Canada on 4 June 1882, on board the *Sarmatian*. Her new lady-in-waiting was the recently bereaved Miss Ina McNeill, whose fiancé had died just before their wedding. Louise had felt sorry for her and the two women would become good friends during their time in Canada. Almost as soon as Louise returned, Lorne and the Prime Minister received coded messages from the Home Office in London warning them of Fenian threats against her life. Louise threw herself back into public events, attending Lorne as he travelled around the country on viceregal business and winning hearts. The Fenians proved less of a threat than Canada itself as, once again, Louise and Lorne narrowly escaped death, this time when they were sailing and their yacht collided with a schooner. The couple returned to Montreal mercifully unharmed and visited the town that Louise would name Regina, in honour of her mother.

In September, Louise and Lorne travelled into the USA. As they neared Sacramento, the couple were involved in yet another dangerous accident, when their train collided with 'a yard engine'. The force of the jolt knocked Louise to the ground, where she bruised her shoulder very badly; she also suffered a minor cut to her face. Yet again, her neck and shoulder were damaged and she was plagued by the headaches that had become such a regular feature of her life. They travelled on to San Francisco, where they were particularly interested in visiting Chinatown. After this they returned to Canada, but with plans to return to the USA as soon as possible.

In 1882 Louise and Lorne visited Vancouver for their first official tour of the region. According to author Colin MacMillan Coates, in *Majesty in Canada*, Louise was so well loved that Robert Beaven, the premier of British Columbia, considered asking her to become queen of a separate kingdom of Vancouver Island. While the couple were on Vancouver Island the papers reported, 'During the visit of the Marquis of Lorne and Princess Louise to the water works to-day, a child fell and broke its arm. The Princess carried it into a house, remaining with it, and endeavouring to relieve its sufferings, until the arrival of a surgeon.' Although the story was laudatory, every time the newspapers wrote about Louise's attitude towards children, it was another reminder that Lorne and Louise were childless.

That the princess and her handsome husband had no children continued to cause debate and gossip throughout their marriage, until Louise was deemed too old to have children. One extraordinary rumour was alleged to have been started by the Campbell family, a claim that Louise had never started menstruating and was physically incapable of getting pregnant. The basis for this rumour is lost in history. The majority of historians who have touched on the subject – even those writing today – seem to attribute the lack of children to Louise's being 'barren', rather than to the possibility that Lorne may have been infertile or that the marriage may have been sexless.

She may not have had children, but Louise had many name sakes, including several Canadian landmarks. At around this time, the Northwest Territories of Canada were being divided and it was proposed that one of them should be named the territory of Louise. She suggested that her middle name, Alberta, would be better and would also honour her father, just as her mother was being honoured by the naming of Regina. Lorne wrote a dreadful poem about the occasion, as he was formally asked to name the new District (later Province) of Alberta:

> In token for the love which thou hast Shown
> For this wild land of freedom, I have Named
> A Province vast, and for its beauty Famed,
> By thy dear name to be hereafter Known,
> Alberta shall it be!

The couple sailed to New Westminster and were greeted by over 3,000 people from local tribes. When both Lorne and Louise shook hands with the wife of the local tribal chief the journalists watched in amazement.

In December, Louise, Lorne and their entourage travelled to California, eager to escape the fierce Canadian winter and spend

Christmas in the sun. They travelled to Los Angeles and San Francisco – where they were introduced to resident Canadians and went on a tour of Chinatown. Then they went on to Monterey, where they impressed the residents by refusing to travel in a carriage and walking from the station to their hotel (the two buildings were four blocks apart). On 24 December they arrived in Santa Barbara to enjoy a 'Mexican style'[58] Christmas. Louise became the first woman ever permitted to enter the sacred garden of its monastery. Louise loved Santa Barbara, where they stayed for a month for her health, but she was sad to miss the birth of Leopold and Helen's first child, Alice. The baby was ostensibly named after her recently deceased aunt; although it is likely Leopold had also wanted to name his daughter after Alice Liddell, who had recently named her son after him. (Queen Victoria surprised even herself by her admiration for Leopold's new daughter, writing to Vicky, 'Though I am not an admirer of babies – I must say this is a beautiful child, so plump and so big with such neat little features and such a complete head of dark hair.')

From Santa Barbara, Louise and Lorne took the train through Tucson, where their train stopped for fifteen minutes in the middle of the night. Unwittingly they made an embarrassing faux pas – the local mayor and other dignitaries had turned out to meet them, but Louise and Lorne were fast asleep and missed the intended ceremony. In Nebraska, however, they charmed the locals. As a local paper reported,

A farmer in Douglass County, Nebraska, writing to a friend says: 'I have had a visit from the Marquis of Lorne. Along with him were the Princess Louise and suite. They came up to my house and stayed for three hours, and the Princess took a sketch of my whole place – farm-house, stabling, wire fence, and all the trees I had planted myself about three years since. The Marquis and Princess both shook hands with me when they left'.

The couple travelled through St Louis to Richmond, where they were expected to meet the Governor of Virginia, but 'owing to a case of

---

[58] This was the expression used by David Duff; he showed the manuscript of his book to Princess Louise at the end of her life and she approved it.

small-pox in his family' the Governor was quarantined and had to send his apologies. From Richmond they continued by sleeper train to Charleston; Louise was still feeling unwell and the local papers reported with scorn, 'The Princess remained in bed until 4 o'clock in the afternoon, at which time she was dressed by her attendants.'

At Charleston the couple parted. Lorne travelled to Washington, where he met the American President, before returning to Canada. Louise, however, was off on another solo adventure. Unwilling to spend another winter in Canada, and supported by the Canadian government whose fears about the Fenian threats to her life were growing stronger, she was off to discover a new part of the world: she would spend the winter months on the island of Bermuda.

CHAPTER 17

Escaping the Fenians in Bermuda

> My sojourn upon these Islands in that 'Eternal Spring, which
> here enamels everything', among such a frank and genial people
> will, I assure you, be ever gratefully remembered by me.
>
> Princess Louise to the Mayor and Corporation of
> St George's, Bermuda

Louise's decision to travel to Bermuda was partly due to the fear that
she was in danger from terrorists, partly to avoid another harsh
Canadian winter, partly to discover a new country with which she
had become intrigued – and to allow herself and Lorne more time
away from each other. She reached the island at the end of January
1883, on board the *Dido*. To thwart any Fenian attempts on her life,
reports had been sent out that she would be spending the winter in
Charleston, Virginia. In an effort to avoid any further editorials about
Louise hating Canada, an official statement was sent to the newspapers,
claiming Louise went to Bermuda 'at the advice of a London physician, and by the express command of Her Majesty'.

As soon as it was known on Bermuda that the princess would be
arriving, there was a flurry of activity to make the island fit for royalty.
The streets were cleaned up, houses were repaired and painted, gardens
and fences tidied up and there was a sudden sprouting of flagpoles.
Shortly after two large welcome arches had been constructed, the
news arrived, via a ship bringing post and newspapers, that the princess
was not coming to Bermuda – she was staying in Charleston after all.
The islanders refused to believe it and continued with their preparations, festooning the island in garlands of flowers and evergreens. At
midday on Monday 29 January, with just forty-eight hours' notice from

another news-bearing ship, the *Dido* arrived in Grassy Bay. A thick red cloth had been laid down as a carpet and a large group of people waited to greet the princess, including the mayor's young daughter, who presented the royal visitor with a bouquet. An observer noted, 'It seemed as if all the inhabitants of Bermuda had poured into Hamilton to bid her welcome.'

There had been a discussion of where the most suitable place would be for Princess Louise to stay. After deciding Government House would not afford enough privacy, local businessman James Harvey Trimingham offered the exclusive use of his family home, Inglewood House. In 1842, the Trimingham family had founded the island's first department store and the current owner was one of the richest men in Bermuda.[59] James was also a member of the Executive Council and of the Governor's Council. The Triminghams moved out of their home and into their old family house, Waterville, at the bottom of the hill below Inglewood, for the duration of Louise's stay.

Inglewood had been built for a large family, so it had twelve bedrooms, ample room for the princess and her small suite of staff, and the grounds boasted a shooting range and tennis court.[60] Louise became friendly with Trimingham and his family, who were welcomed to her parties and social events, and she often went sailing on their yacht. Trimingham's daughter, also called Louise, was a regular visitor to Inglewood, where she often played tennis with Louise's lady-in-waiting. At times her brother would join them and play alongside Louise's equerry. Other local people also recalled being invited to play tennis. Louise Trimingham reported that Princess Louise did not play, but would watch their matches. For someone who loved sport and exercise as much as the princess did, this is surprising, but perhaps it would have been too painful after her sleighing injury. In a repetition of the scarlet fever in Ottawa story, it was noted, with some astonishment, that when James Harvey Trimingham was ill and infectious, Louise went to visit him bearing gifts.

[59] It was the menswear buyer for the Trimingham Brothers shop who invented the now-famous Bermuda shorts – which were based on British military shorts – and introduced them into the store.

[60] The house burned down in 1931. The only part that survives today is the servants' house, a two-storey flat-roofed house separate from the main building.

During her time in Bermuda, Louise was made aware yet again of insidious gossip about the feud between her and Lady Macdonald. Determined to scotch these rumours, she wrote a letter to the Prime Minister telling him how upset she was about the baseless stories, how fond she was of Lady Macdonald and what a perfect wife she thought Lady Macdonald to be – she was, Louise declared, a woman Louise would hold up as an example to all other wives. The sincerity of her letter has often been debated by academics, but the whispers about the two women's supposed animosity are impossible to prove or disprove. (This letter would be made public when Prince Arthur became Governor-General of Canada in the early twentieth century and rumours were still circulating about the supposed feud between the two women.)

Towards the end of February 1883, Louise attended a garden party held by the Governor of Bermuda and his wife. The photographer James B. Heyl, when gathering material for a book about the island which he published in the 1890s, asked people about meeting the princess. Amy Tucker recalled that, as a schoolgirl, she had met Louise at the garden party and remembered her saying 'Everybody in Bermuda has given me such a warm welcome: even the red birds come to my window every morning, and say, "Louise! Louise!"' Amy also remembered what a 'bright smile' the princess had. Interestingly, a local diarist recorded that instructions had been issued to the Bermudian families who were likely to meet Louise and these claimed to be indicative of her personality: 'The public was advised that the Princess had a good mind and was in general serious, but never grave. She had a bright smile with a sense of fun. By inclination, she sailed whenever she could, and avoided dances if possible.' Louise had always enjoyed dancing, so the fact that she was now avoiding it was something very new; perhaps, like the fact that she no longer played tennis, it was because of the severe injuries sustained in the sleigh accident.

As she did in England and Canada, Louise carried out several official engagements on the island, but the pace of her life in Bermuda was far more relaxed. She attended local parties, visited hospitals and schools, opened bazaars, attended regattas, watched amateur theatricals and handed out cups at dinghy races. She spent hours walking around the island (often on her own), sailing or driving out in a carriage with one of her ladies-in-waiting to sketch and paint the views.

One of the most well known stories about Princess Louise's time in Bermuda is still repeated on the island today.[61] Louise often took off on her own to walk and sketch. On one such occasion, she became very thirsty and stopped at a remote house to ask for a glass of water. Inside the house, Mrs McCarthy was alone and busy ironing her husband's shirt. She was bemused by this strange white woman who suddenly appeared, and told her visitor that she had no time to get water until she had finished ironing the shirt. Her mysterious visitor promised Mrs McCarthy that if she would take the time to fetch a glass of water, the stranger would iron the shirt for her. Mrs McCarthy told her that she didn't trust a stranger to do it right and she had to finish the shirt because she had so much to do before tomorrow – as the following day she was travelling to St George to get a glimpse of the princess. When asked if she had already seen the princess, Mrs McCarthy said she'd seen her when she arrived. 'Do you think you would recognise her if you saw her again?' was the enquiry. Mrs McCarthy admitted that she wasn't sure. Louise is reported to have said, 'Well, take a good look at me now so you will be sure to know me tomorrow.' The flustered Mrs McCarthy rushed off to get water – and when she came back she found Louise calmly ironing the shirt. (Shortly after Princess Louise's death, over fifty years later, the McCarthy family were interviewed by a journalist and said that they still owned the shirt.)

Shortly before she left Bermuda, on Easter Sunday, the weather turned cold and Louise requested a fire to be lit in her room. Somehow, the rug in front of it managed to catch fire. Although it was quickly put out and no damage was done except to the rug, the story quickly got into the papers and reports spread around the globe that Louise had narrowly escaped a house fire.

A few days later, on 10 April, Louise reluctantly boarded the HMS *Tenedos* to return to Canada. As on her arrival, the streets and harbour were crowded with cheering well-wishers and yachts were taken out to see the regal ship on its journey. On the evening of her departure, the Mayor of Bermuda – a keen gardener to whom Louise had promised to send a consignment of plants he was unable to get on the

---

[61] Interview with the sculptor Andrew Trimingham and the former archivist for the Bermuda government John Adam in 2012.

island – wrote in his diary that Louise was 'one of the most charming ladies ever to tread Bermuda's soil, so dignified, kind, courteous, thoughtful'. The year after her visit, a new hotel was built in Bermuda. It was named the Princess Hotel, in honour of Louise, and was opened in 1885. Louise may not have been the island's first tourist, but she was certainly the most prominent of her era and she helped to put the island firmly in the centre of the international tourist map. In 1998, Bermuda held the first ever exhibition devoted to watercolours painted by Princess Louise.

CHAPTER 18

Return to London – and tragedy

[Leopold's] life had been hurried & feverish of late, & he never
seemed able to do half he wished to do, or see half the people
he desired to see – But his heart went out to them just the same
– amid all the hustle and unrest of the world.

Major Robert Collins to Max Müller, 31 March 1884

HMS *Tenedos* reached New York City on 14 April 1883 and Louise
travelled straight to Boston, where Lorne was waiting to greet her.
They visited 'the principal points' of the city before travelling to
Montreal where Louise was pronounced 'as brown as a berry' and 'in
the best of health and spirits'. When they reached Ottawa, the mayor
gave a public address to welcome Louise back to the city. The couple
were proud to attend an exhibition at the Royal Canadian Academy
of the Arts. At the exhibition, Lorne purchased paintings by four
Canadian artists whose works he admired and sent them to Queen
Victoria for her ever-growing art collection. In Louise's absence, Lorne
had founded the Royal Society of Canada for the Encouragement of
Science and Literature. Yet despite their apparent popularity, all was
not well, and the threat to the couple's security was worsening. Louise
found the fussing frustrating and claustrophobic and at first she refused
to pander to the need for increased security. After shots were fired in
the grounds of Rideau Hall, however, she took it more seriously. Lorne
insisted she be accompanied at all times by a detective who acted as
her personal bodyguard.

At the end of May, the author Mark Twain arrived in Ottawa, where
he spent five days with Louise and Lorne. He later related that they
'kept him with them almost continually, and were loath to let him

go'. He was there for the opening of Parliament, to which he travelled in a carriage with Louise (Lorne was in the first carriage with his local dignitaries). When the salute to the procession was fired, Twain reputedly turned to Louise and said 'Your Highness, I have had other compliments paid to me, but none equal to this one. I have never before had a salute fired in my honor.'[62] On his return to America, Twain sent both Louise and Lorne copies of his works.

While Louise was enjoying her final months in Canada, a time when the weather was beautiful and she was popular with the general public, the queen had been plunged back into deep mourning and grief. John Brown had died at the end of March from erysipelas. In June, Prince Arthur wrote to Louise, 'Poor Mama has been terribly upset by Brown's death – and her knee has given her so much trouble, she is still very lame.' (The queen had slipped and hurt her knee several weeks beforehand; unable to walk unaided, she had had to be supported at John Brown's funeral by leaning on Beatrice's arm.) Victoria wrote to her grandson (who would become King George V), 'I have lost my *dearest best* friend who no one in *this World* can *ever* replace . . . *never forget* your poor sorrowing old Grandmother's best and truest friend.' Despite her deep dislike of John Brown, Louise felt sadness for her mother. On the anniversary of his death in 1884 she would write the queen a tender letter sending her 'warmest sympathy' for 'the loss of a friend no other can replace'. The queen was very touched by this kindness. (She was struck again by her daughter's thoughtfulness in 1895, when she sent a telegram to Louise who had written to her on the anniversary of her coronation: 'Many loving thanks You are the only one of my children who remembers this day'.)

In mid-September, Louise and Lorne welcomed Louise's nephew, Prince George of Wales, to Canada. They met him in Toronto, where they declared open the city's Industrial Exhibition. He had arrived just as the viceregal couple had started preparing to leave the country. For Lorne, the departure was a huge wrench – yet it was he who had arranged, while Louise was away in Bermuda and without consulting her, to finish his time as Governor-General early. When she returned, to find that they would be returning to England in the autumn, Louise is said to have been furious. She attempted to change

---

[62] Quoted by Albert Bigelow Paine in his 1907 biography of Mark Twain.

the arrangements, writing to her mother to tell her. Louise must have known that it would not be possible to change the date: the new Governor-General had already been named. It seems that her apparent fervour to stay for the allotted time was an intelligent PR move – and worked. Louise left Canada on a wave of good wishes from the Canadian people. Lorne's sadness at leaving Canada was more heartfelt, and he reportedly wept 'like a child' when they departed from Rideau Hall. As Lorne, who had been so happy in Canada, is unlikely to have left early by choice, it is probable that the queen had become deeply concerned about the constant threats to their safety and had ordered them to come home early.

The *Sardinian*, commanded by Captain Dutton, arrived in Liverpool in the late morning of Monday 5 November 1883. For Louise, the most important sight was that of Prince Leopold waiting to greet them. Leopold had travelled by overnight train, accompanied by his former tutor Major Collins, who was now his secretary. Despite heavy rain and a 'cutting northerly wind', the people of Liverpool had turned out to welcome the Lornes, and Leopold's arrival to greet them was 'loudly cheered by the large crowd'. The rain had delayed the ship, which for the ever-seasick Louise was frustrating in the extreme. Eventually, the *Sardinian* was reached by the *Lancashire*, carrying Leopold, the Mayor and other dignitaries. The Princess went against protocol by shaking hands with the captain, much to his delight. Following her precedent, Lorne and Leopold did the same.

At their homecoming a band played 'God Save the Queen' and 'The Campbells Are Coming' and journalists reported that the sight of both Prince Leopold and Princess Louise encouraged the crowd to raise 'hearty cheers'. Lorne was no longer the Governor-General, he was no longer his wife's superior: he was back in England, a commoner and the lowly husband of a princess, outranked as soon as he set foot in Liverpool not only by his wife but by his young brother-in-law. At the mayoral reception, Lorne made a heartfelt speech: 'We have left a land on the other side of the Atlantic which has become very dear to us and have left very many friends . . . but, in spite of the sorrow of leaving Canada, we feel that it is very pleasant indeed to find ourselves among our friends and our countrymen, and to be greeted with those hearty ringing cheers which met us this morning on the streets of Liverpool.' A little later, after a private conversation with his wife, Lorne told the people of Liverpool from the balcony: 'The Princess has asked me to tell you how happy she feels to be again amongst you.'

The party travelled by train to London's Euston station, then went straight to Kensington Palace, which had been renovated during the five years of their absence. The Canadians did not forget the princess easily; the year after Louise had returned to England, Lake Louise was named after her and quickly became a popular tourist attraction. The princess's memory began to be revered and in January 1884 there was a outcry when the special chair that had been built for her, alongside the usual Governor-General's chair, was to be cut down for use as the Speaker's chair. Newspaper articles expressed the nation's fury at such 'vandalism'. A reporter from the *Ottawa Free Press* went so far as to call it 'desecration of the relic', stating that the government should intervene as the people of Canada thought the chair should be placed in a museum.

Louise had been excited to return to England, but 1884 was destined to be one of her most painful years and it would see an already strained marriage severely tested. The couple had grown used to being apart in Canada, an arrangement that suited them. Back in Britain, it was more difficult to manage this without exciting press attention. By the end of the year, their disagreements were obvious outside the marriage.

Louise threw herself into life in London, embracing the new 'Rational Dress' movement and other social changes and advances, such as the International Health Exhibition which opened that year and caused great discussion of its vegetarian restaurant. When Louise had first talked of wanting to become a sculptor, her mother had warned her against spending time with artists because they mix 'with all classes of society' and should be considered 'dangerous'. In that intoxicating world of artistic dangerousness Louise was more than happy to embroil herself once again.

At the start of the year, Lorne was preparing to deliver a series of lectures about Canada, around the country. He had not returned to being an MP at once, as his brother Colin was still in his former seat; Colin, never a popular MP, was lampooned in the press and infuriated his constituents. In 1884, he would also become entangled in a sensational and scandalous court case, damaging his reputation and career even further.

When Lorne chose to travel to the South of France to escape the end of the British winter, Louise decided not to go with him. By the end of March, Lorne was back in England and it fell to him to break the terrible news to his wife that Leopold had suffered a fatal accident. While visiting a club in Cannes, the prince had fallen and, despite its being a minor incident, it had proved fatal for a haemophiliac: Leopold had died within a few hours. He was only thirty years old at the time of his death and his wife Helen was pregnant. Bertie went to Cannes to bring his brother's body home and broke down in tears in public as the casket was placed into the train carriage. Leopold's funeral took place at St George's Chapel in Windsor on 5 April – two days before what would have been his thirty-first birthday.

Nothing in Louise's life – not the death of her father nor that of Sybil St Albans – had been as terrible as the death of Leopold, the brother she had always adored and who had given her nothing but adulation and love. She wrote to Lord Tennyson a distraught letter in which she called Leopold 'the joy and object' of her life. To Lorne's sympathetic Aunt Dot, she described their relationship: 'we were to each other . . . the dearest friend we each had'. Nearly four months after Leopold's death, Lord Ronnie Gower went for lunch at Kensington Palace and was alarmed by Louise's depression. Lorne had no idea how to help her, other than to warn Ronnie not to mention Leopold's name.

That Lorne had no comfort to offer his wife emphasises how stagnant the marriage had become. The queen wrote to Vicky about how unhappy Louise and Lorne were; Louise had told her mother that she wanted a separation, but the queen refused to sanction this. In her letter to Vicky she mentioned Louise's 'perfect aversion' to Lorne and that she was 'bent on separating from him. This dare not be for we cannot have a Scandal in the family!' Louise blamed her mother, writing to her in 1884: 'It was yr wish for two years, that I shd marry Lorne, & because I saw how much it bothered & worried you, that I said I wd see him again. You asked me to choose between him & another, all I answered was that I thought Lorne was the best of those two, if you remember.'

In August of 1884, the same month in which the queen wrote to Vicky, the *New York Times* published a short article about the marriage: 'The continued separation of Lord Lorne and the Princess Louise is again attracting comment. The Princess left England yesterday to spend the Autumn in Germany. Lord Lorne is yachting with his father and mother in the Hebrides.'

In September, Louise travelled to the Tyrol to stay with her eldest sister, who was holidaying there. Some reports claim she and Lorne travelled there together, but in newspaper reports of the time, Lorne's name is conspicuously absent. The queen wrote to tell Vicky it was good that Louise was able to see her sister, who could try and cheer her up; the queen also commented that she believed Louise and Lorne would never live together again and they must do their best to make it as unremarked upon as possible. Louise was reported to have travelled on the mail steamer with Count Gleichen (Queen Victoria's half-nephew) and his daughter. When the sisters met, Vicky was extremely worried about Louise and reported back to her mother how depressed and unwell she seemed to be. In November, the queen commented: 'Louise's aversion [to Lorne] will be permanent.'

The couple did not separate, but their marriage was being exposed as a sham; all the early newspaper reports of the couple having been so in love were starting to look rather foolish. In Canada, Louise had needed Lorne. Now she no longer had to keep up the pretence of being the perfect wife and was as desperate to live alone as when she had been trapped in Buckingham Palace as her mother's companion-secretary. Even the queen seems to have been on her daughter's side, although sorry for Lorne, writing that he 'is totally unsuited to her, very unsoigné, not overfond of soap and water, all of which is very uncongenial to her. He bears her open dislike wonderfully well in public.' That Lorne was an eccentric comes across in the memoirs of family members and friends, who joked about his lack of understanding about what clothes should be worn at which occasions and of inappropriate behaviour, such as refusing to receive honoured guests, most notably – as Elizabeth Longford relates – snubbing the German Emperor, who wanted to bestow upon Lorne the Order of the Black Eagle. Lorne insisted that he did not have time to meet the Emperor as he wanted to have a bath. Many such stories were circulated. As, towards the end of his life, he would begin to suffer from what is believed to have been Alzheimer's or a similar condition, it is possible that he was starting to suffer from dementia earlier than was realised. A sweet and witty letter he wrote to Louise survives from

August 1898 while Lorne was on holiday in France with Lord Ronald Gower and their friend Frank Hird (who was Gower's lover): 'Hird is bathing in the Loire. Ronald and I have had a tub each in our rooms – and I write with nothing on! Clothes are altogether a mistake. I anoint myself with eau de cologne after bathing and remain horizontal till dinner.'

A now-legendary story exists about the state of Louise and Lorne's marriage. Reputedly when they were living at Kensington Palace, Louise became so infuriated by her husband sneaking out at night to try and meet sexual partners, usually soldiers, loitering in the park that she ordered the French windows in their apartments to be bricked up. I was unable to verify this – although I learnt from the staff at Kensington Palace another story which seems to lend credence to the rumour. In the mid twentieth century, Princess Margaret was given the apartments that had formerly belonged to Louise and Lorne. She tried to research the story of the bricked-up window, according to one staff member at the palace; but even Princess Margaret wasn't able to access the records. Elizabeth Longford, who did have access to the Royal Archives, mentions the story in her book and states that Princess Margaret was told 'it had been done on the orders of Princess Louise to keep her husband inside'.

The absence of Leopold was felt very keenly as Louise tried to adjust to being back in England, forced to live closely with her husband and once more under the watchful eye of her mother. She missed her brother and confidant desperately. While Louise was deeply miserable, Princess Beatrice seemed finally on her way to happiness. Despite her mother having thwarted all other attempts at a romance, in 1884 Beatrice met Prince Henry of Battenberg, known as 'Liko'. He was very good looking and amusing – and although everyone knew the queen would never allow her youngest daughter to fly the nest, Liko was willing to marry her.

CHAPTER 19

Keeping up appearances

But their aim, and their claim, which are one and the same,
Are founded in falsehoods of sand, you know.
The Campbells are cunning, oho, oho . . .

Lines from an anonymous poem criticising Lord Colin
Campbell, MP

Lorne's tenure as Governor-General had been such a success that in 1885 he was suggested as the new Governor of New South Wales in Australia. Louise refused to go. So, instead, Lorne returned to British politics, but, following the travesty of his brother Colin's time as MP for Argyll, the Campbells were no longer welcome as MPs in their local constituency. The disappointment of Colin's tenure had led formerly loyal constituents to start parodying him, singing a cynical version of the proud song 'The Campbells Are Coming' as 'The Campbells Are Cunning'.

Knowing he would be thwarted in Scotland, Lorne stood as the Liberal candidate for Hampstead, in London; but the Liberal Party was out of favour and Lorne was defeated by his Conservative opponent, Sir Henry Holland, by almost 900 votes. Lorne felt keenly the vast gulf between his life in Canada and his life back in Britain, once again in the shadow of his wife's mother.

The queen was battling her own demons. Having initially been furious that Beatrice could even think of marrying, she had brokered an agreement whereby Beatrice and Liko promised to live near her. Having persuaded herself that Beatrice's marriage would be acceptable, the queen had not anticipated opposition from the rest of the family. Beatrice's marriage brought out political prejudices from all sides, not least from Vicky and the queen's Prussian relations – Liko was from the House of Battenberg,[63] which Fritz's family thought far too inferior to be allied to by marriage. Added to Vicky's angry snobbery was the reaction of the British people – they were not amused at the idea of yet another member of their royal family marrying a foreigner. It was a difficult time politically. As Beatrice's wedding approached, the situation in the country was becoming increasingly fevered.

The issue dividing the House of Commons and the House of Lords was that of Home Rule for Ireland; the 'Fenian problem' was becoming ever more serious, marking the beginning of a new terror campaign in London. In 1883, Fenian terrorists had bombed the underground train tunnel between Charing Cross and Westminster stations; in 1884 they had caused great embarrassment to the police by the successful bombing of Scotland Yard; now they stepped up the campaign. On 20 January 1885, a Fenian bomb exploded on a train at Gower Street tube station.[64] Just days later, two bombs were detonated at the Houses of Parliament, as well as one at London Bridge and one at the Tower of London (where the bomber was actually witnessed lighting the fuse. He and his accomplice were arrested and later convicted). Early newspaper reports erroneously suggested the bombs had been left by women, who had concealed them under their voluminous skirts. People were living in fear, angry with the government's perceived inability to keep them safe.

The situation was exacerbated by the news of a tragedy overseas: the war hero General Gordon had been murdered in Khartoum. The general had gone to the Sudan to help the Egyptian forces, who were under siege from Sudanese rebels led by Muhammad Ahmed (known as the Mahdi). Gordon had requested urgent reinforcements, but the government and military commanders had been slow to react. He was killed two days before reinforcements arrived, when the rebels broke into the besieged city. When the vivid reports of his death reached Britain the public reacted with fury against the government. Although later historians have blamed Gordon for not getting out of the city, at the time of his death he was seen as a martyr.

---

[63] It was Beatrice who introduced the multicoloured 'Battenberg cake' to Britain.

[64] The station is now known as Euston Square.

During their early married life, images of Louise and Lorne appeared on memorabilia all over the English-speaking world. People could not get enough of the beautiful princess and her handsome husband.

When Princess Louise married the Marquess of Lorne, she was the first member of the British royal family to marry a 'commoner' since 1515.

The media and the public were thrilled by Princess Louise's choice of a British husband. The newspapers were full of articles claiming that this was a romantic love match.

Louise found her new Canadian home dark and oppressive, so she began decorating it. This was the door to her boudoir, which she painted with apple blossoms in a Japanese-style.

Louise was immediately popular in Canada and quickly became renowned for her fashion sense.

Lorne loved his years in Canada and delighted in the freedom he could enjoy whilst in a different continent from his mother-in-law.

A few years after leaving Canada, Louise was commissioned to sculpt a statue of her mother to be erected in Montreal.

Prince Albert instilled in all his children a strong sense of social responsibility. Until the end of her life Princess Louise took her duties very seriously, tirelessly raising funds and awareness for hospitals, schools and other important causes.

Shortly after her marriage, the Argyll and Sutherland Highlanders became known as Princess Louise's regiment. She designed their new regimental badge and took an active interest in their training and activities.

Philip de László was welcomed into London's artistic community, after his arrival from Vienna in 1907. He painted this portrait of Princess Louise in 1915, a year after the death of her husband, wearing mourning.

Beatrice and Liko's wedding took place on 23 July 1885, but it was far less formal than her sisters' weddings and, due to the political situation at the time, was a somewhat muted affair. They were married at St Mildred's Church on the Isle of Wight, where a troop of soldiers from Princess Louise's Argyll and Sutherland Highlanders formed a guard of honour for the couple. Shortly after the wedding, the London correspondent for the *New York Times* wrote an article about the unsuitability of the match and how 'dreadful' Prince Henry of Battenberg was rumoured to be, hinting at having spoken to 'those in the know'. The underlying reason for people believing the marriage to be doomed was that Liko was considered extremely good looking and Beatrice was not. The general consensus was that Liko was bound to stray and would not remain happy for long tethered to the queen's apron strings, as was expected of Beatrice's husband.

Knowing that the queen was initially against the match, Liko had used his charm to win her over to his side. The queen's comment in a letter to the disapproving Vicky is revealing about Liko's and Beatrice's relationship '[Liko] is so modest, so full of consideration for me and so is she, and both are quietly and really sensibly happy. There is no kissing, etc. (which Beatrice dislikes).' An article in the *London Truth*, which was picked up by the American papers, gave an unflattering account of the wedding and the royal family:

> Princess Louise looked well, but she has a very flighty manner.
> Lord Lorne has something of his sire's bantam-like air. He was
> in tartans, but certainly looked very common . . . The Prince of
> Wales . . . seemed ill at ease and out of sorts, and so also did
> the Queen, who looked exceedingly cross and who was dressed,
> as she always is . . . in black satin with a white tulle cap and veil
> . . . [The bridesmaids] looked very pleasing and simple, but there
> was a decided lack of beauty among the group.

The word 'flighty' was one that was often applied to Louise. (In 1880, a Canadian politician had noted, 'Lord Lorne seems to be tolerably happy in the absence of his flighty spouse.')

While Lorne was attempting to resurrect his political career, Louise forged ahead with her charity work and accepted the presidency of the Society for Home Education. The one aspect of their marriage

that was always strong was their desire to make Britain a more egalitarian place, and in their shared belief of the need for better education
for all. The Society homed in on the 'need which was felt to exist for
an improved method of teaching the children of the upper classes, or
those taught at home' and to elevate their home schooling to the level
of that given to boys at fee-paying schools. The bill was aimed specifi-
cally at girls, since sons of the upper classes (unless in delicate health)
were taught at school. Louise wanted sisters to be given the same
educational rights as their brothers. In addition, she continued to work
with the Girls' Public Day School Trust and the Ragged Schools'
Association. In the same year, Louise raised funds for Canadian troops,
and money to send medics out to Canada to aid in the war between
the new settlers and the first nations. She was also involved in fund-
raising for wounded British troops fighting in the Sudan. In the
summer, she laid the foundation stone for the new wing at the Victoria
Hospital for Children, on Tite Street in Chelsea.[65] In this project she
was not merely acting as a figurehead; after visiting the hospital she
had realised the necessity for a new wing, so had lobbied for it to be
built and helped to raise both awareness and funds. The laying of the
foundation stone was the culmination of an achievement Louise could
deservedly be proud of. She also made the newspapers for reports of
bravery, following a carriage accident in London's Covent Garden.
When another carriage ran into Louise's vehicle, the newspapers
reported, 'The horses became restive, and knocked down and injured
two bystanders. The Princess remained perfectly cool, and escaped
unhurt.'

In reponse to the many rumours about their marriage, Louise and
Lorne made a number of high-profile public appearances. They were
seen together at a grand party thrown by the composer Arthur Sullivan,
at an amateur performance of *As You Like It* in the grounds of Archie
Campbell's home in Surrey, at an artists' ball and at numerous society
events. Whilst giving the appearance of being united in public, they

[65] Louise, in common with all artists, knew Tite Street well. This was the street on
which Edward Godwin created Whistler's iconic studio – sadly destroyed in the 1960s
and replaced with an example of deplorably bland architecture. It was also the street
on which John Singer Sargent had his studio. Other notable residents included Frank
Miles, close friend of Lord Ronnie Gower, and Constance and Oscar Wilde.

were leading increasingly separate lives. Louise was spending as much time as possible with her artistic friends. She enjoyed Whistler's parody, in 1885, of the speech made by Royal Academician J.C. Horsley, who took a stand over what he saw as the obscene use of nude models. (*Punch* gave him the nickname 'Clothes Horsley'.) Another artist with whom Louise became friendly was Edward Burne-Jones. Undated letters from the painter to Louise survive, in which he mentions her visiting his studio and his sending drawings or paintings to her at Louise's request. Following the artist's death (in 1898), his devoted wife, Georgiana, wrote to Louise thanking her for her kindness and friendship: 'You knew something of him and what he was to those who lived near him. But I still thank God that no infirmity fell upon him, body or mind, and that before he left us he had done so splendid a day's work.'

Despite the sham that their marriage was in the mid-1880s, the fiction that Louise and Lorne's marriage was a love match was being rekindled, in response to public disappointment in Beatrice's marriage. The papers were thrilled by a perceived romantic reunion in the summer of 1885 when Louise returned to London by train from Balmoral and Lorne met her at the station. The wording of the article in every paper is exactly the same, suggesting that the source of the story was an official news bulletin. The story neatly avoids any mention of the fact that Louise had gone to Balmoral alone. By the autumn, however, the papers had got hold of the story that she was to travel incognito overseas without Lorne, returning to the spas at Aix-les-Bains (where she met old friends and made new ones, including Anny Thackeray, the novelist daughter of William Thackeray). Once again, there was speculation about their lack of children and queries as to whether it would be possible for a woman in her late thirties to conceive for the first time. In contrast, Beatrice's marriage cannot have been as sexually passionless as her mother would have liked to believe, as just four months into her marriage, Beatrice suffered a miscarriage.

CHAPTER 20

Scandal amongst the Campbells

In October I had a severe chill. I was confined to my room . . .
I did not then see much of Lady Colin. On attending a political
meeting at Killmun in Scotland, I got another chill, and was
attended there by the local doctors. Lady Colin did not nurse
me there. I was unwell when she left me.

Morning Post, reporting Lord Colin Campbell's statements
during the Campbell divorce case, 7 December 1886

It was not only the Fenians who had been angered by recent political
decisions: in the mid-1880s many people in Britain were feeling let
down by the government. The gap between the rich and poor showed
few signs of narrowing and unemployment was frighteningly high.
Following the miseries of a cold winter, poverty-stricken families were
growing increasingly desperate. Although the signs of discontent
should have been obvious, the police claimed they were 'taken by
surprise' when the streets of central London exploded in riots.
Following the first day of the riots, in February 1886, journalists
reported, 'The mob, . . . numbering about 5,000, held possession of
the West End for fully two hours, and perpetrated acts of lawlessness
almost unchecked . . . A wanton and vindictive spirit was displayed
by the rioters . . . provisions were taken out of the shops and kicked
into the streets.' Three days later *The Star* reported, 'The panic in
London has subsided this morning, though an uneasy feeling continues
to prevail. The shops are open as usual this morning. The troops and
police are still kept in reserve in readiness for emergencies.'

The papers were also getting ready for the other big story: the
upcoming Campbell divorce case – being fought by Lorne's younger

brother Colin and his wife Gertrude (known as Lady Colin). In 1886, London gossips and newspapers were whispering about every lurid detail.[66] Was it true that Lady Colin had committed adultery with four lovers (a duke, a general, a doctor and the fire chief for London)? Or was Lord Colin attempting to blacken her name to cover up his own behaviour? Was it true that he had married despite knowing he had contracted an 'unmentionable disease', and that he had knowingly infected his wife with the result of his 'bachelor indiscretions'?

That such a scandalous case had close contact with one of Queen Victoria's children gave the gossips a field day. On 30 December 1886, Prince Arthur wrote a sympathetic letter to Louise: 'How sorry I have been for you at all this disgraceful <u>Colin</u> divorce case, there has never been anything so bad before and I am amazed that the Duke, Lorne and all the family ever permitted the matter going before a public court. One is quite ashamed to talk about it and I should think that Colin will be unable to show his face for some time to come.' Usually, it was Bertie and his notorious 'Marlborough House Set' whose name was in the gossip columns. Some years previously, Bertie had been questioned in court during the scandalous Mordaunt divorce case – in which he had been accused of committing adultery with Lady Mordaunt.[67] Despite Bertie having been found innocent in court, the public was not convinced and the case continued to be whispered about later. Now, however, it was not one of Bertie's indiscretions in

---

[66] The family has never been immune from public scandal. In the 1960s, the divorce case of the 11th Duke of Argyll and his wife Margaret was all over the newspapers. Photographs had been published of her performing sex acts on an unidentified man; although both she and the man were photographed without their faces being seen, the duchess was identifiable by her distinctive necklace. It was rumoured that either the 'headless man' (as he became known in the papers) or the man who took the photograph was the actor Douglas Fairbanks Junior.

[67] When Lady Mordaunt gave birth to a daughter who was discovered to be blind, she was so distraught she decided she was being punished for committing adultery. She confessed her affairs to her husband and amongst the men she claimed she had 'done very wrong with . . . often and in open day' was the Prince of Wales. Her husband, Sir Charles Mordaunt, filed for divorce and Bertie was called to attend, as a witness to her defence. Despite having sent her letters and being known to have called on her while her husband was out, Bertie was found innocent of having committed adultery with her. Lady Mordaunt, aged just 28, was ruled insane and committed to an asylum for the rest of her life.

the limelight; it was the turn of Louise, and especially her husband, to be embroiled – by association – in the unsavoury affairs of the divorce court.

Throughout 1886, the couple put on a public show of unity. They were, however, spending as little time together as they could. In the autumn of 1886, Louise returned to Aix-les-Bains. Everyone in Victorian England empathised with the curse of ill health, and the need for a 'cure'. Louise also spent the first few months of 1887 travelling overseas, incognito, with her lady-in-waiting, Lady Sophia MacNamara. Lorne was with her only briefly. Louise visited Malta, Italy and the French Riviera, sailing on the royal yacht *Surprise* and on 'her Majesty's ironclad *Alexandra*, flagship of the Mediterranean Squadron', a ship about which the papers wrote with great enthusiasm. Although Lorne was with his wife when she arrived in Malta, he is not mentioned in any of the later reports of her time there, even though articles that were based on official telegrams all state that he was with her at strategic points of the trip. As Louise was now 39 years old, the gossips were starting to abandon the hope that there would ever be an Argyll heir. Lorne's nephew, Niall, was now recognised as the heir to the dukedom.

In Malta, Louise stayed with Alfred and Marie. Alfred had first visited Malta in the 1850s and 1860s (and it was there in 1867 that he had fallen into disgrace for a 'sexual escapade', the news of which reached the ears of Queen Victoria and caused as much furore in the royal household as Bertie's affair with Nellie Clifden had done). As he was a serving naval officer, Alfred returned to Malta on several occasions. It had caused great excitement on the island when Marie gave birth to one of their children, Princess Victoria Melita, there.[68] By the time of Louise's visit, Alfred been appointed Commander-in-Chief of the Mediterranean Fleet and he and Marie were enjoying a thriving, if small, 'court' in Malta, although their marriage remained unhappy. Louise sympathised with her brother. Not only was she in an unhappy marriage herself, but she had never grown fond of her overbearing sister-in-law.

Malta had long prided itself on its royal and aristocratic associations,

---

[68] Alfred and Marie had four daughters and one surviving son. Their second son was stillborn.

and when Disraeli had visited the island he had written, 'society in Malta is very refined indeed for a colony'. Having a son of the queen living on the island was deemed a very great honour and Alfred was treated more like a king than a commander-in-chief. In January 1887, a grand ball was held to celebrate the anniversary of his wedding. In *The Graphic*'s commemorative issue the front-page illustration shows Alfred speaking to a man wearing a kilt. One can assume the kilted man (whose back is to the viewer) is intended to be Lorne; beside them Louise and Marie, dressed in the latest fashions, look on. Neither woman looks happy, both are pouting and they seem to be looking askance at their husbands. Inside the paper is a brief description of the ball; interestingly, although Louise is mentioned amongst the list of important attendees, Lorne's name is absent from this and from the many other articles about the ball. A few weeks later, Louise celebrated her thirty-ninth birthday, for which Alfred arranged a special event. As the papers reported (again ignoring Lorne): 'Malta has been even more than usually gay this winter. Balls, picnics, and parties of every description have abounded, on many of which Royalty has shed the lustre of its presence. A review of the troops and naval brigade was held in honour of the Princess Louise's birthday . . . Considerable amusement was caused . . . [when] General Davis, who was in command of the troops, called for three cheers for Princess Beatrice instead of the Princess Louise. This little matter, however, was soon put right.'

After leaving Malta, Louise travelled on to Italy; once again a few – but not all – reports state that Lorne was with her. They visited Naples and reputedly stayed at the Hôtel Royal des Etrangers for a week. Louise also visited Rome, where she was inspired by the antiquities and art galleries. Her time in Rome provides an interesting insight into her relationship with Beatrice's husband, Liko. Louise and Liko met up in Rome, purportedly by chance, although it seems likely they had arranged to meet there. Most of the family still disapproved of Liko, despite the fact that Beatrice was apparently very happy. Unfortunately, Beatrice's cosseted and spoilt childhood still rankled with most of her siblings, particularly her brothers, who could not see that it was the queen who was to blame for favouring Beatrice, rather than Beatrice herself. Most of her siblings were jealous of their youngest sister and they distrusted her, nervous of her role as the queen's confidante and, in some instances, the queen's spy. As a result, unflattering letters about Liko continued to be sent between family members.

Most galling to some of Beatrice's siblings was that the queen, so opposed to the match at the start, had been utterly won over by Liko; this felt especially bitter to Vicky, who did not approve of Liko's 'low' family connections. The House of Battenberg was considered 'not of the blood' by Fritz and his family. Others pitied Liko condescendingly because his role as Beatrice's husband meant he was forced to be so completely under the iron thumb of Queen Victoria.

Despite having no recognised children of her own, Louise was always adored by the children (and, later, by the grandchildren) of her siblings, several of whom described her as their 'favourite aunt'. In April 1887, Prince George of Wales wrote a fond letter to Louise: 'My darling Aunt Louise . . . I was dreadfully sorry to say goodbye to you the other day in Malta, but still the few days we spent together were better than none at all. I hope you had some fun after we left and went for some rides . . . I miss you very much, my dear, you are always so kind to me. We must look forward to our next meeting in June, which I am glad to say is not so very far off now.' A letter from his older brother, Prince Eddy, addresses her as 'Dearest Aunt Louise' and ends with 'your ever affectionate old nephew'. Throughout her life Louise had the enviable ability to get on with people of all ages, and children and young people especially loved her. Her siblings who had children of their own but often did not 'understand' their offspring envied her position as adored aunt, and Beatrice in particular often resented how much her children loved Louise.

Three weeks after Louise had left Malta, Prince George wrote to his 'darling Aunt Louise' again, telling her with amusement that one of Marie's ladies-in-waiting, Lady Mary Fitzwilliam, had been shocked by the news that Louise had been 'to Rome with Fortescue and Marsh [two officers under Arthur's command], it amused me very much the way she said it, as much as to say that you ought not to have gone with them and that she did not like it'.

In May he wrote a reply to one of Louise's letters, in which she had told him stories of her travels: she had told George that she had happened to be in Rome at the same time as Liko and that he had teased her about her clothes – Louise remained an artistic and unconventional dresser, pleased with her ability to defy the social expectations of how a princess should dress. George responded indignantly, as though Liko had hurt Louise's feelings, 'I'm very glad you spent a pleasant time in Rome . . . so Liko arrived before you left and began abusing your clothes, you certainly ought to have snubbed him and told him you had not so much money as Beatrice has to spend on your clothes, *damn* his impertinence, he has nothing else to do I suppose but look at people's clothes, poor creature.' The young prince did not pick up on the obvious fact that Liko and Louise felt comfortable enough with each other for him to tease her. Nor did George seem to realise that it was unlikely their meeting was a chance one – or perhaps, given the tone of his earlier letters, he was all too aware and jealous of Liko. From the start, Louise had been fascinated by Beatrice's handsome husband, and he seems to have been equally willing to engage in a flirtation with his attractive sister-in-law. Whether they ever embarked on a full affair is something that has caused speculation ever since.

While Louise was in Malta and Italy, Alix was in need of her sympathetic sister-in-law. When Lorne's mother had died, Beatrice had written to him that it was good he had Louise to take care of him as 'she is so calm and full of feeling'. Alix would have appreciated some of that calming influence while the papers were poking fun at the mental health of her younger sister, who was pregnant while also suffering from post-natal depression (an illness unrecognised at the time). *The Graphic* published a supposedly concerned article, in which the desire to laugh at what the editor obviously found an amusing story is made explicit in the journalist's final sentence:

The Duchess of Cumberland, youngest sister of the Princess of Wales, is seriously ill with melancholia, and is being treated at a private asylum in one of the Viennese suburbs . . . It is stated that she has suffered mentally, occasionally, since the birth of her last child . . . The Duchess's illness being of a comparatively mild form, however, it is hoped that she will speedily recover. The Duke does not see her . . . The Duchess shows much interest in birds, especially pigeons.

Although the newspapers were ostensibly pro-royalty, such sniping articles, with their undertones of cruelty and the sting in the tail, were common – and they were exactly the kind of publicity that Louise was trying to avoid. She already knew how swiftly journalists would latch on to any signs of weakness in her marriage, and she was equally aware how much the journalists would love to link Lorne's story to that of his brother's sordid divorce. That the papers were so reluctant to write about what was obviously a bad marriage is testament to the fact that Louise was so popular with the newspaper-reading public. Had one of her sisters, married to foreign royalty, been experiencing similar marital problems, the newspapers would probably have been far less kind.

On leaving Rome, Louise travelled to Geneva before returning once again to Aix-les-Bains, where she joined the queen, Princess Beatrice and their royal entourage. She stayed for several days ensuring the court circulars would write about her being a dutiful daughter, taking carriage rides with her sister and mother or walking in the grounds of their villa with the ladies-in-waiting. Henry Ponsonby[69] wrote to tell his wife that 'charming' Louise's arrival had finally livened up the family's 'long, dreary evening parties'. Liko arrived a couple of days before Louise was due to depart. She was travelling back to England separately from the rest of her family. One newspaper commented on Lorne being absent from the party at Aix: 'the Princess went on alone to join the Queen at Aix-les-Bains, where she stayed for six days . . . Lord Lorne was not invited to accompany his wife to Aix, possibly because his family are entirely out of favour at Court.'

Louise was back in England by the beginning of May 1887, fully refreshed in time for the rigours of the queen's golden jubilee. For her mother's birthday at the end of the month, Louise sent a silk shawl she had bought in Aix. She also sent a fan she had painted herself, asking her mother to excuse the lack of artistic merit as it was 'my first attempt on gauze so it's not very good'. For the jubilee, Louise, in common with all her siblings, had a vast number of public duties to attend to, either in lieu of the queen or by her mother's side. Shortly before the jubilee a Canadian artist, Frederick Bell-Smith, had travelled to England to paint a portrait of the queen. He gave an interview about his experiences:

[69] Ponsonby had been appointed the queen's' Private Secretary following the death of General Grey.

The sitting lasted a whole hour and the result was 'a common little wooden panel a few inches long'. Mr Bell-Smith and the photographer were waiting for the Queen when in came the Princess Louise, who said 'The Queen wants to know if she shall wear her bonnet?' 'Yes, please' was the reply. Almost at once the Queen entered supporting herself with a heavy cane, and resting lightly on the arm of her Indian secretary. 'I am sorry to have kept you waiting,' said her Majesty, and bade the artist be seated. But there was no chair close at hand, so the Princess Louise was despatched to fetch one. It was, the artist found, very embarrassing, to 'work close to the wrinkles', especially as the Princess watched every stroke over his shoulder, but he was encouraged by such remarks as 'It's very like you, mamma, dear'. The Queen proved to be an excellent sitter, and at the end of an hour she rose, bowed to the painter and left the room.

During the jubilee, Louise and Lorne were ordered to put on a united front. In addition, Louise had an important sculpture to work on – she had been commissioned by the people of Kensington to sculpt a full-length statue of her mother, larger than life size, to commemorate the jubilee. In addition to her public appearances, she needed to devote a great deal of time to working in her studio. She worked on this tirelessly, and a Alfred Gilbert commented how frustrating it was that no matter how hard Louise worked, the public would always claim Boehm had done the work. Like all wealthy artists, she had studio assistants, but according to the contemporary art critic M.H. Spielmann, Louise 'is the master and enforces her own ideas'. She worked on the sculpture in clay (maquettes were also produced in metal), perfecting every detail before the final marble sculpture could be produced.

Because it had been at Kensington Palace that the young Princess Victoria had heard of her uncle's death and her accession to the throne, Louise chose to depict her mother as a nineteen-year-old seated on a throne and wearing her coronation robes. The statue is on a large stone plinth (the base is of buff-coloured stone and the pedestal of fashionable white Portland stone, to match the marble of the statue). A large bronze plaque proclaims that it is the work of Princess Louise. The young, slender queen in her flamboyant robes and jewels, carved from gleaming white marble was a world away from the elderly, black-clad widowed queen who unveiled it. Louise used paintings and illustrations of her mother's coronation to help her design the statue. The statue was placed in Kensington Gardens within sight of the window of the room in which the young Victoria had slept.

Although the statue of her mother was commissioned for the 1887 jubilee, it was not completed and unveiled until 28 June 1893, on the anniversary of the queen's coronation. In the princess's opinion, the committee chosen to organise the event seemed determined to make it dull and formal, so Louise decided it would be vastly improved by the presence of children. She invited twenty-four girls and boys, representative, she said, not only of the queen's own childhood in Kensington, but of the many local children who played in the gardens and would see the statue every day. So that the children would know what to do on the day, they had been invited into Princess Louise's garden at Kensington Palace for rehearsals (and, no doubt, for cakes and sweets). The statue had been veiled with an enormous Union Flag, waiting to be revealed. When the unveining day arrived there was a band playing and large crowds came to witness the spectacle – all of whom were soaked when the heavens opened just as the queen's carriage approached the park. One of the little girls chosen to attend was terrified by the sight of her forbidding monarch. For some reason she became convinced that she was going to be forced to go home and live with Queen Victoria and burst into noisy tears at the very idea of it.

Nina Epton records in *Victoria and her Daughters* that the queen wrote after the ceremony that she 'felt very proud' of Louise. In her speech, the queen commented: 'It gives me great pleasure to . . . witness the unveiling of this fine statue, so admirably designed and executed by my daughter.' It was one of the few moments in Louise's long life when she received glowing praise from her mother.

CHAPTER 21

Celebrating the Golden Jubilee

Had a large family dinner. All the Royalties assembled in the Bow Room, and we dined in the Supper-room, which looked splendid with the buffet covered with the gold plate. The table was a large horseshoe one, with many lights on it . . . The Princes were all in uniform, and the Princesses were all beautifully dressed. Afterwards we went into the Ballroom, where my band played.

Queen Victoria's diary, 20 June 1887

Despite the years of disgruntled comments about the queen's refusal to 'connect' with her people, her golden jubilee was unforgettable. The queen had been something of a recluse for the best part of three decades, so her numerous public appearances in 1887 created a renewed fervour of enthusiasm for the monarchy. The newspapers had been busy with the preparations for months; one of the stories they followed with great excitement was the lengthy journey being made by the Queen of Hawaii, en route to London to join the celebrations. The Hawaiian queen would later publish her impressions of the jubilee in her autobiography. She mentions Louise by name only once, in an interesting passage about Lorne. They were all in attendance at a ball:

Queen Kapiolani and I were conducted to seats on the dais, where the Princess of Wales, Princess Louise of Lorne, and other members of Her Majesty's household, were seated. It was an excellent point from which to see the dancing, which soon began. While watching the dance, I happened to glance down to the farther end of the hall, and saw the Marquis of Lorne bend his arm cordially about that of my husband, Governor Dominis, and pace to and fro with him about the hall, the two gentlemen seemingly much interested in each other as they engaged in prolonged and pleasant conversation.

Louise was kept busy all year, so it was fortunate that public appearances were something she excelled at. The jubilee forced Louise and Lorne to spend much more time with one another than usual. By the end of the year Louise would be suffering from 'exhaustion', causing concern for her health, both in the family and in the newspapers, although the reports seem to suggest that she was emotionally depressed rather than physically ill.

One of their first jubilee appearances was at the American Exhibition in Kensington Gardens, which Louise and Lorne attended on 5 May 1887 with Bertie, Alix and their children. The exhibition caused great excitement in London, although it was not so favourably received by visiting Americans. One reviewer went back to New York, where he wrote disparagingly: 'I am greatly disappointed with it. As a circus or Buffalo Bill show it may pass muster, but as an exhibition representing the abilities and products of the United States it is simply beneath criticism.' Much of his distaste, however, seems to have been the result of his own racism and therefore his disgust with the 'dirty Indians . . . drawing big crowds'. British newspapers were much more favourable and the *Freeman's Journal* wrote with gory glee of the royal party's visit: 'The princesses displayed much interest in the papooses, to the great delight of the squaws. Amongst the relics of Indian warfare exhibited to the Royal party were a number of scalps with hair attached.'

Louise and Lorne were amongst the massed members of the royal family who met Queen Victoria in the East End on Saturday 14 May 1887. The first jubilee event of 'great importance' was the opening of the Queen's Hall at the People's Palace, which had been created for the 'recreation, amusement and education of the people of the East End'. It included a swimming pool, a school, lecture rooms, gardens and a gym.[70] The route of the queen's carriage ride, from Paddington

[70] In 1931, a large part of the complex was destroyed by fire. By the 1950s, its replacement buildings had become part of Queen Mary, University of London.

in central London to Mile End in the east of the city, was thronged with people giving 'thunderous' cheers. The papers were pleased with the 'tact' shown by the queen in choosing to visit the East End on a Saturday, rather than a weekday when people had to be at work. A fashion journalist who signed herself 'A Lady' was not impressed with the queen's sense of style, nor with the fact that the accompanying royal party had not considered how well their outfits would go together:

The Sovereign did not look quite at her best . . . Her dress was not well draped, and, being of several materials suggested what had perhaps be better left unsaid. The Queen's mantle was singularly unbecoming to her figure, which it in no way defined. And, unfortunately, the toilets worn by the attendant Princesses were opposed to each other in colour . . . Next to the Princess of Wales, Princess Louise, Marchioness of Lorne, is the best looking, and has the best taste in dress of any of the Queen's daughters or daughters-in-law. At the opening of the Manchester Jubilee Exhibition, Princess Louise wore a . . . dress of a light shade of terra cotta . . . accompanied by a dark terra cotta plush jacket, with coffee-coloured lace trimmings; bonnet to correspond, with dark green foliage by way of decoration.

Two days after the opening of the People's Palace, Louise and Lorne arrived back in Liverpool, which welcomed the princess as a returning daughter. Louise was there to open the Royal Jubilee Exhibition on behalf of the queen. She requested an extra stop on her itinerary: she wanted to visit the School of Cookery, one of her pet projects promoting the education of girls. (The school also used its teaching rooms to run evening classes for working men and boys.) On the same day, Louise declared open the new buildings of the Deaf and Dumb Institute. Her schedule was exhausting. At the end of May, the organisers of the jubilee fête at Aylesbury in Buckinghamshire were disappointed when Louise didn't show up – unaware that she was opening a new Working Men's Club that day. While she worked through her numerous public engagements with a fixed smile, Louise was longing to get into her studio to work and unwind and to have the time to spend alone with Boehm.

On 14 June, the Jubilee Yacht Race began from Southend Pier, with Bertie's yacht, the *Aline*, one of the entrants. The jubilee began in earnest on 21 June and crowds thronged the streets to get a glimpse of the royal family; the Prince of Wales, once so despised, was greeted by loud cheers as he rode in the procession, in which all the queen's children took part. It was especially exhausting for Beatrice, who was heavily pregnant. Every member of the family covered themselves in glory – except for Lorne who, according to *The Times*, humiliated himself (and his wife) by falling off his horse in full view of the crowds. The queen travelled to Westminster Abbey in a gold-coloured landau carriage; 'drawn by six of my Creams', as she noted in her journal. Vicky and Alix travelled with her, but the others rode in separate carriages. The queen gave her daughters, granddaughters and the wives of her sons and grandsons a special jubilee brooch. When the jubilee procession arrived at Westminster Abbey 9,000 guests had been squeezed into the normally cavernous interior.

The months of June, July and August were spent in constant jubilee activities and Louise and Lorne attended most of them together. On 17 August, Louise travelled to Winchester where she unveiled a bronze statue of her mother by one of her friends, Alfred Gilbert (another of Boehm's pupils).[71] The statue is not a flattering portrait, but it is probably one of the most realistic of all the jubilee statues, showing the queen as she would have looked at the time: an elderly lady with a haughty expression on her face. The queen's throne is surmounted by an ornate canopy composed of a crown held aloft by two female figures. Gilbert had used photographs of the subject to create his realistic likeness, but he also relied on his knowledge of his own mother, saying, 'I realised my deduction of the Queen from my mother, and thus got a more spiritual representation than if I had merely reproduced the Queen's features and form.' The statue not only represents Gilbert's tutelage under Boehm, it also echoes his Parisian training at the Ecole des Beaux Arts. The statue, especially its canopy, was one of the earliest examples in Britain of what would become known as art nouveau. When Louise unveiled the statue, it

---

[71] Alfred Gilbert's most famous work is his statue of Eros (1893), which stands in Piccadilly Circus in London. The statue is actually misnamed 'Eros': Gilbert created it as Anteros, Eros's brother.

was not finished and Gilbert spent another twenty-five years putting the finishing touches to it.

In addition to the official jubilee celebrations, a large number of charity ideas were put into practice throughout the year, including meals being provided for the poor, foundrasing fêtes and parties, the opening of libraries, swimming baths and other public facilities, and prize-giving ceremonies including one at the Princess Louise Home for the Protection of Young Girls in Wanstead (which was presided over by Lorne, on behalf of the absent Louise). The charity had been set up in 1835 and renamed to honour Princess Louise's patronage. Its object was:

> To save young girls (not thieves) between the ages of eleven and fifteen, whether orphans or otherwise, who are, from any circumstance, in danger of becoming abandoned; to educate, train, feed, clothe, and prepare them for future usefulness as domestic servants; to protect them during the most critical period of life; to land them safe into womanhood; to procure situations for them; to provide them with an outfit, and generally to watch over them; to advise, counsel, and reward them, and in every possible way to become their guardians.

The jubilee also encouraged other forms of enterprise; one Manchester philanthropist was so deeply concerned about the dangerous conditions of mining that he offered £600 to anyone able to invent a 'perfect portable electric miners' lamp' by the end of the jubilee year.

Although the jubilee was considered an overwhelming success in Britain, it still had its detractors, not least those who hated the fact that so much money was being spent on pomp, ceremony and numerous statues of the ageing, usually glowering queen. Overseas newspapers were particularly critical in their reporting of the celebrations. One newspaper in Sydney reported,

> It is satisfactory to note by the English papers that the grand old lickspittle movement of grovel and Jubilee has bored down to an abysmal depth of flunkeyism and social abasement absolutely impossible to our colonial Jingoes even in their wildest dreams of sickening silver and abject toadyism. An English print records

that the Prince of Wales attended some football matches last year, the proceeds from which were devoted to charitable institutions. This year, it is reported, he was asked to do the same thing, and consented on condition that the proceeds should be given to swell the funds of the Jubilee Imperial Institute craze!

As soon as the summer of celebration came to an end, Louise left England again for Aix-les-Bains. She was depressed, ill and anxious to be out of the limelight. She also spent a week in Evian, where the papers reported she would 'continue a course of baths for the benefit of her health'. After Aix she travelled to Copenhagen to visit Alix's family, then on to Italy, where she enjoyed a holiday in Venice with Fritz, Vicky and their children. Fritz had been suffering for months with a sore throat and in the autumn of 1887 he was diagnosed with throat cancer.

While Louise was away, Beatrice gave birth to a daughter, Ena[72] (who would grow up to become Queen of Spain). Louise returned to England in time for Christmas 1887, but all was not well. The queen's letters to Vicky from this time are full of concerns about Louise, with her mother fearing that she was emotionally as well as physically unwell; and she reiterated her earlier comments about how unsuited Louise and Lorne were, something she had been writing to Vicky about for several years now. Louise was also being used as a go-between in problems Arthur was having with the queen and Beatrice. Arthur wrote from India (where he and Marie were living) complaining to Louise, 'Of course I know as well as you do that neither Mama nor Beatrice understand children and I fear ours have rather high spirits.' The queen was insisting that the children should come to live with her and Beatrice, and both Arthur and Marie were adamant they should not. In 1886, Prince Arthur sent a letter to Louise in which he wrote: 'Now that Beatrice has got a baby we feel more than ever that our children would be much better away as they must be "de trop".'

While Louise and Lorne's marriage was becoming an obvious travesty, Bertie and Alix celebrated their silver wedding anniversary, on 10 March 1888. Louise (and sometimes Lorne) spent much of 1888 travelling, going back to Malta and Italy and to Algiers, a destination much recommended by doctors in the nineteenth century.

---

[72] She was christened Victoria Eugenie Julia Ena.

As usual, the royal couple attempted to travel in secrecy, but were easily recognised by savvy hoteliers and staff, who often tipped off the papers. When they were staying in Naples, the *New York Times* praised them for being content to travel 'in simple, unostentatious fashion'. Louise made just a few public appearances in the summer and autumn, once to watch a contingent of visiting Canadian marksmen taking part in a competition in Wimbledon. In November she and Lorne travelled to Newcastle where she opened a new wing of the College of Science and presented prizes at Gateshead Girls' School. They also went to stay with the pioneering inventor and engineer Lord William Armstrong at his home, Cragside, the first house in the world to be lit by hydroelectricity.

The world was changing rapidly. As Louise recovered from her depression she was caught up in the excitement of the new styles of art that she and Boehm witnessed as they visited galleries and talked to artists newly arrived in London from other artistic centres, such as Paris and Vienna. An intriguing and unidentified note survives from the summer of 1889: signed simply 'Ted', it is a letter that shows how much a part of easy-going artistic London Louise was: 'My dearest Angel, I beg most respectfully to transmit these beautiful cards for your gracious acceptance. Ever thine most humbly, Ted.' The note may have been from a man or a woman, from a lover or a friend. These brief lines demonstrate perfectly how Louise was perceived outside royal circles and how at home she felt in bohemian London; one cannot imagine any of Louise's sisters (perhaps with the exception of Alice) having been happy to receive such an informal note.

Late Victorian Britain was an inspiring time to be an artist, but for many other people it felt a very frightening place. Crime seemed to have escalated and the world to have become more dangerous. Advances in technology allowed newspapers to report stories from all over the world, so readers who had previously known only what was happening locally were bombarded with faraway tragedies. In the same week, newspaper readers in Britain knew not only that Dumfries in Scotland had been hit by what the papers described as a 'minor' earthquake (in modern measurements, 3.4 on the Richter Scale), but that the Russian imperial family had been involved in a devastating train crash. (Although twenty-one people were killed, the family escaped without major injuries.) It was a time of great advancements and of sharp contrasts. In London in the summer of 1888, around 1,400 female workers – women and young girls – at the Bryant & May match factory went on strike, protesting over their appalling, health-endangering working conditions. In the same year, Clementina Black, the Secretary of the Women's Trade Union League, secured the very first resolution in Britain on equal pay for men and women at the Trades Union Congress. In central London, police were trying to solve the Whitehall mystery – the murder of a woman whose dismembered body was found in several locations; while in the East End, Jack the Ripper was stalking women on the poverty-stricken streets of Whitechapel.

Louise was always affected by the news and the weather. She began the new year craving sunshine, longing to escape the miserably grey British winters as much she had been to escape from the harshly cold Canadian winters. The royal Christmas of 1888 had been tense and the family theatricals, performed in the new year, were notable for Louise and Beatrice's furious bickering. Despite being adults, Queen Victoria's daughters remained incapable of living harmoniously. The diaries of members of the royal household, including Henry Ponsonby and Dr James Reid, record many instances of the sisters falling out with each other: the queen had brought them up to vie with each other for her attention and the learnt behaviour of resentful competi-tiveness blighted their relationships into old age.

For Louise, the first two months of 1889 were spent in a round of official appearances and social engagements, including spending time with Vicky, who was in England, and celebrating the engagement of Louise's niece and namesake. Like her aunt, Princess Louise of Wales had become engaged to a Scottish nobleman, and once again the family was divided, with some members angered by this seemingly 'low' engagement. Princess Louise wrote enviously of her niece to her friend Connie Battersea, 'Fancy marrying a man you love *and* living in that beautiful property!' The thought of having the luxury of marrying for love was intoxicating.

In March, Louise and Lorne travelled to Arcachon in south-west France, where she celebrated her fortieth birthday. The queen, Beatrice and Liko were staying in Biarritz, and on her birthday they sent a special messenger to deliver letters directly to her. The holiday did not lift Louise's spirits and she returned to England grumpy and snap-pish. Perhaps one reason was that, despite Beatrice's reported dislike of 'kissing', her marriage seemed to be the kind of sexual relationship that Louise felt should have been her right. In May 1889, Louise felt surrounded by children: she travelled to Leicester to open a new children's hospital and Beatrice gave birth to her third child, a son. He was named Leopold – and ironically he would be diagnosed with haemophilia. Like his uncle, he was fated to die young.

Louise was unhappy, and as a result her behaviour was so unpleasant that Vicky's daughter, Moretta, was prompted to write to her mother from Windsor Castle: 'Auntie Lou is not right at all – she complains at every sort of thing, but is charming as usual to look at.' The following month, the family learnt that Vicky's husband Fritz had died. When Vicky most had need of her children, Wilhelm was being entirely unsupportive. Queen Victoria wrote in her journal of how unpleasant her grandson was being to Vicky and that his first speech as Emperor indicated a hatred of England. For once Louise was unable to keep an official engagement. She was too ill to travel to Bath, where she was to open the new baths. Her cancellation was notable because it was so unusual; it seems that Louise was suffering a severe depression. Boehm was working exhaustively, mostly on an enormous equestrian statue of Prince Albert, and caring for his wife Frances, who was dying from a debilitating and painful illness. He could spare little time to spend with Princess Louise. By the end of the year, she did not even have her new chosen friend to confide in, because Liko had left the country for three months, leaving Beatrice and the children behind, to go on a sailing trip.

For Bertie and Alix, the year was a mixture of happiness and anger. In the same month that their daughter Louise married the Earl of Fife, their eldest son, Prince Eddy, the future King of England, was implemented in sexual impropriety: the Cleveland Street Scandal. This was not an exploit of which Bertie would have approved, as it involved a male brothel. When the police raided 19 Cleveland Street in central London, several aristocratic men were suspected to have been inside the brothel. The story was suppressed, so the names of only two were reported by the press: the Duke of Somerset and the Earl of Euston. (The former fled overseas, but the Earl of Euston successfully sued the reporter who had named him.) Although Prince Eddy was not mentioned as having been there at the time, it was rumoured that he had visited the brothel before. Whether there is any truth in this is debatable; it is possible that his name was mentioned simply to black-mail Bertie into having the scandal suppressed. Whatever Eddy's involvement (or lack of it), the most damning aspect of the case was that the disgraced Earl of Somerset was Eddy's equerry and a close friend of the royal family. In addition, Bertie was known to have attempted to suppress the information about Somerset. People were convinced there had been a cover-up when the two rent boys, convicted of the crime of sodomy, were handed surprisingly lenient sentences. Although no newspapers in Britain named Prince Eddy, the papers overseas were happy to do so.

The month after the Cleveland Street Scandal, the new Emperor Wilhelm arrived in England, and his family attempted to treat him with civility. He was full of his own importance, now that he had succeeded his father, and Bertie – reminded once too often of his subservience to his mother – in particular found him very trying. Louise was caught in the middle between her brother, whom she adored, and the nephew who described her as his 'favourite aunt'.

At this difficult time, art was the one thing that was keeping Louise happy. She had been thrilled when the collector Henry Tate offered his enviable collection of modern British art, including works by some of her close friends, to the nation, in 1889 – although initially the nation was not at all grateful. The wealthy Tate found himself in the surprising position of having to persuade the nation to accept his generous gift. It was only three years later – after he had offered to build a gallery in which to house his works, at his own expense – that the nation accepted what is now recognised as one of the most impor-tant art collections in the world. (Henry Tate's gallery is now known as Tate Britain.) While Tate was making his generous offer, Louise and her circle of artistic friends were greatly saddened by the inevitable demise of the Grosvenor Gallery. The Palace of Aesthetic Art was a victim of the failed marriage between Lady Blanche and Sir Coutts Lindsay and its doors closed for the last time in 1890. At this time, Louise's work and her relationship with Boehm were the stabilising influences in what seemed in many ways to be a hectic and unhappy life, but that stable part of her world was about to change, dramati-cally, tragically – and in what appears to have been a mysterious scandal.

CHAPTER 22

The princess and the sculptor

The sculptor Alfred Gilbert, who occupied a studio in the same premises, added his weight to their concocted story by taking responsibility for finding the body. Princess Louise championed him for the rest of his turbulent life.

Caroline Dakers, *The Holland Park Circle*, 1999

Just before Christmas 1890, London was shocked by the sudden and unexpected death of Joseph Edgar Boehm. The Sculptor in Ordinary to the queen, who died in his studio, was only fifty-six. The story of his death was made even more newsworthy by early reports that his body had been found by Princess Louise. The newspapers, however, were confused by the order of events, and within a few days several versions of the sculptor's last moments had been published. Was it the princess who discovered the body, or was it Alfred Gilbert, whose studio was next door to Boehm's? Did Louise and Gilbert arrive together and find Boehm at the same time? Was the princess in the room with Boehm when he died? If the princess arrived on her own, how had she managed to get into the studio? Was it true that the princess had sent her lady-in-waiting away before she found her tutor's body and, if so, why? The *Truth* newspaper, which loved a good scandal, rubbished the official version, printed in *The Times*, that Louise could have entered the studio and found Boehm dead; it pointed out that the innovative lock on the door made that an impossibility. Below is a small selection of the reports demonstrating how newspapers around the country covered the event:

Manchester Courier 13 December 1890

Death of Sir Edgar Boehm, the sculptor

Sir Edgar Boehm, Bart., R.A., the famous sculptor, died suddenly last evening at his studio, in the Fulham-road, London. Princess Louise called by appointment at a quarter to six o'clock, attended by Mr. Gilbert, the artist, and they entered the studio unannounced to find Sir Edgar dead in his chair. The Princess who was deeply affected, and terribly shocked by the dreadful occurrence, hurriedly left the studio, and a doctor was called, who found that Sir Edgar had been dead for some time.

Gloucester Citizen 13 December 1890

Sudden death of Sir E. Boehm – Princess Louise finds the body

Sir Edgar Boehm, R.A., the eminent sculptor, was discovered in his studio, in Fulham-road, London, on Friday evening. The discovery was made by the Princess Louise, who went to the studio to inspect a bust of herself, and entering unannounced was terribly shocked to find the distinguished sculptor dead in his chair.

London Standard Saturday 13 December 1890

Sir Edgar Boehm, Bart, R.A., sculptor to her Majesty the Queen, died suddenly last evening at about a quarter to six. The body of the deceased sculptor was found in his studio first by Princess Louise (Marchioness of Lorne). Princess Louise, who used to study the art of sculpture with Sir Edgar at his studio, 76, The Avenue, Fulham-road, paid occasional visits to Sir Edgar, and arrived last evening shortly before six o'clock, having previously intimated her intention to Sir Edgar. As is customary with Royal visitors, her Royal Highness walked straight to the studio, and was horrified to see the lifeless form of her late instructor. Her Royal Highness immediately proceeded to the adjoining studio of Mr. Gilbert, A.R.A., and Mr. Gilbert returned to the studio with the Princess. Finding that the fears of her Royal Highness were apparently correct, he sent without delay for Dr. Macaskie, of Sydney-place, South Kensington, and the deceased's solicitor, Mr. Jno. Gascotte, of Onslow-square, W.

Whitstable Times 20 December 1890

On Friday evening Sir Joseph Edgar Boehm, R.A., the distinguished sculptor, was discovered dead in his studio at the Avenue, 76 Fulham-road. The discovery was made by no less a personage than her Royal Highness Princess Louise, who went to the studio by appointment, about a quarter to 6 o'clock to inspect a bust of herself which had just been finished by this famous sculptor. As this time all the workpeople employed at the place had gone, and there being free access to the studio from a corridor, her Royal Highness, after tapping at the door, was startled beyond description on entering to find Sir Edgar Boehm dead in his chair, no one else being in the room. Her Royal Highness, who was much alarmed, at once rushed to an adjoining studio occupied by Mr. Gilbert, A.R.A., and they both returned together. Dr. McCaskie was quickly summoned from Sydney-place close by, and on his arrival pronounced life extinct. Princess Louise was terribly shocked at the occurrence, and afterwards drove away greatly affected.

Lancaster Gazette Saturday 27 December 1890

I hear on good authority that H.R.H. the Princess Louise went to Sir Edgar Boehm's studio by appointment, and unattended by a lady or a gentleman. She discussed some of the sculptor's latest work with him, and he turned to fetch a bust or something else to show her. The Princess remained studying his latest work, and stood with her back to him. Suddenly she heard a noise and turned to see its cause, when she discovered that the sculptor had fallen close to the sofa. Her Royal Highness showed great presence of mind by unfastening his collar before seeking assistance. Such is the version of this deplorable event that has reached me.

The differences in these reports demonstrate how, even within a few days, rumours were already starting to circulate about the circumstances of the sculptor's sudden death. Even those who didn't know Boehm's name knew his works; these included the equestrian statue of the Duke of Wellington, the monument to the Duke of Kent, the popular statue of Thomas Carlyle, and something that everyone in Victoria's Britain had seen: the 1887 jubilee coin depicting the queen.[73]

Boehm's death was unexpected and shocking. He was a fit, seemingly healthy man with pronounced muscles from his years of hard, physical work; he could have been expected to live well into his eighties. From the very beginning, the story of what had happened was being garbled – some reports state that Louise went in alone, some that she was already in the studio with him when he collapsed, others that she immediately ran to the next-door studio to Alfred Gilbert, and in some versions that she and Alfred Gilbert had entered the studio together to find Boehm dead. One official view of the day of his death, as the queen wrote in her journal,[74] was that Louise had gone to visit Boehm at his studio on Fulham Road, with her lady-in-waiting. The queen wrote that Louise and her lady-in-waiting had entered Boehm's studio and found him dead and that Louise had gone to fetch the doctor. Contradicting itself, the journal also states that the initial version of events as reported in the newspaper was not true and that 'poor Louise' had not been the person to find him dead.

Several years later, the account had been changed to such an extent that Louise didn't even make an appearance, with the person who found the body being named as Alfred Gilbert, and Louise turning up much later. On Boehm's death certificate, it is stated that Alfred Gilbert was the person who had found the body. That there were so many versions of the sculptor's death, from the very beginning, made it apparent that something was being covered up. In letters to concerned (and disapproving) family friends, Louise protested that she had not been alone as the papers had suggested, that she had been with her lady-in-waiting and all was therefore entirely respectable. She blamed the story on salacious journalists not getting their facts right. Yet this

[73] Not everyone was a fan of Boehm's work. The artist Kate Perugini (née Dickens) wrote to her great friend Anny Thackeray Ritchie in 1905 bemoaning how dreadful most of the portraits were of Anny's father, William Makepeace Thackeray, and mentioning 'that awful thing of Boehm's'.

[74] There is some speculation as to whether this entry was genuinely written at the time or was added in later. As Jehanne Wake points out in her biography of Louise, it is not known whether the account of Boehm's death in the queen's journal is the original version told her by Princess Louise at the time, or the edited manuscript version made years later by Princess Beatrice, who then destroyed the originals.

in itself contradicts the story in the queen's own journal which claims Louise wasn't in the studio to find him.[75] A letter written by Louise a few weeks after Boehm's death to the Dowager Duchess of Atholl also supports this view:

> It was a terrible shock, doubly so as he was quite well when he met me in the long passage: as you see I did not go (unattended and unannounced) as all the papers pleased to say. Lady Sophia and I were talking to him some 20 minutes and then Sophia said 'as your carriage will be here in a minute I think I will walk home' and in much less than 5 I heard that awful cry. Sir Edgar had carried a bust to show me wh I entreated him not to, also pushed some heavy things & he must have overexerted himself. It was found to be aneurism of the heart.

The very first version of events – that Louise arrived to visit Boehm and went unannounced into his studio, where she found him dead – had to be changed after people who knew the studios started musing about it. They wondered how Louise had managed to enter the studio if Boehm was already dead; his studio was one of a group of artists' studios on Fulham Road and it was well known that they were all fitted with a new type of lock, which locked automatically when the door was shut. Any visitor would either need a key or need the person inside to open the door for them. Louise could not simply have opened the door and walked in. Alfred Gilbert was good friends with both Boehm and Louise. This was why the story began to be changed, and why later reports state that Louise arrived for her intended visit to her tutor and found Gilbert at Boehm's studio, where he had discovered his friend's body. Louise and Gilbert remained close friends and she helped promote his career to the end of her life. Like so many of Louise's male friends' wives (or girlfriends), Gilbert's wife became increasingly jealous of how much time her husband spent with Louise, famously calling her 'that tiresome princess'. The *Dictionary of National*

[75] The queen's journal entry for 13 December 1890 states: 'Terribly shocked at the news, that good, excellent talented Sir Edgar Boehm had died suddenly yesterday and that poor Louise had found him dead, which latter turns out not to be true from what I have learnt from her.'

Biography writes of Gilbert's later career: 'After Boehm's death . . . Gilbert emerged as the most famous sculptor in England . . . he was a picturesque character of the 1890s in his flamboyant black cape, felt sombrero and walking stick.'

In *The Holland Park Circle*, Caroline Dakers points out that, following Boehm's death, Louise gave Gilbert even more help than she had done before. In the 1920s, after he had declared himself bankrupt, Louise had her studio at Kensington Palace converted so that Gilbert could live and work there. Gilbert's biographer Adrian Bury describes it as 'the last, most secure and peaceful home of his life'. Louise was a renowned patron of the arts and artists, it was not at all unusual that she should help out those she knew were struggling, yet there was no other artist for whom the princess found accommodation within her own royal palace. There are very strong suggestions that Louise was expressing her gratitude for Gilbert's having helped to save both her and Boehm's reputations and for helping to staunch the flow of gossip. Letters written by Gilbert's first biographer, a Scottish journalist named Isabel McAllister, to her friend Marlon Harry Spielmann survive in the Royal Academy's archives. McAllister wrote that Princess Louise had been an 'invaluable friend' to Gilbert, that she had attended to his final wishes and had visited him the day before he died.

Those who have attempted to write about Boehm are often frustrated by the lack of material available. According to his biographer Mark Stocker this is because of the 'sensational circumstances of Boehm's death . . . for his executors destroyed all but a handful of his personal papers'. Within a very short time, the gossips of London's artistic world were whispering that Louise had been with Boehm when he died and that he had died from the exertion of making love to her.

In 1952, archivists at the Fitzwilliam Museum in Cambridge opened a box that had been bequeathed to them thirty years previously. The box contained private papers and diaries from the diplomat and diarist Wilfrid Scawen Blunt who had died in 1922. Blunt had left the box to the Fitzwilliam with a condition stipulating that it should not be opened for another three decades; he knew much of its contents would be considered historically explosive. In 1952 the curators read through his legacy for the first time. After analysing the papers, they made the decision to keep the contents of the box hidden from members of the public for another twenty years. Since 1972, the papers have been available to researchers, but much of what is in them is still little known as the diaries have never been fully indexed and researchers need to know what they're looking for before requesting one of the many volumes.

Blunt's diaries are fascinating: they are politically acute, forward thinking and laced with the type of Victorian scandal that today's gossip magazines would envy. Blunt had travelled widely and was far less inhibited than many of his contemporaries; his years of living overseas had allowed him a far greater freedom than those of his era who remained within the confines of British Victorian society. Blunt was interested in world religions and was unusually understanding of other cultures for a man of his time; one of his books is entitled *The Future of Islam*. He campaigned for Irish Home Rule and for Egyptian Independence. Blunt's many correspondents included Jane Morris,[76] T.E. Lawrence, Ezra Pound, E.M. Forster, Winston Churchill and Lord Alfred Douglas (about whose literary efforts and personality Blunt is often scathing).[77] Through his friendship with 'Skittles' – Bertie's former mistress, Catherine Walters, who had revealed the scandalous story of Louise and John Brown at Balmoral – Blunt found himself on the periphery of the royal circle and the receiver of many royal secrets. These secrets came to Skittles via one of the royal doctors, Sir Francis Laking, who was personal physician to Bertie (King Edward VII by the time of Blunt's later diaries).

During King Edward VII's reign, his former lover was elderly and ill and was having radium treatment for cancer. Blunt visited her regularly, as did Laking and, until his death, the poet Swinburne. Skittles loved talking to Blunt about her life, knowing that he was as unshockable as she and that he was recording everything she said in his diaries (in which Blunt always refers to Skittles as 'XX'). On 4 June 1909 Blunt begins his account with the words:

[76] Jane or 'Janey' Morris was a favoured model of the Pre-Raphaelites. Born Jane Burden in an impoverished part of Oxford, she ascended through the social classes by marrying the founder of the Arts & Crafts Movement, William Morris.

[77] Lord Alfred Douglas, nicknamed 'Bosie', was a would-be poet of Uranian verses, best known as the lover of Oscar Wilde. It was Bosie's father, the Marquess of Queensberry, who brought about Wilde's arrest and imprisonment. Although he was known to be Wilde's lover, the son of the marquess escaped prosecution.

Called on XX whom I found almost convalescent, the radium treatment having been pronounced a success so far . . . We got onto the subject of the sculptor Boehm and his death and burial . . . The story is so important historically that I cross-questioned her pretty closely as to test its accuracy and found that in all essentials it held well together and was the same that she had given me so long ago.

Boehm had also been one of Skittles's lovers and through him she had been introduced to many of the most prominent artists of the day. She described the sculptor as having been 'very good looking and distinguished in manner' and told Blunt that Boehm had admitted to her that he had been so very impoverished as a student in Paris that he had barely been able to afford to eat. She said once he moved to England, he had started to enjoy success, and that the queen had wanted to commission Boehm not simply because of his talent, but primarily because he spoke German. Boehm was also commissioned by Bertie to sculpt an Aesthetic-style naked statue of Skittles, as the Venus de Milo. She stood for the sculpture in a seductive pose, with her arms thrust back behind her head and her breasts jutting forward.

When Skittles told Blunt the earlier story about Boehm and Louise and the queen discovering them at Balmoral, she went on to recount how the queen had decided Louise should be married as soon as possible. The first two men she had hoped would marry the princess, Lord Cowper or Lord Hastings, were already taken, so the queen turned in desperation to Lord Lorne. As Skittles summed up, 'The marriage however was not a success as Lorne was unsatisfactory as a husband, and the Princess took other lovers, especially Sir John McNeill whom she took to Canada with her when Lorne was Governor General there, and Boehm with whom she renewed her intimacy, going to visit him constantly at her studio in London.'

Skittles's summing up of Boehm's death was told by Blunt as follows:

while he was making love to her Boehm broke a blood-vessel and died actually in the Princess's arms. There was nobody else in the studio or anywhere about, for she had sent her lady in waiting away, and the Princess had the courage to take the key of the studio out of the dead man's pocket, and covered with blood as she was and locking the door behind her, got a cab and drove to Laking's whom she found at home and took him back with her to the studio. Boehm was dead and they made up a story between them to the effect that it had been while lifting or trying to lift one of the statues that the accident had occurred. Princess Louise was so shocked at this that she has not since had a lover. She busied herself to such effect about Boehm with the Prince and his friends that she got him buried at Westminster Abbey.[78]

Skittles said that it was Laking who had told her the full story, but that Bertie also knew all about it and had helped Louise to hide the scandal. Skittles said of Bertie, 'He was fond of his sister and says he and she were of the same temperament.' Blunt's summing up of the situation mocks the hypocrisy of Queen Victoria's reign: 'So all has been hushed up and Boehm lies sepulchered in the Abbey [sic]; and a memorial is being built for "Victoria the Good" in front of Buckingham Palace, and the Queen's life is held up as a model for us all, and for future generations.'

Blunt was aware that Skittles embellished the stories she told him, but whereas most accounts of this story (in books whose manuscripts have been checked before publication by the Royal Archives) dismiss everything the former lover of Edward VII said as mere gossipy lies, Blunt considered the situation differently. He wrote in his diary: 'I don't suppose all that she says is accurate but I fancy it is mainly true. Her memory is good in spite of all her bodily infirmities.'

The story is often discredited, but the persistent rumours did not originate with Skittles's story in Blunt's diaries. They were hidden away in the bowels of the Fitzwilliam until 1972 and yet the story was being discussed decades before the Blunt files were opened to the public. The inconsistencies in the story of Boehm's death, such as those in the confusing newspaper reports, added to the lack of transparency right from the beginning; it is these inconsistencies that ensure the rumours still exist. The closing of Princess Louise's files in the Royal Archives only serves to make this story seem more likely.

During my research I was very fortunate to be introduced by a

---

[78] Boehm was actually buried in St Paul's Cathedral.

mutual friend to a writer whose work I admire and whose area of research takes her close to mine. Henrietta Garnett is the granddaughter of the Bloomsbury artists Vanessa Bell and Duncan Grant. One of her books is a biography of William Thackeray's eldest daughter, the novelist Anny Thackeray Ritchie. I wrote the biography of one of Anny's closest friends, Charles Dickens's younger daughter, the artist Kate (usually known as 'Katey') Perugini. In conversation with Henrietta, I told her I was researching Princess Louise, who inhabited the same artistic and bohemian world as Anny, Katey and their circle. Henrietta told me that her grandfather, Duncan Grant, had related to her the story of Joseph Edgar Boehm's death as he had heard it. Bearing in mind that Grant was born in 1885, just a few years before Boehm died, he had heard the story second hand, but the death had long been gossiped about within the Bloomsbury Group – almost all of whom were blood relations of people who were a part of Boehm's, Louise's and Gilbert's inner circle. Duncan Grant also heard his, albeit outlandish, version of the story long before any researchers had been able to read Blunt's diaries.

Grant told his granddaughter that Boehm and Louise were not at his studio, they were at Louise's studio in Kensington Palace. They were having sex, with Boehm on top of her. While he was still physically inside Louise, Boehm had a stroke, or an aneurism, and died very suddenly. Louise, trapped underneath him, was terrified. Louise was tall, but she was far more slender than Boehm and she found it extremely difficult to get him out of her and to roll him off her. Duncan Grant's version of the story is that Louise then had to call her 'most discreet lady-in-waiting'. He claimed that, together, the two women rolled up Boehm's body in a carpet 'Cleopatra style' and hired a discreet cab to take them to the doctor's house. From there, they took Boehm back to his own studio and pretended he had died there while lifting a heavy statue.

The story has many typically Bloomsbury embellishments, not least the moving of the body – we know from the employees of the studios that Boehm was working in his own studio that day and had told them when they left at around 5p.m. that he was expecting 'the princess' to visit him. That was mentioned in several of the earliest newspaper reports and is something that doesn't change. The story of Boehm dying in the middle of having sex with Louise and of her being unable to get out from underneath him has been reported by several sources and seems likely to have been true, not least because of Alfred Gilbert's chivalrous attempts to cover up the fact that Louise was in the studio alone with Boehm.

In a tactic she had learnt from her mother, Louise began to blame her lover's death on the queen herself. In an ironic parody of the way in which the queen had blamed Bertie for Prince Albert's death, Louise blamed her mother and a statue of her father for Boehm's untimely demise. Writing to a friend and warning 'we must not tell the queen', she surmised that Boehm had been over-exerting himself through work for so long that he had made himself ill and that the 'cause of his death' was having to work so hard on the enormous equestrian statue of Prince Albert that had been unveiled in Windsor Great Park just a few months earlier. *The Graphic*, which wrote of the statue that its likeness to the prince was 'considered excellent', mentioned that it was 33 feet high including its pedestal of Aberdeen granite, 'which weighs nearly twenty tons'.

Louise wrote that 'the shock and the whole thing made me very ill, I am not yet strong'. Her mother also commented that she was worried about Louise following Boehm's death. She wrote to friends that it was quite natural for Louise to be so upset following the death of a 'very kind friend' and emphasised to her correspondents that Louise had been a 'pupil' of the dead sculptor, placing their relationship entirely on a formal, respectable footing.

Louise longed for her lover to be given the full honours he deserved, and although many were against it, Boehm was buried in St Paul's Cathedral, thanks to Louise petitioning the queen. A letter written on 15 December 1890 begins in a rushed fashion and goes into pleading:

Dearest Mama, I telegraphed you the feeling there was in favour of good Sir E. Boehm being buried at St Paul's. Frank Holl the painter was, and young Caldecott, the man who drew those charming illustrations of children's books, a very clever young fellow. I think you ought to express your desire that he should be buried there, as he did more for modern art, than any one of the day. If you remember 22 years ago it was dull heavy and bad classic, he was almost the first to introduce life and action into his work, also it is very important that those who want to try and ignore him, should be shown by <u>you</u>, the Queen, what you thought. It is *not* asking an unusual thing, as you see these two artists who died so lately were buried there.

Perhaps in a bid to prevent Beatrice from interfering, Louise requested in the letter: 'Please communicate <u>direct</u> with <u>me</u>, it will save time, and is better.' She also praised Alfred Gilbert for his care and help and for his 'thoughtfulness and devotion to the memory of his friend'. Gilbert had been to the chapel of rest and sat with his friend's body for a long time. He had also re-dressed Boehm for burial in the clothes he had been wearing on the day he died; it was decided that he should not be dressed up in finery for his coffin; instead he should be buried in his working clothes 'as he fell'.

Louise praised John Everett Millais and William Blake Richmond too, who had been 'most kind' to her; she was not, however, impressed with Frederic, Lord Leighton, the President of the Royal Academy, who had 'not shown much generosity, or feeling!'. The queen agreed to Louise's pleas, writing to Vicky that 'good and ever-to-be-regretted Sir E. Boehm will be laid to rest in St Paul's'. Much was made in the newspapers of Louise 'breaking protocol' to attend Boehm's funeral; although the newspapers should really have been used to the princess ignoring royal protocol, just as her eldest brother had been doing for so long.

A few weeks after his father's death, the sculptor's son, Edgar C. Boehm, wrote letters to Louise; very stiff and formal but gracious, the style suggests he was extremely nervous about writing to royalty and was not quite sure how to address her. In the letters he talks about his father's work and wants to know which things from his father's studio the princess would like and which he could be permitted to keep for himself. He commented in one letter, in a manner which suggests that Louise might have heard otherwise, 'I also beg to assure Your Royal Highness how deeply sensible I am of the kindness which you have shewn to my sisters and to me.' What Boehm's son really felt about the princess is debatable.

CHAPTER 23

Trying to dull the pain

Aunt Louise . . . got on well . . . with any man – she ran after everything in trousers. Louise liked Louis Battenberg too . . . oh, all the men.

Princess Alice, Countess of Athlone, in conversation with
Nina Epton

Louise entered the second year of the 'naughty nineties' in a daze of mourning her tutor, friend and lover. Even Elizabeth Longford, who disliked to think that the two had been anything other than teacher and pupil, wrote in *Darling Loosy*, 'Boehm was curly-haired, blue-eyed, urbane . . . Louise, like many an art student, fell under her master's spell.' At around the time of Boehm's death, Louise was photographed by the fashionable photographer Frederick Hollyer (the photograph is in the archives at the V&A). She is exquisitely fashionable, in a dress richly embroidered with what appear to be pearls; it has a low-cut neckline, leaves her arms exposed, and she is heavily corseted. She wears a very pronounced bustle and looks every inch the woman of fashion. She also looks extremely serious and severe.

While everyone else was gossiping about Bertie and the Marlborough House Set, in particular the 'baccarat scandal' that hit the headlines in early 1891,[79] Louise did what she always did when in pain: she went

---

[79] During a country house party at Tranby Croft, the home of wealthy shipbuilder Sir Arthur Wilson, Bertie was one of the gamblers playing an illegal game of baccarat. A scandal ensued when one of the guests, Sir William Gordon-Cumming, was accused of cheating. Sir William was confronted and agreed to give up playing cards; in

overseas in search of sunshine. The queen and Beatrice were visiting Grasse, where they stayed at the Grand Hotel. (There was an outbreak of smallpox nearby and Dr Reid insisted on vaccinating the royal party Louise also went to Grasse, with her close friend Constance, Lady Battersea,[80] and stayed with Constance's cousin, Alice de Rothschild (who offered the entire royal party use of her private gardens to walk in, in case they could find no privacy at the hotel). Constance, like Louise, was a fervent social campaigner and the two women shared a number of interests. Constance had grown up in a home with both Christian and Jewish relations and had an intriguingly honest and refreshing view of religion. She described Louise as 'truly attractive and gifted', though sometimes despaired of her mercurial nature and worried about her 'queer and capricious character'.

To Alice de Rothschild, Louise was a less than perfect guest. She demanded stimulation and amusement to bring her out of her gloom. On discovering that a regiment was stationed nearby, and on meeting an attractive young officer, Louise immediately invited him and his fellow officers to a tea party at her hostess's house. Alice complained that Louise (who, despite believing herself to have egalitarian principles, enjoyed pulling rank) ordered her about constantly, and was also irritated – as many would be throughout Louise's life – by the princess's constant lateness. Louise complained that Alice pestered her and was tiring. In most circumstances, the princess far preferred the company of men. She could be acidly disapproving of women she was jealous of, once commenting that the successful composer Ethel Smyth 'advertises herself and thinks more of her talents than others do'. In *Serving Victoria*, a study of the royal servants, Kate Hubbard comments of Louise: 'Men found her "fascinating"; women mistrusted her.' It would be unfair, however, to assume that Louise did not like other women; she had many very close female friends and was able to inspire just as much admiration from women as from men – as long as they were women she liked. A letter from the 2nd Lord Tennyson (son of the

---

return the scandal was hushed up. When the story leaked out, Sir William, whose position in society was becoming untenable, sued those who had accused him, for libel. Bertie was called as a witness.

[80] Lady Battersea, née Constance de Rothschild, married Cyril Flower, a friend of Louise and Lorne's, who later became Lord Battersea.

poet), sent on 6 November 1894, comments, 'How can I thank you enough for all your kindness to my wife . . . she writes that she was very heavy-hearted at leaving your Royal Highness. If I may venture to say so, you have certainly inspired a romantic and devoted affection in her.' Lady Ashburton wrote to Thomas Carlyle in 1875, 'I am quite bewitched by her – [she has] so much intelligence.'

Throughout Louise's life, there are numerous mentions of her being a 'flirt', a term generally used in an icily derogatory manner by disapproving women. Men found her 'charming', which was the word used time and again about her, up to the end of her life. In 1870, Lord Granville wrote to the queen that 'Princess Louise was charming last night, and won the hearts of everybody', listing the men who had appeared to be enamoured of her. William Ewart Gladstone wrote to thank the queen for allowing Louise to attend one of his parties and commented on her 'gracious demeanour' and how popular she had been. In 1891 Lady Wolseley, a guest at an entertainment at Osborne House, wrote angrily to her husband that Louise broke protocol to sit with the 'members of the household' instead of her family (and Lady Wolseley). She was convinced Louise's behaviour had nothing to do with the princess's desire to treat everyone in the same way, and everything to do with Louise's desire to 'flirt' with a member of the royal household.

In *Darling Loosy* Elizabeth Longford noted that 'Louise's very natural capacity for falling for any handsome young man in her entourage . . . was beginning to attract attention.' Louise certainly enjoyed being surrounded by attractive men. When she and Lorne had set up their first home, assisted by Henry Ponsonby, Louise told Ponsonby that the most necessary members of their household staff were footmen. She was insistent that she be allowed to choose the servants herself as she had a horror of 'an absurd man in a kilt following me about everywhere'. In Grasse, the discovery of a regiment stationed nearby was enticing. Her much-adored lover had died. Her husband was unable – or unwilling – to sleep with her and she found him physically unappealing. She was more than happy to be surrounded by attractive young officers. It was not only the soldiers who had excited her interest; Louise also found herself increasingly drawn to Beatrice's husband, the dashing Liko. In turn, Liko was bored out of his mind at having to be one of the queen's lapdogs and eager for excitement.

In the summer of 1891, six months after the death of Boehm, the

New York Times made much of the fact that at a special performance at the Royal Opera House in London, in the presence of the Emperor and Empress of Germany, Louise chose to sit not only separately but 'far away' from her husband. Louise sat beside her niece, the former Princess Louise of Wales, now the Duchess of Fife, while Lorne and the Duke of Fife sat some way off. People were still talking about the Lornes' marriage – and even though the scandal and stories continued to attend the Colin Campbells, the papers longed to have another sensation in the now much-derided aristocratic Scottish family to write about. Louise never forgave Colin for the way he had behaved. Several royal historians have claimed that she was surprisingly conventional in her views on divorce and that was why she shunned her brother-in-law. The suggestion, however, that the thoroughly modern woman who had been bold enough back in the 1870s to want to help Josephine Butler in her reform of the Contagious Disease Acts, and had actively angled to meet the scandalous George Eliot who was openly 'living in sin' with a married man, was offended by the mere idea of divorce, seems puerile. Louise may have been living in the puritanical Victorian age, but she was anything but a puritan herself. That she refused ever to see Colin – for the rest of his life, if she were expected in Scotland, he had to leave the castle before she arrived – seems to have had far more to do with the way in which he had treated his wife, than with Louise being offended by his divorce. The fact that Colin had knowingly infected his wife with a dangerous and painful sexually transmitted disease would have been far more likely to have angered Louise, the champion of women's rights, than the fact that he had exposed the family name to the shame of the divorce courts (although she was furious that the scandal touched on her via her husband – she and Lorne had plenty of their own sexual secrets they did not want people to pry into).

Even the queen, who was so rigid in her views on divorce and scandal, felt compassionate about Lady Colin, writing in a private letter to Prince Arthur, 'Ld Colin must be a horrid creature. Whatever faults Ly may have, she has been most cruelly used, & the case trumped up agst her.' It was an unusual stance for the queen to take; Louise's opinions about the matter influenced her mother. That the queen wrote so kindly about Louise's sister-in-law seems doubly extraordinary when one considers that while the *Campbell* v. *Campbell* case was being fought, Victoria was still refusing to accept the wife of John Everett Millais, one of her favourite artists and a pillar of the establishment. Millais had married Effie three decades earlier, but the queen had never forgiven Effie for having been previously married to John Ruskin. Even though John and Effie Ruskin were not divorced – Effie sought and received an annulment, a respectable agreement from the Church that the marriage had never existed – the queen was still disapproving. The scandal of the court case (in which Effie had petitioned for annulment on the grounds of 'non-consummation' of their very strange marriage) had been enough to persuade the queen that Millais's sweet, unassuming, shy Scottish wife was *persona non grata*. Why, when she continued to invite Millais but not Effie to royal events, did the queen write such understanding words about Lady Colin Campbell? Was it perhaps because Lord Colin was a member of the clan Campbell with whom the queen was now extremely angry? Or was it because, like Louise, she was disgusted that a man should have knowingly infected his wife with 'a loathsome disease'?

Louise must have had a very low opinion of the Campbell men: her once-adored father-in-law had proved himself tyrannical,[81] upsetting everyone by insisting that his second marriage take place less than a year after the death of his much-mourned first wife. Then there was Lord Colin Campbell, who had given his wife a sexually transmitted infection before fabricating lies about her having multiple lovers. In doing so he had blackened not only his wife's name but also the innocent men he had cited, caring nothing about the consequences for them and their families. Even though the court found there was not enough evidence to substantiate his allegations, the reputations of Gertrude (Lady Colin) and her four reputed lovers were tarnished for ever by the case.[82] Finally, there was Louise's own husband, the

---

[81] In 1895, Lord Colin Campbell died at the age of 42. Lord Ronnie Gower was shocked see that the Duke of Argyll did not seem to be 'affected . . . at all' by the death of his son.

[82] Gertrude did have a sexual relationship with at least one of them, the Duke of Marlborough, but there is no way of knowing if this affair began before or after the court case. She may also have slept with Shaw, the fire chief for London (and the father of one of her friends) and possibly also had an affair with a Dr Bird – although it is more likely that they simply enjoyed a flirtation he was too embarrassed to

Campbell who had married her despite being gay.[83] In years to come, Louise and Lorne would become devoted to one another – she called him 'my darling Lorne' – and start to enjoy one another's company more often, even becoming co-conspirators against the rest of Louise's family when she needed an ally. This closeness had not yet developed.

Throughout 1891, Louise threw herself into officialdom, trying to dull the pain of Boehm's death by keeping herself busy. For most artists, working in their studio would have been one method of working out the pain – but for Louise her studio was a constant reminder of her dead lover. She went to the Isle of Wight to launch a lifeboat; to the Lake District where she opened 'a fancy fair' in Kendal and an 'industrial, arts, crafts and loan exhibition' in Barrow; and to Edinburgh where she 'formally opened' the Edinburgh School of Cookery and presented diplomas to successful students. This pattern would be repeated throughout the coming years, with Louise lending her name to numerous charities and causes and responding to a stream of requests that she hand out prizes, lay foundation stones and attend balls and fund-raising dinners. Many of the charities she supported were concerned with health reform, education and the rights of women and girls. Refusing to shy away from the stigma attached to mental illnesses, she actively raised money for asylums as well as hospitals. She was president or patron of numerous charities, including the Girls' Public Day Schools Company, the Victoria Hospital for Children, the National Society

---

explain to his wife. The fourth named co-respondent, the general, was too upset even to be in England during the court case, let alone enter the witness stand. Snide journalists claimed this proved his guilt, yet he was a deeply religious and apparently happily married man who barely knew Gertrude and it seems highly unlikely they had ever had any kind of intimate relationship.

[83] There are claims by those who still insist the couple were in love and that no scandal ever touched them that Lorne 'must' have been heterosexual because there were rumours that, as a young man in Scotland, he pursued local girls and was a 'ladies' man', and even stories of illegitimate children fathered before he married (these putative children are unnamed and unclaimed in any of the reports I've read). There must be very few gay men (or women), living in a country and an era where homosexuality was illegal, despised and harshly punished, who have not tried to 'cure' themselves of their sexual impulses by attempting to make themselves attracted to the opposite sex. Perhaps, like Oscar Wilde, Lorne was bisexual.

for the Protection of Young Girls, the Kensington District Nursing Association, the Kensington Philanthropic Society, the Soldiers' and Sailors' Family Association,[84] the Women's Emigration Society, the Irish Distressed Ladies' Fund, and the Home Education Society. She took an active interest in the Ragged School Union, the Boys' Brigade, the Recreative Evening Schools Association, the Lifeboat Fund, a newly formed homeless charity called the House of Shelter, the East End Mothers' Home, the Gentlewomen's Employment Association and a large number of schools, hospitals and asylums around the country. When the operetta star Eugène Oudin died unexpectedly in 1894, Louise joined a committee to raise money for his bereaved family. She was also involved with several quirkily intriguing charities, including the British Institute at Brussels, which aided 'all Englishwomen earning their livelihood in Belgium', and the Young Men's Friendly Society.

Louise allied herself to a number of artistic and artisan charities, including the Scottish Home Industries Association, the Ladies' Work Society (which helped poor women earn a decent living from their needlework skills) and the Royal Female School of Art. In 1894, Lord Ronnie Gower recorded in his journal his observations on Beatrice and Louise, when the princesses attended the same charity fête but on different days. Princess Beatrice, Gower noted, 'looked cross and extremely bored and produced an unfortunate impression'. Princess Louise was, however, 'in every way a contrast to her younger sister, being most gracious and charming everyone'.

Throughout the 1890s, Louise's name pops up tirelessly in the newspapers, less because of her court life than for her numerous public appearances and her artistic career. In fact, she was so renowned for the lack of 'royalness' in her diary that in 1895, when the queen was ill, the papers reported with open astonishment the news that 'Princess Louise will hold the fifth and last Drawing Room of the season at Buckingham Palace on Wednesday next'. Neither Helena nor Alix was available, so Louise had stepped in. As the papers reported, 'It is many years since Princess Louise held a Drawing Room, and the esteem in which her Royal Highness is held will ensure a large attendance.' She impressed those who attended with her usual

---

[84] The earliest incarnation of what, today, is known as SSAFA.

flamboyant dress sense: a lace-trimmed dress of cream satin, adorned with flowers, emeralds and diamonds and completed by a dramatic black velvet train decorated with embroidery, feathers and a pink satin trim.

Despite her numerous public engagements Louise had managed to devote much of 1895 to art. In November, she sent an unnamed present to Arthur Sullivan, who responded with a delighted letter: 'Nothing could be of greater value to me – nothing give me more real and lasting pleasure – than to possess something done with your own hands and head – a part of yourself.' He was in Berlin overseeing a production of *Ivanhoe* and his letter continues wittily about how much the press hates him because he is a 'foreigner' and how furious the people of Berlin are that an English composer's work is being performed in their opera house. He writes of missing his home and friends and 'longing to get back to London'.

By the early 1890s, Queen Victoria was in her sixties and had begun to experience a number of health problems, one of the most worrying of which was a deterioration in her vision. As Beatrice had a very young family (another baby was born in 1892), Louise found herself back in the role she had played in the early 1870s, standing in for her mother at official functions, usually with one of her brothers. Louise was still very much *the* member of the royal family whom the people had taken to their heart; she was accessible to them, and they turned out in their droves every time she appeared at an event. (In the early 1890s, the sporting pages are littered with mentions of a popular racehorse named Princess Louise.)

At the start of 1892, Louise was summoned to help Bertie and Alix through a heartbreaking tragedy. On 14 January, the country was shocked to hear of the death of their future king: Bertie and Alix's eldest child, Prince Eddy. The young man whose name had been whispered about in connection with the Cleveland Street male brothel three years before was now reported to have died of influenza and pneumonia. The year in which he died should have been the year in which he married. Eddy was engaged to Princess May of Teck (May being the diminutive of Mary) and their wedding date was just a few weeks away. Princess May received the sympathy of the people when she placed on Prince Eddy's coffin a wreath made of her bridal flowers. (She would go on to become Queen Mary when on 6 July 1893 she married Eddy's younger brother Prince George, who became King George V.)

From very early on, there were rumours about Eddy's death, the most outlandish of which was the claim that he had had his throat cut by a male lover, with his parents said to have covered up his murder to avoid a scandal. The rumours seem to have begun because Bertie had told the queen not to visit Sandringham when Eddy was ill. If Eddy genuinely died of influenza, the doctors would almost certainly have suggested that the queen, whose health was already failing, should not be exposed to the risk of infection. There are also rumours that Eddy died of a fatal venereal disease, the most common of which at the time was syphilis, which often led to early death from associated complications such as heart disease. In her biography of Lady Colin Campbell, the author Anne Jordan writes about the early death of the Duke of Marlborough, from a heart attack, and comments that a number of unexpected deaths of seemingly healthy young or middle-aged men are most likely to have been the result of syphilis, or complications caused by syphilis. Few doctors would have written the name of such a disease on the death certificate of anyone except a pauper. What is often overlooked, however, is that at the time of Eddy's death Britain was in the grip of an exceptionally virulent and deadly strain of influenza. Official statistics record that almost 17,000 people died in 1891 and almost 16,000 in 1892.[85]

For some time, Bertie and Alix had not been getting on well and although the death of their son drew them very closely together for a while, the marriage was suffering. Louise, who loved both of them, was caught in the middle of their constant arguments – as were their servants, who were seldom dismissed from a room before the couple broke into a furious row. Alix's health had not been good for some years: a slender, frail woman, she had never recovered fully from the demands of pregnancy and childbirth, and suffered from agonising rheumatic fever. She had also lived for many years with debilitating hearing problems, and was becoming increasingly deaf. Both she and Bertie were made irritable by the problems caused by her deafness

[85] Because influenza was not a notifiable illness, many more people may have died as a result of the flu epidemic than those whose deaths were officially attributed to flu.

– and she found it more and more difficult to turn a blind eye to his constant infidelities, not least because so many people knew about them. One of the stories that Catherine Walters ('Skittles') related to Wilfrid Scawen Blunt was about Alix and Mrs Keppel, who became Edward VII's mistress in the late 1890s:

> She [Alix] naturally enough does not like Mrs Keppel. On one occasion, when she had been obliged to receive her and her husband, Mrs Keppel came to take her leave at the end of a three days visit and made a little speech of thanks, to which the Queen responded with a few conventional phrases of politeness, but the moment she had turned away the Queen cocked what boys call a snooky at her. [Dr] Laking was there and saw it.

The 1890s saw great advances in engineering and technology making travelling easier and faster. In 1892, the royal family's overseas visitors included both the King of Romania and a former slave from Tennessee. When she visited England, Martha Ann Ricks, who had left the United States to live in Liberia, said that she had been saving for fifty years to travel to England and meet the queen, because she wanted to thank her in person for the Royal Navy's role in preventing slave ships from reaching the shores of Africa and taking people captive.

In the year of Martha Ann Ricks's visit, Louise was working feverishly again. This was not only on her sculpture (in Boehm's absence, with the help of Alfred Gilbert), but also on paintings. At a party held by the musician George Henschel, Louise was introduced to a young Polish pianist who was taking London by storm. Ignacy Jan Paderewski was renowned both for his talent at the piano and for his romantic good looks. His lustrous red hair, so fashionable in a post-Pre-Raphaelite world, and strong facial bones made artists long to paint him and Louise was no exception. When the actress Ellen Terry met Paderewski at a party hosted by the Alma-Tademas, she noted in her diary 'Mrs Alma-Tadema's "At Home". Paderewski played. What a divinely beautiful face!'

Paderewski had become a friend of Lawrence Alma-Tadema, so when the eminent artist asked to paint him, the pianist agreed quite happily. In his memoirs Paderewski recalled:

It was probably the most exacting and elaborate posing for a picture that has ever been done, because at the first sitting I found, to my surprise, that there were three people making my portrait! . . . Princess Louise, Sir Lawrence himself, and Lady Alma-Tadema, and all three were furiously painting me at the same time.

Paderewski remembered all three of the artists repeatedly imploring him to turn in *their* direction, which he found impossible, and he described it not as a 'sitting' but as a 'moving'. Louise wanted Paderewski to sit to her again. In 1892, in a round of newspaper interviews Paderewski was reported as saying that the princess had told him that, as he was so busy, she required only 'three sittings of two hours each', that these took place in her studio in Kensington Palace and that Paderewski was 'very much delighted with the kind reception he received at Kensington Palace'. Reporters also claimed Paderewski had told them Louise had attended every one of his recitals and concerts that season, armed with her sketchbook and pencil.[86] Of the three paintings created in Alma-Tadema's studio, the pianist commented that Laura Alma-Tadema's painting was very small, Lawrence Alma-Tadema's was 'a masterpiece' and that Louise's was 'not successful as a likeness, because, quite evidently, I was not turning enough *her* way!'. It may not have been an ideal likeness, but the painting is stunning. The *Boston Evening Transcript* claimed: 'Princess Louise considers her greatest artistic achievement is the portrait of Paderewski exhibited by her in London . . . Paderewski, with his shock of red Pre-Raphaelite hair, dreamy green eyes and sensitive clear-cut features, stares out of the canvas straight into futurity.'[87]

While her portrait of Paderewski was being exhibited, Louise, in common with other artists, was working tirelessly in advance of the 'World's Fair' of 1893, which was being held in Chicago. Louise sent to Chicago a bust of her mother as well as paintings which, the papers reported, 'will, after the exhibition, be sold, the proceeds being given to some of the charitable institutions in this country in which she takes so much interest'. She was not the only member of the royal

[86] The Royal Collection contains two photographs of Paderewski taken in 1891, which may well have been props used by Louise when finishing her painting.
[87] Louise bequeathed the painting to the people of Poland.

family to send artwork to the fair; the queen and several of the princesses sent paintings and embroideries. Despite an angry strike by over 1,500 of its workers in April 1893, the World's Fair (also known as the Columbian Exposition) opened on 1 May and stayed open until 31 October. It was in the style of the Great Exhibition of 1851 and the queen felt proud that her husband's efforts to unite nations through art and industry were continuing.

Louise was becoming increasingly involved with her regiment, of which she had been made honorary Colonel-in-Chief; it was a role she took very seriously, aware of what an honour it was for a woman and a non-Scot to have been appointed. She must also have enjoyed the chance to spend the time with so many handsome young men – and not only because she enjoyed flirting, but also because, to the younger men, she could take on the maternal role that led her nieces and nephews to adore her. A number of former soldiers from this regiment have written about her regular visits to their barracks, and of how interested she was in them and their lives. In 1977, F. Maclellan Orr still remembered vividly the time he met the princess:

In the latter half of 1915 I was serving in the . . . Argyll and Sutherland Highlanders stationed in Dunbarton Castle when H.R.H. Princess Louise, our Colonel-in-Chief, inspected the battalion. She very kindly requested that anyone who had already been in action in France, or elsewhere, should be presented to her, and as I had earlier returned as a casualty from the 1/9th Battalion, I came into this category. She addressed a few words to me and offered her hand to shake and as I was carrying a claymore I had to flick it quickly with the left hand, shake hands, return the sword and salute, a complicated manoeuvre, during which I was terrified that I should drop the sword . . . Although I have now reached my 82nd year, I remember the occasion well.

Today she is honoured at the regimental museum in Stirling Castle, where there are a number of Princess Louise objects on display. One is a stunning portrait of the princess (a copy of the original by Hubert von Herkomer). In the painting she looks every inch an Aesthetic beauty, wearing an unusual and very fashionable crimson bodice over an ivory-coloured blouse, together with a simple gold-and-pearl neck-lace. Louise is seen in left profile: her hair is swept back over her ear, but the whole of her right side, including the ear she injured in the sleigh accident, is hidden. The princess looks wistfully up and out of the painting, as if deep in thought. Every surviving photograph of Louise following her time in Canada shows her either from the left side or with her hair covering her right ear.

Lorne, meanwhile, was back in the world of politics, trying to repair the damage his brother had caused to the Campbell name and to promote the Liberal cause. Wisely avoiding any attempt to regain the Scottish seat that until Colin's residency had been such a popular Campbell stronghold, Lorne focused his attention on England and, in 1895, was named the MP for Manchester South in the Liberal Unionist Party. The location of his constituency provided the perfect excuse for spending time away from London. Although throughout the first half of the 1890s, the Court Circular sections in the newspapers suggest that Louise and Lorne were often together, the reality seems to have been rather different. The columns would record their arrival together – for example at Windsor, Osborne or Balmoral – and their departure together, yet often Lorne went away and Louise remained with her family on her own. It seems the official bulletins were intended to suggest the couple spent much more time together than they did; a ruse often belied by later announcements that Lorne had arrived somewhere he should already have been several weeks earlier. The same seems to have been true of their travelling plans. Every winter, the couple – in common with most of the royal family – would set off to warmer climes, usually the French Riviera and Italy. The fashion for the royal family 'wintering' overseas smarted with social reformers and radical journalists. One of their number, who had not yet recovered from his anger at Beatrice marrying yet another German – whose income was being paid by British taxes – wrote a caustic article in 1894 in *Reynolds's Weekly Newspaper*:

Meetings of the unemployed and starving will be held presently. The Queen, the Prince of Wales, and the others of that ilk, are in the meantime making arrangements to depart for warmer climes to escape the rigour of an English winter. The money spent on these trips would provide a living and luxuries for all the hungry and distressed. Moral: it is better to be a German pauper in a strange land than to be an English pauper in one's native country.

On their holidays, Louise and Lorne would stay independently of the queen, usually at a hotel close to whichever grand home the queen had been lent for her holiday. Often they were accompanied by Lord Ronnie Gower, as well as at least one of Louise's ladies-in-waiting, usually Lady Sophia MacNamara. Louise would travel incognito as the Countess of Sundridge. Since the death of Boehm, her health had been poor and her spirits low; just as she had done when living in Canada, when she became depressed she began spending more and more time overseas. Lorne and Ronnie would travel with Louise until she was settled, then take off on their own. This agreement suited all of them, not least because Louise was having to spend increasing amounts of time helping her mother – Louise's childlessness and Beatrice's fecundity meant that Louise was being sucked back into the role she had so detested. The role was less difficult now, as the queen was mellowing in her older age. She was far more indulgent of her grandchildren than she had ever been of her own children and she and Louise began to enjoy a less antagonistic relationship as Louise grew into middle age. When Boehm died, her mother would have been able to understand Louise's grief, having lost both her beloved Albert and John Brown. She, perhaps more than anyone, could have identified with Louise's misery and loneliness.

When Louise was in London she was part of a social life that revolved around theatre, opera and dinner parties (fitted in between regular visits to Osborne and Windsor). She and Lorne had a wide circle of friends, many of whom they shared with Bertie, and the couple were always in demand. When they visited Wolverhampton for an official engagement, they attended the opening night of Oscar Wilde's *A Woman of No Importance*. The papers were thrilled to report on the procession that followed the royal carriage: 'Among the private carriages at the rear of the procession was one drawn by a pair of greys . . . having in the windows the announcement, in large letters, "This carriage is reserved for a Woman of No Importance".' Louise, Lorne and Bertie were also guests of Arthur Sullivan at the music festival in Leeds.

The Court Circular announcements of the time are full of stories of Louise and Lorne attending events together, often with Louise as the only woman in the party, with Beatrice's and Helena's husbands making up a four. (On one occasion, the newspapers printed the shocking announcement 'The Princess Louise and Prince Henry of Battenberg visited the Haymarket Theatre last night.' A couple of days later an embarrassed amendment was printed, claiming it had been Beatrice and not Louise who had attended the theatre with Liko, but whether this was damage limitation or the truth is debatable.) Louise was also there to help Lorne through a wounding and humiliating time with his father. Once again Lorne's father had been widowed – Duchess Mimi had died at the start of 1894. Less than a year later, at the age of 72, the duke announced he was marrying for a third time, to a woman over twenty years younger, who had been one of Louise's attendants in Canada. The third duchess, Ina McNeill, was disliked by all the duke's children and every one of them boycotted the wedding. Louise, who had come to know Ina very well in Canada, tried to play peacemaker and mediator, but the situation just became worse and, the two women ended up not speaking. Lorne was incensed with his father and deeply unhappy, and Louise was angry on her husband's behalf.

Yet despite this show of solidarity, of Lorne accompanying Louise to public events and she standing by his side when he was running for parliamentary office, there were still rumours about their marriage. On 13 May 1894 the gossip column of the radical *Reynolds's Weekly Newspaper* printed a brief article; a couple of lines long, it simply poses the unanswered question: 'Princess Louise lives in a suite of rooms at Kensington Palace. But where does her husband, the Marquis of Lorne, live?'

CHAPTER 24

Scandal in the royal household

> She is my constant companion and hope and trust will never leave me while I live. I do not intend she should ever go out as her sisters did (which was a mistake) but let her stay (except of course occasionally going to theatres) as much as she can with me.

> Queen Victoria writing about Beatrice in 1875

Ever since the queen's eyesight had started to fail, Louise and Beatrice had been forced to spend more time together. The two sisters had, to all appearances, been growing closer, yet despite the frequent references in the newspapers to the sisters 'driving out' with their mother and sailing together between Portsmouth and the Isle of Wight, Beatrice and Louise did not enjoy a trouble-free relationship. This was exacerbated for Beatrice by the obvious mutual attraction of her husband and her pretty, always slim older sister. Since she had grown out of the infantile golden curls stage of her early childhood, Beatrice had never been a beauty. Like her mother, she disliked pregnancy and childbirth and found herself growing increasingly fat; also like her mother, Beatrice found it difficult to curb her love of food. Conversely, Louise had astonishing willpower when it came to eating, and often denied herself food precisely because she refused to end up like her rotund mother and sisters. When, as a young woman, her siblings ridiculed her constant need to exercise, Louise retorted that when they were all old, she would be the only one who had not succumbed to the portly Hanoverian physique. In 1895, when Louise was 47, a story in the newspapers revealed her latest exercise regime:

[Princess Louise] has been taking advantage of the semi-emptiness of Battersea Park lately . . . to continue her bicycle lessons. She drives usually to the Trafalgar Club, alights there, and then, putting herself into the hands of the most fashionable instructor of the moment, goes round and round the Park in the most energetic way possible. Occasionally, still accompanied by her instructor, of course, Her Royal Highness ventures out of the solitude of the Park into the traffic of the streets. Princess Louise rides in the neatest coat and skirt, and holds herself splendidly.

That Louise needed excitement and attention is obvious throughout her life and there has been speculation ever since the 1890s as to whether she had an affair with her sister's husband. She and Liko enjoyed flirting with each other, but whether it ever went further will remain a mystery. When she ended her startling revelations about Boehm's death to Wilfrid Scawen Blunt, Skittles remarked with relish that the shock of her lover dying in her arms meant that Louise had not had a single lover since. Such a bombastic announcement smacks of pure embellishment – apart from anything else, Dr Laking could not possibly have known that Louise had not slept with anyone since – yet the experience of her lover dying while having sex with her must have caused serious psychological scars for Louise. As for Liko, his marriage was obviously not satisfactory. He was spending increasing amounts of time on his own: taking off on sailing trips for months, or escaping to London when his wife and children were at Windsor, he was happy to go anywhere he could enjoy a social life that didn't revolve around Queen Victoria. Whether Liko and Louise's mutual attraction ever became physical or not, Beatrice was growing antagonistic to her sister and her dislike came to a head at the end of 1895.

To look at the next scandal in the royal family, we need to return to the summer of 1879, when the young Arthur Bigge had appeared at the royal court for the first time. He was the soldier who had served in the Zulu Wars with the Prince Imperial (the ill-fated son of the deposed Emperor and Empress of France) and had brought to the palace the news of the prince's death. Bigge was an attractive and charismatic man and the queen had immediately taken an interest in him. When Sir Henry Ponsonby became very ill in 1895 and the role of private secretary needed to be filled, Bigge (now a respectably married man with children), was chosen. He and Louise got on very well and enjoyed working together.

Perhaps Beatrice was irritated by the ease with which all men were attracted to her sister, or perhaps simply with Louise herself, but Beatrice became suspicious that her sister and Queen Victoria's private secretary were having an affair. Instead of talking to Louise, Beatrice sent for Sir John Reid, the queen's physician and advisor. As Beatrice knew would be the case, Reid had no option but to go to the queen and tell her of Beatrice's concerns. Matthew Dennison, Beatrice's biographer, who is usually very empathetic towards his subject, describes the chaotic incident as the result of Beatrice's 'determined exposure' of what she believed was Louise's love affair. In his view, Louise suffered from 'a persecution complex' about her sisters. When Helena joined forces with Beatrice about the Arthur Bigge scandal, Louise was hurt and claimed they were ganging up on her.

Louise was certainly overly sensitive, but Helena and Beatrice were extremely jealous of their sister. That Beatrice deliberately passed on the rumours about Louise, rather than asking her sister herself, and that, instead of trying to cover up the scandal, she exposed it, was vindictive and intended to wound. Beatrice took pleasure in being able to cause trouble. With such a brace of sisters, it is not surprising that Louise felt 'persecuted'. Liko also took part in the discrediting of Arthur Bigge and his sister-in-law, relating that he had heard Bigge, at a dinner, drinking Louise's health (often an indication of an affair).

When Louise discovered what her sisters and Liko had done she was so shocked and hurt that she made herself seriously ill with 'nerves': the severe headaches and neuralgia she had been plagued with ever since her sledging accident in Canada had never abated and always grew worse at times of stress. The row that ensued after Beatrice's betrayal left Louise utterly incapacitated; even the queen became deeply concerned about her daughter's health. Dr Reid found the prolonged incident wearying, as he was forced to listen to complaints from all sides. He wrote in his diary that Louise was convinced there was a 'smear' campaign against her.

When she was well enough, Louise spoke to her mother about the incident, telling her (as she had told Reid) that Liko was to blame. Her brother-in-law, she explained, had attempted to seduce her. She had refused him and he had become irate. She insisted that Liko had then gone to Beatrice with lies about her and Arthur Bigge in revenge. Within a few days of Louise's confession to her mother, Lorne had arrived at Windsor Castle, summoned to fetch Louise. The couple returned at once to Kensington Palace. For several weeks afterwards, it is notable that the queen was accompanied in her carriage either by Beatrice or Louise, never the two together. Unusually, at the end of 1895, Lorne is often named as having accompanied the queen and Louise on these rides.

Whether Louise slept with Liko or with Arthur Bigge, or was having affairs with both of them, is unknowable, but Bigge made it obvious that he found her attractive and Liko made it apparent that Bigge's attitude affronted him. Sexual tension had reached fever pitch and what must have angered Beatrice was that the only one who did not seem to have been caught up in the heated sexual atmosphere was Liko's *hausfrau*. Elizabeth Longford, whilst seemingly refuting all suggestions of Louise's adultery, wrote the intriguing paragraph: 'For Louise the 1890s were not exactly "naughty" – rather, full of temptations, to some of which she would succumb. Two of those who have seen private papers agree that in her forties she was at her most "alluring".'

Louise was forced to spend time with her trouble-making younger sister at the end of 1895, due to the death of Sir Henry Ponsonby, whose funeral took place at Whippingham Church on the Isle of Wight. Louise had been very fond of him and his death depressed her. Louise and Lorne were forced to stay at Osborne for the funeral, living uncomfortably alongside Beatrice and Liko. The situation was so unbearable that Liko came up with a solution: he was leaving the country. Although his military service had, so far, been little more than honorary, Liko persuaded his mother-in-law to permit him to serve in Africa, in what was known as the Fourth Anglo-Ashanti War.

Beatrice and Liko's eldest son, Drino (Alexander) would claim as an adult that his father had spoken to him before he left England and told him that he was going away because he had to 'escape the attentions' of an unnamed 'lady'. This added fuel to the speculation that Liko and Louise were having an affair, with Drino's obvious implication that his father was the less willing of the two. Drino was nine years old when his father left and he never saw him again. It seems unlikely that a Victorian father would have shared a sexual secret with such a young child, and far more likely that Drino believed what he was told in later years by his mother. If Liko did genuinely tell his son that he was 'escaping' from unwanted attention, this makes it more likely that Louise had rejected him. Had he genuinely rebuffed her, he would have had no cause to be jealous of her and Arthur Bigge; instead one would have expected him to have been relieved and not to have joined in his wife's jealous crusade to expose Louise's secret.

When Liko left for Africa, the family was about to celebrate Christmas. It was a muted affair for Beatrice and her children, and this December Louise and Lorne spent much more time in London than had been usual in recent years. Liko had little time to enjoy his freedom and was never able to win the glory of being a hero. Within a few weeks of leaving England he had contracted malaria. He died, without ever seeing military action, on 20 January 1896. Beatrice and the queen, who were at Windsor, heard the news on 22 January. Louise, who was in London, was told of Liko's death on the following morning, whereupon she immediately cancelled her engagements for the day and went into mourning. She mourned sadly the friend she had grown so close to in recent years and with whom she had fought so bitterly just before he left. In a letter to a friend, she described her grief: 'He was almost the greatest friend I had – I, too, miss him more than I can say.'

On 28 January, Louise left Kensington Palace for the Isle of Wight. Liko's body was being returned to England and Beatrice was planning his funeral. This meant Louise was away for the funeral of fellow artist Frederic, Lord Leighton, President of the Royal Academy, which was held at St Paul's Cathedral on 2 February; Louise was represented by Colonel Collins. Ever since Leighton's cool attitude towards Boehm's death, Louise had not been impressed with him. He, it seems, had been aware of his faux pas and had attempted to build bridges in their relationship, but although the two were, ostensibly, friends, she had never really forgiven him. A letter of his survives from 1893, written when Louise was planning a trip to Italy. It was a country Leighton knew very well and he sent her suggestions for artistic places to visit. After pages of ideas, he ended with 'I trust these brief notes may be of some little use to Your Royal Highness. Although I gather there is little hope of my having the honour of seeing you next week at my studio'; obviously hopeful that she would change her mind, he mentioned that both Vicky and Bertie would be visiting him on the following Friday.

Liko's funeral was held on 5 February. He was buried in the church at which he and Beatrice had been married. Much was made in the newspapers of the image of the two dumpy, black-clad widows, mother and daughter, now locked together just as they had been when Beatrice was an unmarried daughter-cum-companion. On the same day as the family funeral at Whippingham Church, a memorial service was held in Westminster Abbey. Many of London's theatres closed as a sign of respect for the princess's husband; the queen sent the managers a formal message of gratitude for their kindness.

Instead of being brought together in their grief, Beatrice and Louise were still at loggerheads. Smarting from her sister's betrayal over the Bigge affair and depressed by her own misery at Liko's death, Louise lashed out at Beatrice. The household was in shock as yet another family scandal threatened to break. As the Duchess of Teck wrote to a friend, the court was in uproar: 'Louise has alas! *frisséed* [Beatrice] terribly by calmly announcing that she was Liko's *confidante* and Beatrice nothing to him, indicated by a *shrug* of the *shoulders!*' Whether Louise intended the inference or not, the entire household was gossiping that she was claiming to have been Liko's lover. Sadly, the likelihood of Liko having found Louise a more sympathetic confidante (in the true meaning of the word) than Beatrice is very high. Having been brought up so closely by her mother, Beatrice was far more like Queen Victoria than Prince Albert. She was as unmaternal to her children as her mother had been to her older children (an odd circumstance when one considers that Beatrice was the only child towards whom Victoria *was* maternal). Perhaps Louise's bitchy assertion was a very badly timed moment of truth. Once again, Louise and Lorne returned swiftly from the Isle of Wight to Kensington Palace.

Interestingly, instead of causing a long-standing rift between the sisters, Louise's outburst, and any repercussions that followed, managed to heal the wound caused when Beatrice summoned Sir James Reid to tell tales about Louise. As soon as she could, Beatrice took her children to the South of France to help them through the grief of losing their father. Within a couple of weeks, Louise had been invited to join them. From that time on, the two sisters became increasingly close. Louise suggested that they commission Alfred Gilbert to make a memorial for Liko's tomb. Beatrice gladly assented. In the same year, Louise would begin a grave memorial of her own, a monument to honour Mary Ann Thurston, one of the royal children's nurses. It can be seen today at Kensal Green Cemetery, in London. When it came to real friendship, Louise was immensely loyal, and always aware of how important to her own life the royal servants had been. She remembered those who had been kind to her, especially during her childhood, and went out of her way to ensure that they received appropriate gifts and had no financial worries. For years she had visited the elderly Mrs Thurston regularly, taking her gifts, gossip and amusing friends – such as Lord Ronald Gower – until the old lady's death, in her eighties. At the end of her life, Mrs Thurston had been living very close to Kensington Palace, so Louise was able to keep an eye on her and send help if it were needed.

One of Queen Victoria's ladies-in-waiting, Marie Mallet, described Louise as 'a complex character', noting that although she could be spoilt and difficult, Louise was 'at her best when people are in trouble'. This adult desire to be needed harks back to Louise's childhood and Lady Bruce's comment of 1861, that the adolescent Louise 'is so happy to be made a little of'. She craved attention and affection and those who gave it to her, truly, were to be rewarded.

In March 1896, Louise and Lorne reached a milestone: their silver wedding anniversary. While lavish gifts piled up at Kensington Palace, the couple spent the culmination of twenty-five years of marriage apart. On the anniversary itself, Louise was in Cannes, on board the royal yacht *Britannia* with Bertie, and Lorne was with a large party staying at Sandringham with Alix. In the 1920s, Colin F. McFarlane, who had been tutor to one of Princess Louise's nieces, recorded the following entry in his diary:

They talked too of the Duchess of Argyll who was from the first the rebel of the Queen's family, taking always her own line and refusing to be led or driven. When her Silver Wedding Day came, she was abroad, no one knew where, not even her husband who was staying at Sandringham. The Queen gave him a silver rose-bowl which he forgot as he was leaving till Aunt Alix came out with it at the last moment saying: 'Better not forget your pot, Lorne'.

Shortly after their un-shared anniversary, Louise went off on another holiday without her husband, taking her friend Maggie Ponsonby (daughter of Sir Henry Ponsonby).

That year, Louise was working on an interesting new project. When the Duke of Argyll had told his children that he would need to sell off some of his properties, Lorne had bought Rosneath Castle in Argyll and Bute and its surrounding land (home to many dependent tenants). Although the property was ostensibly purchased by Lorne, the money used to buy it was Louise's. It rankled with Lorne that Louise therefore made the decisions about their new home, but everyone was in agreement that Lorne had no idea of style (his lack of fashion sense had become a joke amongst his friends and family).

Louise had become an admirer of the work of the architect Edward ('Ned') Lutyens, and was keen to commission him to renovate the castle and the local pub, the Ferry Inn, to which she wanted him to add an extra wing. Queen Victoria was scandalised when she discovered how familiar Princess Louise was with the locals in the pub and that she proposed in future staying at the small house next to the refurbished Ferry Inn if she was in Rosneath on her own, so that she didn't have to go to the inconvenience of opening up the big house. When a cartoon appeared in *Punch* depicting Louise serving behind the bar, with the local for whom she was drawing a pint saying 'A pint please and how's your old mother?' the queen forbade her daughter to stay in the house beside the pub.

Louise grew fond of Lutyens because, as she explained, he treated her like everyone else, he was not 'a courtier'. That Lutyens liked Louise was a source of great annoyance to his wife. Like Alfred Gilbert's wife, she became irritated by the beautiful princess who seemed to have dazzled her husband. The situation was not helped by Lutyens himself describing the irresistible charm of spending time with Louise; 'one makes believe and has jokes innumerable', he reported. Louise evidently was not 'safe' as far as wives were concerned. In the early 1920s, a young man named Herbert Ward was one of Lutyens's pupils. Several decades later he recalled a story that Lutyens had told him:

He had to travel with Princess Louise either to or from Scotland. He inadvertently left his silk hat on the seat which she decided to occupy. A crowd of people had collected and she started bowing right and left. Lutyens took the first opportunity of explaining that she was sitting on his hat, whereupon, still bowing vigorously right and left, she whispered, 'For God's sake don't make me laugh; for God's sake don't make me laugh before all these people.' He was certainly very fond of her.

Throughout the spring and summer of 1896, Louise was concerned about her friend, John Everett Millais. The artist, who had become President of the Royal Academy following the death of Lord Leighton, had been given little time to appreciate the honour. He was suffering from throat cancer and his doctors knew there was nothing more they could do for him. In the May of 1896, Millais pretended he was well enough to greet the Prince of Wales at the Academy, though as the artist's son would later write, by that date 'the disease had made such rapid advance that he could hardly walk round the room'. Louise visited Millais, and his family remembered with fondness that, during his final months, she made 'frequent enquiries' and sent 'lovely flowers'. The queen counted Millais amongst her favourite artists and told Louise to ask if there were anything she could do to ease the discomfort of her illustrious subject. When Louise, as instructed, told her friend this Millais reputedly replied that the one thing the queen could do for him would be to receive his wife. Ever since the couple had married in 1855, the queen had held firm to her bigoted conviction that Effie, as a woman who had caused scandal (no matter how innocently) by seeking an annulment from her first husband, was not to be tolerated. On his deathbed, Millais outsmarted the queen. She had no choice but to grant his dying wish and Effie was duly invited to the royal court. Like his friend, Lord Leighton, just a few months previously, Millais was buried in the artists' section of St Paul's Cathedral. He had died on 13 August 1896 and his funeral took place exactly a week later.

The end of the year was marked by a milestone for Queen Victoria. On 23 November 1896 she wrote in her journal: 'To-day is the day on which I have reigned longer, by a day, than any English sovereign.' The century was heading towards its close and, against all the odds, it seemed the ageing queen would live to see the new one. Already ten years had passed since her golden jubilee.

Throughout the first six months of 1897, the year of Victoria's diamond jubilee, the royal family went through the same frenetic preparations as they had witnessed during the golden jubilee. Celebrations started in the middle of June and continued for a month. For Louise, as for all of them, it was exhausting, but exhilarating. One reason why Queen Victoria is often held up by historians as an example of a monarch who was loved by her people is the diamond jubilee. It was a landmark for both queen and people. They had grown used to her and, although she made far fewer public appearances than they had hoped, at least now, with the venerability of infirmity and old age, she had an excuse for her reclusive behaviour. The queen wrote in her journal: 'No one ever, I believe, has met with such an ovation as was given to me, passing through those 6 miles of streets . . . The cheering was quite deafening & every face seemed to be filled with real joy. I was much moved and gratified.'

The family, however, was unable to live without either a scandal or a tragedy for long. In January 1899, Alfred and Marie were celebrating their twenty-fifth wedding anniversary with a family party at Schloss Rosenau, the castle in which Prince Albert had grown up, near the town of Coburg. Their eldest son, also named Prince Alfred, was just 24 years old and had fallen in love with a woman his parents disapproved of. During the family party, the young prince shot himself. He survived, but was very badly injured. Immediately he was sent to the Sanatorium Martinsbrunn at Meran, in nearby Austria, but he died there a fortnight later. Louise wrote a loving letter to her brother, reminding him of happier times and memories. He responded: 'Heartfelt thanks for your dear sympathy in my terrible grief. You knew my dear boy so well and . . . know how lovable he was so that you will appreciate what a fearful blow his loss was to me . . . You remind me of Eastwell and all those happy days and how all my hopes are gone and crushed. It is awfully hard to bear.' Alfred found solace for his son's death in his usual way, by drinking. Louise found it hard to bear the knowledge that her much-loved brother had such an unhappy existence, married to an abusive disappointed wife and addicted to alcohol. A few months later Arthur wrote to Louise that

'Affie is in great monetary difficulties. Mama and Bertie are in an awful state about it.'[88]

With the memories of the ill-fated silver wedding party still haunting them, it was a muted group of people who gathered at Windsor Castle just four months later to celebrate the eightieth birthday of Queen Victoria. The death of young Prince Alfred brought back memories for many royals of a similar tragedy a decade earlier, when their relative Crown Prince Rudolf of Austria had died at his hunting lodge in Mayerling; he was discovered shot through the head next to the body of his teenage mistress. Although this death was ruled a suicide, many believed that it was a political assassination, an attempt to bring down the house of Habsburg. Rudolf had been the son and heir of Emperor Franz Joseph I and his charismatic wife Elisabeth (better known by her pet name of Sisi). To add to the tension of the queen's birthday, her eldest grandson, Vicky's difficult and combative son Wilhelm, was angry not to have been invited to his grandmother's party. When he arrived to visit his English relations in November 1899, the atmosphere was tense. The second Boer War[89] had just begun and Wilhelm had made his allegiance to the Boers politically obvious.

Louise was now very much back in the public eye, carrying out royal duties and working tirelessly, with her siblings, to try and make up for the absence of their mother, who was growing more unpredictable as old age began to take its toll. The young artist and book illustrator Kate Greenaway met Princess Louise that year. She recorded the meeting in a letter to her friend and patron John Ruskin on 9 May 1899:

Then the Princess Louise came and I was introduced to her. She is so pretty and looks so young. I actually remembered to curtsey (which I always forget), and I was just congratulating myself on having behaved properly, when all my money rolled out of my

---

[88] In the same letter Arthur thanked Louise for sending 'charmingly painted matchboxes' to a charity bazaar.

[89] The first Boer War had taken place in 1880–1; the war usually referred to in Britain as the 'Boer War' is that of 1899–1902. The war was between the British Empire, which governed parts of southern Africa, and the residents of two Boer states: the Transvaal and the Orange Free State. The Boers were Dutch settlers, who spoke Afrikaans. They wanted to rule themselves and not be governed by the British.

purse onto the ground. The Princess laughed and picked it up. Wasn't it nice of her?

Louise remained as unconventional as ever, and as charming: the artist William Blake Richmond told Louise when she was an elderly widow, 'You could never bore me.' Nor had Louise lost her desire to flirt, or her 'flighty' reputation. In 1898, Marie Mallet described a handsome man to her husband and commented, 'I am sure [Louise] will . . . pounce on him at once.'

The royal Christmas of 1899 was spent at Windsor Castle, and Louise and her siblings spent much of their time knitting socks and scarves to be sent out to the soldiers, and raising funds for war charities. The wounded had already started to be sent home and Louise became involved in helping to set up special Hospital Homes for the injured troops, persuading people to turn their buildings over to the war effort. She proved how persuasive her powers of charm were when she managed to secure several rooms for the wounded at the Savoy Hotel (thanks not only to her royal connections but to her friendship with Arthur Sullivan). As the London Standard reported: 'Princess Louise . . . has received from the Directors of the Savoy Hotel an offer to provide rooms and board for six wounded officers or non-commissioned officers, with nurses and attendants, free of all cost, for so long a period as may be thought desirable.' She visited the proposed sickrooms to ensure they really were suitable for invalids as opposed to hotel guests, and reported back to General Wolseley that 'they seem very suitable and comfortable, having two lifts to the kitchen and stillroom, two bathrooms and a storeroom'. She herself undertook to provide (and pay for) properly trained nurses and other medical attendants. She also arranged for one of the wings of Rosneath, her and Lorne's home in Scotland, to be turned into a military hospital so that injured Scottish soldiers could be cared for close to their families. Once again she reported to General Wolseley and was thrilled that her home's proximity to a pier meant the patients could be transported with the minimum need for painful movement: 'the steamers can come up near, and the patients wheeled to the door of the building'. She threw her artistic skills into practical use, designing architectural plans for the patients and medical staff's accommodation.

Louise had not forgotten the people of Canada; she also raised funds and arranged for supplies to be sent out to Canadian troops fighting in the war. Louise was always at her best when mentally and physically active and able to be useful. People knew they could approach her and ask for favours, such as the woman who asked for her help because her wounded son was in a hospital so far away from his family that they could not afford to visit him. Louise took this on as a personal mission, writing to her influential friends and querying why families were expected to pay full-price train tickets, something that could cripple their finances; she wanted charitable funds to be made available and, if possible, for men to be nursed closer to their homes. She understood, in common with all her sisters, the importance of good practical nursing, and how important it was to take care of the 'whole' patient, mentally as well as physically.

By the end of the nineteenth century, Louise had become more contented. The worst times of her and Lorne's marriage seemed to be past, the queen no longer wrote of her worries that they would separate or of Louise's insistence that she wanted to live 'apart' from her husband. As they advanced in years, people who knew them commented on what a good wife she was to him – although the steward who was with her for many years, John James, cruelly remarked when Louise was in her final illness that she had not been kind to her husband and was dreading meeting him in the afterlife. (John James had not known Lorne well and, as was usual for Victorian men, he seemed of the opinion that men could get away with pretty much any type of behaviour but women had to be patient and long-suffering and never assert their independence.) Marriage, for Louise and Lorne in old age, was the devotion of old friends, of people who knew each other's foibles and forgave each other's defects. They had been through a great deal together and knew each other as well as they knew their lovers. The couple had settled into a routine, accepting of each other's independence and lifestyles. There are so many different types of marriage. Theirs was never the romantic 'love match' that the purple-prose journalists of the 1870s had proclaimed, but it had endured almost three decades of what had often seemed insuperable difficulties. As their thirtieth wedding anniversary approached, Louise and Lorne had learnt to live together and to miss each other when they were apart. He wrote letters addressed to 'Alba', his pet name for Louise, and relied upon her for advice. Their correspondence in the 1890s grew increasingly friendly and solicitous, evincing the respect of a couple growing older together and discussing their health problems and sharing witty stories. In 1906, after Lorne had been spending time in Inveraray, he wrote to his wife that 'It will be heaven for me to see you again.' Louise seems to have become maternal towards Lorne, writing to him as her 'boy', fussing about his clothing and whether he was taking enough exercise and attempting to lure him into eating, as though he were a child. Most notably in recent years, Lorne had been on Louise's side through the crisis with Bigge, Beatrice and Liko; in return she had accepted him as the man he was.

CHAPTER 25

A new century and the end of an era

All my deep sympathy with you in the loss of one to whom you
have so nobly and so long devoted your life

Telegram from Princess Louise to Joan Severn at Brantwood,
following the death of Ruskin on 20 January 1900

The new century began with the death of John Ruskin and with
depressing news from Africa. Despite her friendship with Whistler,
Louise had not abandoned Ruskin after the disastrous court case; this
was largely because when her brother Leopold was at Oxford, Ruskin
had become one of his most trusted friends. Louise had remained
grateful to Ruskin ever since (despite his years of unreasonable and
often unpleasant behaviour, caused by mental illness, when many of
his former friends shunned him). She sent a wreath to his funeral and
a letter to his cousin Joan Severn, who responded: 'My darling was
so loyally devoted to you – and all the Royal Family – but especially
to Prince Leopold – and your words would have gratified him.' After
the funeral Joan wrote again: 'Your beautiful wreath was laid on my
darling's coffin while he rested in the church, and was lowered into
his grave with one sent by G.F. Watts RA . . . and to-day I placed
yours on his grave – at his head.' The death of Ruskin, such a pillar
of the Victorian art world, seemed indicative of the old being replaced
by the new – in art and in society. Louise was embracing the new
century, but she was keenly aware of how much the world was
changing, how much she was feeling her age and how many of the
people she loved were no longer alive.

News from Africa, where the war was still raging, was extremely
worrying and Louise spent the first year of the twentieth century

visiting wounded soldiers and attending fund-raising events in aid of
the war widows and orphans fund. This was a cause to which many
of her artistic and theatrical friends became allied, holding special
performances and exhibitions to raise money for those families left
poverty stricken by the death of the family breadwinner in the Boer
Wars. Everyone in the royal household was exhorted to start knitting
for the soldiers – even the queen took up her knitting needles and
made warm clothing for her troops.

Louise and the queen also contributed paintings to an exhibition
at the Guildhall Art Gallery, which Louise was invited to open. (Louise's
painting entitled Sketch of Botzen sold for 44 guineas.) The exhibition
included works by some of the country's top artists, including Sir
Lawrence Alma-Tadema and Sir Edward Poynter. A charity both Louise
and Lorne had become interested in was the Gentlewomen's
Employment Association and they continued to show their support
for general suffrage, and for equal rights for both genders. (Queen
Victoria vociferously opposed this: when she heard that Lady Amberley
had become president of her local suffrage society, she declared that
she should be given 'a good whipping'. She also complained every
time one of her newborn children or grandchildren turned out to be
a girl.) One of Lorne's sisters, Lady Frances Balfour, was a prominent
member of the National Union of Women's Suffrage Societies and
her husband was the brother of Arthur Balfour. (Louise grew to have
a great affection for Arthur Balfour and supported him in his political
career. She became renowned in the family for her little presents; in
1916 when Balfour had a great many speeches to make and was sleeping
badly, Louise sent him a present of Ovaltine. He sent her a witty and
amused thank-you letter.) Frances had fallen under Louise's spell as
soon as they were introduced; an adoration fed by the fact that Louise
was the first person to notice how much Frances was struggling with
everyday life. She realised it was because Frances's eyesight was failing
and arranged for her to receive her first pair of glasses. For this, Frances
would remain grateful and say that Louise had changed her life for
ever.

Despite Lorne and Louise's close connections with some of the
most important suffrage campaigners of their day, their marriage was
not an example of gender equality. Lorne attempted to impose his
will on Louise's behaviour, just as her mother had done – most notably

refusing to allow her to play billiards, something he was extraordinarily strict about. Just as Louise ignored her mother's orders not to smoke, she ignored this dictate of her husband – but she only played billiards in secret. Even as late as 1905 one of her ladies-in-waiting wrote to her husband that Louise was 'afraid' anyone would mention this to Lorne. Ironically, knowing his sister's love of the game, Bertie had given Louise and Lorne a billiards table when they married.[90]

As the new century dawned, Britain was painfully divided by the fighting in Africa. Many of Victoria's subjects were patriotically behind the armies and the government, but there was a growing voice of those who thought the war and its aims were wrong. Many voiced concern that the Boers were being treated in a 'barbaric' fashion and that those in power were guilty of allowing atrocities to happen. The anger was felt across Europe, and in Ireland many felt an affinity with the Boers, as fellow sufferers of British oppression. In the spring of 1900 amid increasing political tension, Bertie and Alix found themselves the target of an assassination attempt. While they were travelling by train across Belgium, their would-be assassin took advantage of the train's stopping in Brussels. As it was about the leave the station, an Italian gunman jumped up on to the step of their carriage and fired directly at them. He missed. Newspapers described him as 'an anarchist', but he was simply a 15-year-old boy, named only as Sipido, reacting to the news from Africa and nursing a hatred of the British as a result of the war. Although Bertie and Alix escaped unhurt, the war did not leave the royal family unscathed. Many members of the royal family served in the military (as both Prince Alfred and Prince Arthur had done) and in the Boer Wars Helena's eldest son, Prince Christian Victor, joined the fighting. He contracted malaria in Africa, and died of what was described as 'enteric fever'.

While Louise was busying herself with war relief work, one of her large-scale statues of her mother was making its way to Canada, where it would be unveiled with great ceremony in Montreal. The

---

[90] In the 1870s, Josephine Butler wrote to Mrs Ford, a suffrage campaigner, advising her not to put Princess Louise on the spot by asking her to join a campaign, and explaining that she had caused her embarrassment once. In addition to the queen's disapproving of Louise allying herself openly to the suffrage cause, Butler wrote that she was sure 'that little prig Lord Lorne' would prevent the letter from reaching his wife.

newspapers continued their love affair with Louise, writing proudly about their princess's statue being placed 'at the imposing entrance to the Royal Victoria College for Higher Education of Women' (where it still stands today). Louise retained a strong connection to Canada and saw herself as an ambassadress between the two countries. She regularly attended Canadian events in London and invited visiting Canadians to her home. On one such occasion, a journalist interviewed Canadians who had attended a lunch at Kensington Palace. He reported that the visitors had enthused about the kindness and friendliness shown by the princess: 'she talked to me and all the rest just as if we were her brothers', one remarked. Lorne's success as Governor-General of Canada was still being discussed, and at the start of 1900 it was suggested he should be sent out to Australia as Governor-General. Before anyone could speak to Lorne about it, the queen refused. Louise's health, she said, could never stand it.

Lorne's future, however, was about to change regardless. At the end of April 1900, the 8th Duke of Argyll died. He had not reconciled himself to his son and heir (the situation between the duke and all his children had deteriorated steadily ever since his third marriage) and Lorne refused to go to his father's funeral. Duchess Ina attempted to prevent all of the children and their spouses from attending, but Louise went anyway. She had tried, and failed, to change Lorne's mind. Reportedly, Louise 'hid' in the church with several other Campbell relations and when Ina saw them, she stalked out and did not return to the service. (Louise and her Campbell in-laws had several nicknames for Ina, including 'Bitchina' and 'Hell Cat'.)

Following the 8th Duke's death, it was discovered that Lorne, now 9th Duke of Argyll, had inherited an estate in financial crisis. Inveraray Castle would have to be let out (as the only alternative to its being sold). Between his father's financial mess and his brother's political and social disgrace, Lorne had inherited a very difficult title. He was also in dispute with his brother-in-law. Lorne's decision not to attend the funeral infuriated Bertie. He was disgusted by the 'bad form' Lorne displayed by refusing to go and, for several months, the two men would not speak to each other. Whenever Bertie invited Louise to an event, she had to attend alone; the future king made it very clear that the 9th Duke of Argyll was not welcome.

In the year in which she celebrated her eighty-first birthday, Queen

Victoria was beginning to suffer serious health problems. Then the family was rocked by two deaths, the news of which reached them on the same day. The first was of the assassination of King Umberto of Italy. Soon afterwards they were informed of the peaceful, but shockingly sudden, death of Prince Alfred, fourteen months after the suicide of his son. The queen wrote in her journal, 'It is merciful that Affie died in his sleep without any struggle, but it is heartrending.' In her biography of Bertie, Jane Ridley writes poignantly: 'Affie had been Prince Albert's favourite son; so much cleverer than Bertie as a boy, in middle age he was a friendless alcoholic.' Louise and Arthur in particular had been very concerned about Alfred and with their encouragement he had tried taking 'cures', being sent off to rehabilitation centres, but nothing had worked. The alcoholism contributed enormously to his ill health and he died at the age of only 55. It was just a few weeks later that the family learnt of the death of Helena's son, Prince Christian Victor, in Africa.

In addition to the deaths of her brother and her nephew, Louise was informed of the deaths of two of her close friends. The composer Arthur Sullivan died suddenly, aged 58, at his home. Not only had he been a friend of hers; he had been a particular friend of Prince Alfred (before Alfred's marriage to the disapproving Marie). Sullivan and Louise had often corresponded and spoken about the twin tragedies of Prince Alfred's life: his alcoholism and his very unhappy marriage. An undated heartfelt letter from Sullivan, written to Louise from France, reads as a letter from a friend about a friend, forgetting all about 'protocol'. Louise had responded to an earlier worried letter from Sullivan, which he had regretted as soon as he sent it in case it was too informal, but her response made him realise that she felt the same way he did about Prince Alfred.

The composer thanked her for 'the kind tone, and the true womanly sympathy evident in every line' of her response. Now, shortly after the death of his unhappy friend, the composer had died too. Louise was devastated by the loss of another good and kind friend.

The queen, urged by her daughter, requested that Arthur Sullivan be buried at St Paul's Cathedral. A memorial was unveiled three years after Sullivan's death, in Embankment Gardens in London. The sculpture, designed by William Goscombe John, is placed a short walk from the Savoy Theatre, where Gilbert and Sullivan's operettas were staged.

Leaning against the pedestal that supports the bust of Sullivan is a curvaceous weeping woman, beautifully sculpted in flowing art nouveau style. She is usually identified as the grieving Muse of Music, but she is also symbolic of the women Sullivan loved. Sullivan did not marry, but he had many lovers. His final mistress, Fanny Roberts, was summoned when Sullivan became ill, but she arrived too late to see him before he died.

On Christmas Day 1900, Louise was devastated to hear of yet another death, that of her great friend Lady Jane Churchill. It had been a truly miserable year. Perhaps it was Louise's unhappiness that made Bertie and Lorne realise they *had* to end their argument. How the reconciliation was effected is uncertain, but on 18 January 1901, Bertie arrived at Kensington Palace to have lunch with his sister *and* her husband. The reconciliation was timely. The day after their Kensington Palace lunch, the newspapers posted their first bulletin about the grave state of Queen Victoria's health.

Four days previously, the queen had carried out what would be her last official engagement. She had received Field Marshal Frederick Roberts, who had just returned from commanding British forces in the Boer Wars. The frail queen, who remained seated in her chair throughout the meeting, made him a Knight of the Garter. She also took the unusual move of granting his daughter the right of inheriting his title – because his only son, Freddy, had died in action in Africa. Earlier in the year, Roberts had written a letter in which he had commented, 'Honours, rewards and congratulations have no value to me. So very different to what they were when I used to think of the son who would bear my name.'

Bertie, Alix and Louise were summoned to Osborne House, while Lorne stayed in London, waiting for telegrams and instructions from his wife. Kaiser Wilhelm also arrived to visit his dying grandmother, still resentful of his uncle Bertie and desiring to cause problems within the family he believed had rejected him.

At half past six on 22 January 1901, the longest-reigning monarch in British history died. It was four decades since she had written despairing letters about her longing not to see old age but to die as soon as she could after her beloved Prince Albert. As her life came to an end, the queen was surrounded by many of her children and grandchildren, including Wilhelm, and Beatrice's 12-year-old daughter

Ena. Bertie sent a telegram to Lorne, summoning him to Osborne. Louise, shell-shocked by the death of her seemingly indomitable mother – the mother who had clung so tenaciously to life that she had confounded doctors for several days – began the arduous administrative tasks that had to be performed on the death not only of a parent, but of a monarch. The queen had left very specific instructions about her death and burial. She had stipulated that certain precious items be placed in her coffin and buried with her. The person she relied upon to do this was Dr James Reid, by now her senior Physician in Ordinary and one of her most trusted confidants; he had been with her right to the end.

The Reid family papers show that when he was alone with the queen's body, the doctor carried out her secret instructions to him. The numerous possessions she wanted to be buried with her included rings and other jewellery, photographs, handkerchiefs and plaster casts made of her husband's and children's hands. She also requested several other photographs, including:

> A coloured profile Photograph in a leather case of my faithful friend J. Brown, his gift to me – with some of his hair laid with it and some of the Photographs which I have marked with an X and have often carried in a silk case in my pocket, to be put in my hand. *All* these objects, which have been so dear to me during my life time and have never left me – I should wish to be near my earthly remains.

In addition, she had instructed her doctor to bury her with a simple golden wedding ring, which she said had belonged to John Brown's mother and which she had 'worn constantly' since Brown's death. (The queen's constant wearing of this ring had led to much speculation, including rumours that the queen had married John Brown in a secret ceremony. In 1872 a Scottish Presbyterian minister named Dr Norman Macleod had died; his sister later claimed that, on his deathbed, he had confessed to having performed a marriage ceremony for the queen and John Brown.) Queen Victoria had asked that two handkerchiefs be placed on her body: one had belonged to Albert, the other to John Brown. Dr Reid placed the leather-bound photographs of John Brown in the queen's right hand, then covered it and the handkerchiefs with Alix's mourning flowers, so that the relatives would not be aware of everything that had been placed inside the queen's coffin. He then tenderly covered with her wedding veil the face of his queen, who for so many years had refused to wear anything except black.

The queen's funeral procession began on 1 February, and Louise, her sisters and the new Queen Alexandra walked solemnly behind the coffin for important parts of its journey. The coffin began its journey at Osborne, from where it was taken to the royal yacht *Alberta* and across the Solent to Portsmouth. The royal family spent the night at Gosport. On 2 February, the coffin and its melancholy procession reached London from where it was taken to Windsor for a ceremony at St George's Chapel. At the queen's request, the gun carriage on which her coffin was placed was pulled by eight white horses. The horses detailed to carry the coffin through the streets of Windsor got into difficulties and broke their harnesses; because the Royal Horse Artillery was unable to re-harness them, the naval guard of honour was detailed to pull the coffin on its carriage themselves. On 4 February, Queen Victoria's coffin was laid to rest beside that of Prince Albert. On 21 April 1901, Princess Louise would write to her friend, Audrey Tennyson: 'The sorrow . . . never wears off.' Within the space of a year she had lost her mother, a brother, a nephew and several friends. It was a desperately lonely time as she tried to adjust to what life would be like without her indomitable mother.

Ten days after the queen's funeral, Louise stood by her brother's side as Bertie opened Parliament for the very first time as King Edward VII. Despite his mother's wish that he make the name Albert that of a British king, Bertie insisted on being known by the already regal name Edward (his second name).[91] No longer could his mother make him bend to her will.

Full mourning was observed for the queen until 24 July 1901. Vicky had been unable to attend the funeral as she was extremely ill and unable to travel and, shortly after the family had stopped their official mourning for her mother, Vicky was also dead. Her health had been problematic for some time and Queen Victoria had long been

---

[91] Bertie commented that his title had come too late for him to truly enjoy being king and he wished he had been twenty years younger when acceding to the throne.

convinced – ever since Vicky's confinement with Wilhelm – that the Prussian doctors were not as skilful as British doctors. This seemed to have been confirmed when Vicky visited Balmoral in 1899 and her debilitating illness that had defied the Prussian court's medical establishment was diagnosed by the queen's physicians as cancer. As soon as he was able, following his mother's death, Bertie had travelled to visit his sister, taking with him Dr Laking and a large amount of morphine: the Prussian court doctors were nervous of prescribing high doses of morphine and Vicky had suffered agonies as the dosage was woefully inadequate to ease the pain of her final months. It was thanks to this visit from Bertie that Vicky was able to ship back to England (in secret) private family papers, including all the correspondence she had received from her mother. Vicky died on 5 August 1901, at the age of sixty.

Unlike Princess Beatrice, whose role in the family became difficult and unhappy once Edward VII had ascended to the throne, Princess Louise was a vital part of her brother's official court. Queen Alexandra was suffering very poor health, so, when necessary, Louise accompanied her brother to official events – it was just like the old days of the 1870s when the rebellious brother and sister attended public events and covered up for their mother's shortcomings, gaining the affection of the newspapers and the public. Once again, it was Louise and Bertie standing together.

In April 1901, Louise went to Windsor for the first time since her mother's funeral. The dinner parties held at Windsor by King Edward VII could not have been more different from those ponderous, dull dinners presided over by a stern Queen Victoria and so complained about by Henry Ponsonby in letters to his wife. Under Queen Victoria's watchful eye no one had dared to smoke in public. On 4 May 1892, the *Auckland Star* had printed an extraordinary paragraph: 'Queen Victoria smokes! This is a fearful strain on our Loyalty. The *Tobacco Trade Journal* says so, and mentions the gift of a silver cigarette case to Her Majesty by the frisky Princess Louise, who certainly does smoke and apparently makes no secret of it.' With regard to Victoria the newspaper article was certainly not true. The queen had always adhered to Prince Albert's strict dislike of smoking. She had attempted to stop her sons from smoking (she ordered any rooms in which Bertie could have smoked to be locked up for the duration of his visits), and refused to countenance even the idea of her daughters taking up such a masculine habit. Now, under the reign of the new king, all guests, male and female, were positively encouraged to smoke and Edward VII was seldom seen without his signature cigar.

For Princess Louise, lighting up a cigarette in the Green Drawing Room at Windsor Castle was a symbol of the freedom of the new century. For Lorne, the death of his mother-in-law gave him licence to publish a book he had been working on for many years: *The Life of Queen Victoria*. For once the new British king and the Kaiser of Germany were united – they were both scandalised by the 9th Duke of Argyll's literary endeavours.

For Beatrice, the new reign was a time of misery. Bertie had never got over the inequality of his mother's treatment of her children and now Beatrice bore the brunt of the king's anger. The homes that she had once been mistress of were now the property of her brother, and she was made to feel unwelcome. Louise, who did not have her sister's strong ties to Osborne House, was not especially unhappy with Bertie's plans to give the property to the nation, but Beatrice was devastated. Bertie remained unmoved by her pleas; Beatrice, in his view, had had her own spoilt way for far too long. Louise and Beatrice both had their own properties on the Isle of Wight and, as far as Bertie was concerned, that was all Beatrice needed. Osborne House was costly and too far away to be of real use to him. After decades as the overlooked child, at last he was king and Beatrice was his subject – and whatever he wanted, finally, was what was going to happen.

It was not only Beatrice who was relegated to her rightful place; Bertie also got rid of a servant whose presence had galled the family as much as that of John Brown had done: 'the Munshi'. His real name was Abdul Karim and he had arrived from India in 1887, for the queen's jubilee, at the age of just 24. For four years, the queen had been mourning John Brown and by the time of Abdul Karim's arrival she was ripe to fall under the spell of another strong personality. Within a remarkably short space of time the Munshi had captivated the monarch, who was forty-four years his senior, and had made himself invaluable, teaching her to speak Urdu and Hindi and advising her both on politics and family matters. He became her most trusted advisor on Indian politics – which led to accusations that he was a spy. Just as John Brown had done, the Munshi drove a wedge between the monarch and her children; now that his mother was dead, Bertie was determined to erase all memories of her 'shameful' relationship with the young (and married) man. Although Abdul Karim was seen prominently in the queen's funeral procession, he knew his situation at court was precarious. It was not only the queen's family who disliked him; he had also become deeply unpopular with the queen's courtiers.

Within a few days of the queen's funeral, Bertie had ordered soldiers to seize and destroy everything that the queen had written to the Munshi. He also ordered Abdul Karim and his wife to return to India. They left as quickly as possible, moving to Agra where the queen had purchased land for him – she had been fully aware that after her death his position in England was likely to become impossible. Paranoid (and rightly so) that the Munshi had managed to smuggle out private documents concerning his life at the British court, Bertie sent detectives to India to keep an eye on the former servant. Yet despite these precautions, Abdul Karim managed to keep at least one of his precious British diaries a secret, bequeathing it to future generations of his family living in what is now Pakistan.

Louise threw herself into the renovation of her own Isle of Wight property, Kent House. Initially, she had thought of hiring Lutyens, but their relationship was now less close and, in common with many of his former clients, she felt that Lutyens was charging far too much for his expertise. For some time Lutyens had been working in an unequal partnership with fellow architect Baynes Badcock, but the partnership had recently come to an unamicable end. It was Badcock whom Louise commissioned to work on Kent House, working closely with him on the plans. She then sent him to Scotland to oversee the renovations at Rosneath Castle. (Lutyens was hurt and unimpressed by the way he felt the princess and his former 'assistant' had abandoned him, at one of the busiest times in his career.) Lorne did not share Louise's or Badcock's taste and fought them every step of the way – but the money being used for the much-needed renovations of Rosneath was not the duke's, it was his wife's. Lorne's father had left the estate in such financial ruin that Lorne had no choice but to let Louise have a free hand, although he challenged Badcock constantly. Many local residents were struck by how artistic the princess was and how proficient in organising the renovations. (Surprisingly, a document

written in the 1970s by a resident of Rosneath made the claim that
Princess Louise was 'a qualified architect'.)

A child who lived near Rosneath at the time when Louise and Lorne
were in residence recalled in adulthood: 'There was an <u>enormous</u> wall
completely surrounding the garden . . . it could have been 12' to 15'
high and the wall was <u>completely round</u>. I can remember that striking
me at the time as having been very cleverly built . . . I can remember
the pink[?] trees on the inside of the wall all very beautifully pruned
and each branch fixed to the wall at the proper angle – all so tidy.'
Another local story was that when Louise wanted any building work
done, she used a local man named David Buchanan Spy. Having realised that he felt very awkward in her presence she said to him, 'You
are never very sure what to call me when you come to see me, sometimes you call me Your Grace, sometimes it is Your Highness and
sometimes it is Ma'am, so in future when we are in private, as we are
now, I'm Mrs Argyll and you are Mr Spy.'

Not all the local residents were happy with Louise's plans. Charles
Warr, who knew from childhood what it was to be one of Louise's
favourite people, included in his book *The Glimmering Landscape* several
stories about the princess. His accounts are warm and full of love,
but he was aware how difficult she could be. One incident concerned
a new bicycle shed, which Louise saw as an eyesore and wanted to
replace with an aesthetically pleasing alternative:

A good friend of the parish, Mr Wilfred Thom, offered to erect
a bicycle-shed in a small laurel grove in the church precincts
where worshippers from a distance could house their bicycles
on rainy days . . . It was an unobtrusive wooden structure with
a corrugated-iron roof, and painted dark green to blend in with
the surrounding laurels. But when Princess Louise first saw it
she was very much incensed. Accustomed to call a spade a spade,
she declared it a hideous monstrosity. She said that it was a blot
on the landscape, and insisted upon its immediate demolition.
She also said that in its place she would build an attractive stone
bicycle-shed in the clachan which would harmonise with the
surroundings. My father pointed out that the bicycle-shed was
a gift . . . to supplant it with another would be a grievous insult
to the donor . . . The Princess remained obdurate. Interminable

arguments took place between her and my father, in which the Duke wisely took no part. Eventually the Princess resolved to take a chance. One day the beadle came to the manse and said that carpenters from the estate were about to pull down the bicycle shed on the instructions of H.R.H. My father . . . sent for the village constable and instructed him to . . . arrest the first man who dared to lay a hand on it. This was immediately reported to the Princess by a local factor. The factor recalled later that, on hearing the news, H.R.H. was immediately seized with an immoderate burst of laughter. She laughed till the tears ran down her face. 'I'd have pulled it off,' she declared, 'if only I'd had a different sort of parson to deal with'.

Another tale was recalled by the daughter of a captain in Louise's regiment. Captain Macarthur, recently returned from fighting in Africa, invited Louise to lunch with him and his wife. The couple were excited about entertaining royalty, but had not counted on their dogs. 'All was prepared and the housemaid announced the luncheon was served. The Princess on father's arm entered the dining room – four spaniels were on the table, two tearing a side of ham apart, the other two eating a roast of beef, the silver meat covers lying on the floor! The Princess laughed and said she had plenty of time and was enjoying herself – and something else could be cooked!'

The second Boer War had come to an end in 1901 and the country was looking forward to a celebration of a new and peaceful century. King Edward VII and Queen Alexandra held their first official court on 14 March 1902 and their coronation was due to take place on 26 June. The plans for the coronation were thwarted at the last moment, however, when the new king developed what was said to be appendicitis just before the celebrations were to start. For some time, his subjects feared he would die before he could be crowned. Once again, churchgoers around the country began praying for Bertie's safe recovery. Jane Ridley, his biographer, has scotched all rumours that the illness was appendicitis, confirming that the king's appendix was not removed and that the operation – which the doctors feared might reveal a tumour – was for a very large and painful abscess.

A date in August was set for the coronation and the souvenir sellers had their work cut out, creating an entirely new set of memorabilia.

Louise was kept busy with two important jobs: while Bertie was convalescing, she had to perform a number of his public appearances as well as her own. The artist Sydney Prior Hall produced a popular illustration for *The Graphic* (19 July 1902) entitled 'Princess Louise Reviewing Twenty Thousand Children in Battersea Park', recording a special children's parade at a coronation fête.

Louise was also overseeing the creation of Alix's coronation robes: no queen consort had been crowned in living memory, so no one was certain what the etiquette for her robes should be. Louise designed the robes and employed one of her favourite charities, the Ladies' Work Society, to bring the ideas to fruition. The design for the delicate gold-thread embroidery incorporated symbols to represent England, Scotland and India. On top of her perfectly coiffed wig, Alix wore a crown she had commissioned – complete with the Koh-i-noor diamond which Queen Victoria had worn so proudly at Vicky and Fritz's wedding. The month of the coronation was, however, a time of great sadness for Louise and her siblings, as they were struggling to cope with the news of Vicky's death just four days previously.

CHAPTER 26

The death of Henry Locock

The Lady Frances Balfour, who is coming to Devonshire to address four meetings in support of the cause of Women's Suffrage, is the daughter of the late Duke of Argyle [*sic*] . . . She is, consequently, the sister-in-law of Princess Louise . . . For many years she has been a member of the National Union of Women's Suffrage Societies, which has dissociated itself wholly from the militant section.

Exeter and Plymouth Gazette, 19 February 1909

Throughout Edward VII's reign, Louise and Lorne continued to work towards emancipation and suffrage for both genders and all classes, travelling around the country to make public appearances. Their work had to be kept mostly in the background as they added their weight to campaigns and fund-raising efforts and promoted the causes of female education and equal rights for women in the workplace. Much as Louise may have longed to have been at the forefront of the marches and rallies, she was never able to be. Despite her early support for Josephine Butler and the Garrett sisters, Louise could not take as full a part in the suffrage campaign as she had wished – at first because her mother, the queen, was so fervently against it and then because her brother, the king, was far less enthusiastic than his sister at the prospect of female emancipation.

Bertie railed against the changes that were taking place and looked back longingly to an age when women were more compliant and submissive, when they did not chain themselves to railings or throw stones through MPs' windows. When the king heard that some women were abandoning the practice of riding side-saddle in favour of riding astride a horse in the same manner as men, he announced that any woman who rode in the masculine style was no longer welcome at court.

To keep the peace, Louise and Lorne tried to keep their political opinions out of family events, but Louise was very happy to cut ribbons, make speeches and promote the cause of female-oriented charities and educational establishments. By the start of the twentieth century, both Louise and Lorne were heading towards their sixtieth birthdays and were feeling older; both suffered from poor health. Louise was feeling the strains of the physical work of sculpting in a way that she never had when she was younger; for Lorne it was more than the physical signs of ageing. His mental health was also suffering. His behaviour was becoming erratic and the strain of looking after him and coping with his temper led to a recurrence of Louise's debilitating headaches and neuralgia. She also suffered from insomnia, an affliction that often affected her at times of stress. Their marriage, which had been so much improved, was in trouble again as Lorne was fighting what may have been Alzheimer's disease.

Louise was still held in great affection by the public, loved just as much for being the artistic sister of the king as she had been as the unconventional daughter of the queen. Glasgow University awarded her an honorary degree in recognition of her work to further the cause of women's education and she felt gratified that, at last, Glasgow University had agreed to treat female staff and students as full members of the college. Louise's life was a constant round of visits to schools and orphanages and hospitals. She opened new buildings, and campaigned for help with fund-raising. She was involved with the Boy Scouts, the Boys' Brigade and the Territorial Army. Bertie was growing more worried about the possibility of a war with Germany; Louise was worried that she was powerless to help.

Even before Vicky's death, her son had been showing increasing antagonism to his mother's country, but since Vicky had died Wilhelm's hatred for the British, and particularly the uncle he had fallen foul of so many times in his youth, became more marked. Bertie, aided by his excellent French, began to spend more time in France, intending to create a strong alliance between the two countries, in the hope that they would unite against a belligerent Germany. He encouraged visits to England from foreign royalty and heads of state, including the King and Queen of Italy and the imperial family from Japan; Louise often presided over these events with her brother and sister-in-law.

In the spring of 1905, Louise was exhausted by the erratic behaviour of her husband and from the physical rigours of creating her memorial to those who had died in the Boer Wars. The memorial, commissioned by the Colonial Troops Club and the Boer War Memorial Committee, can be seen at St Paul's Cathedral, in London. Louise created a finely sculpted grieving angel, its huge wings (huge only in relation to the angel itself) seeming to offer shelter to those who died in the conflict. The angel raises up to Heaven the dead Christ, emblematic of Britain's dead soldiers. The figures owe more of a debt to the sculptural styles of Lord Leighton and Alfred Gilbert than to Boehm; the flowing draperies evoke later Pre-Raphaelite paintings and are reminiscent of Simeon Solomon's *Love in Autumn*. The model for the lithe angel was a professional model named Mrs Lloyd, who was recommended to Louise by Sir William Blake Richmond, a friend of many Pre-Raphaelites and Aesthetic artists and an adherent to the Pre-Raphaelite movement.

At the same time that Louise was using Mrs Lloyd as a model, she was helping the artist Edwin Abbey with his painting of King Edward VII's coronation. She lent Abbey the clothes she had worn on the day so he could paint them from life and helped him with his portraits of her relatives. In return, Abbey sent her the details of a male model for the study of the dying Christ (naked except for drapery), explaining that he was 'a tall, thin model – a restless person, to whom repose, unfortunately, means sleep. In the pose you require, however, Madam, this failing may not be a drawback.' Modelling the statue was hard, physical work and Louise complained of aching muscles and pain in her arms and hands.

The model Louise ended up using for the figure of Christ was an Italian named Antonio Corsi, who had modelled for her on previous occasions and has left revealing insights into what it was like to work with the princess. Corsi modelled for some of the most famous artists in Britain and America, including Alma-Tadema, Burne-Jones, Sargent and Felix Moscheles. In an interview given in 1908, Corsi explained that he found posing for the princess's Boer War sculpture extremely demanding, and that his limbs would start to shake from the exertion. Princess Louise, he revealed, would hold a cigarette to his lips, to allow him to smoke without changing his position and to alleviate the shaking. Corsi had a well-muscled physique.[92] The story of the princess standing close enough to her almost nude model to place a cigarette between his lips was one that would have shocked readers of the newspaper – but would have surprised no one who knew her.

On 17 December 1905, shortly after he finished posing for the Boer War memorial, an interview with Corsi appeared in the *New York Times*. In it he spoke both about the princess and her mother. He talked of taking tea with the princess every day for months at a time on the days that he modelled for her. He talked of two earlier occasions on which he met the queen and candidly revealed that he had chatted with her about the princess's ability. It is a surprisingly frank interview, but by this date Corsi had left England to live in America, following a scandal. If the interview can be believed, it also reveals the queen's disloyal attitude to her family, gossiping about her daughter with a man she barely knew. In the interview it was claimed that, on one occasion, Corsi saw the queen alone. The journalist reported:

It seems that she asked Corsi what he thought of the work of her daughter.

'The Princess is a very clever woman,' Corsi answered.

'But there are better sculptors, are there not?' the Queen asked.

'Your Majesty, to be frank, I think there are,' Corsi replied.

In early 1905, needing to escape her exhausting husband and schedule, Louise left for her first overseas trip in several years. Unlike Lutyens's wife, Baynes Badcock's wife had become very friendly with Louise and it was Ethel Badcock whom Louise took with her on an incognito tour through France, Switzerland and Italy. Although Ethel found the princess at times difficult and tiring, she also commented 'She has a wonderful heart and sympathetic character' which, she said, more than made up for her defects. Louise's enthusiasm for travelling was infectious and Ethel noted how she could suddenly become as giddy as a child with excitement (though their other, more staid, companions found the princess's mood swings exhausting). The Royal Collection owns a large number of paintings and sketches by Louise showing

---

[92] Antonio Corsi's naked body appears in many famous works of art, including Edward Burne-Jones's *Wheel of Fortune* (1883).

Italian landscapes and figurative scenes. Most are undated, so it is impossible to say on which of her several trips to Italy each was done, but whenever she went travelling, she took her painting paraphernalia and relaxed by sitting outside and painting or drawing the scenes that unfolded in front of her. In September 1905, after her return to England, Louise travelled north to Blackburn to unveil a statue of her mother (sculpted by Bertram Mackennal); the visit was filmed by the cinematographic pioneers Mitchell & Kenyon and the enthusiastic crowds can be seen welcoming her with affection. Buildings were draped with banners that proclaimed 'Welcome to Princess Louise' and 'Welcome Royal Lady'. (There are a number of Mitchell & Kenyon films in existence recording Princess Louise's official duties.)

Some years earlier Louise had decided to start trying to publish her writing, and under the pseudonym Myra Fontenoy she submitted articles to newspapers and magazines. In 1899 the *Sydney Morning Herald* published an article in which they claimed 'Princess Louise, the Marchioness of Lorne, has published a good deal of poetry . . . She has also written notes on art and literature for London weeklies. One editor reputedly accepted articles in art matters from her before he discovered the identity of his contributor. The Princess said that the proudest moment of her life was when she received a cheque – made out to "Myra Fontenoy" – for literary work sent in and accepted in the ordinary manner.' In 1906, Louise published an article entitled 'The Art of Childhood'. In the same year, one of her paintings was featured in the New Zealand International Exhibition, alongside works by several deceased artists, including Lord Leighton, Millais, Watts, and Louise's mother.

Her continental trip had rekindled Louise's love of travelling and, in 1906, she decided to undertake an epic journey. This time her destination was North Africa. A couple of years previously, Beatrice, devastated by the loss of Osborne House and unable to bear the spectacle of it being handed over to the nation, had spent several months wintering in Egypt. Beatrice's stories and sketchbooks had enthralled her family and had ignited in Louise a desire to see this fascinating country for herself. She and Lorne, with their entourage, followed in Beatrice's footsteps. Two of Louise's nephews also visited Egypt in the spring of 1906.

The Lornes left England in early January on the same steamer as Louise's nephew Arthur (her brother Arthur's son), who was travelling to Asia. At the end of January 1906, the newspapers remarked on how few members of the royal family were in England that winter: 'The Prince and Princess of Wales are absent in India, the Duke and Duchess of Connaught and Princess Patricia are in South Africa, Prince Arthur of Connaught is en route for Japan, Princess Louise Duchess of Argyll is in Egypt, Princess Henry of Battenberg and Princess Ena of Battenberg are in the South of France, and Princess Louise of Schleswig-Holstein is touring in the East.'

For Louise, one of the highlights of their travels was a trip along the Nile. In the Royal Collection are a number of sketches by Louise dating from, or inspired by, her time in Egypt. She was intrigued by the people, their clothing, the animals and the landscape, all of which were so different from anything she had witnessed before. She made studies of the palm trees, the heavily laden working donkeys, the architecture of Egyptian buildings, riverside scenes of boats and boatmen, and studies of the different types of turban worn by Egyptian men.

For Louise, the extended holiday was inspiring and relaxing. She loved the Egyptian climate in January and welcomed the pleasurable feeling of being too hot, after the always cold London winter. As his wife basked on the sunny deck, sketching the scenes on the riverbanks and marvelling at the historic sights, Lorne grumbled about the heat and locked himself firmly away from the sunshine in his cabin. Many of his friends believed that Lorne had never truly settled back into life in England; his sister commented 'His heart is always in Canada', and even while they were in Egypt, Lorne's thoughts were turning to Canada and the book he wanted to write, which he hoped would be a less controversial one than his biography of his mother-in-law. He would go on to publish *Yesterday and Today in Canada* in 1910. Lorne was nostalgic for the great happiness he had felt while living in Canada, where he had been the most important person in the country, had received adulation and his word was law. Ever since their return, he had been merely the husband of a princess. Although he was now a duke in his own right, he was nonetheless an impoverished duke, reliant on his wife's money for any changes to the ducal estate. The renovations at Rosneath and Louise's easy command of them still rankled. The man whose poor dress sense had caused his wife and oldest brother-in-law to squirm when he was young remained a man whose taste, even in decorating his own castle, was constantly questioned.

The party travelled to the Sudan and then on to Alexandria. Although Louise did pay a formal visit to the Egyptian Khedive and Khediva, this was not a state visit, it was a holiday and a chance to be real, sightseeing tourists. They spent two months in Egypt before leaving Alexandria on 15 March and Louise celebrated her fifty-eigth birthday on the journey to Naples. Lorne's mood did not improve until they had left Egypt. Louise, however, had found the holiday inspiring and had filled several sketchbooks with her artistic impressions of the country. A newspaper column entitled 'A Royal Artist' revealed:

> I am told that the Princess Louise . . . has brought away with her from Egypt a velvet portfolio of drawings in water-colour, which she will finish during her residence at Kensington Palace within the next few weeks. Her Royal Highness was greatly interested in the examples of ancient enamel jewellery which are preserved in Cairo; and there is reason to anticipate that she will turn her studies to account by devising some jewelled objects in African designs. The Princess Louise is much benefited by her trip along the Nile Valley.

Lorne, who most certainly did not feel he was 'much benefited', was relieved to be back in Europe. Together, they travelled around Italy, visiting the ruins of Pompeii and Herculaneum and returning to Rome and Florence. They arrived in England to join in family celebrations. While they had been away, Beatrice's daughter, Princess Ena of Battenberg, had become engaged to King Alfonso of Spain. The family were happy, but the public were not. The marriage of another English princess to a foreign royal might not have caused such controversy in Britain had it not been for Ena and Alfonso's religious differences. When Ena converted to Catholicism in order to marry the Spanish king, Anglicans in Britain were appalled; despite the centuries that had passed since Henry VIII had broken away from the Church of Rome, the very word 'Catholic' still invoked in many Britons the fear of a 'takeover' of the monarchy. Since the mid nineteenth century, 'Catholic' had become painfully associated with the Fenians.

The situation in Spain was even more inflammatory. Initially, the royal wedding seemed to be hugely popular with the Spanish people. Triumphal arches were erected all over Madrid, bearing messages of welcome to the new queen, and 700,000 visitors were estimated to have arrived in the city, whose streets were 'a bright mass of flowers, drapery and flags', hoping for a glimpse of the king and his bride. It was reported with glee in the papers that Ena had turned, spontaneously, to embrace her mother, moments before the ceremony. The reporters also made a point of noting that she had signed her married name with a 'gold fountain pen . . . presented to her by Spanish journalists'.

Following their wedding ceremony, the newly-weds were being driven through Madrid, from the church to the royal palace, when a bouquet of flowers was thrown at their carriage. The man who threw it was an anarchist[93] and his flowers disguised a lethal bomb. Although the king and his new queen escaped relatively unharmed, they would suffer for years to come the emotional scars of the scenes they witnessed. Ena was horrified to see a bystander having both of his legs blown off. Several horses were killed or maimed by the bomb and one of the outriders accompanying the couple's carriage was decapitated.

The newspapers proclaimed the tragedy: 'The crowd so obstructed the traffic that with difficulty the Red Cross men were able to attend the injured. Shouts of indignation were raised by the crowd every time a dead body or injured man was carried out . . . Four soldiers were killed on the spot.' As a tribute to those who had died, within days of the attack Queen Ena's wedding dress, splattered with the victims' blood, had been placed on display at the Church of Almádena, close to where the bombing had taken place.

After their return from Egypt and Italy, Louise and Lorne attended necessary public functions together, but both seemed to be more keen on travelling with friends than with each other. Louise's next holiday was less exotic than Egypt, but equally artistic: she spent several days sketching in August 1906, eluding journalists. She stayed secretly in Buxton, with the daughter of her friends Lawrence and Laura Alma-Tadema. The papers were only alerted to her visit once she had left her hotel (the reason for her precipitate departure for London was given as 'the break-up of the weather' in Buxton). Lawrence Alma-Tadema had also generously agreed to display one of his paintings,

---

[93] He was later named as Manuel Duran, also known as Mateo Moral. The newspapers made much of the surprising fact that those who knew him had described him as 'well dressed'.

Caracalla and Geta, at a charity exhibition to raise funds for Princess Louise's Soldiers' Home at Rosneath.

Louise continued her round of public appearances, performing the opening ceremony of Wandle Park, in south London, opening the new children's ward at Essex County Hospital and naming the king's new and very fast yacht in honour of her favourite sister-in-law. As she cut the yacht's cord and smashed the bottle against her side, Louise called out, '*Alexandra*! Good luck to you!' At a royal garden party – 'the largest garden party on record at Windsor Castle' – to celebrate the visit of the King of Siam and princes from Russia, Greece, Germany and India, Louise drew admiring comments from fashion journalists. Despite heading towards her sixtieth birthday, she was still the best-dressed woman at the party, in 'a blue and white striped dress, with a white hat worn far back on the head'.

It was estimated that 8,500 guests attended the party and, the papers reported, 'The scene . . . was one never to be forgotten . . . and Bohemian society had mustered in full force.' Among the guests was the actress Ellen Terry, one of the group of Aesthetic friends whom Louise had made during the first years of her marriage. The country's favourite actress caused a sensation by arriving with her new husband. At the age of 60, she had returned from a triumphal tour of America newly married to James Carew, an American actor twenty-nine years her junior.[94] Another notable guest was Mark Twain, who was happy to renew his friendship with Louise and Lorne. Someone had leaked a story to the newspapers that Twain was in England because he wanted to buy Windsor Castle, and its grounds, and that he was trying to persuade the king to sell it to him, so he could have it dismantled and shipped back to America. In an interview with a journalist after the

---

[94] Ellen Terry, who was a year older than Louise, had been married to the artist G.F. Watts while she was in her teens and he was 47. The marriage was never consummated, and failed within a year, whereupon he sent her home to her parents but refused to divorce her. She lived for several years with the Aesthetic architect Edward Godwin and they had two illegitimate children. By the time Watts finally agreed to divorce her, because he wanted to marry again, Godwin had left Terry to marry a young heiress. Terry married fellow actor Charles Kelly, but the marriage failed, largely due to his alcoholism and erratic behaviour. When she married James Carew, Ellen Terry was marrying a man who was almost as many years younger than she as her first husband had been older. The marriage lasted three years.

garden party (at which, the papers noted, he and the king and queen chatted animatedly and roared with laughter together), the author admitted that it was he who had leaked the 'false rumour' to the papers.

By the end of 1907, Louise was obviously under strain. She was forced to cancel some of her engagements through 'indisposition', was suffering problems with her eyesight and was feeling depressed. One problem concerned a new friendship Lorne had made. He had become friendly with Frank Shackleton, the brother of the great explorer, Sir Ernest Shackleton. Frank was a very different character from Ernest. By the end of 1907, King Edward VII was trying desperately to keep his brother-in-law's name out of the papers when Frank Shackleton (who was known to be homosexual), was implicated in the shocking and daring theft of the Irish Crown Jewels.[95] At the same time, Louise and Bertie were trying not to show their hostility to their nephew, Kaiser Wilhelm. The situation between Wilhelm and his English relations was growing strained and Louise, whom the kaiser openly called his 'favourite aunt', had to try and play the peacemaker between nephew and uncle – not only for the sake of family harmony, but in an attempt to prevent the two countries going to war.

At the end of the year, Louise heard about the death of her son, Henry Locock. He was killed on 9th December 1907, when he fell out of a moving Canadian Pacific train. Henry had gone to Canada to buy some land, as he had relatives living there who were advising him about the best places to invest in. A member of the Collett family, relatives of the Lococks, was waiting at the train's final destination to meet him. The train arrived, bearing his luggage, but Henry was not on it and the alarm was raised. Louise must have wondered – as many people have

---

[95] The Irish Crown Jewels were a star and a badge made of diamonds, emeralds and rubies; mounted in silver, they were better known as the insignia of the Order of St Patrick. In 1907, the jewels were stolen from the safe at the Office of Arms in Dublin; several other items belonging to members of the household of the Ulster King of Arms were also stolen. At the time, the Ulster King of Arms was Sir Arthur Vicars, a friend of Frank Shackleton, who in turn was a close friend of Lorne. Shackleton was one of several men who fell under suspicion. Although a thorough investigation was begun, much of the official paperwork from the investigation disappeared and the case was never brought to fruition. It was widely believed that King Edward VII had ordered a cover-up to protect his brother-in-law (and, by association, Louise) whose friendship with more than one of the suspects was well known.

wondered since – if there was also another reason for him to be visiting the country. Walter Stirling had emigrated to Canada. Was Henry Locock on a mission to find him? After falling from the train, his body was later discovered on the rails at Montreal West. Although there is no suggestion that Louise attempted to maintain maternal contact with him beyond the age of 16 (as Henry Locock told his children), she and all her family saw the Lococks as family friends and the two families did keep in touch following the deaths of Sir Charles Locock and Queen Victoria. Frederick Locock had received an annuity until the time of Henry Locock's death. The annuity had begun after his adoption of the baby in 1867, and – just as mysteriously – following Henry Locock's death a trust fund was set up for his children. The Locock family have assumed that the money came from Princess Louise.

At the time of his death, Henry Locock was declared to be 39 years old, because of the date written on his adoption certificate. However without a birth certificate it is impossible to know his true age. If Louise gave birth to him some months before he was adopted, he would have been 40 at the time he died. He had married some years earlier; his wife and six children were living in England.

When I was researching in Canada I was told of conspiracy theory rumours that had suggested Henry Locock was murdered, to prevent him from finding out the truth about his parentage, but the inquest showed that he had been drinking heavily and it found that his death was simply a tragic accident. Henry was last seen in the dining car, after which he walked off along the train and, somehow managing to open the wrong door, fell out on to the tracks.

The inquest on the death of Henry Frederick Leicester Locock was held in Montreal on 12 December 1907. The post-mortem report stated that Henry had been 'under the influence of liquor at the time of the accident . . . The statements go to show that he fell off some car ahead of the diner, probably the colonist coach as he was seen to go in that direction and was not seen afterwards.' Achille Peyfer, who examined the body, gave the following evidence: 'On the deceased I found 47 piastres & 53 cents; a gun-metal watch and chain; a silver matchbox; two gold rings; one cigarette box; two bunches of keys.'

Henry Locock's body was returned to England and buried in the Locock family vault at St Nicholas Church, Sevenoaks, in Kent.

CHAPTER 27

The king, the kaiser and the duke

In deepest admiration and esteem for one who devoted her whole
life and energy to the advancement and welfare of her
fellow-countrymen

Inscription on Princess Louise's wreath, for Octavia Hill's funeral

In the autumn of 1908, matters grew even worse between the kaiser
and the king. However much Bertie attempted to grit his teeth and
tolerate his much-loved sister's son, the two men had never liked one
another. Marjorie Crofton, one of Louise's former ladies-in-waiting,
recalled several stories about the antipathy between the uncle and
nephew: 'H.R.H. told me how on one occasion at Sandringham they
were all waiting in the hall for the Kaiser who was late. King Edward
hated unpunctuality. At last the Kaiser appeared on the stairs rather
decked out with feathers in his hat. So King Edward saw him [and] in
his loud voice said 'What a mountebank the man looks' and the Princess
said 'Wasn't it awful? William heard and never forgave his uncle'.

Another of Marjorie Crofton's reminiscences reveals the sad cause
behind Wilhelm's arrogant personality, which was used to mask the
lack of confidence caused by his disabled left arm:[96]

One story about the King and the Kaiser was that the latter liked
to shoot, but because of his withered arm he was no good at it,

---

[96] Wilhelm's arm had been irreparably injured during his very difficult birth, in which
the German doctors gave up both Vicky and her baby for dead. Reputedly it was
the Scottish doctor sent out by Queen Victoria who managed to save both of them,
but he was unable to prevent the baby's arm from being damaged.

so always brought a man with him who was a crack shot and stood behind him and fired at the same moment and of course brought down the bird or rabbit. The Kaiser then boasted of his prowess, especially if he had a bigger bag than King Edward who was an excellent shot. The King said afterward, 'We would all be so sympathetic if he couldn't hit his mark, but this boasting absolutely sickens me'. So he wouldn't praise him.

During Wilhelm's visit in 1907, Louise, aware that she was one of the few family members who had any influence with her nephew,[97] made her best attempts at diplomacy, having lunch with the German ambassador and taking Wilhelm to art galleries. The kaiser was reported to have particularly enjoyed the Wallace Collection, where he 'displayed the keenest interest . . . in the German sixteenth century armour'. (He also cast doubt on the authenticity and provenance of one of the gallery's most proud exhibits, which flustered the curators.) Wilhelm's itinerary included shopping on Oxford Street, visiting the German Athenaeum, to which he gave a portrait of himself, and sending flowers to the ailing and elderly Florence Nightingale, who had been bedridden for many years.

By the end of 1908 Wilhelm's behaviour had grown even more unpredictable. As Wilfrid Scawen Blunt recalled in his diary, the *Daily Telegraph* published 'a new manifesto by Kaiser William . . . It is most compromising in regard to past history. The most remarkable things in it are when he declares that the French and Russian Governments proposed to him in the winter of 1899–1900 to intervene against England in favour of the Transvaal which he refused to join in doing – and that he then supplied the English Government with a plan of campaign against the Boers which was the one adopted successfully . . . The whole of Europe is up in arms against the Emperor Wilhelm for his pronouncement – especially his own people in Germany . . . There never was a moment when the complications of European diplomacy were more difficult for an outsider to unravel.'

In addition to his political worries, Bertie's marriage had become increasingly volatile. Alix was incensed by his continuing affair with

[97] Marjorie Crofton wrote in the 1970s: 'The Kaiser said that Princess Louise was his favourite aunt, I don't think he was her favourite nephew.'

Mrs Keppel. Things came to a head in the spring of 1909, when one of Bertie's former mistresses died in Paris. She had hoarded compromising letters Bertie had written to her in his youth, and her friend, Charlie Kettlewell, who found them after her death, used them to try and blackmail the king. What already seemed an impossible situation became even worse when Kettlewell died and Bertie found himself in the even more worrying situation of not knowing who had the letters.

In comparison to that of the king and queen, Louise and Lorne's marriage appeared relatively strong. But they were continuing to spend a great deal of time apart. The newspapers reported that Lorne had been in Scotland while Louise was in London and that he was returning to Kensington just as Louise was about to leave the country for 'a few weeks'. Louise began 1909 with a series of colds and illnesses that prevented her from making several public appearances. She was run down and unhappy about Lorne's irascible behaviour and her awareness that he had a serious mental illness that was changing his personality. His mood was not helped by the opening of a new art exhibition at the start of the year, entitled Fair Women. As well as portraits of some of the country's most famous beauties, including Ellen Terry and Jane Morris, and one of Burne-Jones's masterpieces, The Mirror of Venus, the exhibition included a portrait of Lady Colin Campbell.

Alongside her usual commitments, Louise had become interested in a relatively new charity. The idea of the National Trust was born in 1884, when the philanthropist and social campaigner Octavia Hill had been asked to help save a threatened garden in south-east London. Octavia Hill and Princess Louise shared a love of gardens, architecture and history. Louise was frequently found working in her garden and stories, especially from Lorne's tenants in Scotland, make regular mention of her pruning the roses and clearing the paths instead of relying on gardeners to do all the work for her (she shocked one of her Scottish gardeners by her use of the coarse word 'dung' instead of the expected 'manure'). One local farmer recalled that when Louise was asked 'Why do you not let the gardeners prune the rose bushes?' she responded, 'If you want a thing done right, do it yourself!'

Louise joined Octavia Hill in her campaign to preserve the country's heritage, helping to raise funds to buy Samuel Taylor Coleridge's cottage and presiding over meetings on the preservation of endangered buildings on the Windsor Castle estate. She was also involved with the Royal Horticultural Society and, in December 1909, opened the annual exhibition of Colonial Fruits and Vegetables, at which great excitement was caused by the appearance of frozen fruit from New Zealand. The papers were astonished to report that, despite having been frozen for twelve months, the fruits 'appeared to be as sound as when packed'. (The exhibition also introduced crystallised fruits into the country for the first time.)

Although Louise's primary concern at the start of 1910 was for the health of her husband, it was her brother who was fated not to survive the year. At the start of May, Louise was summoned to Buckingham Palace with the news that the king was dying. He had been suffering from emphysema and had had a series of heart attacks; he survived for only a few hours after his sister's arrival. Alix was devastated by his death, and the papers reported that her grief was 'pathetic' (with the word used in its true sense). She reportedly clung to his body, refusing to allow it to be removed. The decision was made that the king's coffin would lie in state at Westminster Abbey for the public to pay their respects. At his funeral on 20 May eight kings and an emperor were in attendance. Many members of Bertie's family were shocked by the behaviour of Kaiser Wilhelm who inappropriately rushed up and kissed the mourning Alix, pushing ahead of all other mourners. The mourner who most fully captured the public's imagination, however, was Caesar, the king's dog, which walked behind the coffin. Dogs had always played an important role in the life of the royal family. The queen and Prince Albert had portraits painted of their dogs (most notably by Landseer) and all the children gave dogs a special place in their lives. Louise was seldom without her dogs, which she adored. In 1894 the queen had written her daughter a touching reply when Louise had written to her mother in misery following the death of her much-loved pet: 'Darling Loosy, Many thanks for your dear letter received yesterday and which made me so sad. I do feel so deeply for you. The loss of a dear, faithful darling dog is that of a devoted friend – almost of a Child!'

Shortly after her brother's death, Louise appealed to the National Trust to make the viewpoint at Grange Fell in Borrowdale a memorial to her brother. She began the fund-raising by making a very large donation of her own. The viewpoint is marked with a memorial stone, which reads:

In loving memory of
King Edward VII
Grange Fell is dedicated by his sister
Louise
as a sanctuary of rest and peace.

Here may all beings gather strength
Find in scenes of beautiful nature a cause
For gratitude and love to God giving them
Courage and vigour to carry on his will.

Louise had always found solace in nature and, almost as soon as her brother's funeral was over, she travelled to Scotland. She had invested much in the renovations of Rosneath, not only money, but her artistic and horticultural expertise, as well as her time. She was heartbroken to hear, at the start of 1911[98], that a fire had broken out while she and Lorne were in London. Louise's studio and all the works inside it were destroyed. Part of Rosneath House was gutted, but most of the building was saved by the people of Rosneath, who battled to extinguish the fire. Everyone who had helped was rewarded with a present from Louise and Lorne, engraved with personal messages of thanks for their bravery.

Louise had planned on spending much more time than usual in Scotland to help with the cleaning up and renovations at Rosneath, but following her nephew George's coronation, as King George V, Lorne became very ill with bronchitis and Louise gave up her plans of escaping to Scotland in order to stay at Kensington Palace and nurse him. (Her nephew retained his fondness for his unconventional aunt, still signing his letters to her, despite being the king, as 'your devoted nephew Georgie'.) Lord Ronnie Gower, who had recently been through the public humiliation and social disgrace of the bankruptcy courts, was one of Lorne's most faithful visitors at this time, and he was shocked both at Lorne's wandering mind and erratic temper and at the effect Lorne's illness was having on Louise. Lorne was also jealous that his brother-in-law Prince Arthur (the Duke

[98] In September 1911, Louise was saddened by the news of another death, following so closely after the death of her brother, that of Leopold's former tutor the Reverend Robinson Duckworth. She sent a touching telegram to his bereaved brother, Sir Dyce Duckworth, expressing her condolences.

of Connaught) was about to leave for Canada, where he had been appointed the very first royal Governor-General.

Arthur kept Louise in touch with what was happening in Canada and consulted her regularly by letter. Ever since Leopold's death, Louise had been growing closer to Prince Arthur, and even more so after Bertie's death. The siblings had started to spend as much time as possible together and Louise often chose to attend events with Arthur instead of her husband; she missed him dreadfully when he moved to Canada. In a letter to her about the *Titanic* disaster in 1912, Arthur wrote, 'I am very grateful to say that very few Canadians lost their lives and those belonged almost entirely to Montreal . . .' He knew she would understand his feelings about the problems between the British-owned and French-owned areas of Canada. (He also told her that a letter she had sent to him in the diplomatic bag was lost on board the ship.) It seems likely that during his year in Rideau Hall he went through the archives and destroyed (or returned to England) any sensitive information about Louise and Lorne's time in Canada.

Lorne's memory was seriously affected by his illness, and his dementia was becoming more pronounced. Niall Campbell[99] wrote that his uncle was becoming increasingly 'queer'. Lorne exhausted Louise and Ronnie by constantly repeating himself and by firing angry questions at them. By the start of 1912, Lord Ronnie's fears about Louise's health were also becoming more apparent. She had been diagnosed with a heart condition and had succumbed to both laryngitis and a debilitating attack of influenza. Her doctor recommended that she go abroad to a warmer climate for her health, so she returned to the French Riviera to recuperate. In the warmer climate she seemed to improve and was able to return to England in the spring. At the start of May she travelled to Blackpool, where she declared open a new promenade named after her, Princess Parade. Louise's visit was the first royal visit to Blackpool and the city put on a magnificent display of its now-famous illuminations to mark the occasion. Around 10,000 light bulbs were used – and the display proved so popular with residents and tourists that the council decided to stage a similar display a few months later.

Soon afterwards, it was Lorne's turn to leave for the continent, for

[99] Niall was the son of Archie and Janey Campbell and heir to the dukedom. He and Louise were good friends.

his health. While he was away, Louise began working on one of her pet projects. Her country home, at this date, was Ribsden Hall near Windlesham in Surrey. On a visit to Suffolk, she had seen a derelict half-timbered building, in the town of Lavenham, known as the Old Wool Hall. It had been built during the reign of King Henry VII and was falling into ruins. Deciding she wanted to restore it, the princess bought it – then made the extraordinary decision that she would remove the building brick by brick and have it rebuilt in Surrey.[100] Not surprisingly, there was public fury in Lavenham. According to the locals and Louise's friends, as soon as the princess became aware of the outcry she apologised, halted the removal process at once and returned everything that had been moved so far, insisting that the Old Wool Hall be returned to its original state. Today, the beams still bear the numbers that were written on them at the time Louise was arranging for their removal, intended as a guide to the builders, so they knew where each one was to be placed during the rebuilding.[101]

One of Louise's close friends at this time was Mrs Edith Bruce Culver (three years previously, Louise had become godmother to Mrs Culver's son). Louise presented the building to Mrs Culver 'to use as she wished'. As Mrs Culver's daughter later recorded, 'My mother formed a small committee and most skilfully restored and adapted the building as a convalescent home for railway women and the wives of railway men – and in 1921 . . . she presented it to the Railway Convalescent Homes (for men) of which father was secretary. This met with the Princess's warm approval, for she had already taken a keen interest in this work and had opened an extension to the first Railway Convalescent Home at Herne Bay.' In the 1960s, the railway was closed and, as a consequence, the railway home was closed too.[102] In 1913 Princess Louise returned to Lavenham by train, to visit the neighbouring town of Sudbury and unveil a memorial to Thomas

[100] Local sources in Lavenham claim that the building was intended to be removed to near Ascot, but Celia Culver-Evans, the daughter of Mrs Edith Bruce Culver, wrote of her mother's involvement in the project and confirmed that the Old Wool Hall was intended for the Windlesham estate.

[101] For this information I am indebted to the very helpful management and staff at the Swan Hotel in Lavenham.

[102] The building was purchased by Trust House Forte and is now part of the adjoining Swan Hotel.

Gainsborough. Although her previous association with the town could have made her unpopular, people had been so impressed by her quick turnaround that, when she arrived at Lavenham station, she was given 'a ceremonial welcome'.

The year 1912 ended on a sad note, with the death of Louise's former lady-in-waiting, friend and loyal confidante, Lady Sophia MacNamara. Louise mourned the loss of the much-loved 'Smack' with whom she had shared so much. In January, the papers reported that Louise was to leave for Italy for the remainder of the winter, yet the Court Circulars record that she was in England throughout the next few weeks. Once again, she threw herself into work to alleviate her sadness, and carried out an astonishing number of public appearances in 1913. She was, by now, in her mid-sixties, which, in the early twentieth century, was considered 'elderly'. She was kept busy by the new king, who seems to have appreciated Louise's presence at his parties as much as his father had. She attended the first 'private ball' to be held at Buckingham Palace during King George V's reign, where, it was reported, there was a complete 'absence of ceremony' and the royal family joined in the dancing with enthusiasm. The new king recognised his aunt's contribution to the country by agreeing to keep paying her the annual income that his father had provided her with.

A few days before her sixty-fifth birthday, Louise was present at Buckingham Palace for an intriguing invention: to witness Mr J.P. Bickerton presenting 'a series of cinematograph pictures of Mr Paul J. Rainey's African hunt'. A few weeks later she was in Stepney Green to open a tuberculosis dispensary, which she named in honour of her recently deceased brother. It was one of three planned dispensaries, and Louise commented in her speech that she hoped their work would be successful and that 'London would soon banish the dreadful disease of consumption, which was felt so severely by the poorer classes'.

Louise's many engagements included laying the foundation stone of the new children's hospital in Birmingham, where she unveiled a statue of King Edward VII; presenting the 'Princess Louise Prize for animal drawing' at the Royal Drawing Society exhibition; and laying the foundation stone of the South London Hospital for Women. She attended the Royal Irish Industries Association exhibition, opened a bazaar in Nottingham in aid of 'waifs and strays', attended a fund-raiser for the Boy Scouts and Girl Guides, a garden party in aid of the Jubilee Institute for Nurses, and opened a Military Bazaar at the Horticultural Hall in Westminster. This frenetic working life was a way of masking the difficulties she was experiencing at home, as Lorne's illness made him problematic to live with. At this time, Louise must have felt very keenly the loss of her mother and the lack of children to help deal with Lorne. She was always wary of confiding too closely in Helena and Beatrice, who still had a tendency to 'gang up' against her and, with Arthur in Canada and so many of her friends now dead, she felt very lonely.

Her work schedule continued to be punishing – until she was forced to stop by another violent attack of influenza. She had become so run down and stressed that her recovery was slow and painful. Lorne too was feeling unwell and was anxious to leave London and recuperate on the Isle of Wight. Unfortunately the journey to the island proved cold and damp and made him even weaker. Louise, still recovering from the flu, was summoned to Kent House to care for him. On Wednesday 29 April, the official bulletin from Kent House declared: 'The Duke of Argyll . . . is suffering from double pneumonia, and his condition is serious.'

The 9th Duke of Argyll died on 4 May 1914, at the age of 68. The announcement of his death was posted on the gate of Kent House and all flags on the island were lowered to half mast. Louise's great-niece, Princess Louise of Battenberg (Alice's granddaughter), arrived on the Isle of Wight to console her aunt. Louise was also comforted by Lorne's sister, Lady Frances Balfour, and his nephew, of whom Louise was very fond, Niall Campbell, now the 10th Duke of Argyll (to whom she once confided that 'poor Mama [was] so deluded by Beatrice . . . and by Helena'). As preparations were being made to transport Lorne's coffin from the island, Louise was gathering flowers and greenery from her gardens to create a wreath of her own design. A memorial service was held in Westminster Abbey on Friday 8 May;[103] but Lorne's body was taken to Scotland, where his funeral was held exactly a week later; it was estimated that over 9,000 mourners arrived to pay their respects to the chief of the Campbell clan. Lorne's body was placed in the Campbell family mausoleum at Kilmun. An obituary in *The Times*, written by an

---

[103] King George V ordered that all court mourning for Lorne be suspended for five days, as the King and Queen of Denmark were arriving for an official visit on 9 May.

anonymous author who had been at Eton with him, described the schoolboy Lorne as having been 'remarkable for his manly beauty of a fine Celtic type'. Princess Alice's daughter, Irene (now Princess Henry of Prussia) wrote to her sister Victoria (Princess Louis of Battenberg), 'poor dear Aunt Louise she must have gone through terrible days till the end came and will miss him sadly I fear in spite of all, after such a long married life'. The strangeness of Louise and Lorne's married life had not escaped the notice of the younger generation.

Edith Bruce Culver told her children an interesting story about Lorne's memorial service. Louise had said that she was not up to coping with the memorial service and asked if Edith would represent her. Edith's daughter wrote down the following account:

> My mother sat in the Household pew, immediately behind that reserved for the Princess. As the service began, she was astonished to see a heavily veiled figure in black, walk up the aisle and enter the Princess's pew – her walk and carriage typical of the Princess . . . After her arrival home, my mother telephoned the [Kensington] Palace and spoke to the lady-in-waiting. 'So, the Princess attended the service after all?' 'Indeed, she did not: I have been with her the whole time'!

Following the funeral, the 66-year-old Louise became very ill and was diagnosed with laryngitis and 'exhaustion'. She told her lady-in-waiting her 'loneliness [was] quite terrible'. Exactly three months after the death of her husband, Louise watched helplessly as the country she loved went to war against her nephew's country. Within a few months, the family heard the melancholy news of the death of Beatrice's son, Maurice, at Ypres. He was 23.

Louise was rocked by widowhood, grief for her nephew and the overwhelming miseries of war. Just before Christmas she wrote to Ethel Badcock, 'I cannot get over my loss at all . . . I am, apart from the sorrow, utterly lost[,] and desolation is all around me.' Alix wrote to her on 20 April 1915, almost a year after Lorne's death, apologising for having complained of her own troubles to her sister-in-law 'when you poor darling Louise were so sad and lonely! With a fit of the blues as you call it . . . My poor dear Louise, I am so awfully sorry for you in your terrible loneliness which at times must be almost too great a burden to bear!'

CHAPTER 28

Widowhood and war

Yesterday the House of Lords presented quite a martial appearance by reason of the fact that some of its members appeared in khaki . . . The influence of the war was apparent to-day, but in another respect altogether. There were a few peeresses in the aide galleries . . . One of these ladies of high degree evidently thought that the occasion could be improved by a little useful knitting. Accordingly she produced from a bag the now familiar needles and the no less familiar wool and resumed the knitting of a muffler. Her example was speedily followed by a lady in the gallery opposite.

Western Daily Press, Friday 8 January 1915

Louise had been convinced for some years that England and Germany would end up at war. While others talked with blind optimism of agreements being brokered, Louise had spent time convincing her friends, including Edith Bruce Culver, to prepare for war and it was thanks to the efforts of so many of these women – most of whom had been denied the chance to work until now – that the VAD (Voluntary Aid Detachment) was so successful. The organisation had been formed in 1909 and Louise was a prominent advocate of the movement. She was more aware than most of her friends of the escalating hostility between Britain and Germany, through her close association with the king and her knowledge of the personality of the kaiser, her nephew. The war would prove, for Louise, a deeply testing time. Widowed and lonely, she must have spent many hours pondering over whether she, or anyone else in the family, could have behaved differently and therefore helped change the kaiser's angry attitude to his mother's country. Remembering Vicky and imagining what she would have thought of her two countries going to war must have been heartbreaking for Vicky's siblings.

Like so many women of her generation, Louise was galvanised by the adrenalin-fuelled years of what would become known by the ironic title of the Great War. She, like many of her peers, was caught up in the fever of needing to be busy. Within months of the start of the war she had sent a number of sculptures and oil sketches to be exhibited at the War Relief Art Exhibition (to which Queen Alexandra also sent a watercolour), alongside works by artists including Sargent and Poynter. One reviewer gave an unintentionally patronising critique of Louise's works, describing them as 'some very pretty and characteristic specimens of her art as a sculptress'. Over the ensuing years, the War Relief Art movement held exhibitions to raise funds for the Red Cross, St John Ambulance and other wartime charities. Her great-nephew, the future King Edward VIII, wrote to thank Louise on 9 August 1914 for a donation of £1,000 for the National Fund: 'How good and kind of you to send such a magnificent sum in response to my appeal,' he wrote, ending his letter 'I remain ever, your most affectionate nephew, David'.[104] Louise also donated a number of her own precious possessions to be sold at auction houses to raise money for the war effort. To one such sale, at Christie's, she donated a beautiful jade bowl and an oak day bed dating from the reign of King Charles II. To a sale of rare books and papers in aid of the Red Cross, she donated a letter from her collection, sent in 1815 by William Wordsworth to Coleridge. Some years later, she donated a carved ivory box which had belonged to Queen Victoria to a sale that was raising money for the Victoria Docks Settlement.

At this time Louise owned a property named Ribsden, near Windlesham.[105] As almost all her gardeners had been called up, Louise, to keep the garden as it should be, tired herself out working in it. When her lady-in-waiting told her, on a dark and cold autumn afternoon, that she was doing too much, Louise responded, 'If the work has to be done it doesn't matter who does it, so we shall finish it.'

---

[104] Although known in the family as David, when he became king he was crowned King Edward VIII.

[105] Louise bequeathed this house to Prince Arthur's daughter, Princess Patsy.

Louise was brutal about other people's gardens, telling them in no uncertain terms if she disliked or disapproved of their horticultural choices. The postmaster at Rosneath, Mr Eakin, would often tell people of the time the princess visited his home Kilarden. As they took a walk around the garden she criticised a sweet briar he had planted. Mr Eakin was very proud that he managed to convince her that 'the scent was so beautiful that one could overlook its drawbacks'. One of Louise's goddaughters recalled that whenever Louise visited, 'She used to bring a saw in her car and if she didn't like any of our trees the poor chauffeur was made to cut it down, regardless.' According to this goddaughter, 'she was very good to children and always refused invitations unless we, as well as our mother, were included'.

Louise continued her hospital visiting, often doing so on behalf of the king and carrying messages of his thanks to the wounded troops. She supported financially, and became patron of a charity that had been set up to finance the production of artificial limbs for wounded soldiers. A number of hospitals throughout the British Isles are indebted to Princess Louise and several were named after her, including the Princess Louise Hospital for Scottish Limbless Sailors and Soldiers.

In the summer of 1915, while recuperating from another debilitating illness, she made an official tour of south-west England, spending time in Devon and Cornwall, where she admired the architecture of Exeter Cathedral and visited Launceston Castle. She returned to London via Sussex, where she visited military wards and schools. After she had opened up her own home to the wounded, her great-nephew David wrote in response to her birthday letter to him: 'It was a sad day this year with this ghastly war on, and so many of one's friends killed . . . How splendid of you having had all those wounded officers in your house; what a real rest and change it must be after the trenches. I suppose some of them must have been pretty bad.'

A few years before the outbreak of war a new artist had arrived in London from Hungary, who would produce one of the most striking portraits ever painted of Princess Louise. Following the tragic death of their baby, Philip de László and his wife Lucy had decided to leave Hungary and move to Vienna (where Louise's lover Boehm, who was half Hungarian, had also lived and trained). In 1907 the de Lászlós had moved again, this time to England, where they settled in London and raised their five sons. This was the age of fashionable portraiture, led in London by artists including John Singer Sargent and Giovanni Boldini. De László's unique style of portraiture was immediately successful and he was taken up by King Edward VII. He became a friend of Louise's and would often visit her at Kensington Palace. In 1915, he painted a portrait of Louise dressed in widow's mourning, but a beautifully draped, aesthetically pleasing version of the black mourning. Resting on her chest are loops of pearls and a large, irregular, thick silver cross, possibly (judging from their description) the same piece of jewellery that had so impressed the visitors to Osborne House when Louise was young, a necklace she had made herself. Her hair is artistically and fashionably arranged and, at the very centre of her forehead, just at the point where her hair is swept up and back, rests one long, pendulous pearl. It draws the viewer's eye directly down to Louise's penetratingly blue eyes, that gaze not at the viewer but just off into the distance. She looks piercingly intelligent and indomitable, the image of elegance. This is not a portrait intended to flatter (although it does) or to dissemble – it is a portrait of an independent and single-minded woman who is living through the horrors that everyone else is experiencing and empathising with their plight. It depicts a grand old lady of the British Empire and one who, the viewer may imagine, will still be standing strong when the troops return. De László's Princess Louise is going to endure.

Louise still visited Scotland regularly, staying at Rosneath. Inveraray Castle was now the property of the 10th Duke of Argyll and another of Louise and Lorne's Scottish homes, Dalchenna House,[106] was doing its bit for the war effort, having been lent to the Women's Land Army. On her regular journeys between London and Scotland, Louise not only visited schools and hospitals; now she also inspected munitions factories, about which she reported back to the king. These visits were extremely important to her because she wanted to show female solidarity and express how proud she was of the women working in the factories. A contingent of journalists visited one such factory shortly after Louise. Under the headline 'Women Better than Men' a reporter

---

[106] At the start of 1919, Dalchenna House, still occupied by the Women's Land Army, was destroyed by fire. Fortuitously, the previous autumn, Louise had visited to remove her valuables from the house.

commented on how 'remarkable' it was that this hastily trained, formerly unskilled workforce was able to achieve such impressive results. One woman interviewed had been given merely 'three hours' instruction' before starting her job. 'In several cases the girls were asked what had been the effect of the sudden change from domestic conditions to the factory from the point of view of strain. "A little trying for the first few days," was the invariable reply, "but we now find the work most interesting, and should be sorry to leave it".'

In 1917, Louise travelled to Bristol to open the newly enlarged YWCA hostel on Whiteladies Road, which was vital for the many women who travelled to the city to work in the factories. Helena's husband, Christian, died just a few days before Louise's intended visit and the people of Bristol feared she would cancel, but Louise turned up as arranged and spoke of the 'beautiful comradeship' found in all-female institutions.

During the war, Louise became patron of several charities that sound intriguing, including the Duty and Discipline Movement[107] and the Soldiers' and Sailors' Dental Aid Fund. She also declared open the first Soldiers' and Sailors' Hut for Rest and Refreshment, at King's Cross station in London. Several of these refreshment huts were set up by the YMCA. On her way to open another one, Louise was involved in a car crash on the Fulham Road. Her car was hit by what the newspapers described as 'a heavy lorry' and the front of her vehicle was completely caved in. Louise, her chauffeur and her lady-in-waiting escaped uninjured and, as the accident had happened right by the gates of the hospital where the hut was to be opened, she continued on to her appointment. She also participated in a public education programme, opening an exhibition on Domestic Economy at the Institute of Hygiene, which it was hoped would help eliminate the wasting of food through 'carelessness and ignorance' at a time when every scrap was precious. In her speech she talked of 'the importance of domestic economy' that was at last being widely recognised 'under the pressure of this terrible war'.

At regular intervals throughout the war Louise was forced to give up her public appearances because of poor health. In addition to

---

[107] The movement, set up by a friend of Lord Baden-Powell, was intended to 'preach patriotism instead of politics'.

catching regular coughs and colds she was prey to crippling sciatica, but she always went back to work as soon as possible. She maintained her close connections with Canada and paid regular visits to wounded Canadian troops in British hospitals. In 1916 she presented a silk banner (or flag) and silver shield to the people of Canada, at a ceremony in Kensington. These had been donated by the 'women and children of the United Kingdom' as thanks for the selfless help Canadian troops had given to the British war effort. Louise was also a regular visitor to the Weir Hospital at Balham, where she took particular interest in all overseas soldiers, knowing how desperately they must want visitors yet having no family near enough to visit them. According to a nursing assistant, Louise frequently used to visit a hospital in Palace Green, Kensington, where she would slip in without anyone noticing her, bringing flowers from her gardens. The sister at an East End hospital also recalled Louise visiting her ward: 'She was very bright and cheerful to all the patients and chatted away to them quite easily and was very sprightly and bright with the children.'

On the first anniversary of the atrocities at Gallipoli, Louise attended a special ANZAC matinée at Her Majesty's Theatre, in London, at which four soldiers were awarded the Distinguished Service Medal.[108] She also took a special interest in her own regiment, as one of the soldiers, W.A. Morgan, remembered many years later:

I served in the 13th London Regiment during the war of 1914–18 . . . On the outbreak of the War the Regiment recruited for a second Battalion, and the Countess of Ilchester gave permission for the grounds of her house, Holland House, to be used for drill purposes. Now the Countess considered that the Holland House Dog Show was of more importance than the drilling of recruits. Our then Colonel, later Brigadier Maclean, approached Princess Louise in the matter and she at once gave permission for the training to take place in the grounds of her residence Kensington Palace.

In 1914, Louise had begun sharing her Kensington Palace apartments with one of her nieces, Helena's daughter Princess Marie-Louise of

[108] In 1916, 25 April was officially declared ANZAC Day.

Schleswig-Holstein. After the end of the war, Princess Beatrice and her haemophiliac son Leopold also moved into the palace. Early on in the war, Louise gave up Kent House on the Isle of Wight to one of her favourite relations, as Lord Louis Mountbatten recalled with great fondness:

> my great aunt, Princess Louise . . . to me she was a most affectionate and charming great-aunt, indeed more of an aunt than a great-aunt. We used to have regular rooms in her apartment at Kensington Palace when my family came to London. I remember my uncle Lorne (the Duke of Argyll) fairly vividly too. I can only say that she was very kind and considerate in spite of her rather gruff voice. Nothing was too much trouble. In particular, I remember, that although she had arranged to leave Kent House in the Isle of Wight to my mother in her Will . . . when my father had to resign from the Admiralty at the end of October 1914 and we had nowhere to go, she immediately made Kent House over to my mother at once. A typical kind thought of hers.[109]

Louise's 'gruff voice' is one of the most often remarked-upon characteristics, particularly by those who were young when she was elderly. A number of people who responded to the researcher Michael Gledhill's newspaper advertisements of the 1970s commented on how Germanic Louise's accent was, especially in any words containing the letter 'R'. One of Lorne's nieces said how much she enjoyed hearing Louise call for her husband, as somehow she managed to imbue the word 'Lorne' with a rolling Germanic R. The same comment was often made about King Edward VII's voice. Queen Ena's daughter, Maria Cristina, however, remembered Louise's accent as slightly softer than those of her siblings; she attributed this to Louise's having been married to a Scot and to having spent so much time in Scotland.

---

[109] Louise did the same for her great friends in Scotland, the Warr family. When Charles Warr's father died in 1916, Louise immediately offered the widow and her children a property she owned, Clachan House, to make use of for as long as they needed it. In 1916, she also lent another of her properties, Rhu Lodge, to a shell-shocked soldier to recuperate in.

The relationship between Louise and Beatrice was still not entirely harmonious. They were very different personalities, and the differences between them were exacerbated by age. Louise was growing ever more cantankerous and she enjoyed creating a fuss – she had never lost her love of shocking people. Louise's lady-in-waiting during the First World War wrote:

> one occasion she and princess Beatrice were to attend a memorial service for soldiers who had died in hospital and each was to drive up separately and be received by the Mayor of Kensington at the door of St Mary Abbots Church. At the last moment she said that she was going to walk there, when I protested she said that 'Beatrice could get all the kudos, which she liked' and that she wished to walk. So we set off and went to a side door and quietly entered the empty church. At once we were spotted by one of the church wardens who not recognising her ordered us out most officiously saying that Royalty was expected and that we had no right to butt in like that. I managed to stop him and explain who she was. Then of course he recognised her and said 'How naughty of you your Royal Highness.' We were put in a front seat and she thoroughly enjoyed it all.

It was felt by Louise's staff that Louise was jealous of Beatrice for having children. Beatrice's granddaughter, Maria Cristina, however, felt that the jealousy was not one-sided. In a letter written in 1978, she remembered her great-aunt with obvious fondness:

> . . . what I can remember of my charming old Aunt Louise. A beautiful face, smooth pale skin and lovely white hair – very like my granny, her youngest sister Beatrice – only a straight nose and wider mouth and a cordial smile and not a bit timid like her sisters. She was charming and not frightening at all. One felt at once she liked children and not watching to see if we were well brought up . . . tailor made clothes, scarfs and felt hat, when the others wore ribbons and flounces. I only saw her at Kensington Palace informally for teas and lunch when she visited her sister – once we were scolded for having devoured everything on the tea table, after we thought our elders had finished. And the dear

old soul stuck up for us and said 'Stop this nonsense, the poor children are happy and it is only fair after having to sit in silence, I would have done the same' – and then the sisters started an argument over how to educate children etc and we felt so guilty but touched at the defence of the old Aunt. As a result of her understanding we asked how many children she'd had. Another disaster! My mother felt like murder. Granny choked over our tactlessness and we were bid to return to our rooms. Seeing our confusion, the Aunt said. 'I was just leaving (for something or other) so please children will you help me down the stairs?' And later she said 'It was always my greatest pity not to have any children and I'm happy when I see them' – so we hugged her so warmly, we nearly knocked her off balance and she laughingly said 'I said help me, not throw me down them!!' Dear old lady.

Maria Cristina finished her letter to Michael Gledhill with the words: 'I hope I have helped to give you the impression that in spite of Q. Victoria this lady [Louise] was human and had a sense of humour. All say her husband was a bore – but she loved her simple life.'

During the war, the British royal family, so many of whom had grown up with German as their first language, refused to speak any German. A member of Louise's staff recalled an occasion when Prince Arthur, returned from Canada, came to visit during the war: '[he] came for tea and they talked of the old days at Balmoral and in the nursery when the Prince [Albert] came in to play with them . . . they both got more and more guttural in their pronunciation, but never a word of German.'

Kaiser Wilhelm was now despised by his English relations. In 1917, the 10th Duke of Argyll visited Louise and as they talked she railed with fury about her nephew. The king had taken the decision that the family should dispose of their old Hanoverian associations: the family's new name was to be Windsor. At around this time, Louise was growing deeply concerned about her niece Alexandra (Alice's daughter), who had married the Tsar of Russia. After receiving a letter from her niece, in which Alex confided her adoration for the monk Rasputin, Louise fretted even more. She told members of her household, 'I don't like the affair at all for Alex can be so foolish and unwise. I shall write at once and tell her to be very careful, she is no judge of characters.'

During 1917, both Helena and Arthur were widowed. All the surviving children of Queen Victoria were now on their own again, and they turned to their siblings in the same way as they had in childhood. Arthur's wife, Louischen, died a few months before Helena's husband, Prince Christian. Following the death of Louischen, Arthur and Louise grew even closer and, from this time onwards, the brother and sister often went on holiday together.

The war was still raging when Louise celebrated her seventieth birthday, on 18 March 1918. A few weeks later, her nephew, the king, formally recognised her indefatigable contributions to his people by making Louise a Dame Grand Cross of the British Empire in the King's Birthday Honours List. This was for her work as 'Member of the Council and President of the Kensington Branch of the British Red Cross Society'. As the war moved into its final months, King George V and Queen Mary celebrated their twenty-fifth wedding anniversary and Arthur, Helena, Louise and Beatrice jointly presented them with a painting by John Lavery. He was an Irish artist who had studied in Paris and London, moved in the same Aesthetic circles as Whistler and Princess Louise and who, in 1917, had been appointed an Official War Artist. The painting selected for the silver wedding gift was Lavery's *Air Station, North Queensferry, 1917* (1917). The prince and princesses paid the artist 75 guineas.

The Great War came to an end on 11 November 1918. On Tuesday the 26th, Louise, Arthur and Helena attended a thanksgiving service at St John's Church in Clerkenwell, which was led by the Archbishop of York. In early December, several members of the royal family waited at London's Cannon Street station to welcome home repatriated prisoners of war. A journalist who interviewed the returning men on the day they met the royal family wrote passionately: 'A private in the Royal Fusiliers said that right up to the signing of the armistice the Huns behaved like wild beasts to the British. "No torture or insult was too great for us. Hundreds will never return alive to their friends. When the Government sent us food recently German women offered us jewellery in exchange for their rations. 'Let us be friends,' they begged, but none of us would accept their handshakes."'

While Arthur and Alix welcomed the troops back to London, Louise was waiting in Scotland. She stood proudly on the docks at Leith to welcome home over 1,000 POWs (including thirty Americans). Forty of the prisoners were so brutally injured that they had to be transported in cots. These prisoners had been incarcerated in a camp in West Prussia. Journalists reported that the returning men 'presented an emaciated and pitiful appearance. Her Royal Highness chatted with many of the men as they were being hospitably entertained.' Louise could never quite stop feeling guilty for being the aunt of Kaiser Wilhelm.

CHAPTER 29

The Grande Dame of Kensington

Louise spent much of the last twenty years of her life at Kensington Palace. In her ninety-eight roomed home in the broad Gardens.

David Duff, *The Life Story of H.R.H. Princess Louise,*
Duchess of Argyll, 1940

I have read several accounts of Princess Louise's life which claim that, following the death of her husband, Louise barely left her home. Some describe her as having become 'a hermit'. That is, quite simply, wrong. Even well into her eighties she was making regular public appearances. Perhaps it was the many long, debilitating periods of illness, which left her unable to leave her home for weeks at a time, that gave rise to this erroneous opinion of her final years. Looking at the newspapers and official records, it is surprising to see quite how much travelling Louise did in her seventies and eighties and how many times successive monarchs relied on her to stand in for them on official occasions, just as she had once done for her mother. She was a grand old lady of British royalty and the public appear to have felt towards her in much the same way as they did towards Queen Elizabeth, the Queen Mother, in the late twentieth century.

Princess Louise's love of exercise and her strict diet had been overseen by her personal attendant, Mme Klepac, an Austrian health and nutrition specialist, who in twenty-first-century language would be described as a 'personal trainer'. When Mme Klepac no longer worked for Louise (she had left the princess's employment in 1912), she gave an interview to a newspaper in which she revealed her former employer's obsession with staying slim and talked about her strict diet and exercise regime. While Beatrice, who was nine years her junior, grew increasingly infirm, Louise remained astonishingly capable and sprightly. She did, however, grow more envious of youth and its ability; one lady-in-waiting remembers feeling as though she was in disgrace because she was so quick and able. 'At times,' she recalled, 'she could be very gay and we had quite a lot of laughter together, but there was always a tinge of jealousy about my youth. When I ran downstairs when she called she said "oh how ridiculously young you are".'

That Louise was at times obsessive about retaining a trim figure is something that comes across in many reminiscences of her. Princess Alice of Battenberg,[110] Louise's great-niece, remembered one occasion at a dinner when Princess Louise ate the sum total of four brussels sprouts while everyone else tucked into an enormous meal. Whenever Louise was teased about refusing fattening foods or taking exercise in inclement weather, she would say 'I'll outlive you all'. If she ever faltered in her regime, she would scare herself with the fear that she would start to look like her short, fat mother.

The British Pathé website contains a short film of Louise visiting Glasgow some time between 1910 and 1920 (although the date is unknown, Louise's clothing suggests it was towards the end of that date range). She was filmed inspecting troops and planting a tree. In the footage, making allowances for the jerky movements of the film, Louise's gait appears uneven, as though she has a limp or perhaps pain in her hip; it may well have been caused by her sciatica. Despite this she remains energetic, wielding the spade with the strength of an expert gardener then ably supporting the tree while the remaining earth is packed in around it. She is also shown walking to, and then nimbly climbing into, her waiting car, without assistance – reaching the car some moments before her aide was there to hand her inside. Most notably, the footage shows Louise smiling and laughing spontaneously.

The princess was a woman with both a very public and a very private persona. Those who worked for her often spoke of her bad temper; as one lady-in-waiting complained, Louise often bullied her

---

[110] Princess Alice of Battenberg was Queen Victoria's great-granddaughter and the mother of Prince Philip, consort of Queen Elizabeth II. I am grateful to Hugo Vickers for sharing this anecdote with me.

(although the lady-in-waiting's letters also suggest that having a difficult and volatile personality was a trait the two women shared), but all agree that when she was in a good mood she was the most enchanting of companions. As she grew older, Louise became more like her mother than she probably cared to realise. Interestingly, the accounts of Louise's bad moods (or 'a real royal rage', as one acquaintance called it) all seem to be given by women who could be as feisty as the princess. It seems Louise chose to surround herself with strong women who would be able to stand up to her when she was at her most unpleasant – and she could be very unpleasant when she wanted to. Edith Bruce Culver's daughter, Celia, wrote of one such spat between the princess and her attendant:

> One day the Princess took my mother with her, on a drive to visit her brother, the Duke of Connaught, and on arrival went in alone. My mother, somewhat piqued . . . went for a short walk, and on her return was dismayed to see the Princess already in the carriage, sitting very upright and looking distinctly annoyed. No greeting was given, just the order to drive on! Presently, with a side-long look at the Princess, my mother exclaimed 'You look very handsome when you're angry, ma'am!' Whereupon the Princess burst into laughter and all was well!

Celia Culver-Evans also recalled how kind Louise was to her and her sister: when her mother was called to work with Louise, the princess always made sure that the girls were kept amused by sending out members of her staff to play with them and make them laugh.

One of Louise's most loyal servants was her steward, John James. He claimed that he and Louise shared an interest in spiritualism. Very little has been written about this, but Lorne was known to have been interested in the subject. It is unknown whether Louise shared Lorne's enthusiasm or whether it became important to her after she was widowed. Another former member of the royal household commented that Lorne would arrange for mediums to visit Kensington Palace. This is a side to Louise's life that has been very difficult to investigate. In 1922, Professor Conrad Lisle, a palmist, placed an advertisement in a newspaper to alert people to the fact that he had opened new consulting rooms; in the advertisement he states that he has read the hands of the Prince of Wales and Princess Louise. One letter about Louise's spiritual beliefs explained that, because she was always so closely related to the reigning monarch, and the monarch was the head of the Church of England, Louise's interest in mediums and spiritualism had to be kept a secret from the eyes of the press. It does not, however, seem to have been a very great love of hers, more something that, in keeping with the bohemian spirit of the age, she showed an interest in, rather than being a strong aficionado.

During the last decades of their lives. Princess Louise and Princess Beatrice – although retaining strong differences – seem to have clung together. They, Helena and Arthur had become the last bastions of the Victorian age. (After Helena's death, Beatrice was always the 'extra' when the three of them got together and she never developed the closeness to Arthur that Louise did. Throughout the 1920s, there was a trend in the papers to write about the trio in terms of their advanced age; for example, 'their combined ages are 247 years old'.) They were seen by the modern generation as fascinating dinosaurs, relics of a bygone age. Most of the Bright Young Things would have been amazed if they had known the truth about the aged princess's life and love affairs.

Far from becoming a hermit, Louise, or 'the grand old lady of Kensington Palace', as she became, seems to have embraced the new era of peace with its promise of universal suffrage. She enjoyed being 'the artistic one' right up to the end of her life, and fashion journalists would continue to comment on her dress sense and style. In 1919, Louise had used her fashionable reputation to help boost British industry, giving her patronage to a glove-maker Mr W. Pinkham, who was setting up a new factory in Chelmsford. This was not only about fashion: before the war, German imports had dominated the glove industry, meaning that few British glove-makers had survived. Pinkham's new factory would provide not only an important British product but many new jobs – mainly for women. Louise was very keen to support any ventures that helped women to achieve independence.

In the same year she attended the wedding of her niece, Arthur's daughter Princess Patricia of Connaught. Like her aunt, Patsy married a commoner, Alexander Ramsay, upon her marriage relinquishing her titles of Princess and HRH (although the public still continued to call her Princess Patsy). The papers reported that Louise wore to the wedding 'blue chiffon velvet, gracefully draped to show an under-dress of black satin. The coat of the same velvet was finished with a large collar of soft grey fur, and she wore a becoming hat to correspond.' In 1922, when Louise attended the wedding of her grand-niece Princess Mary to Viscount Lascelles, she was reported as looking 'very lovely in a rich gown of mole-coloured panne with steel embroideries and rosy lights running through it . . . [she] might also have been the fairy godmother of the occasion, with that kindly twinkle in her grey-blue eyes'. (Princess Mary touched the hearts of the people by asking a soldier to lay her bridal bouquet on the Cenotaph in honour of those who had died in the war.) A few weeks later, Louise attended the king and queen's garden party at Buckingham Palace at which she wore '[a] crêpe-de-chine dress . . . of a very rich tone of brown with hand-some lace panels and trimmings. She also wore a brown lace hat with flower shading from deep yellow to primrose colour, and the shoes and parasol were en suite.' One cannot help wondering if she and Beatrice had not had the foresight to consult one another before dressing for the wedding of the Crown Prince of Sweden and Lady Louise Mountbatten in 1923. The newspapers tactfully reported that the sisters were, 'both dressed in sapphire-coloured gowns of varying but harmonious shades, with sable stoles'.

The war meant that Louise had been forced to curtail her love of travelling. As soon as it was safe to do so, she crossed the English Channel and spent a month in the spring of 1919 in and around Nice. This became the pattern for the rest of her life. By the end of the same year, she and Helena were amongst the royals who gathered to welcome the French President to London, a visit during which much was made of the strong ties between Britain and France in this post-war era.

Louise continued her community work, particularly among young people. In the summer of 1920 she reviewed 1,000 Salvation Army Life Saving Guards in Hyde Park (aged between 11 and 18), she visited Chelmsford to inspect a Girl Guides' rally and, together with Arthur, attended an international Scouts jamboree in London. A few weeks later, she and Helena attended a moving ceremony for the unveiling of a memorial on London's Victoria Embankment 'as an expression of Belgium's thanks for Britain's hospitality to her war refugees'. She also lent her support to an ambitious fund-raising plan to raise £500,000 for the Royal Free Hospital and School of Medicine for Women. The newspapers reported that she would be taking part in 'A unique luncheon . . . There are a hundred hostesses and each is under an obligation to entertain a representative male guest, who is expected to contribute handsomely to the fund.' She was continuing, despite the infirmities of old age, to work as an artist. In 1920 the publisher John Murray wrote to thank her for the present she had sent him, one of her paintings: 'Your very beautiful picture has just arrived . . . It is especially refreshing after a recent visit to the Cubist deformities in Burlington House.'

The following year, in which Louise celebrated her seventy-third birthday, she presided over a luncheon for Mrs Lloyd George and the wives of Dominion prime ministers, held by the British Women's Patriotic League. She was still remembered by the Dominions and in 1921 a ship named *Princess Louise*, 'the largest passenger ship ever built in British Columbia', was launched at Wallace Shipyards. It was the only 'Princess' ship to be designed and built in Vancouver.[III]

At the end of the year, Louise was back in the newspapers, as the caring face of the royal family. It was a couple of weeks before Christmas and a cold December day when Louise travelled to Holloway in north London, to open a bazaar in aid of the Royal Northern Hospital. After the opening, a journalist reported, Louise was 'making her way through the cheering crowd when she caught sight of a working man carrying a child, who looked ill. The Princess insisted on the man being taken in out of the cold weather to the warmth of the gaily lighted bazaar, and when he left later the baby was hugging a large bottle of sweets, the gift of the Princess.'

Louise's fear that she would be permanently blamed for the kaiser had proved unfounded. In the post-war era, public adoration of Louise seems to have reached the height it had done when she was in her early twenties. She felt, however, that she was less appreciated by her family. In a depression, in 1922, she sent a sad letter to Dr James Reid claiming, 'I am feeling very much that some of my family would be

[III] According to the Vancouver History Society, 'The *Louise* was on the run for 40 years without incident, a record, before being sold in 1955 to become a restaurant in Long Beach, California, where she sank in 1990.'

glad if I were out of the way. It's always been so but I am not as
strong as I was and I cannot throw it off so easily . . . One can rise
above minding, and I try to.' It is not known which family members
she was talking about, or if there was any reason for her to have felt
as she did, but she was growing older and less able and that upset
her. As the princess had written, she was no longer 'strong' and her
childhood sadnesses still plagued her.

One family project that Louise was involved in wholeheartedly was
the creation of the remarkable Queen Mary's Dolls' House. Louise's
role was to contact notable artist friends and request them to contribute
miniature versions of their works.[112] Although the journalists who
wrote about Louise at this time had a tendency to assume she was
now too old to be anything other than a 'hobby' artist (often making
such comments as 'the Princess used to be an artist') she still took an
active interest in the artistic scene, entertaining artists to lunch at
Kensington Palace and attending private views and openings of exhibitions; sadly much of her involvement now included sending wreaths
to artists' funerals, such as that of William Blake Richmond in 1921.
Louise had started to break up her own art collection, giving items
to friends or to galleries. In 1923 she donated to the Victoria and Albert
Museum an Italian sculpture named Centurion; she and Lorne had
bought it in Florence on their honeymoon.

In June 1923, Princess Helena died at her home in London. Louise,
Arthur and Beatrice were now the only remaining children of Queen
Victoria – and Louise had attained the dubious honour of being the
oldest surviving member of the British royal family. Helena's funeral
was held at St George's Chapel in Windsor. Louise's public appearances were noticeably lacking in the few months following her sister's
death. She and Beatrice spent much of their time together at
Kensington Palace, mourning their older sister and one of their last
ties with the world in which they had grown up. In November, Louise
resumed her public engagements, and back in Scotland she visited
Glasgow to declare open the War Memorial Club of the Argyll and
Sutherland Highlanders. In December, in London, she attended a
special party at East Ham Palace for 'hundreds of local school children
. . . [The princess] received an ovation from the boys and girls . . .

---

[112] Queen Mary's Dolls' House is on display at Windsor Castle.

and watched with interest the distribution of bags of sweets and fruit as the audience filed out after the performance'.

In 1924, London was buzzing with excitement and people were flocking to the city just as they had in the time of Victoria and Albert for the Great Exhibition of 1851. This time they were travelling not to Hyde Park, but to Wembley, to visit the new Empire Stadium where the British Empire Exhibition was opened by King George V and Queen Mary on St George's Day (23 April). The stadium could be reached by a new branch of the railway line and had a smart new station to connect it to central London. Newspapers reported that when the princess 'visited the walled city of West Africa at Wembley for the first time, she was particularly interested . . . in the beautiful timber . . . and the exquisite work in leather of the Africans at Kano, the chief city of the Emir of Kataina. HRH bought a leather cushion, one of those articles which society is making popular just now.'

While Louise was visiting the Africa pavilion at Wembley, Beatrice was making plans to visit Africa itself. She travelled to South Africa to spend Christmas of 1924 with Helena's daughter Princess Alice and her husband the Earl of Athlone (the recently appointed Governor-General of South Africa). Louise and Arthur also spent that Christmas overseas. Arthur had bought a villa at Beaulieu at Cap Ferrat on the French Riviera, and had begun spending a large portion of each year out there, usually during the winter months. Louise was one of his most regular visitors. After returning to London, Louise became seriously ill with bronchitis and was forced to cancel a number of engagements, taking over a month to regain her health. She did, however, manage to submit a painting to an exhibition of the Royal Society of Painters in Watercolours; it was a landscape of a garden in Scotland. A couple of years later, she sent some of her work to the Applied Arts and Handicrafts Exhibition at the Royal Horticultural Hall in Westminster.[113]

In early April 1925, as soon as she was well enough to travel, Louise returned to Cap Ferrat, where she remained for a month. Even the overseas travel was not a truly effective cure and for much of the next few months she felt unwell and depressed. The newspapers assumed

[113] The exhibition's press release proclaimed, 'All the last-word novelties will be on view, from handbags to evening gowns, and lingerie to sunshades.'

this would be Princess Louise's last illness, but she defied the rumours and determined to get better and back into her usual routine. She was aware that living in a cold, grey climate was one of the triggers for her illness and depression. In sunshine, she invariably felt better, so she was particularly interested in a new facility which had opened in London: the Sunlight Clinic established by the British Humane Association. In August 1925, the Maharajah of Patiala and his brother, Baro Raja Birendra Singh, were paying a state visit to the capital and one of the institutions they visited was the Sunlight Clinic. Although Louise was not well enough to accompany them, she did send a message, and requested that it be read out to the Maharajah: 'It must seem strange to the Maharajah that what comes as a matter of course in India should have to be cultivated here with much science and care; but we find that satisfactory results can be obtained, and that artificial sunlight has much the same power of doing good as the natural sun's rays have in the Far East.'

By the end of the year, Louise's health had recovered enough for her to start attending public events again, but she was devastated on 20 November by the news that Alix had died at Sandringham, at the age of 80. Louise described her as 'the dearest of sisters and friend[s] to me'. The elderly princesses attended their sister-in-law's memorial service together at Kensington Parish Church; Beatrice was infirm and Louise was openly grieving. They were a melancholy sight.

At the start of January 1926, Louise returned to the French Riviera. One journalist commented, 'The Duke's villa *Les Bruyeres* is one of the most attractive of the many around Beaulieu, and the princess will find many friends already installed nearby . . . Most artistic of our princesses, the Duchess will be able to indulge her taste for sketching, for the view from the Duke's villa is superb.' A newspaper noted that the elderly princess had been working very hard recently, often standing in for the much younger queen, and she was in need of a rest. Louise spent most of the spring of 1926 happily with her sole remaining brother, basking in the sunshine, sketching, painting and attending parties. All the time she was away, she kept in touch with her friends and family by sending regular illustrated letters. These letters had become such a feature of her personality that everyone was talking about them. A newspaper article was even written about Louise's epistolary talent:

She has a considerable amount of 'big' work to her credit, but I fancy that what her family most appreciate are the hastily dashed-off sketches accompanying this royal globe-trotter's letters home. These impromptu illustrations lend piquant point to her racy, informative chats covering many pages. The Princess writes as naturally as she talks; and she can talk as wittily and amusingly of life and letters as of people and places. I have heard it said that in the Royal Family it is Princess Louise's letters that are most laughed over.

Back in London, Louise was full of praise for a new invention, which she described on several occasions as a 'miracle'. This was the radio, or 'the wireless', and Louise was fascinated by it. At the end of April 1926, she was present for the opening of a new hospital radio system: '. . . and HRH, besides showing how deep the impression the marvel of modern broadcasting had made in her mind, spoke of the value of wireless in hospital wards, where it relieved the monotony of the sick bed . . . the Princess rightly held that the resulting influence should be a help towards recovery.' Louise gave a speech over the hospital radio; outside the hospital, people who owned radios had been told of the occasion in advance and her broadcast could be heard throughout the country by anyone who wanted to tune into the frequency. A week later she took part in a radio concert, in aid of London hospitals, and her speech was, again, transmitted all over the country by the power of radio. Now even more of the king's subjects were able to hear the distinctive, deep 'guttural' voice of the oldest member of the royal family as she embraced the newest technology. She had not lost her love of the new and exotic.

At the start of July, Louise was ill again and unable to lay the foundation stone of a church that was being built as part of a new housing estate, but she had recovered enough by the end of the month to lay another foundation stone, of the new wing of the Latymer Road Mission, in west London. At the ceremony she gave a moving speech which included the words, 'Whatever we wish for ourselves we should wish for our neighbours, and our love for our neighbours should be at least equal to our love for ourselves.'

CHAPTER 30

'This remarkable lady'

> Bob, Princess Louise's dog . . . has sat outside Kensington Palace, close to the policeman on duty, for the past 14 years. He has such a partiality for policemen that he goes off and on duty with them, and asks for nothing better than to sit on his elderly haunches, quietly musing, in the shade of a pair of dark blue trousers. 'In fact,' said Mrs Wheelerbread, 'Princess Louise often says that he is not her dog any longer, but belongs to the police force'.
>
> *The Ottawa Citizen*, 1937

In the autumn of 1926, *The Spectator* published an unexpected book serialisation – the memoirs of the former kaiser. The autobiography of the now-disgraced German leader appears to have been written in such a way as to appeal directly to his estranged family in England (or, at least, that was the way in which it was serialised in Britain). Wilhelm described Queen Victoria as 'the perfect Queen and . . . the perfect woman, mother, and grandmother . . . [she was] a real grandmother, and our relations to one another were never changed or dimmed to the end of her life'. He also makes the startling claim that Sir James Reid, the queen's physician and confidant, told Wilhelm that the last visit Wilhelm made to his grandmother, shortly before she died, was the queen's 'last great joy'.

One newspaper reported: 'The ex-Kaiser says his favourite uncle was always the Duke of Connaught and says of the loss of their friendship . . . [that] "the war broke the bond, a grievous loss to me". He says he always loved and admired Princess Louise, and for him she remained "the indulgent auntie". "But this bond has been severed too," the ex-Kaiser adds.' If Wilhelm was hoping for a joyous family reunion, he was to be disappointed. Louise and Arthur were disgusted by their nephew and would never be interested in patching up the severed 'bond'.

Back in full health, Louise was also back on her official rounds and continuing her work with children. In 1926 she opened the Kensington Memorial Recreation Ground, a children's playground that had been bought with funds raised in memory of those who had died in the war, and laid the foundation stone for the Princess Louise Hospital for Children.[114]

She spent much of the summer of 1926 at Rosneath, her home in Scotland, working in the gardens. Since Lorne's death, her visits had been sporadic, but her influence remained as strong as ever. As an article written in 1928 shows, Louise was ever present in the landscape around her husband's former estate: 'On the Argyll estates at Roseneath [sic], is a delightful inn, which was reconstructed and furnished to her designs, and she painted the swinging signs which hung over the door. Even the spoons used in the dining room were designed by her.' The journey to and from Scotland and the harsher climate took its toll, however, and after returning to London that autumn she became, once again, ill and confined to her rooms in Kensington Palace. Beatrice had also been unwell and it was a measure of how much more elderly the youngest princess looked than her older sister that a newspaper, when writing that Louise was expected to visit her brother in Cap Ferrat again in the new year, got their ages muddled up and described Louise as 'the Duke's youngest sister'. Arthur had been given a new lease of life by the villa in Beaulieu. He was finally over his grieving for Louischen and wanted to enjoy life to the full. As such, he had commissioned builders to extend and improve his home, Les Bruyères, to make it fit for a bigger party of guests and to ensure that Louise would always have room to stay with him, no matter who else he had invited as well.

By November, Louise was fully recovered and back on her hospital and charity rounds. She had become involved with the Ladies' Guild

[114] Louise had been calling for years for a new children's hospital for the impoverished area of North Kensington. The hospital was opened by King George V in 1928. The architects were George A. Lansdown and J.T. Saunders.

of the Lifeboat Institution and attended their fund-raising meetings. Louise was also the proud possessor of a motor car, another recent invention which she had embraced with fervour – it was perfect for the princess who had always wanted to drive her horse carriage as fast as possible. Just as charities today hand out badges to those who have donated money, it was fashionable at the time to fix a charity or institution's badge to one's car. Louise, in common with several other members of the royal family, bought the RNLI's 'motor mascot in the form of a lifeboatman', which her chauffeur attached to her car. Within a few months it had been joined by the motor badge in support of the National Association for the Prevention of Tuberculosis – a disease that was taking a frightening hold once again in the towns and cities of England. Louise also became a patron of the Margaret-Street Hospital for Consumption in central London.

Another charity of which she had agreed to become president was the Women's Farm and Garden Association, a body that helped women attain degrees or diplomas in agriculture. The intention was that many more women would end up running their own farms (the war having laid waste to the able-bodied men). That December, Louise attended another party at the East Ham Palace, this time for over 2,500 children. The children of the East End had become used to the smiling face of this elderly princess. On the same day, Louise visited Queen Mary's Hospital for the East End and once again used hospital radio to talk to the patients in all the wards.

At the start of 1927, Louise was with Arthur at Les Bruyères, together with his daughter, Princess Patsy. Aunt and niece spent many happy days sketching and drawing together. A photograph survives of Louise from this year. It was taken by the photographer Mary Galsworth and shows Louise seated and contentedly reading a book. It is a very attractive and informal photograph, in which Louise appears much younger than her 79 years. She appears absorbed in her book and has a slight smile on her face, her clothes are fashionably simple and in addition to her pearl choker, she wears the fashionable 1920s jewellery of a long string of beads, possibly black pearls.

Back in London, Louise celebrated her birthday in March, presenting the London County Council with sixteen Cornish elms for the Kensington Memorial Recreation Ground. Once again, however, soon after returning to the colder climate of England, Louise became ill with bronchitis. She was nursed back to health in time to take part in the Empire Day Parade and service at St Paul's Cathedral on 21 May. On that day, almost 3,000 members of the British Empire League – an organisation intended to promote harmony and friendship throughout the empire – marched through the streets of London. Louise stood proudly on the steps of St Paul's Cathedral to receive the procession as it arrived for the service.

That summer, Louise paid her first visit to the Isle of Wight in many years. As the Mountbatten family now had Kent House as their home, the princess stayed in Beatrice's Osborne Cottage. Local newspapers remarked wistfully how seldom the island received royal visitors now and how the younger set of royals did not seem to appreciate Britain's coastal beauty, preferring to head off to the warmer climes of the Mediterranean.

Her artistic ability affected by the process of ageing, Louise had begun to turn again to one of her first loves: music. She attended festivals and would eventually become president of the Stratford Music Festival. At the end of 1927, after attending the British Music Festival, she had told the papers how tired she was of hearing jazz[115] and that she abhorred the way it dominated the British music scene. She was quoted as saying, 'It would be much to the good if some of the fine old English music were more often heard.' She also championed the work of fellow sculptors, some of whom she hired to work in her studio. One of these was Peter Russell McCrossan, the visiting modelling master at St Martin's School of Art. Although he was much younger than the princess he predeceased her by over a decade. His students erected a memorial plaque to him and Louise unveiled it and praised his talent.

Louise was not always so magnanimous in her praise, however – and she did not always give credit where it was due. One art student recalled how, just before the First World War, Louise had 'got into difficulties' while designing an embroidered table cover. The girl had been a student at the Glasgow School of Art and had a diploma in Design and Decorative Art. She was invited to Rosneath, where she

---

[115] Louise was not alone in her distaste for jazz; Henry Fielding Dickens (son of the novelist), who was born less than a year after Louise, wrote in his memoirs, 'I can only regard jazz as a passing phase in music, and not one that is likely to endure.'

and Louise spent some time improving the design (the girl admitted to her sister that she didn't think much of Louise's original design). The table cover was exhibited and when the student read a review of the exhibition it mentioned the princess's work but with no reference to the help she had received.

A more favourable mention of the princess's patronage was revealed in the newspapers by a Mr and Mrs Wheelerbread. After leaving the navy, Mr Wheelerbread was struggling to support his family on his small pension; as he had been a cook, he began making and selling sweets from a stall near Kensington Gardens. His wife ran a second stall, but they were not making much money and knew that they were in danger of being prosecuted for trading illegally. When Princess Louise stopped to chat with Mrs Wheelerbread one day, she was told their history and immediately 'granted them permission' to trade in the park. 'And she bought a penny packet of chocolate,' added Mrs Wheelerbread to a journalist. 'Whenever she is going on a hospital visit she stops and buys supplies of chocolate and sweets.' For many years, on Princess Louise's birthday, Mrs Wheelerbread would go to the tradesmen's entrance of Kensington Palace and deliver a pot of daffodils. Mrs Wheelerbread told the journalist, 'Whenever she passes she never fails to stop and ask me how I am.'

On 18 March 1928, Louise celebrated her eightieth birthday. She was in good health and was feeling contemplative about the past. A few weeks later, she made an impromptu announcement about her childhood, surprising everyone with her sudden and genuine outburst: 'Luckily the habit of moulding children to the same pattern has gone out of fashion. It was deplorable. I know, because I suffered from it. Nowadays individuality and one's own capabilities are recognised.'

That summer, she was the guest of honour at the Costers' and Street Traders' Show. The display of East End culture had travelled across London, as the participants had been invited to show off their wares in Kensington Palace Field. Louise handed out prizes to the pearly kings and queens, chatted with them and their families and visited the stalls. A British Pathé film shows the fashionably dressed princess smiling and laughing, stroking one of the costermongers' donkeys and looking as though she is genuinely enjoying herself. Soon afterwards, she spent three days in Kent with her regiment, of which she had been made the Colonel-in-Chief. The reports of her schedule proclaimed, 'On Monday night the "Retreat" was carried out; on Tuesday an inspection of the Battalion; and on Wednesday rifle practice.' A few days later the elderly princess attended an antiques fair at Olympia, in London, and once again made the newspapers: at one stall she picked up a piece of valuable antique china to examine it, whereupon a policeman immediately asked her to put it down. Louise reportedly said, with chagrin, 'You are quite right' and moved on to the next stall. Journalists gleefully reported that once the stallholder had explained to the policeman whom he had just admonished, the policeman said dispassionately 'Orders is orders.'

At the end of 1928, the country was poised for bad news. The king and his aunt were very ill, both suffering from a 'severe chill'. As their obituaries were being prepared, George V and Princess Louise rallied and at the start of the new year, Louise was once again at Victoria station to take the boat train to France. There she remained for several months, and in April Arthur held a special music party with visiting musicians including Auguste Mangeot – who had recently established the Ecole Normale de Musique de Paris – and the pianist Lyell Barbour. Although she returned to England in time for summer, Louise carried out few public engagements, although she did preside over the British Empire Union garden party in July. That autumn, she and Beatrice went to stay with Arthur, but this time at his imposing country home Bagshot Park in Surrey. In October, Louise officially opened the new isolation hospital at Hendon and in November she attended the wedding of the youngest daughter of the Duke and Duchess of Devonshire (she gave one of her watercolours as a wedding present).

The following year, Princess Louise became the very first royal subject to pose for a newly fashionable photographer, Cecil Beaton. She is photographed holding a book and wearing simple but fashionable clothes. Beaton discovered that she had very decided opinions not only on her own art, but on his as well, as she offered him many suggestions on how best to light his photographic subjects and told him what she was not happy with in some of the photographs. She took an active interest in his career and it is largely due to Louise's patronage that Beaton became a household name. On her eighty-first birthday, a journalist from the *Daily Telegraph* shared his own portrait of the venerable princess: 'This remarkable lady . . . walks briskly, has a cheery smile for everyone, and greets any joke with a hearty laugh.

Moreover she is still able to keep up her hobby of painting . . . "And," she told a friend the other day, "I have been opening bazaars for 66 years".'

At the start of 1931, Beatrice suffered a serious fall at Kensington Palace. Louise sent a message to tell Arthur that she could not come and join him as usual; she would have to delay her trip to France until Beatrice had recovered. It was several weeks before Beatrice was fit enough for her sister to feel comfortable about leaving her, but Louise was able to celebrate her eighty-third birthday with Arthur on the French Riviera. On this holiday, she visited Nice, where she spent time with John Shirley Fox (a portrait painter from Bath) and his wife; at some point that year, he painted her portrait. By mid-April she was back in England, distributing prizes to artistic children at the Dulwich Picture Gallery. This was a scheme she had helped to set up in her role as president of the Royal Drawing School; the scheme had been given the nickname the Children's Royal Academy.

Louise saw out the end of the year at the exclusive Fortfield Hotel in Sidmouth, Devon. It was a new discovery of Arthur's, who was finding the travelling to and from France rather arduous. He and Louise would become some of Sidmouth's most regular visitors. The town was thrilled. When Louise returned to London from Devon, it was because Beatrice was about to have a cataract operation. It was a success and Beatrice recuperated at Kensington Palace, but, hindered by a heart condition, it took a long time for her to regain her full strength. By contrast, Louise seems to have been in good health throughout the coming year. She attended several weddings, travelled back and forth to visit Arthur in Devon and Bagshot, attended art galleries and went to parties with the king and queen. By the autumn, however, missing her usual months of Riviera sunshine, Louise was at a low ebb. The following spring, she was determined to go back to Cap Ferrat. The *Western Morning News* announced: 'The Duke of Connaught is to have as his guest for two or three weeks his favourite sister, the Princess Louise, who left London yesterday to join him at Bruyere, Cap Ferrat . . . Her Royal Highness was 86 last month and is two years older than the Duke, who will be 84 in May next, but both are wonderfully active for their years.'

The holiday seems to have worked its magic and Louise once more threw herself into public appearances. She went to the East End to

see the pearly kings and queens at home and much was made of
Princess Louise meeting 'Princess Norah' the nine-year-old granddaughter of the Pearly King of the Old Kent Road. In July, she went
for lunch at Buckingham Palace and attended a garden party and in
August drove out to the Croydon Aerodrome as the official welcome
party for Princess Ingrid of Sweden. Louise was still a tireless hospital
visitor – and an ardent appreciator of male beauty, as Dr Mavis
Stratford attested:

In 1934 I was House Surgeon at the Princess Louise Hospital for
Sick Children in North Kensington and my fellow house man was
Dr William Strain,[116] a Northern Irishman from Queen's University
Belfast. The Princess often visited "her" hospital, but liked it to be
a surprise – but Matron had a pact with one of the footmen at
Kensington Palace, who telephoned her directly the Princess gave
instructions "Drive to my hospital" – consequently there was a panic
rush for all the wards to be tidied up and the children's faces washed,
and all the nurses rushed for clean aprons and we two doctors for
clean white coats, to be presentable when the Princess arrived for
her "surprise" visit. She was very charming to the children particularly if one was playing with a Teddy Bear which she called "Bruin"
with a German accent. She took a great fancy to my colleague . . .
We both enjoyed her visits – so did the children.

The year ended, however, on a sad note. Louise's long-term friend
Alfred Gilbert died on 4 November; Prince Arthur sent Louise a letter
of condolence for what he described as 'your natural grief at the
rather sudden death'. Gilbert had been her last tangible contact with
Boehm and she felt his loss keenly. She wanted his ashes to be placed
in the crypt at St Paul's Cathedral, alongside many of his peers. Initially,
this request was refused, but Louise persevered and was triumphant,
attending his memorial service at St Paul's Cathedral and seeing his
ashes interred there so close to the remains of her lover.

At around this time, Louise was made privy to a family scandal,
learning that the king was furious with his son, David, the Prince of
Wales. The prince had invited his scandalous married lover Wallis

---

[116] The handwriting is difficult to decipher in the letter. I think the surname is Strain.

Simpson to Buckingham Palace and had attempted to introduce her to his parents. King George V had refused to meet her. The family detested Wallis Simpson and the way that David was behaving. A letter from Prince Arthur to Louise a couple of years later includes the comment 'Your American joke about Mrs S. and the only <u>throne</u> that she would ever sit on, is very funny and <u>very strong</u>.'

The king had been preparing for his silver jubilee. As part of the celebrations, Louise was honoured by the borough in which she had lived for so long: she became the first honorary freeman of the Royal Borough of Kensington. Despite being in her late eighties, Louise carried out a number of official jubilee functions, returning to Deptford to mark the fiftieth anniversary of the laying of the foundation stone of the building that she had declared open in 1886. She accompanied the king and queen to several events, including the opening of the Summer Exhibition at the Royal Academy; attended weddings and memorial services; and became godmother to the son of the Duke and Duchess of Kent.

At the end of the year, the jubilee celebrations were marred by the death of Louise's niece, Princess Victoria. The monarch survived his younger sister by only a few weeks. King George V died on 20 January 1936 and was succeeded by his wayward son, King Edward VIII. Directly after her nephew's funeral, Louise left London for Bath to join Arthur; they stayed at the Pulteney Hotel. Her arrival in the city was warmly anticipated, but the reception was necessarily muted, because of the mourning period for the king. Instead of loud cheers, Louise was met by the spectacle of people raising their hats in silent greeting as she passed by. Still trying to distance herself from the royal gossip that was buzzing around London, Louise spent the summer in Scotland. Although the British newspapers were more discreet, those on the continent and in America were filled with stories of the new king's summer holiday with a group of friends including Ernest and Wallis Simpson. The king and Wallis had been photographed by the paparazzi several times on their own.

CHAPTER 31

One last rebellious command

Probably few people who travelled by the 10.20am train from Bath LMS Station on Tuesday realised that a Royal personage was among their fellow-passengers. Fewer still who looked casually at a tall lady walking briskly, albeit with dignity, from the waiting room to a first-class compartment on this train would have believed that she was in her 91st year . . . HRH has been staying at Chavanage House, Tetbury, as the guest of Mrs Lowsley Williams. She came to Bath by car and was on her way to Bournemouth. Her hat and coat were black. She took a window seat facing the engine when she entered her compartment at Bath station.

Bath Chronicle, Saturday 29 October 1938

When Louise returned to London in October 1936, the city was agog with the news that Ernest and Wallis Simpson had begun divorce proceedings. Louise's wayward great-nephew had rented for his royal mistress a beautiful home in Regent's Park. On 16 November, the king told Stanley Baldwin he was prepared to abdicate if the government opposed his intended marriage. Perhaps it was coincidence, but a couple of days later Louise was forced to cancel an engagement through ill health – she had been intending to hear a performance by a Salvation Army home choir, composed of twelve of her contemporaries, a group of female singers, almost all of whom were over 90 years old.

On 3 December 1936 the story of the king and Mrs Simpson finally broke in the British newspapers. A week later, the king signed the Instrument of Abdication and Stanley Baldwin announced the news

to the House of Commons. On 11 December 1936 the king's abdication was endorsed by Parliament and King Edward VIII broadcast his
decision to the nation via the BBC. The following day, the former
king's brother (known in the family as 'Bertie') was declared King
George VI. Although most members of the royal family thought that
Edward VIII would not have been a good monarch, it was not an easy
transition and the public was shocked. For all members of the royal
family, it was a deeply worrying time. The scandal made Louise
depressed and frightened. She was already well aware that things were
not as they should be in Europe, that Germany was once again
becoming a threat to Britain and that her great-nephew, who was
thankfully no longer the king, had sympathies more akin to those of
Herr Hitler than to his British subjects. For all those who had lived
through the First World War, the late 1930s was a time of shock and
disbelief; no one wanted to believe that 'the war to end all wars' had
only been the precursor of a new war about to be played on the
battlefields of Europe.

Over the next three years, Princess Louise, now in her late eighties,
began to disappear from public life. Queen Elizabeth, the Queen
Mother, the wife of King George VI, was asked in the 1970s what her
memories were of Princess Louise. A lady-in-waiting wrote the reply:
'The Queen Mother told me that the Princess lived a very quiet life,
doing a lot of painting, and Her Majesty very rarely saw her.' By this
time, Princess Louise was living vicariously through the lives of her
younger friends, one of whom was Charles Warr, who had adored
the princess since childhood. When King George VI was crowned in
1937, Louise lent the Duchess of Kent the beautiful train that she had
worn for the coronation of her brother, King Edward VII. Warr
attended the coronation and recalled some years later, 'I had promised
to telephone Princess Louise that evening . . . She was most concerned
to know how the Duchess of Kent had looked. I said, "Radiantly
beautiful, as always!" To which the Princess replied, "Of course, she
was wearing my train!"'

For the last two years of her life, Louise became increasingly incapacitated. As she approached her ninety-first birthday, she was
exhausted and depressed by the awful news from Europe. The world
was, once again, heading into the misery of war and for an elderly
lady who had lived through so many wars already, it was time to give

in to the inevitability of old age. She refused to agree to have an air-raid shelter built for her, fully prepared to take her chances with any bombs that might fall and insisting she would trust only to the thick old walls of Kensington Palace to protect her.

Princess Louise, the Duchess of Argyll, died at 6.50a.m. on Sunday 3 December 1939, at her home in Kensington Palace. For many listening to the wireless that day, the important news would not have been the death of a child of Queen Victoria, it would have been one of the many horrific stories about the Second World War; but to those who remembered her, Louise was one of the last great Victorians.

In her will Louise had left specific instructions: if she died in Scotland, her remains should be interred beside Lorne. If she died in England, she should be interred near her parents in Windsor. Either way, she desired to be cremated. This wish was her last rebellious command. Cremation was still a very controversial subject. Many Christians were firmly against the idea, and for a princess to request it was a deeply divisive issue. Her wishes were respected, however, and a very private cremation was carried out at Golders Green Crematorium in north London. The urn containing her ashes was then transported to the Albert Memorial Chapel in Windsor.

On 12 December 1939, a funeral service was held at St George's Chapel in Windsor. The princess had requested that people send no flowers to her funeral, but donate the money instead to the Princess Louise Kensington Hospital for Children, or to Charing Cross Hospital. Her funeral was attended by royalty, the military and her artistic friends – and she was also mourned, on the streets outside the chapel, by some of the poorest people from the East End of London, showing their appreciation of the charity work she had done on their behalf. The following day, Louise's ashes were interred at the family mauso-leum, Frogmore.

The princess's steward, John James (who had left Louise's employ-ment in 1915 but remained a regular visitor to the household) related what he called 'an extraordinary story' to the former lady-in-waiting Marjorie Crofton. James told Crofton that Louise had made him promise he would remove her wedding and engagement rings from her fingers before she was cremated, so they were not destroyed by the heat. He was then to place the rings in the urn with her ashes, to be buried with her. Following Louise's death, however, James was forbidden to touch her body or remove the rings so she was still wearing them when she was placed in her coffin to be cremated. As Crofton wrote many years later, 'after the cremation when the ashes were brought to him, the curate said "An extraordinary thing has happened, here are the two rings found intact, it is a mystery how they survived the heat." So in the end the rings were placed as H.R.H. had wished.'

Epilogue

By the time the Second World War and its attendant horrors finally drew to a close, Princess Louise was little remembered, except by those who had known her well. Prince Arthur had died in 1942 and Princess Beatrice in 1944; there were no more reminders of Queen Victoria and her family. The world and its politics, society and art had changed immeasurably. People wanted to look forward to a brighter future and, in many ways, to try and forget the past.

The centenary of Princess Louise's birth, in March 1948, was not marked and she seemed to have been forgotten. Her story, however, was so unusual that, from time to time, her name has come back to prominence. At around the time of the fiftieth anniversary of her death in 1989, there was a flurry of activity and several books were written about her and Lorne, yet despite the interest and the number of researchers wanting to find out about her, Louise's story has been whitewashed and sanitised, with the most important elements often hidden away. Instead of looking into the truth of what happened, it became common to dismiss her as 'unpleasant' and a liar, as the discordant element in the family. The more I read of these books, the more I realised there appeared to have been a concerted attempt to change the public perception of the princess who had been so loved in her lifetime; it seemed to be a deliberate attempt to stop anyone from wanting to seek any further.

It seems that all the children of Queen Victoria were so emotionally damaged that each of them, at times, could be extremely unpleasant. Louise, far from having been the discordant element in an otherwise harmonious family was named the 'favourite sister' of Bertie (after Alice's death), Arthur *and* Leopold and usually got on well with Vicky and Alice. Although there were regular arguments with her sisters, and – particularly with Beatrice – the arguments could be vindictive and spectacular on both sides, it is testament to all of the princesses' personalities that even the angriest of disagreements was always made up.

Among the many obituaries of Princess Louise, one contained the words: 'Although in her early years she suffered from the austerity of her family life, the modern trend of thought found in her a sympathetic friend. Regarded as the most unconventional member of the Royal Family in her earlier years, she was yet the most meticulous upholder of the dignity of the Crown.'

One reason why Princess Louise's contemporaries found her so difficult was that she was a woman ahead of her time. From her first 'public' appearance at the age of two, through to the exhausting schedule she still pursued in her late eighties, she was an indomitable force. She stood alongside three successive monarchs, all of whom relied upon her to be the acceptable and kindly face of the British monarchy, smoothing over troubles just as she had during her mother's darkest years of depression. In her roles as an artist, the wife of a politician and the friend of many impassioned social thinkers, Louise embraced the modern world and was an active voice in calling for change. She was genuinely concerned about the plight of the people she represented and fought constantly for the rights of those who were unable to fight for themselves. She was a champion of women's and children's rights long before the most famous suffragists and suffragettes made the cause fashionable and, in an age before the National Health Service and free education for all, Louise insisted on the creation of more, and better-run, hospitals and schools. She insisted that boys and girls should be treated equally and – as the testimony of the many children she knew shows – she attempted to improve the lives of every child who came into her world. Princess Louise paved the way for the royal family of the twenty-first century, her example instilling in future generations the need for royalty to have a more accessible, approachable side than they had ever had before.

In terms of the legacy that Louise attempted to bequeath, however, there is still a long way to go. That the life of a woman born in 1848 remains so hard to research is a sad testimony to the fact that, in many ways, the trappings of monarchy are still stuck in the era of Queen Victoria. That a woman who was so innovative and independent continues to have some of the most important aspects of her life bowdlerised and shrouded in secrecy is an ironic and rather sad end to the story of one of our country's most fascinating princesses and one of the most intriguing of Victorian women.

Princess Louise was a remarkable woman. She intensely disliked excessive formality and kept to a minimum the etiquette associated with her exalted station in life. Yet she was royal to her finger-tips. No one would have dreamed of presuming upon her gay approachability. She was greatly gifted and her personality was vital and magnetic . . . Had she been born half a century later, with the larger freedom that our times afford to royalty, she would have been one of the most outstanding women of her day. (Charles Warr, *The Glimmering Landscape*, 1960)

Bibliography

A member of the Royal Household, *The Private Life of King Edward VII (Prince of Wales, 1841–1901)*, Appleton & Co., New York, 1901

Bailey, John (ed.), *The Diary of Lady Frederick Cavendish*, John Murray, London, 1927

Bennett, Daphne, *Queen Victoria's Children*, Gollancz, London, 1980

Bigelow Paine, Albert, *Mark Twain: A Biography*, the personal literary life of Samuel Langhorne Clemens, Harper & Brothers, London and New York, 1912

Bolitho, Hector and the Dean of Windsor (eds), *Later Letters of Lady Augusta Stanley 1864–1876*, Jonathan Cape, 1929

Bousfield, Arthur and Garry Toffoli, *Royal Tours, 1786–2010: Home to Canada*, Dundurn Press, Toronto, 2010

Blunt, Wilfrid Scawen, *My Diaries: Being a Personal Narrative of Events, 1888–1914*, Secker, London, 1919

Bunsen, Marie von, *The World I Used to Know, 1860–1912*, Butterworth, Thornton, 1930

Bury, Adrian, *Shadow of Eros: A Biographical and Critical Study of the Life and Works of Sir Alfred Gilbert, R.A., M.V.O., D.C.L.*, Macdonald & Evans, London, 1954

Byng of Vimy, Viscountess, *Up the Stream of Time*, Macmillan, Toronto, 1945

Camp, Anthony, *Royal Mistresses and Bastards: Fact and Fiction, 1714–1936*, privately published, 2007

Casteras, Dr Susan P. and Colleen Denney, *The Grosvenor Gallery: A Palace of Art in Victorian England*, Yale University Press, New Haven and London, 1996

Dakers, Caroline, *The Holland Park Circle*, Yale University Press, New Haven and London, 1999

Dennison, Matthew, *The Last Princess: The Devoted Life of Queen Victoria's Youngest Daughter*, Weidenfeld & Nicholson, London, 2007

Denney, Colleen, *At the Temple of Art: The Grosvenor Gallery, 1877–1890*, Fairleigh Dickinson University Press, Madison, New Jersey, 1999

Duff, David, *The Life Story of H.R.H. Princess Louise, Duchess of Argyll*, Stanley Paul & Co., London, 1940 and 1971

Epton, Nina, *Victoria and her Daughters*. Weidenfeld & Nicholson, London, 1971

Festing, Sally, *Gertude Jekyll*, Viking, London, 1991

Fishman, Paul and Fiorella Busoni (eds), *Dinner at Buckingham Palace*, Metro Publishing, 2007

Fulford, Roger (ed.), *Dearest Child: Letters Between Queen Victoria and the Princess Royal, 1858–1861*, Evans Brothers, London, 1964

Fulford, Roger (ed.), *Dearest Mama: Letters Between Queen Victoria and the Crown Princess of Prussia, 1861–1864*, Evans Brothers, London, 1968

Gower, Lord Ronald, *My Reminiscences*, Kegan Paul & Co., London, 1895

Gwyn, Sandra, *The Private Capital: Ambition and Love in the Age of Macdonald and Laurier*, McClelland & Stewart, Toronto, 1984

Hall, Mrs Matthew, *The Royal Princesses of England*, Routledge & Sons, London, 1871

Hamilton, Lord Frederic, *The Days before Yesterday*, Hodder & Stoughton, London, 1921

Harper, J. Russell, *Painting in Canada*, University of Toronto Press, Toronto, 1977

Heald, Henrietta, *William Armstrong: Magician of the North*, Northumbria Press, Newcastle, 2010

Heyl, James B., *Bermuda Through the Camera of James B. Heyl, 1868–1897*, Robert MacLehose & Co, London, 1951

Hibbert, Christopher, *Queen Victoria in Her Letters and Journals*, John Murray, London, 1984

Honour, Hugh and John Fleming, *The Venetian Hours of Henry James, Whistler and Sargent*, Walker Books, London, 1991

Horan, David, *Oxford: A Cultural and Literary Companion*, Signal Books, 1999

HRH Princess Louise and Walter Douglas Campbell, *Auld Robin the Farmer*, David Douglas, Edinburgh, 1984

Hussey, Christopher, *Life of Sir Edwin Lutyens*, Country Life, London, 1950

Jacobs, Arthur, *Arthur Sullivan: A Victorian Musician*, OUP, Oxford, 1984

Jekyll, Gertude, *Gertrude Jekyll: A Memoir*, Jonathan Cape, London, 1934

Johnston, Lucy, *Nineteenth-Century Fashion in Detail*, V&A Publications, London, 2005

Jordan, Anne, *Love Well the Hour: The Life of Lady Colin Campbell*, Matador, Leicester, 2010

Kerr, John, *Queen Victoria's Scottish Diaries: Her Dream Days*, Eric Dobby Publishing, Orpington, 1992

Legge, Edward, *King George and the Royal Family*, Richards, London, 1918

Liliuokalani, Queen, *Hawaii's Story by Hawaii's Queen*, Lee & Shepard, Boston, 1898

Longford, Elizabeth (ed.), *Darling Loosy: Letters to Princess Louise 1856–1939*, Weidenfeld & Nicholson, London, 1991

Lutyens, Mary, *Edwin Lutyens: By his Daughter*, Black Swan, London, 1991

MacKenzie, John, M. (ed.), *Imperialism and Popular Culture*, Manchester University Press, Manchester, 1986

MacMillan Coates, Colin (ed.), *Majesty in Canada: Essays on the Role of Royalty*, Dundurn Press, Toronto, 2005

Marillier, Henry Currie, *Dante Gabriel Rossetti: An Illustrated Memorial of His Life and Art*, George Bell & Sons, London, 1901

Martin, Brenda and Penny Sparke (eds), *Women's Places: Architecture and Design 1860–1960*, Routledge, London, 2003

Martin, Theodore, *The Life of His Royal Highness the Prince Consort*, Smith Elder & Co., London, 1875

Maurice, Edmund C. (ed.), *Life of Octavia Hill as Told in her Letters*, Macmillan & Co., London, 1913

Millais, John Guille, *The Life and Letters of Sir John Everett Millais*, Methuen & Co., London, 1899

New British Institution, *New British Institution First Winter Exhibition of Water-Colour Drawings*, London, 1870

Packard, Jerrold M., *Victoria's Daughters*, Sutton Publishing, Stroud, 1998

Ponsonby, Arthur, *Henry Ponsonby: Queen Victoria's Private Secretary, His Life from his Letters by his Son, Arthur Ponsonby*, Macmillan & Co., London, 1943

Rappaport, Helen, *Queen Victoria: A Biographical Companion*, ABC-Clio, Oxford, 2001

Rose, Lionel, *The Erosion of Childhood: Child Oppression in Britain, 1860–1918*, Routledge, London, 1991

Rushton, Dr Alan R., *Royal Maladies: Inherited Diseases in the Ruling Houses of Europe*, Trafford Publishing, Bloomington, Indiana, 2008

Shoumatoff, Alex, 'The Grand Cascapedia and Its Endangered Atlantic Salmon', *Travel & Leisure Magazine*, July 2005

Spielmann, M.H. and G.S. Layard, *Kate Greenaway*, Adam & Charles Black, London, 1905

Squire, Geoffrey, *Simply Stunning: Pre-Raphaelite Art of Dressing*, Cheltenham Art Gallery & Museums, Cheltenham, 1996

Stamp, Robert M., *Royal Rebels: Princess Louise and the Marquis of Lorne*, Dundurn Press, Toronto, 1988

Staniland, Kay, *Royal Fashion: The Clothes of Princess Charlotte of Wales and Queen Victoria 1796–1901*, Museum of London, London, 1997

Stocker, Mark, *Royalist and Realist: The Life and Work of Sir Joseph Edgar Boehm*, Garland, London, 1988

Summers, Leigh, *Bound to Please: A History of the Victorian Corset*, Berg, Oxford, 2001

Tisdall, E.E.P., *Unpredictable Queen: The Intimate Life of Queen Alexandra*, Stanley Paul & Co., London, 1953

Wake, Jehanne, *Princess Louise: Queen Victoria's Unconventional Daughter*, Collins, London, 1988

Warr, Charles Laing, *The Glimmering Landscape*, Hodder & Stoughton, London, 1960

Wilkinson, H.C., *Bermuda from Sail to Steam: The History of the Island from 1784 to 1901*, OUP, Oxford, 1973

Zeepvat, Charlotte, *Prince Leopold: The Untold Story of Queen Victoria's Youngest Son*, Sutton Publishing, Stroud, 1998

Zuill, William Sears, *Bermuda Journey: A Leisurely Guidebook*, Robert MacLeshose & Co., London, 1946

Index